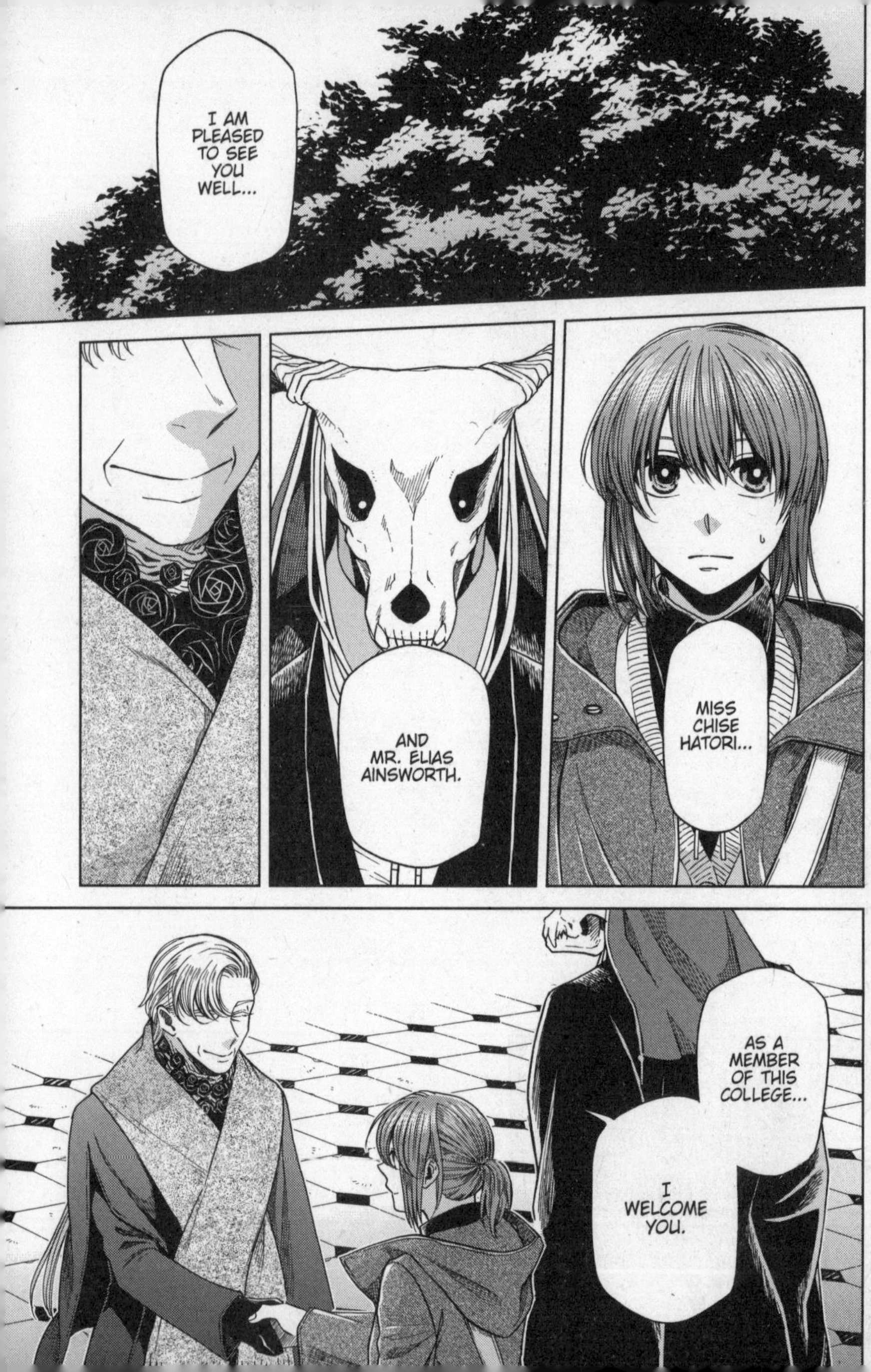
I AM PLEASED TO SEE YOU WELL...
MISS CHISE HATORI...
AND MR. ELIAS AINSWORTH.
AS A MEMBER OF THIS COLLEGE...
I WELCOME YOU.

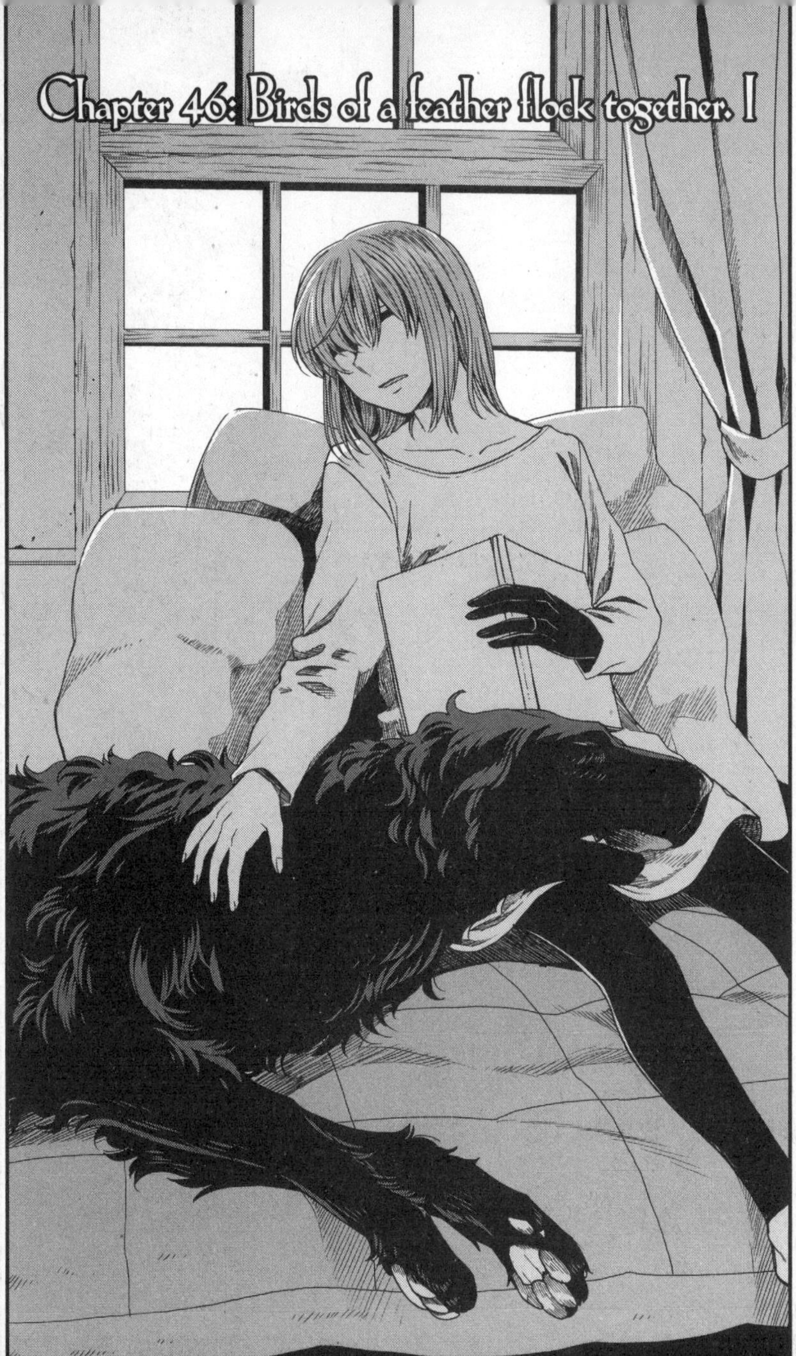
Chapter 46: Birds of a feather flock together. I

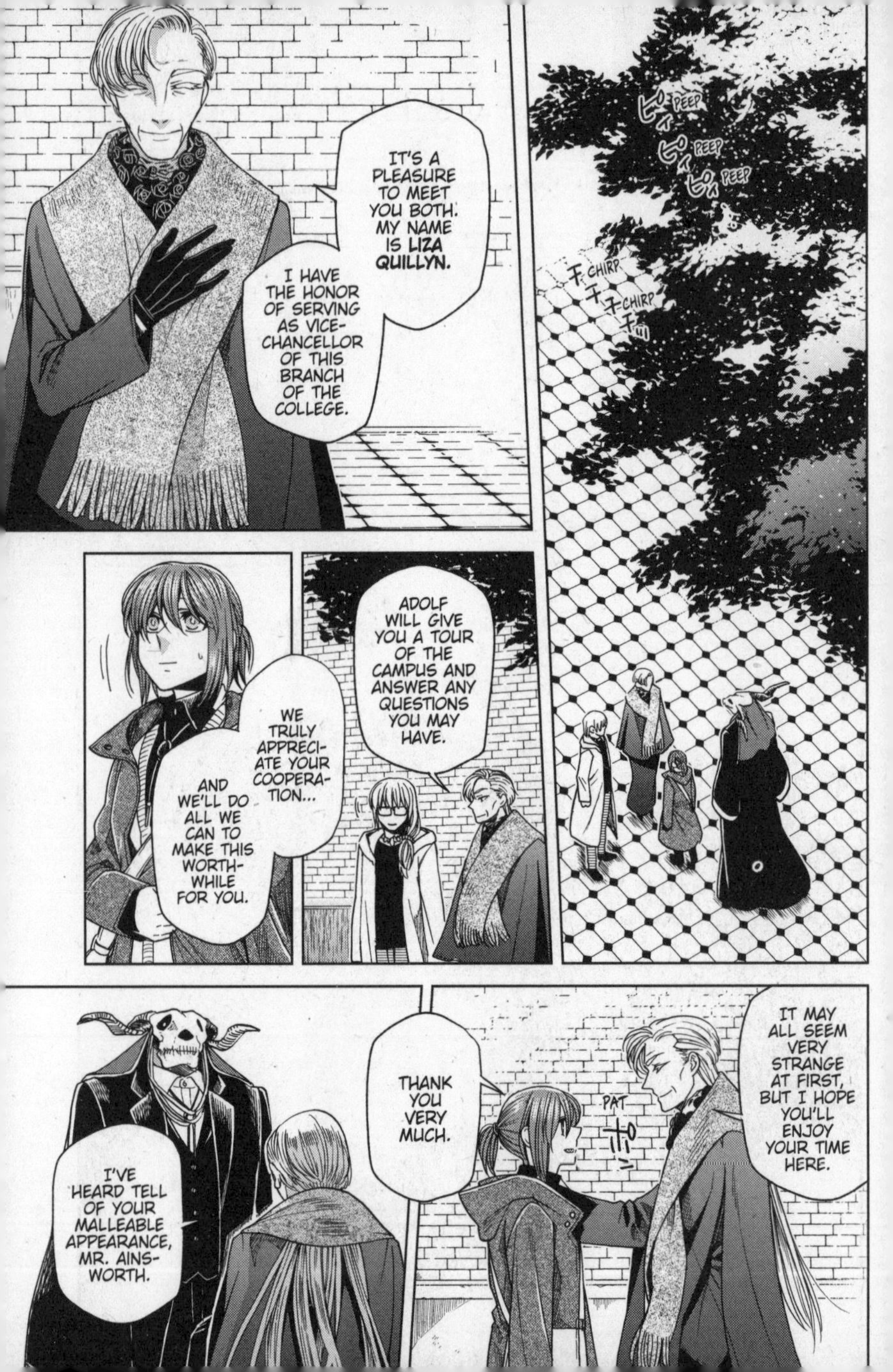
PEEP
PEEP
PEEP
CHIRP
CHIRP
IT'S A PLEASURE TO MEET YOU BOTH. MY NAME IS **LIZA QUILLYN.**
I HAVE THE HONOR OF SERVING AS VICE-CHANCELLOR OF THIS BRANCH OF THE COLLEGE.
ADOLF WILL GIVE YOU A TOUR OF THE CAMPUS AND ANSWER ANY QUESTIONS YOU MAY HAVE.
WE TRULY APPRECIATE YOUR COOPERATION...
AND WE'LL DO ALL WE CAN TO MAKE THIS WORTHWHILE FOR YOU.
IT MAY ALL SEEM VERY STRANGE AT FIRST, BUT I HOPE YOU'LL ENJOY YOUR TIME HERE.
PAT
THANK YOU VERY MUCH.
I'VE HEARD TELL OF YOUR MALLEABLE APPEARANCE, MR. AINSWORTH.

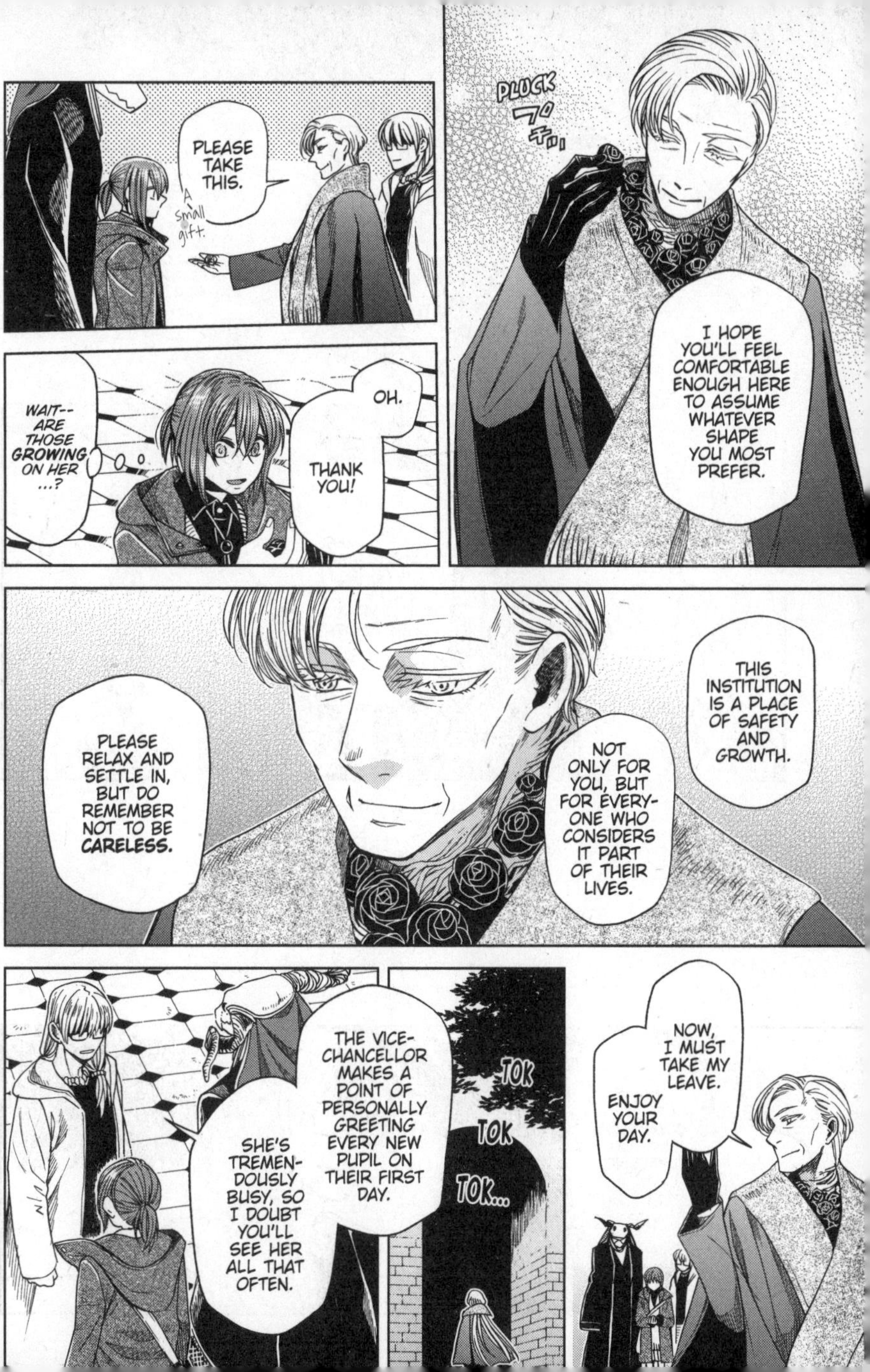
PLUCK
I HOPE YOU'LL FEEL COMFORTABLE ENOUGH HERE TO ASSUME WHATEVER SHAPE YOU MOST PREFER.
PLEASE TAKE THIS.
A small gift.
OH.
THANK YOU!
WAIT-- ARE THOSE GROWING ON HER ...?
THIS INSTITUTION IS A PLACE OF SAFETY AND GROWTH.
NOT ONLY FOR YOU, BUT FOR EVERY-ONE WHO CONSIDERS IT PART OF THEIR LIVES.
PLEASE RELAX AND SETTLE IN, BUT DO REMEMBER NOT TO BE CARELESS.
NOW, I MUST TAKE MY LEAVE.
ENJOY YOUR DAY.
TOK
TOK
TOK...
THE VICE-CHANCELLOR MAKES A POINT OF PERSONALLY GREETING EVERY NEW PUPIL ON THEIR FIRST DAY.
SHE'S TREMEN-DOUSLY BUSY, SO I DOUBT YOU'LL SEE HER ALL THAT OFTEN.

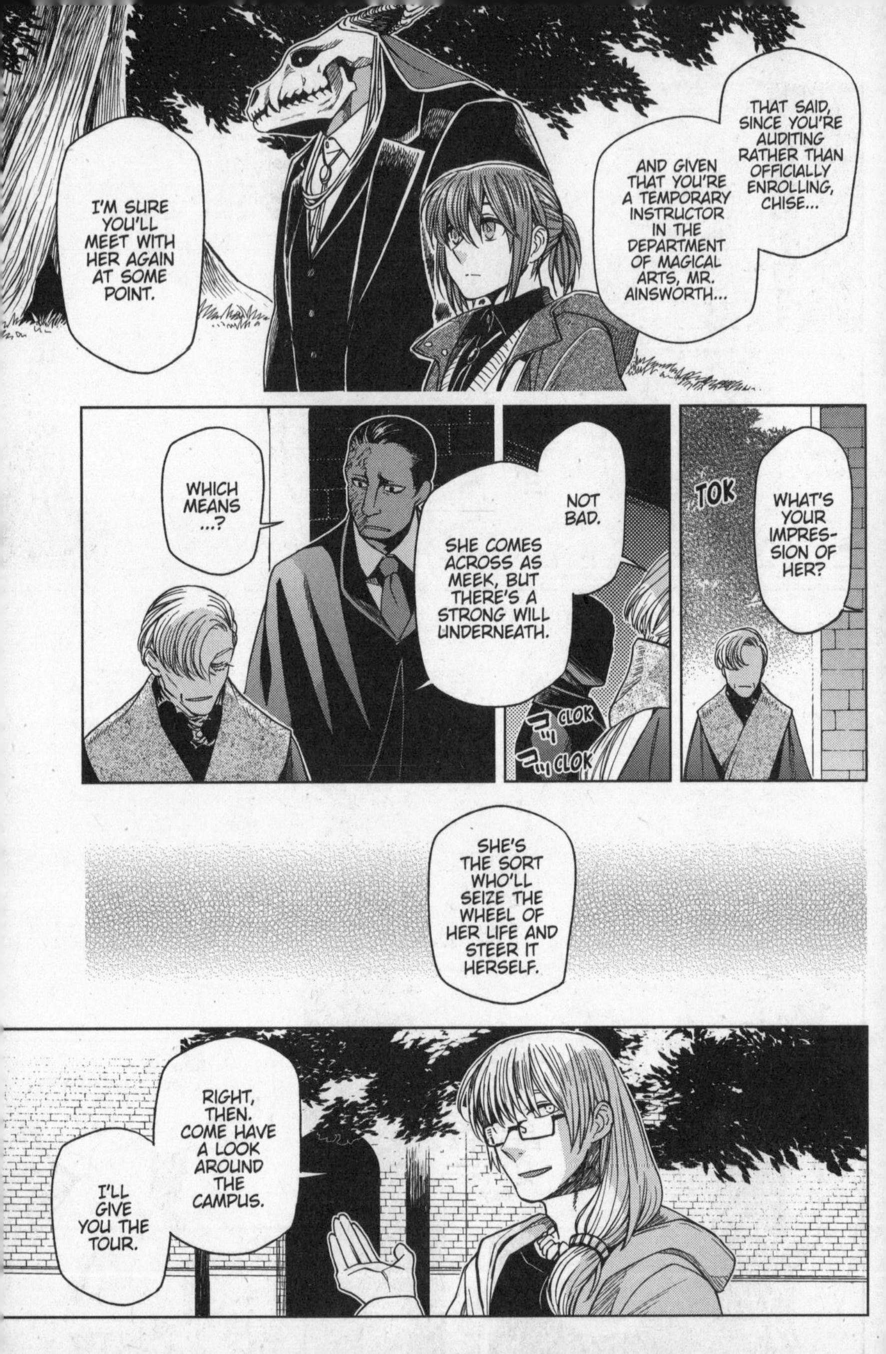
THAT SAID, SINCE YOU'RE AUDITING RATHER THAN OFFICIALLY ENROLLING, CHISE...
AND GIVEN THAT YOU'RE A TEMPORARY INSTRUCTOR IN THE DEPARTMENT OF MAGICAL ARTS, MR. AINSWORTH...
I'M SURE YOU'LL MEET WITH HER AGAIN AT SOME POINT.
TOK
WHAT'S YOUR IMPRES-SION OF HER?
CLOK
CLOK
NOT BAD.
SHE COMES ACROSS AS MEEK, BUT THERE'S A STRONG WILL UNDERNEATH.
WHICH MEANS ...?
SHE'S THE SORT WHO'LL SEIZE THE WHEEL OF HER LIFE AND STEER IT HERSELF.
RIGHT, THEN. COME HAVE A LOOK AROUND THE CAMPUS.
I'LL GIVE YOU THE TOUR.

GREAT! THANK YOU.

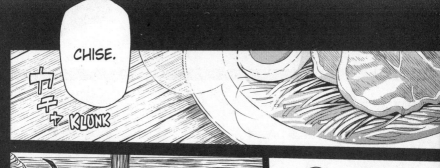

CHISE.

ナ
チ
ナ KLUNK

THE SILVER LADY WOULD LIKE YOUR ATTENTION.

HUH?

W-SH

CHISE ...?

HAH!

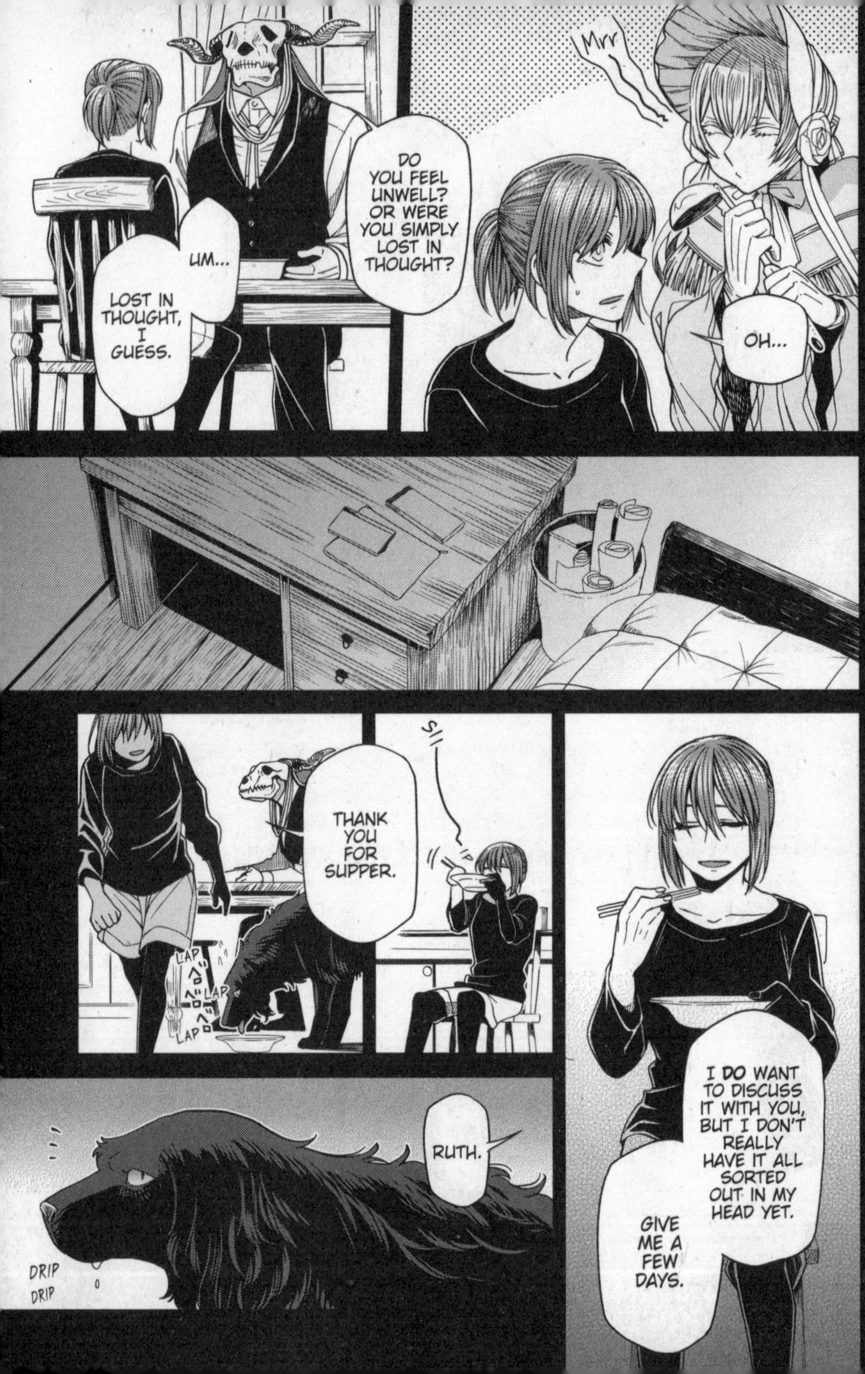

Mrr
OH...
DO YOU FEEL UNWELL? OR WERE YOU SIMPLY LOST IN THOUGHT?
UM...
LOST IN THOUGHT, I GUESS.
I DO WANT TO DISCUSS IT WITH YOU, BUT I DON'T REALLY HAVE IT ALL SORTED OUT IN MY HEAD YET.
GIVE ME A FEW DAYS.
THANK YOU FOR SUPPER.
LAP
LAP
LAP
RUTH.
DRIP
DRIP

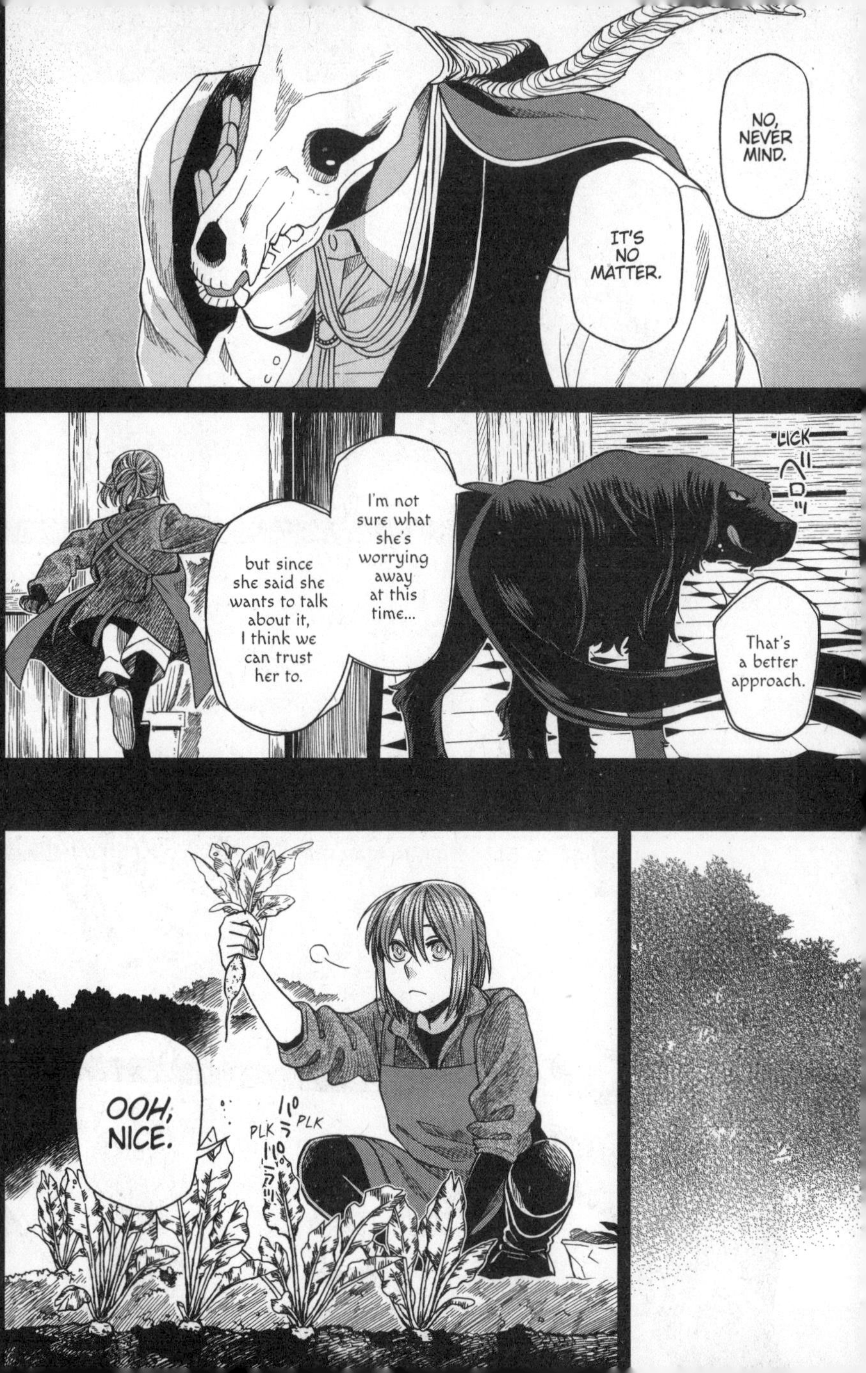
NO, NEVER MIND.
IT'S NO MATTER.
LICK
That's a better approach.
I'm not sure what she's worrying away at this time...
but since she said she wants to talk about it, I think we can trust her to.
OOH, NICE.
PLK PLK

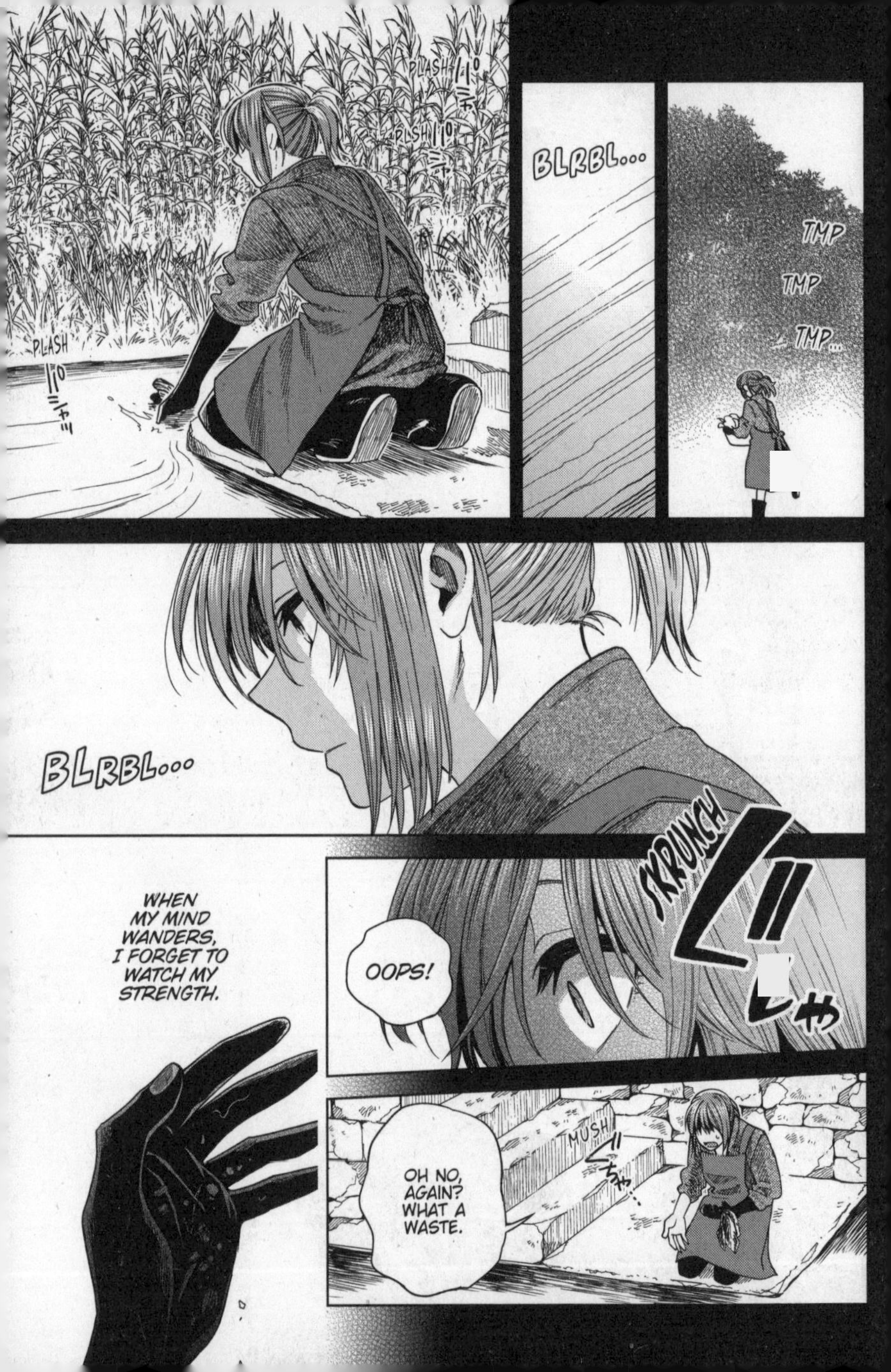
TMP
TMP
TMP...
BLRBL...
PLASH
PLASH
PLASH
BLRBL...
SKRUNCH
OOPS!
MUSH
OH NO, AGAIN? WHAT A WASTE.
WHEN MY MIND WANDERS, I FORGET TO WATCH MY STRENGTH.

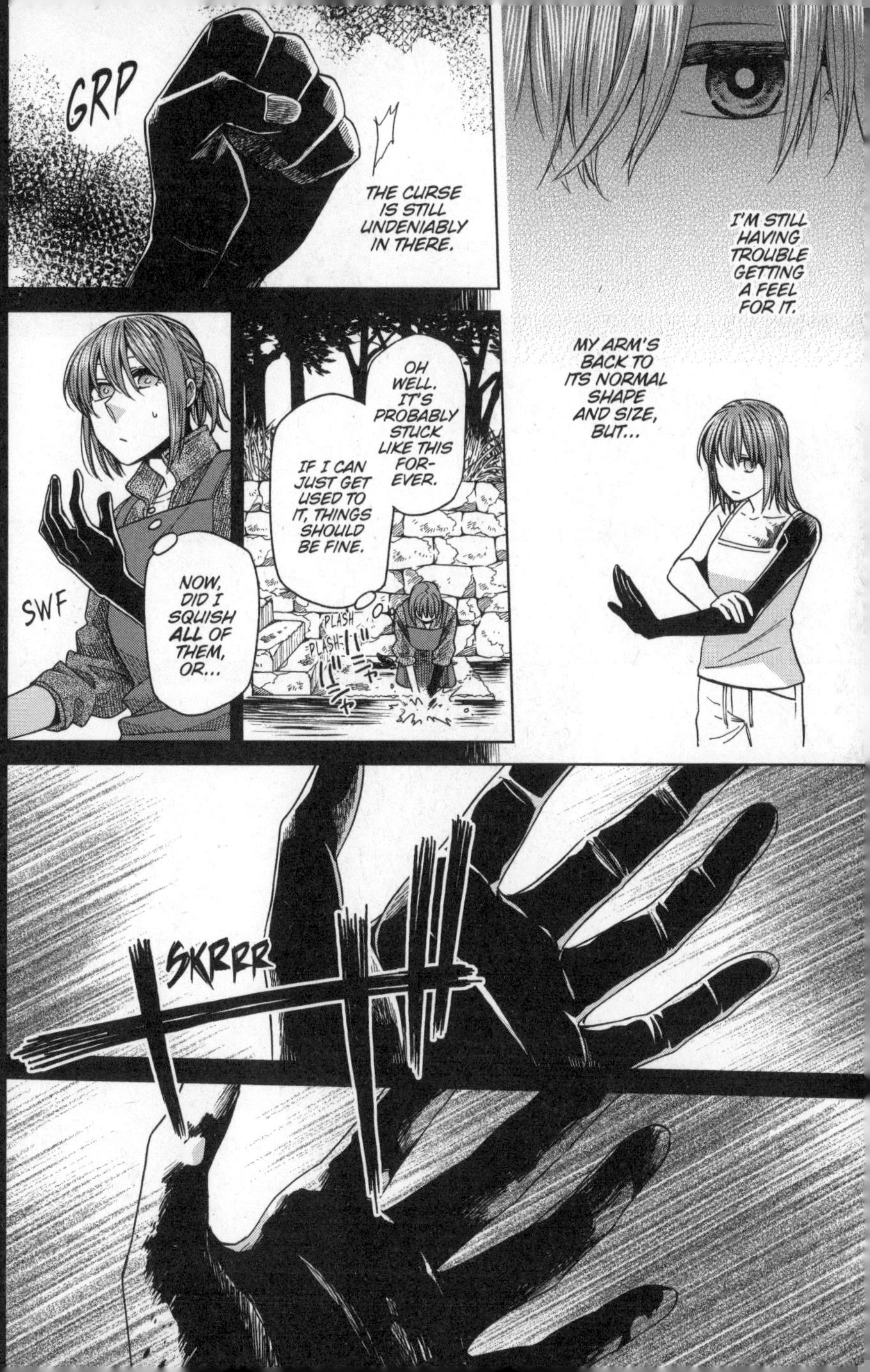

I'M STILL HAVING TROUBLE GETTING A FEEL FOR IT.
MY ARM'S BACK TO ITS NORMAL SHAPE AND SIZE, BUT...
GRP
THE CURSE IS STILL UNDENIABLY IN THERE.
OH WELL. IT'S PROBABLY STUCK LIKE THIS FOR-EVER.
IF I CAN JUST GET USED TO IT, THINGS SHOULD BE FINE.
PLASH
PLASH
NOW, DID I SQUISH **ALL** OF THEM, OR...
SWF
SKRRR

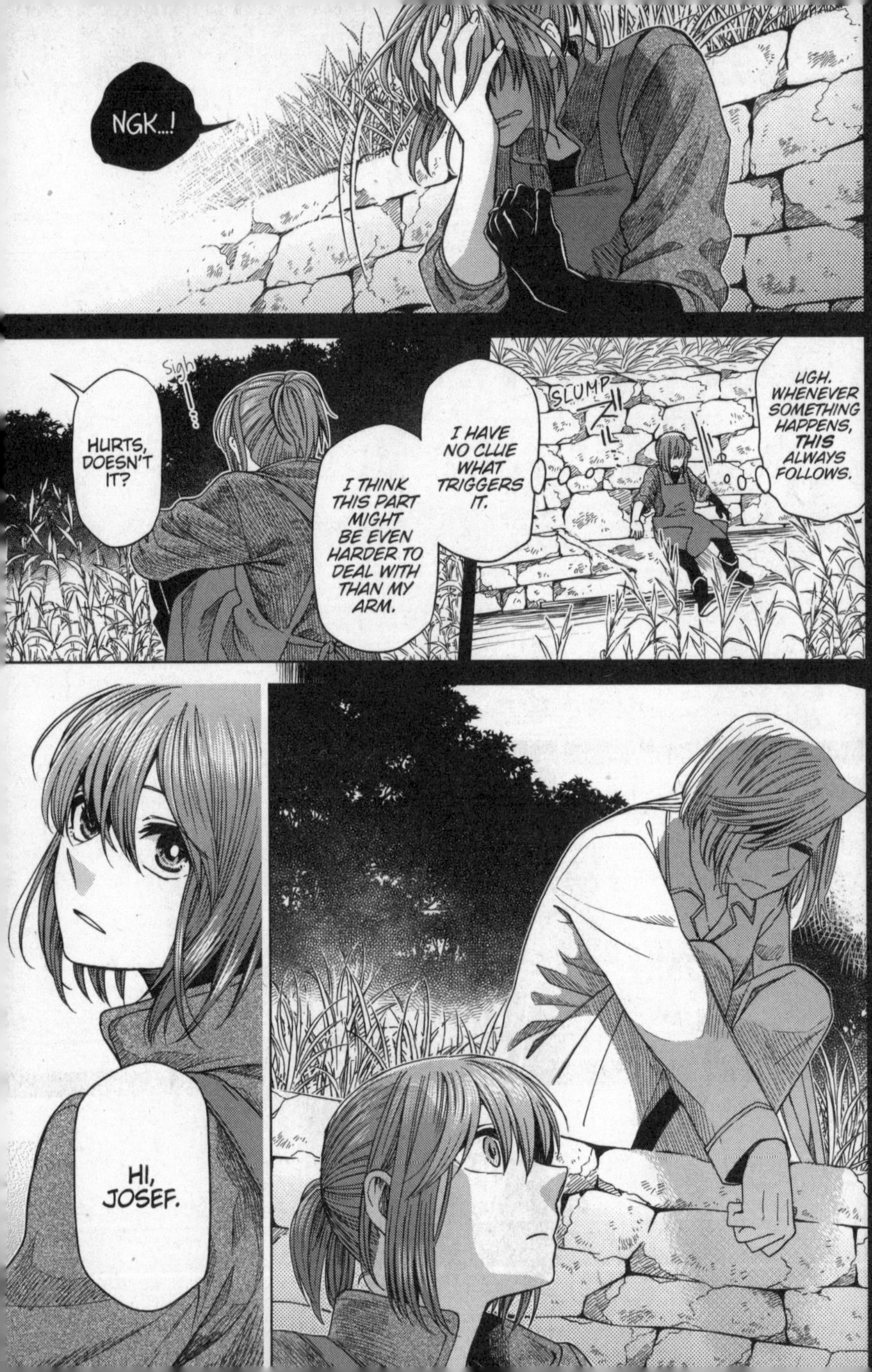
NGK...!
UGH. WHENEVER SOMETHING HAPPENS, THIS ALWAYS FOLLOWS.
SLUMP
I HAVE NO CLUE WHAT TRIGGERS IT.
I THINK THIS PART MIGHT BE EVEN HARDER TO DEAL WITH THAN MY ARM.
Sigh...
HURTS, DOESN'T IT?
HI, JOSEF.

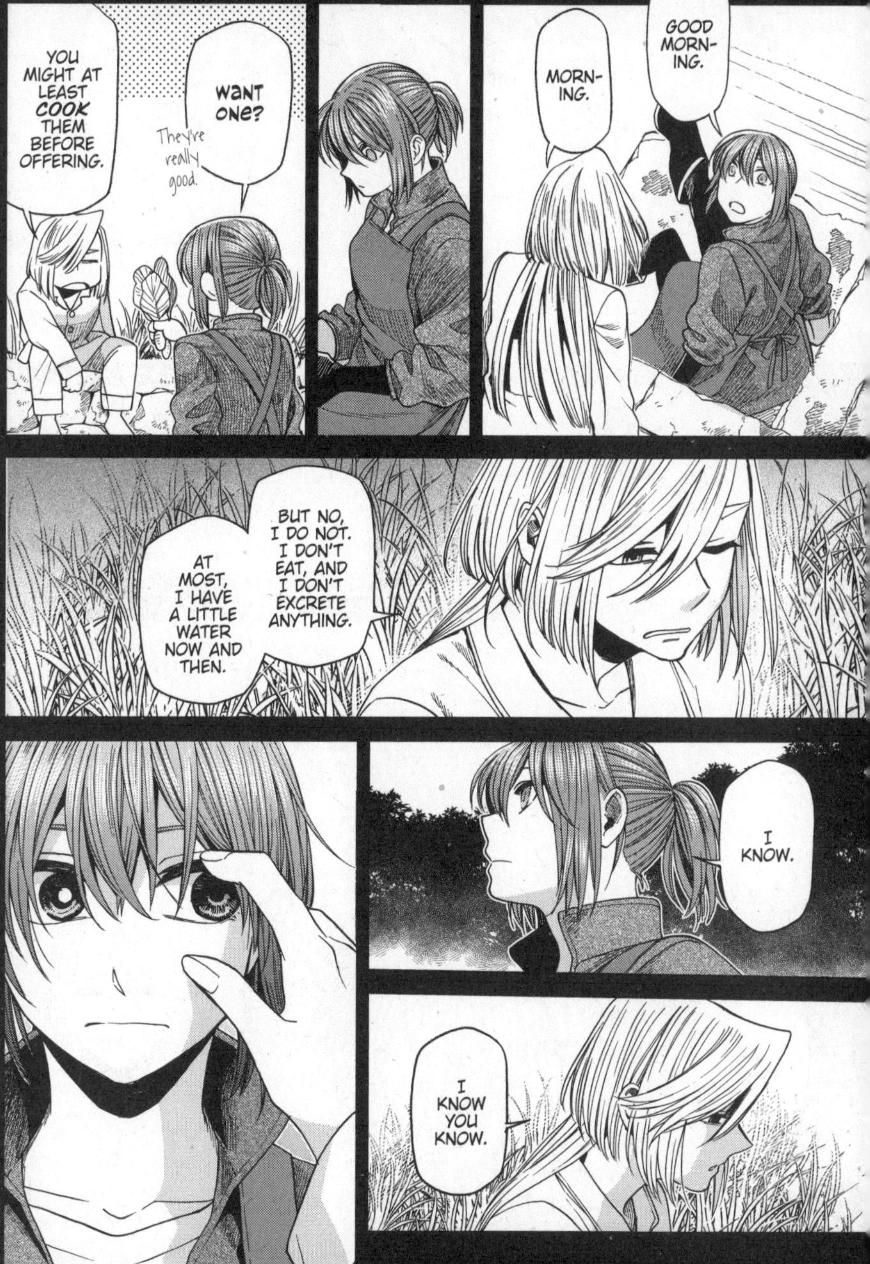
GOOD MORNING.
MORNING.
Want one?
They're really good.
YOU MIGHT AT LEAST COOK THEM BEFORE OFFERING.
BUT NO, I DO NOT. I DON'T EAT, AND I DON'T EXCRETE ANYTHING.
AT MOST, I HAVE A LITTLE WATER NOW AND THEN.
I KNOW.
I KNOW YOU KNOW.

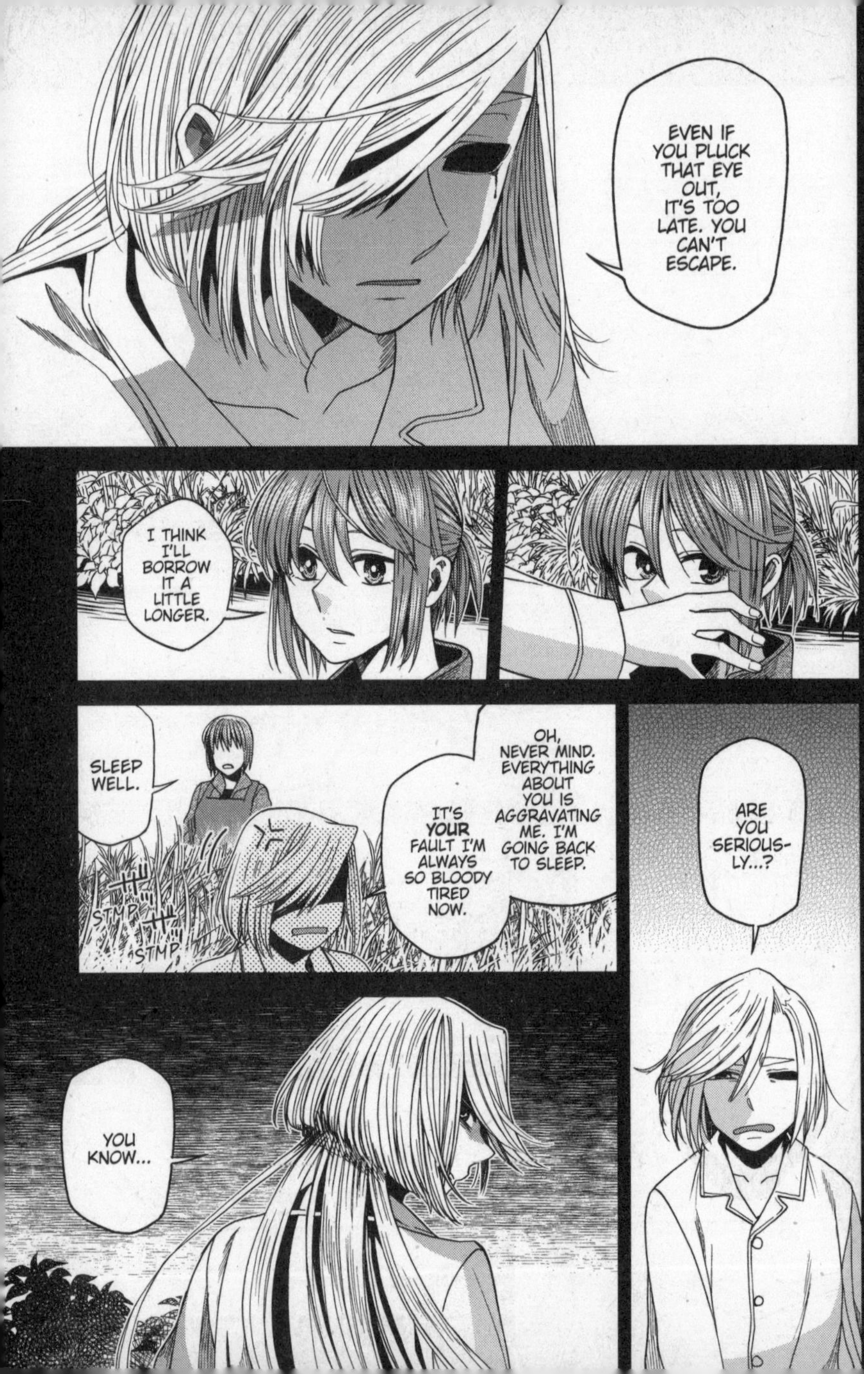
EVEN IF YOU PLUCK THAT EYE OUT, IT'S TOO LATE. YOU CAN'T ESCAPE.
I THINK I'LL BORROW IT A LITTLE LONGER.
ARE YOU SERIOUS-LY...?
OH, NEVER MIND. EVERYTHING ABOUT YOU IS AGGRAVATING ME. I'M GOING BACK TO SLEEP.
IT'S **YOUR** FAULT I'M ALWAYS SO BLOODY TIRED NOW.
SLEEP WELL.
STMP STMP
YOU KNOW...

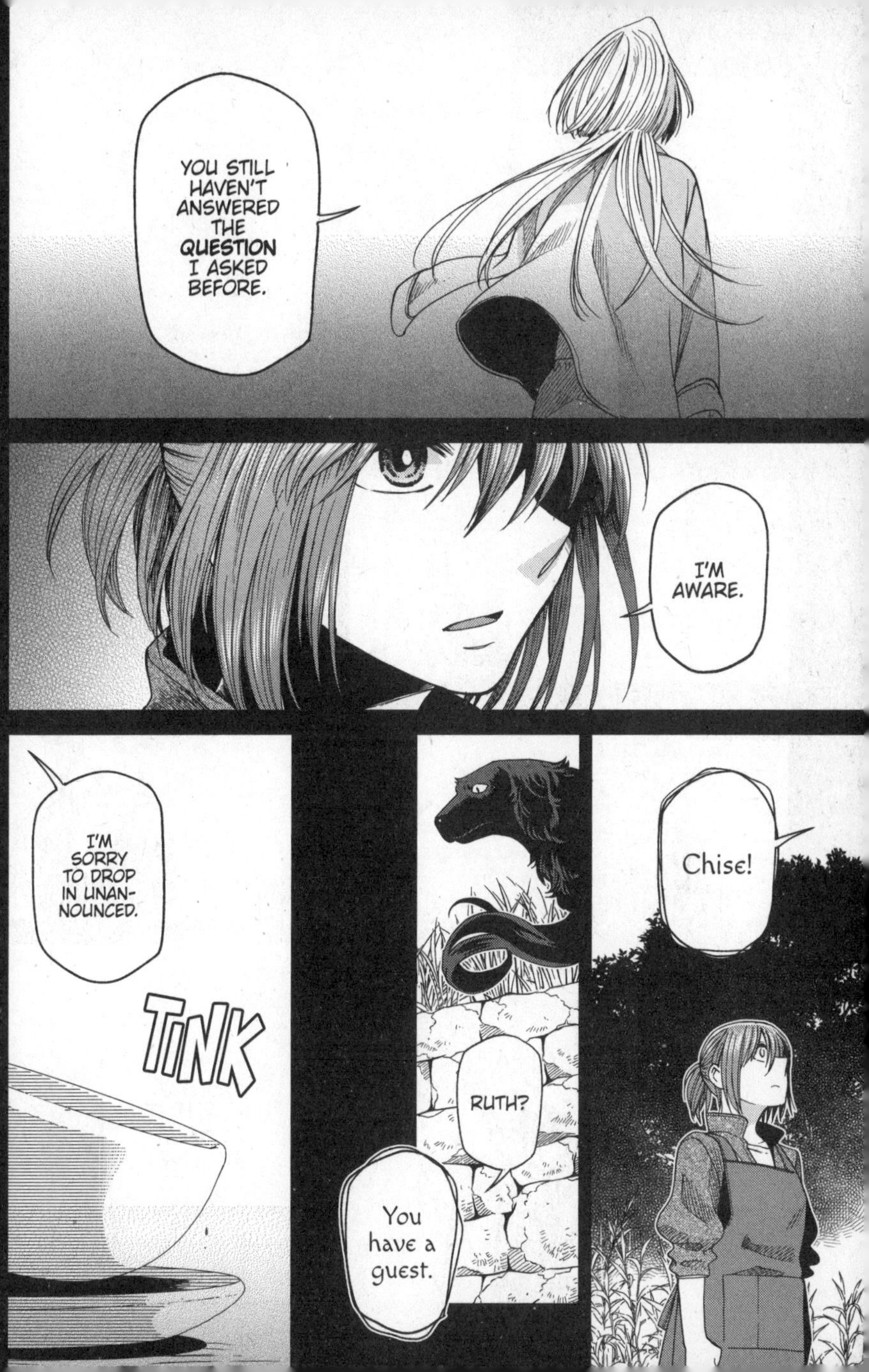
YOU STILL HAVEN'T ANSWERED THE QUESTION I ASKED BEFORE.
I'M AWARE.
Chise!
RUTH?
You have a guest.
I'M SORRY TO DROP IN UNANNOUNCED.
TINK

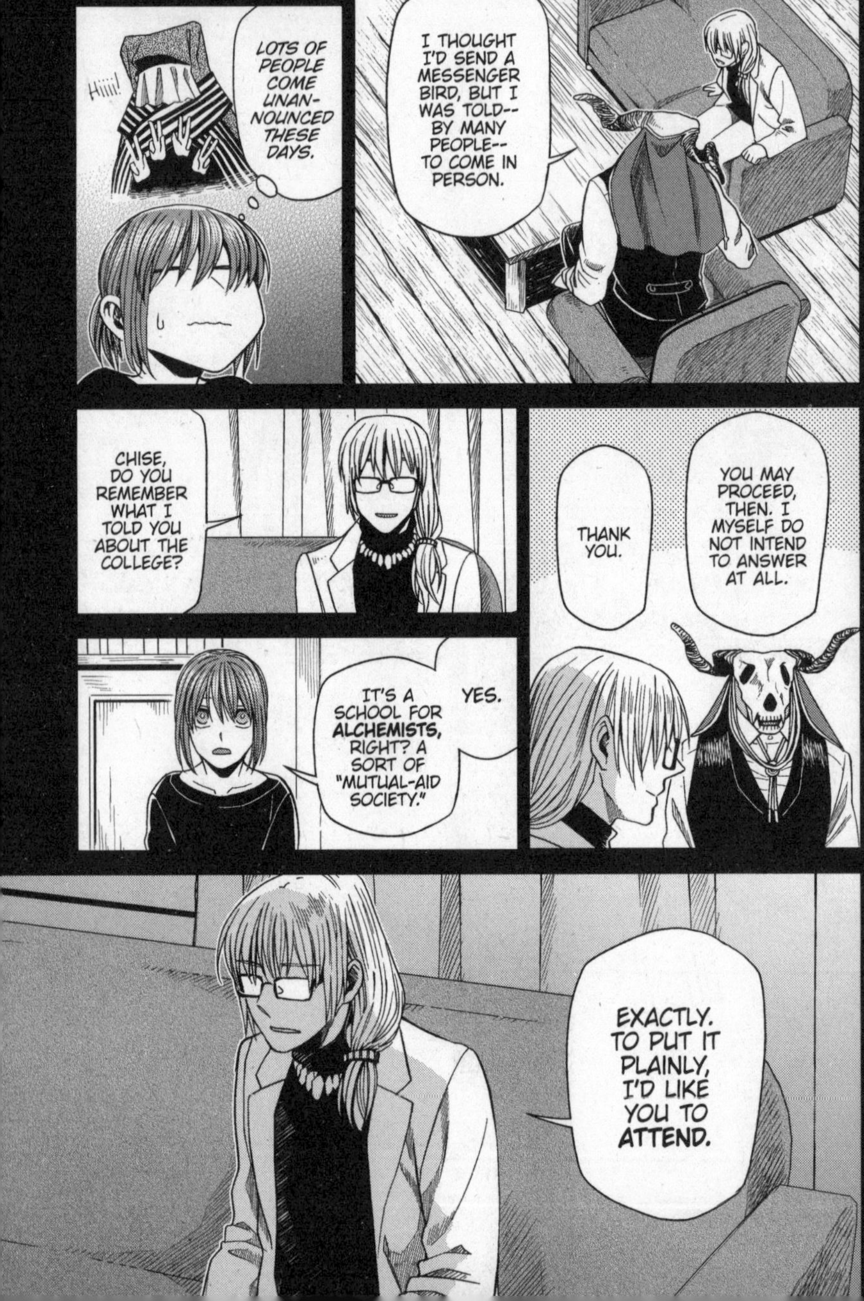
I THOUGHT I'D SEND A MESSENGER BIRD, BUT I WAS TOLD-- BY MANY PEOPLE-- TO COME IN PERSON.
LOTS OF PEOPLE COME UNAN-NOUNCED THESE DAYS.
Hiiii!
YOU MAY PROCEED, THEN. I MYSELF DO NOT INTEND TO ANSWER AT ALL.
THANK YOU.
CHISE, DO YOU REMEMBER WHAT I TOLD YOU ABOUT THE COLLEGE?
YES.
IT'S A SCHOOL FOR **ALCHEMISTS**, RIGHT? A SORT OF "MUTUAL-AID SOCIETY."
EXACTLY. TO PUT IT PLAINLY, I'D LIKE YOU TO **ATTEND**.

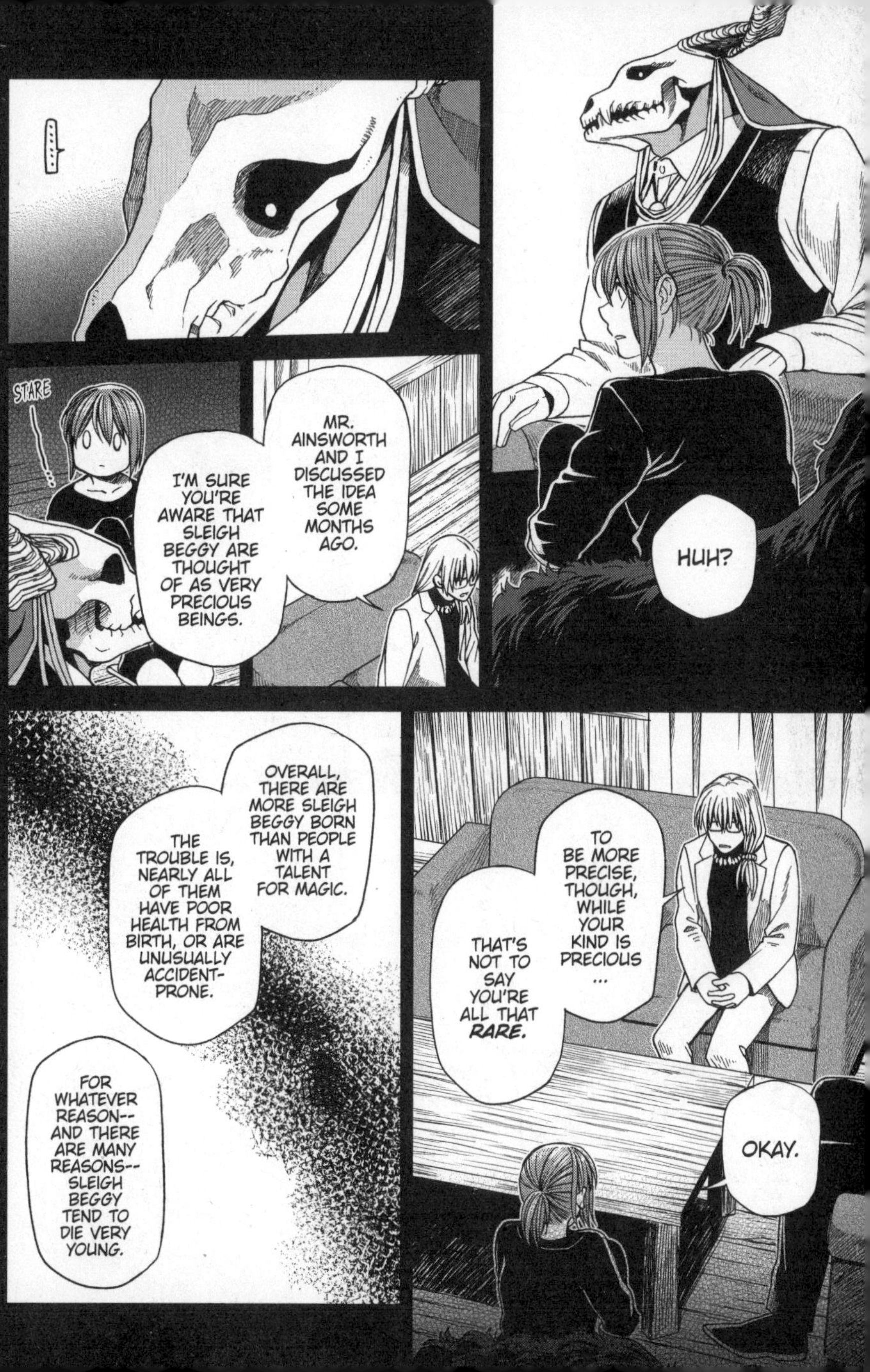
HUH?
......!
MR. AINSWORTH AND I DISCUSSED THE IDEA SOME MONTHS AGO.
I'M SURE YOU'RE AWARE THAT SLEIGH BEGGY ARE THOUGHT OF AS VERY PRECIOUS BEINGS.
STARE
TO BE MORE PRECISE, THOUGH, WHILE YOUR KIND IS PRECIOUS...
THAT'S NOT TO SAY YOU'RE ALL THAT RARE.
OKAY.
OVERALL, THERE ARE MORE SLEIGH BEGGY BORN THAN PEOPLE WITH A TALENT FOR MAGIC.
THE TROUBLE IS, NEARLY ALL OF THEM HAVE POOR HEALTH FROM BIRTH, OR ARE UNUSUALLY ACCIDENT-PRONE.
FOR WHATEVER REASON--AND THERE ARE MANY REASONS--SLEIGH BEGGY TEND TO DIE VERY YOUNG.

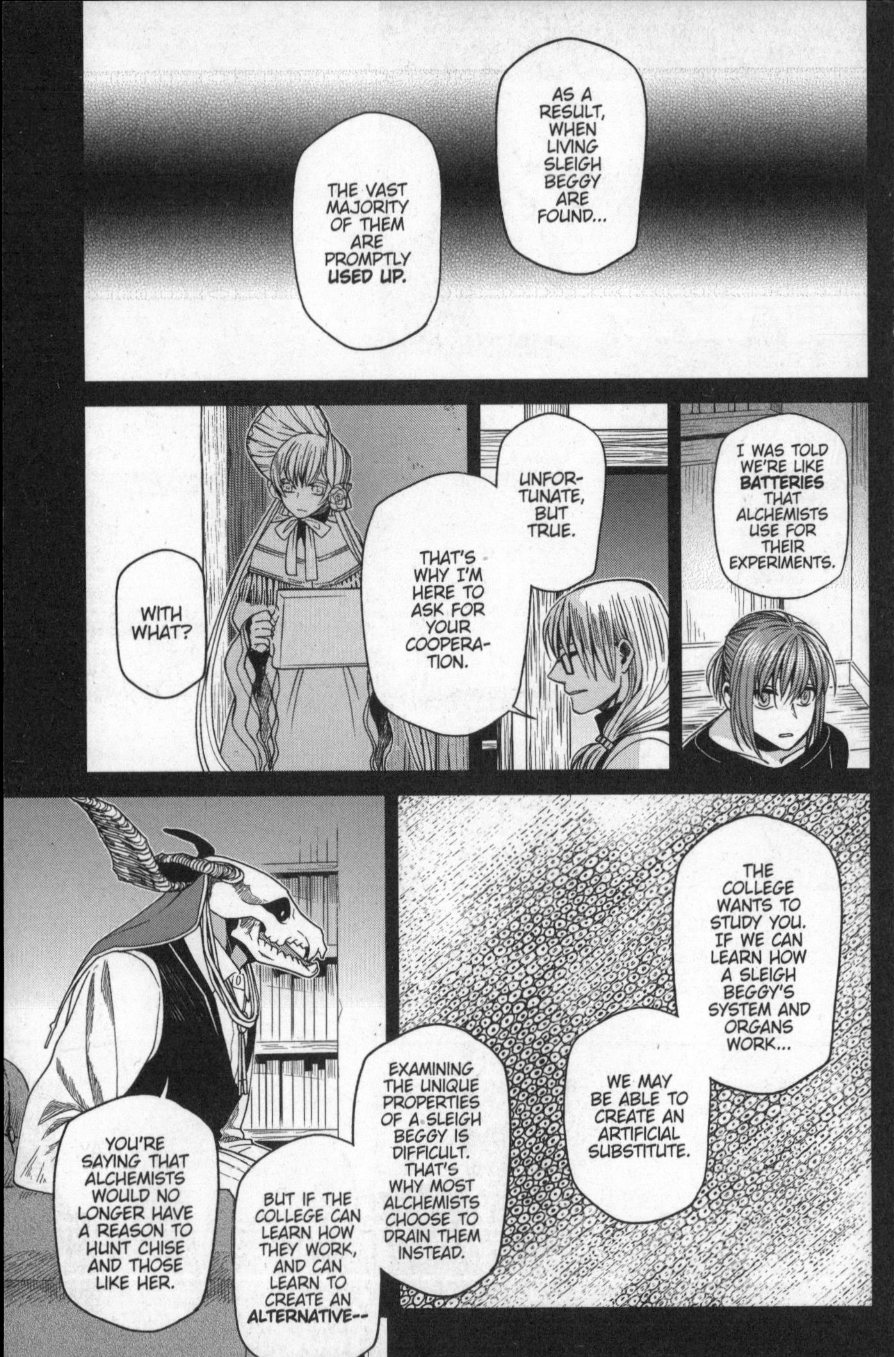
AS A RESULT, WHEN LIVING SLEIGH BEGGY ARE FOUND...
THE VAST MAJORITY OF THEM ARE PROMPTLY **USED UP.**
I WAS TOLD WE'RE LIKE **BATTERIES** THAT ALCHEMISTS USE FOR THEIR EXPERIMENTS.
UNFOR-TUNATE, BUT TRUE.
THAT'S WHY I'M HERE TO ASK FOR YOUR COOPERA-TION.
WITH WHAT?
THE COLLEGE WANTS TO STUDY YOU. IF WE CAN LEARN HOW A SLEIGH BEGGY'S SYSTEM AND ORGANS WORK...
WE MAY BE ABLE TO CREATE AN ARTIFICIAL SUBSTITUTE.
EXAMINING THE UNIQUE PROPERTIES OF A SLEIGH BEGGY IS DIFFICULT. THAT'S WHY MOST ALCHEMISTS CHOOSE TO DRAIN THEM INSTEAD.
BUT IF THE COLLEGE CAN LEARN HOW THEY WORK, AND CAN LEARN TO CREATE AN **ALTERNATIVE--**
YOU'RE SAYING THAT ALCHEMISTS WOULD NO LONGER HAVE A REASON TO HUNT CHISE AND THOSE LIKE HER.

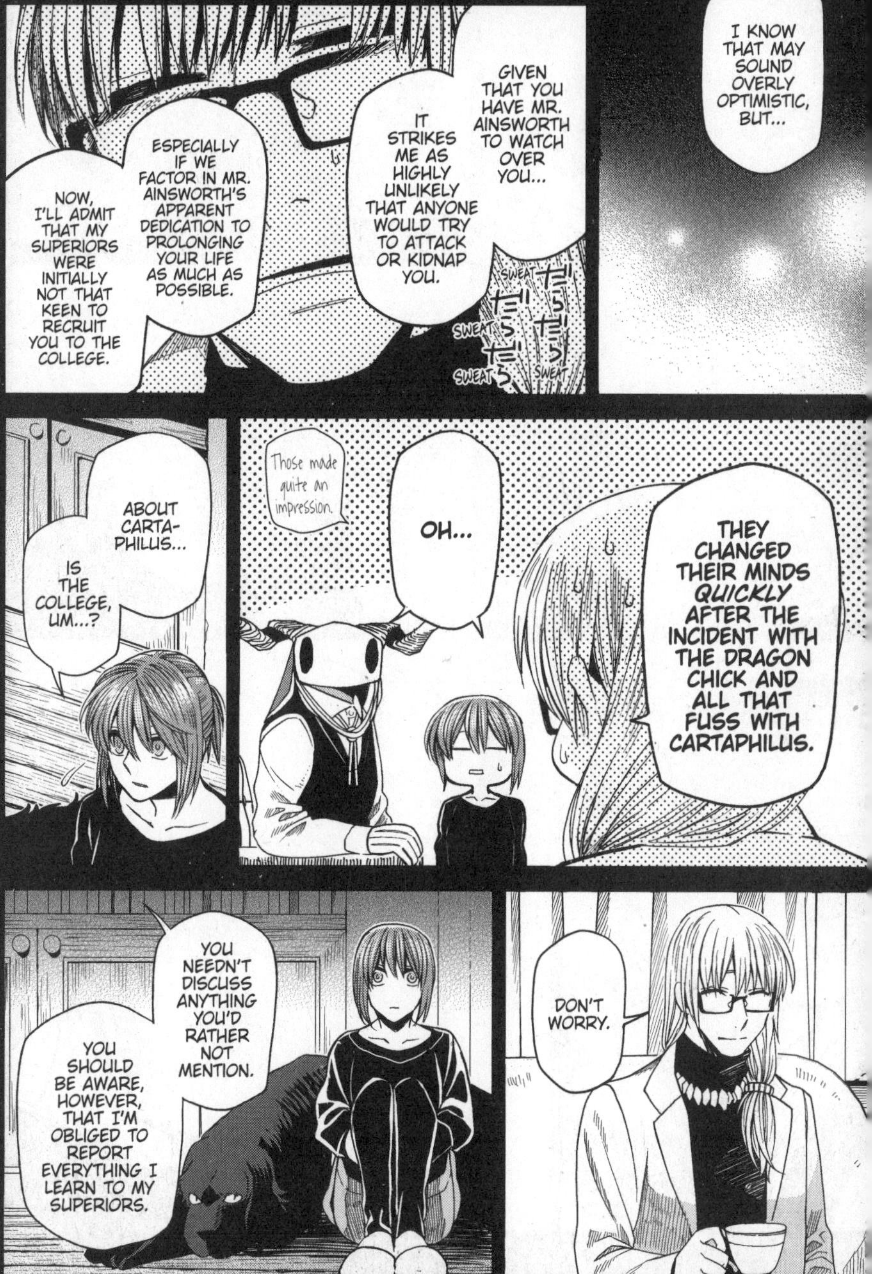
I KNOW THAT MAY SOUND OVERLY OPTIMISTIC, BUT...
GIVEN THAT YOU HAVE MR. AINSWORTH TO WATCH OVER YOU...
IT STRIKES ME AS HIGHLY UNLIKELY THAT ANYONE WOULD TRY TO ATTACK OR KIDNAP YOU.
SWEAT SWEAT SWEAT SWEAT
ESPECIALLY IF WE FACTOR IN MR. AINSWORTH'S APPARENT DEDICATION TO PROLONGING YOUR LIFE AS MUCH AS POSSIBLE.
NOW, I'LL ADMIT THAT MY SUPERIORS WERE INITIALLY NOT THAT KEEN TO RECRUIT YOU TO THE COLLEGE.
THEY CHANGED THEIR MINDS *QUICKLY* AFTER THE INCIDENT WITH THE DRAGON CHICK AND ALL THAT FUSS WITH CARTAPHILUS.
OH...
Those made quite an impression.
ABOUT CARTA-PHILUS...
IS THE COLLEGE, UM...?
DON'T WORRY.
YOU NEEDN'T DISCUSS ANYTHING YOU'D RATHER NOT MENTION.
YOU SHOULD BE AWARE, HOWEVER, THAT I'M OBLIGED TO REPORT EVERYTHING I LEARN TO MY SUPERIORS.

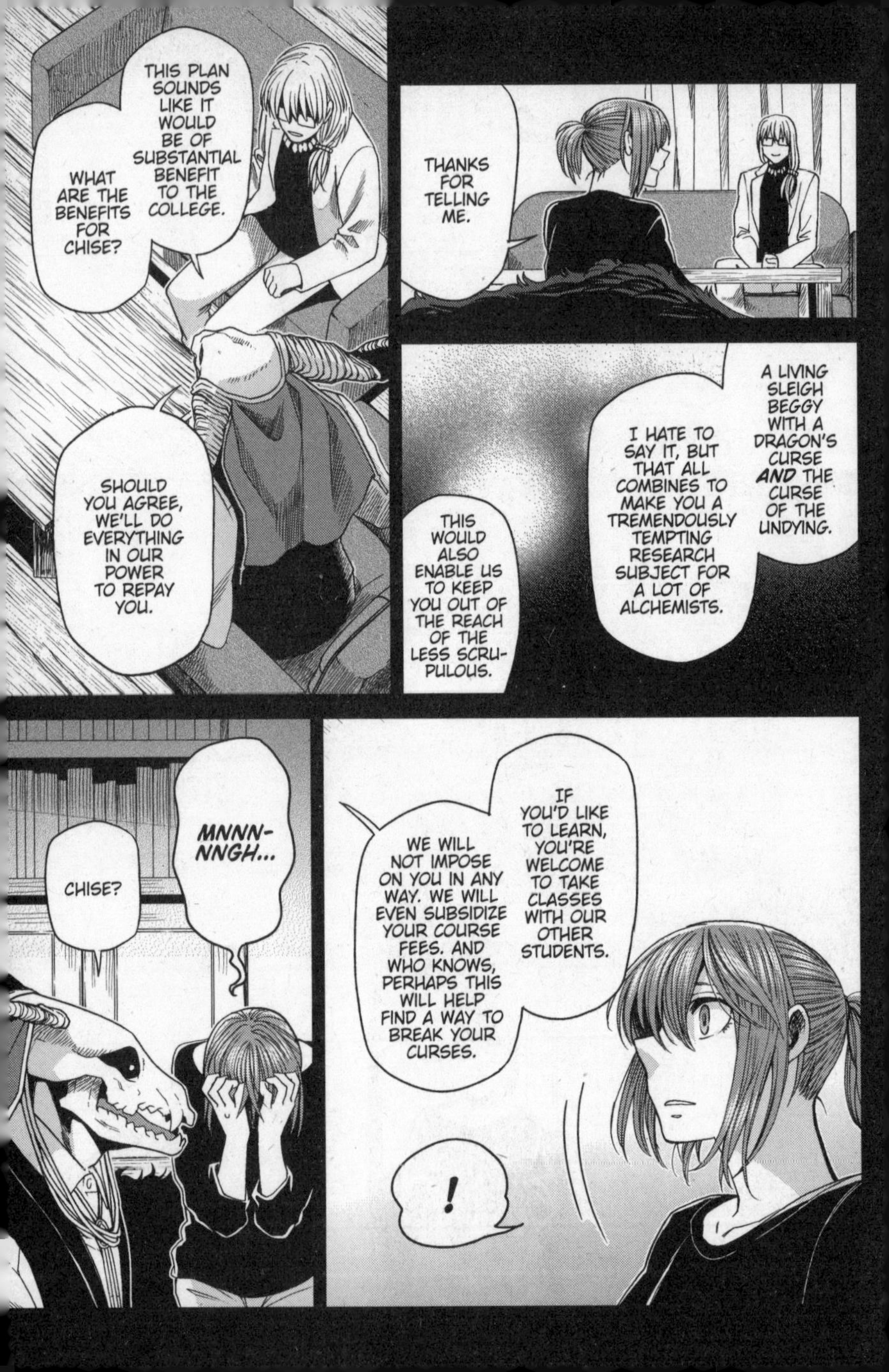
THANKS FOR TELLING ME.
A LIVING SLEIGH BEGGY WITH A DRAGON'S CURSE *AND* THE CURSE OF THE UNDYING.
I HATE TO SAY IT, BUT THAT ALL COMBINES TO MAKE YOU A TREMENDOUSLY TEMPTING RESEARCH SUBJECT FOR A LOT OF ALCHEMISTS.
THIS WOULD ALSO ENABLE US TO KEEP YOU OUT OF THE REACH OF THE LESS SCRU-PULOUS.
THIS PLAN SOUNDS LIKE IT WOULD BE OF SUBSTANTIAL BENEFIT TO THE COLLEGE.
WHAT ARE THE BENEFITS FOR CHISE?
SHOULD YOU AGREE, WE'LL DO EVERYTHING IN OUR POWER TO REPAY YOU.
IF YOU'D LIKE TO LEARN, YOU'RE WELCOME TO TAKE CLASSES WITH OUR OTHER STUDENTS.
WE WILL NOT IMPOSE ON YOU IN ANY WAY. WE WILL EVEN SUBSIDIZE YOUR COURSE FEES. AND WHO KNOWS, PERHAPS THIS WILL HELP FIND A WAY TO BREAK YOUR CURSES.
!
MNNN-NNGH...
CHISE?

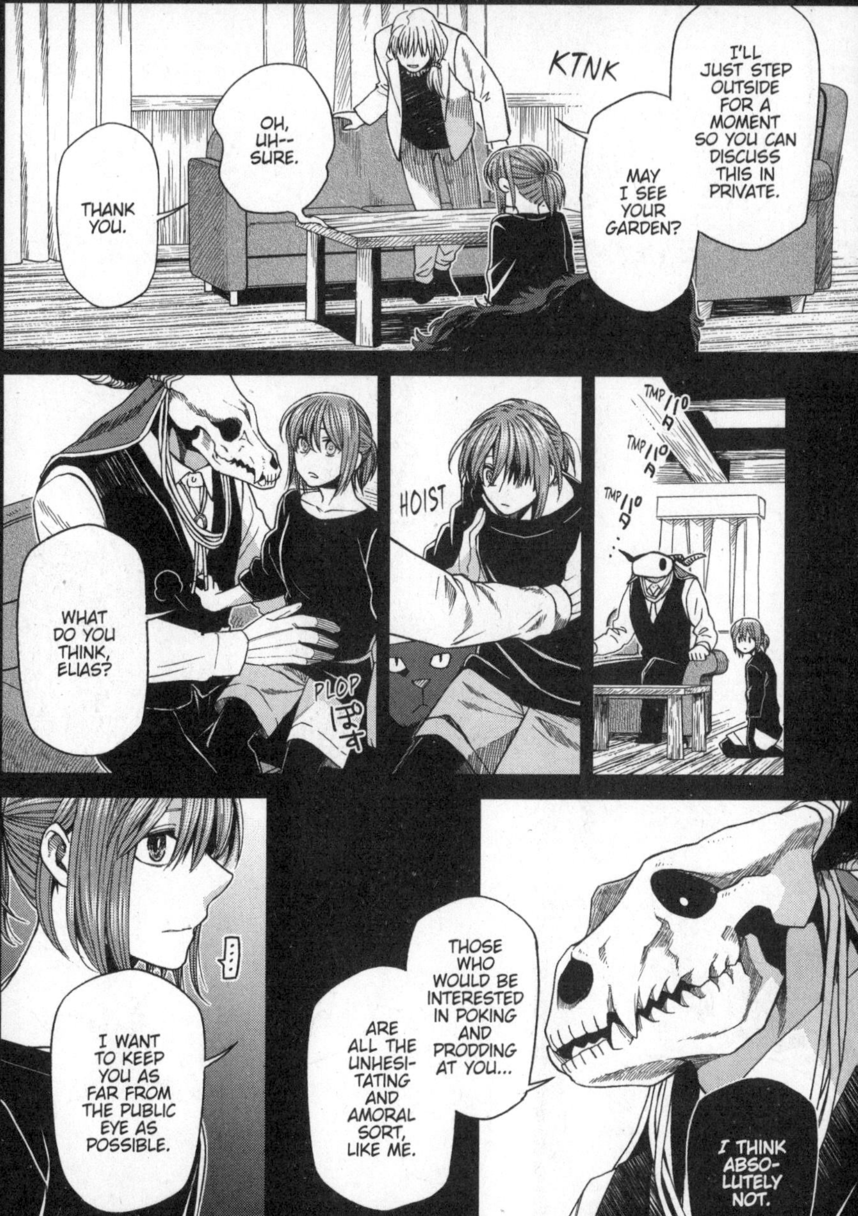
I'LL JUST STEP OUTSIDE FOR A MOMENT SO YOU CAN DISCUSS THIS IN PRIVATE.
MAY I SEE YOUR GARDEN?
KTNK
OH, UH-- SURE.
THANK YOU.
TMP パタ
TMP パタ
TMP パタ
...
HOIST
WHAT DO YOU THINK, ELIAS?
PLOP ぽす
THOSE WHO WOULD BE INTERESTED IN POKING AND PRODDING AT YOU...
ARE ALL THE UNHESITATING AND AMORAL SORT, LIKE ME.
I THINK ABSOLUTELY NOT.
...
I WANT TO KEEP YOU AS FAR FROM THE PUBLIC EYE AS POSSIBLE.

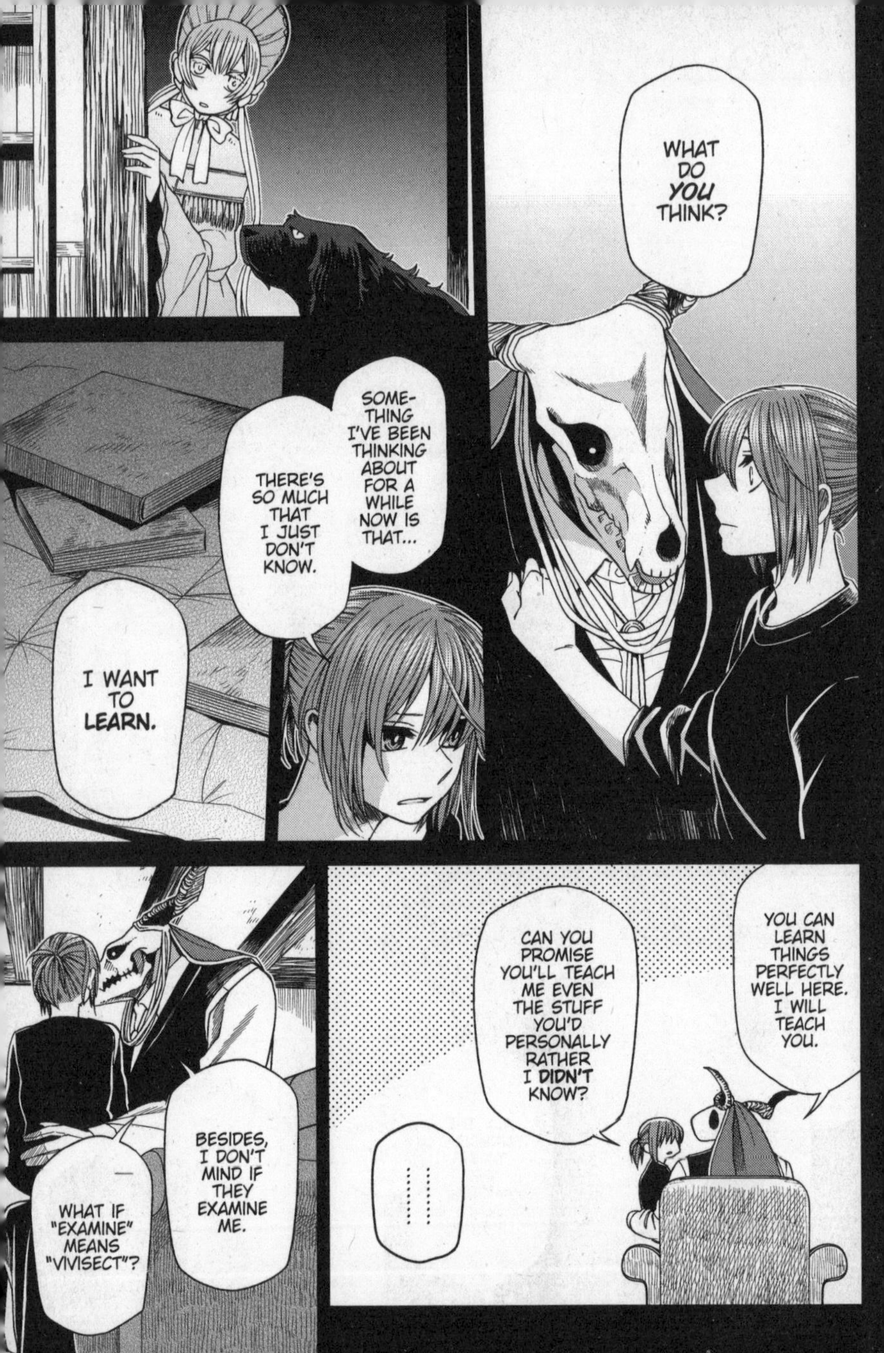
WHAT DO YOU THINK?
SOME-THING I'VE BEEN THINKING ABOUT FOR A WHILE NOW IS THAT...
THERE'S SO MUCH THAT I JUST DON'T KNOW.
I WANT TO LEARN.
YOU CAN LEARN THINGS PERFECTLY WELL HERE. I WILL TEACH YOU.
CAN YOU PROMISE YOU'LL TEACH ME EVEN THE STUFF YOU'D PERSONALLY RATHER I DIDN'T KNOW?
......
BESIDES, I DON'T MIND IF THEY EXAMINE ME.
— WHAT IF "EXAMINE" MEANS "VIVISECT"?

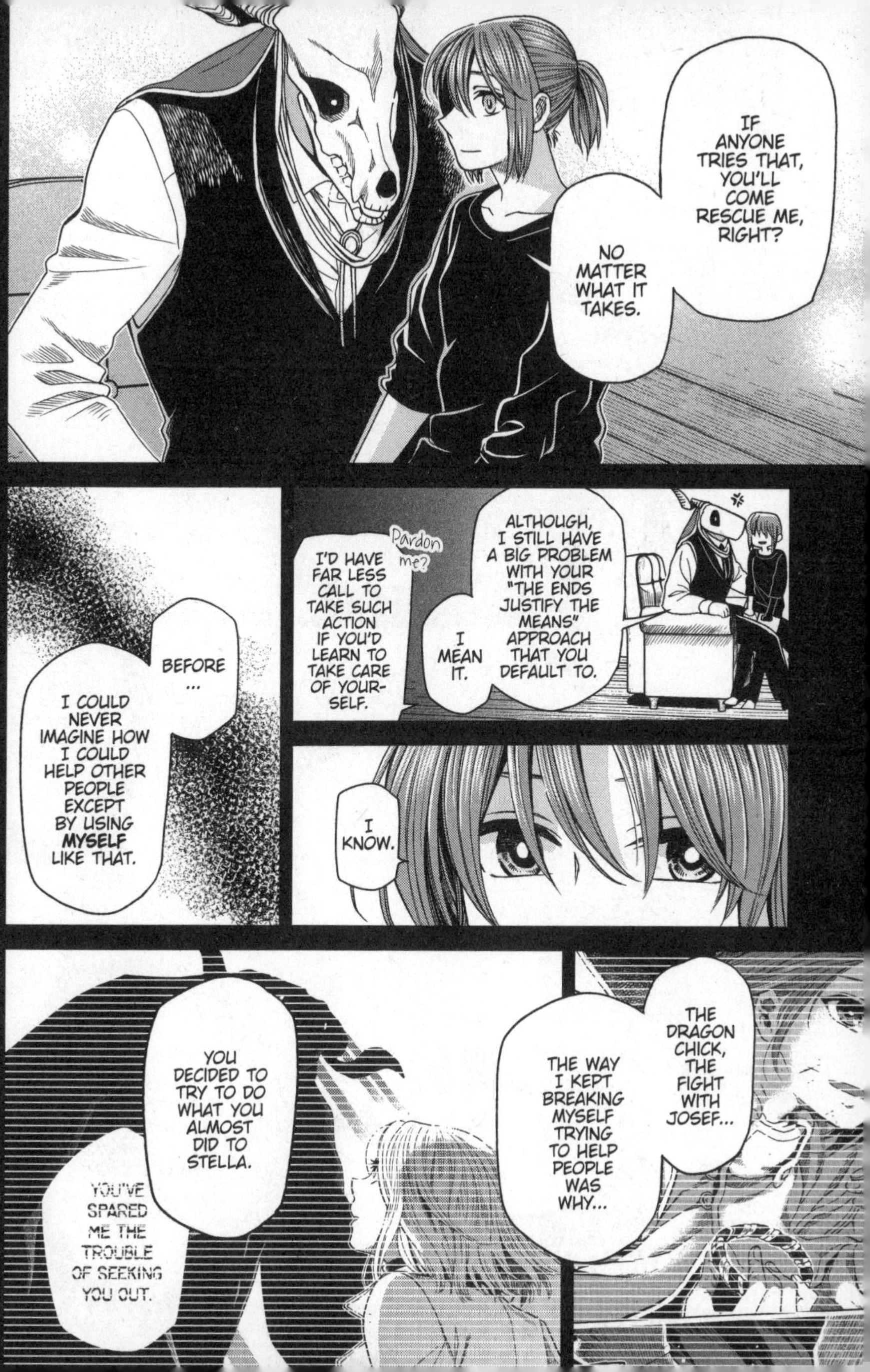
IF ANYONE TRIES THAT, YOU'LL COME RESCUE ME, RIGHT?
NO MATTER WHAT IT TAKES.
ALTHOUGH, I STILL HAVE A BIG PROBLEM WITH YOUR "THE ENDS JUSTIFY THE MEANS" APPROACH THAT YOU DEFAULT TO.
I MEAN IT.
Pardon me?
I'D HAVE FAR LESS CALL TO TAKE SUCH ACTION IF YOU'D LEARN TO TAKE CARE OF YOURSELF.
I KNOW.
BEFORE...
I COULD NEVER IMAGINE HOW I COULD HELP OTHER PEOPLE EXCEPT BY USING MYSELF LIKE THAT.
THE DRAGON CHICK, THE FIGHT WITH JOSEF...
THE WAY I KEPT BREAKING MYSELF TRYING TO HELP PEOPLE WAS WHY...
YOU DECIDED TO TRY TO DO WHAT YOU ALMOST DID TO STELLA.
YOU'VE SPARED ME THE TROUBLE OF SEEKING YOU OUT.

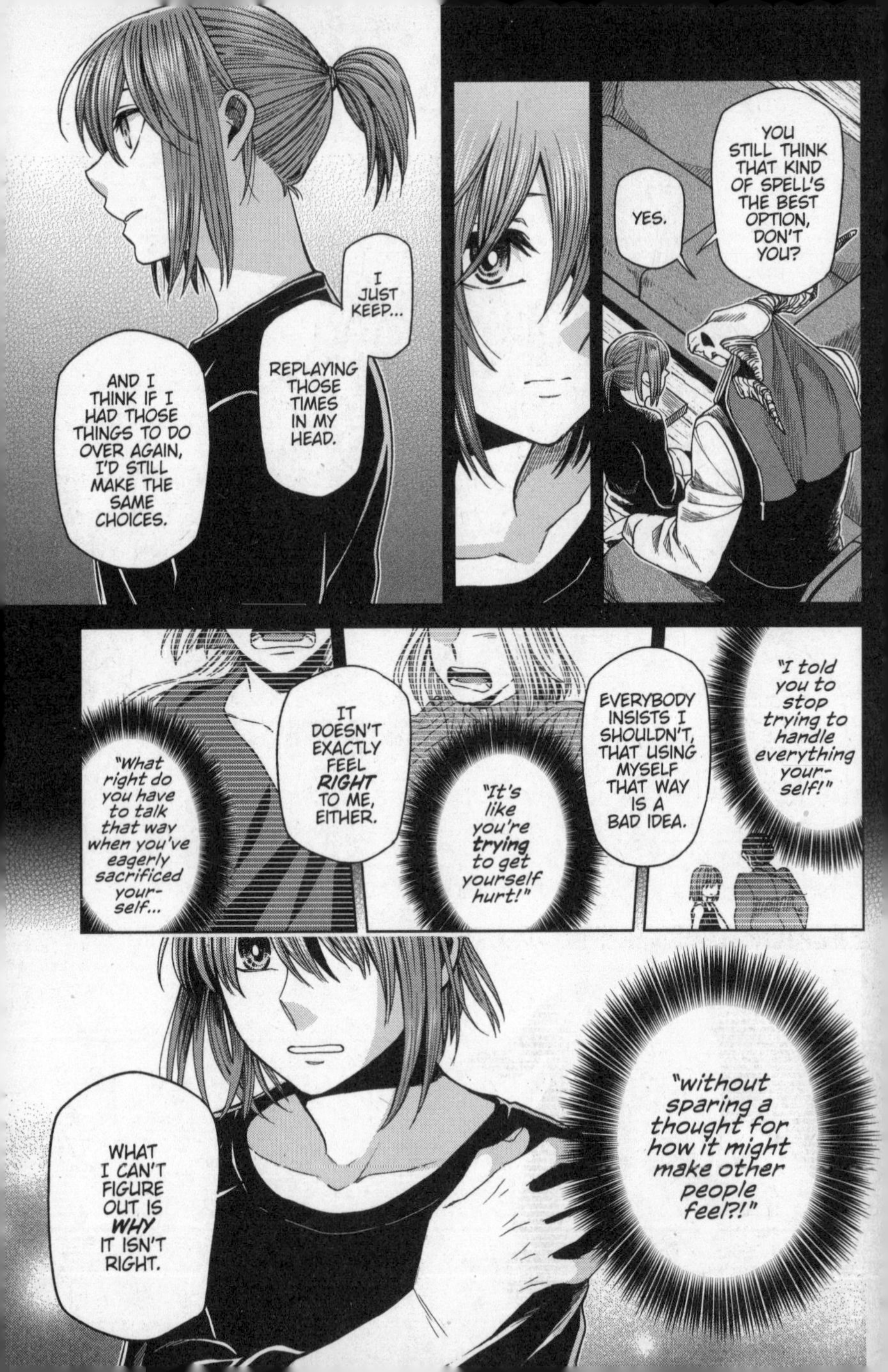
YOU STILL THINK THAT KIND OF SPELL'S THE BEST OPTION, DON'T YOU?
YES.
I JUST KEEP...
REPLAYING THOSE TIMES IN MY HEAD.
AND I THINK IF I HAD THOSE THINGS TO DO OVER AGAIN, I'D STILL MAKE THE SAME CHOICES.
"I told you to stop trying to handle everything your-self!"
EVERYBODY INSISTS I SHOULDN'T, THAT USING MYSELF THAT WAY IS A BAD IDEA.
"It's like you're **trying** to get yourself hurt!"
IT DOESN'T EXACTLY FEEL **RIGHT** TO ME, EITHER.
"What right do you have to talk that way when you've eagerly sacrificed your-self...
"without sparing a thought for how it might make other people feel?!"
WHAT I CAN'T FIGURE OUT IS ***WHY*** IT ISN'T RIGHT.

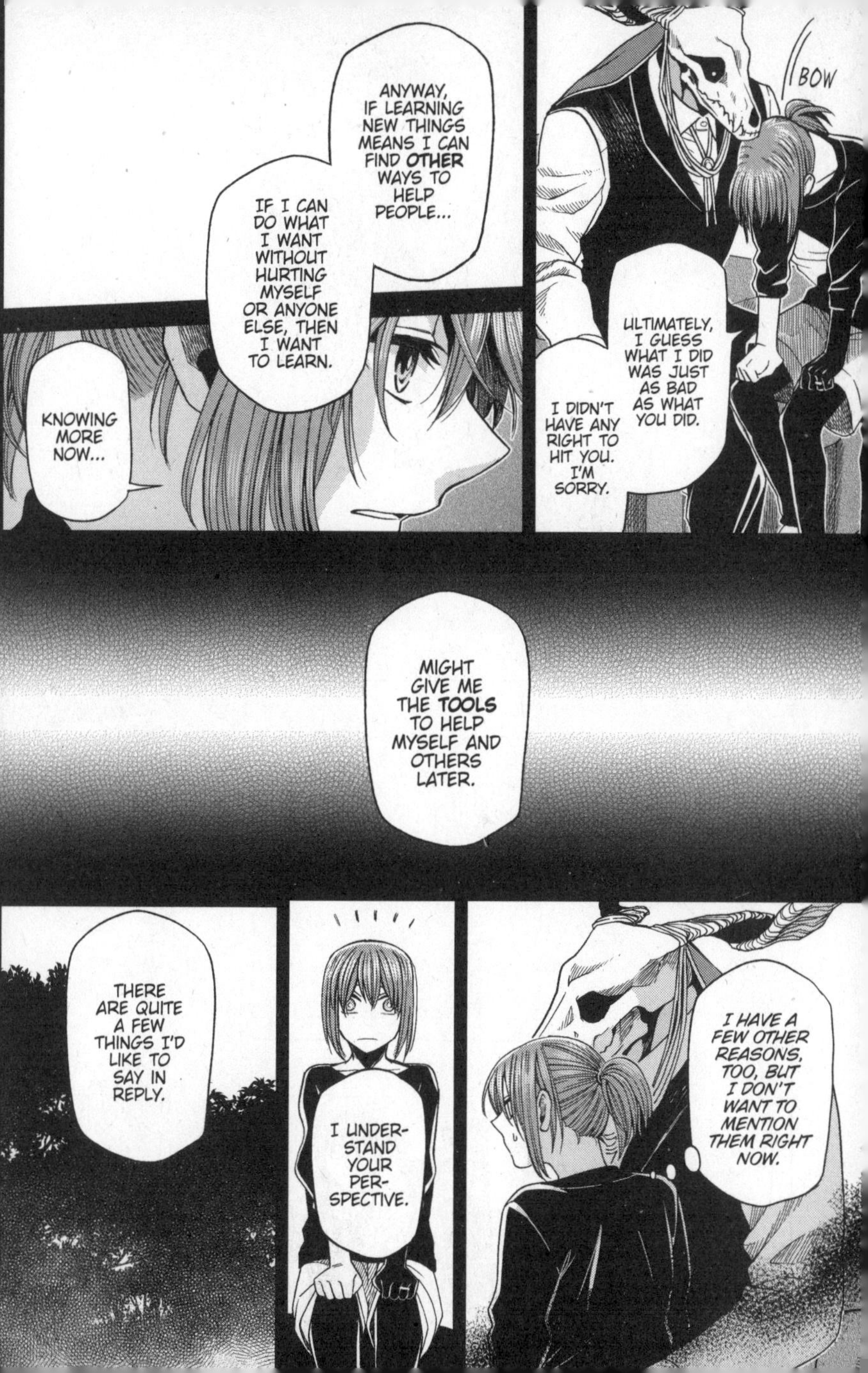
BOW
ULTIMATELY, I GUESS WHAT I DID WAS JUST AS BAD AS WHAT YOU DID.
I DIDN'T HAVE ANY RIGHT TO HIT YOU. I'M SORRY.
ANYWAY, IF LEARNING NEW THINGS MEANS I CAN FIND **OTHER** WAYS TO HELP PEOPLE...
IF I CAN DO WHAT I WANT WITHOUT HURTING MYSELF OR ANYONE ELSE, THEN I WANT TO LEARN.
KNOWING MORE NOW...
MIGHT GIVE ME THE **TOOLS** TO HELP MYSELF AND OTHERS LATER.
I HAVE A FEW OTHER REASONS, TOO, BUT I DON'T WANT TO MENTION THEM RIGHT NOW.
I UNDER-STAND YOUR PER-SPECTIVE.
THERE ARE QUITE A FEW THINGS I'D LIKE TO SAY IN REPLY.

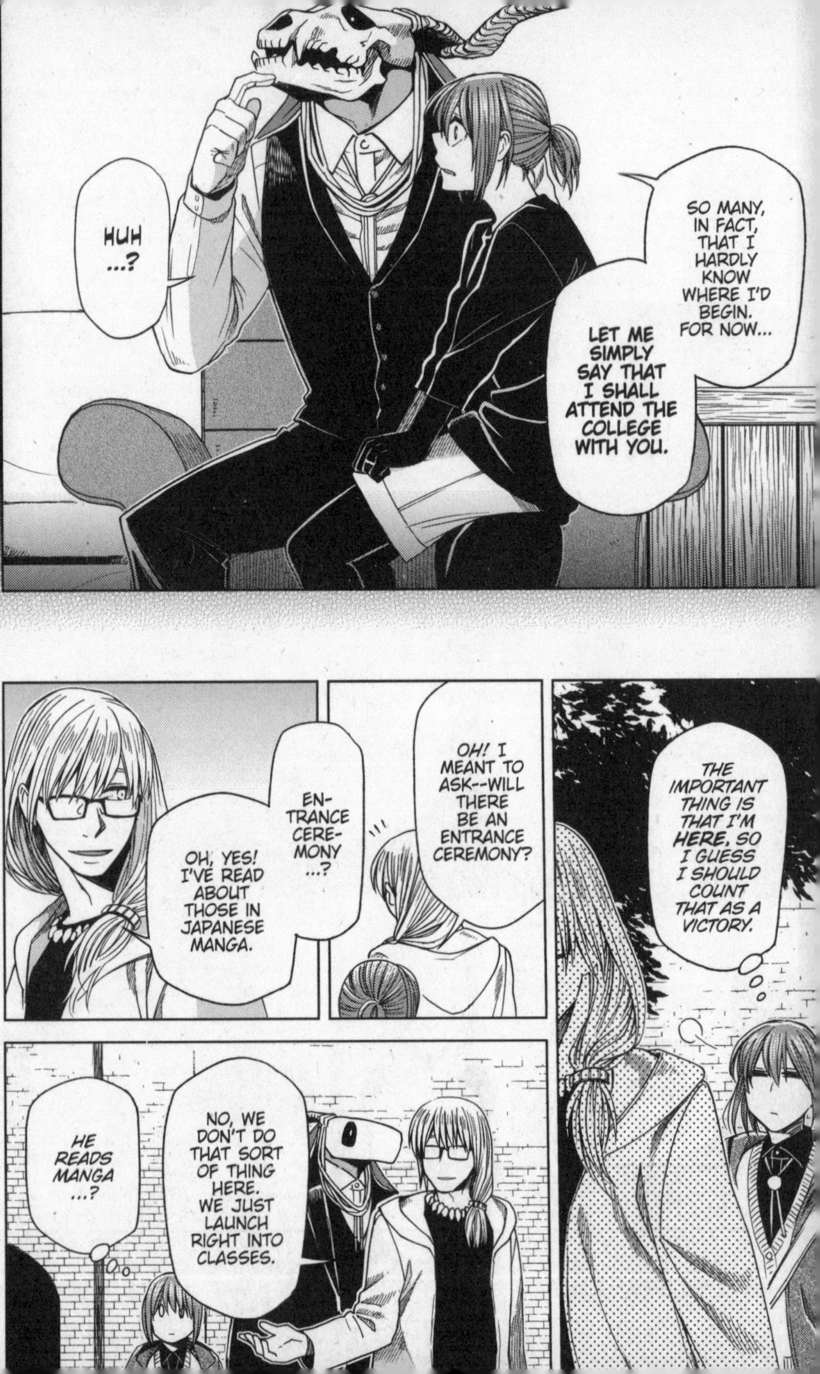
SO MANY, IN FACT, THAT I HARDLY KNOW WHERE I'D BEGIN. FOR NOW...
LET ME SIMPLY SAY THAT I SHALL ATTEND THE COLLEGE WITH YOU.
HUH ...?
THE IMPORTANT THING IS THAT I'M HERE, SO I GUESS I SHOULD COUNT THAT AS A VICTORY.
OH! I MEANT TO ASK--WILL THERE BE AN ENTRANCE CEREMONY?
EN-TRANCE CERE-MONY ...?
OH, YES! I'VE READ ABOUT THOSE IN JAPANESE MANGA.
NO, WE DON'T DO THAT SORT OF THING HERE. WE JUST LAUNCH RIGHT INTO CLASSES.
HE READS MANGA ...?

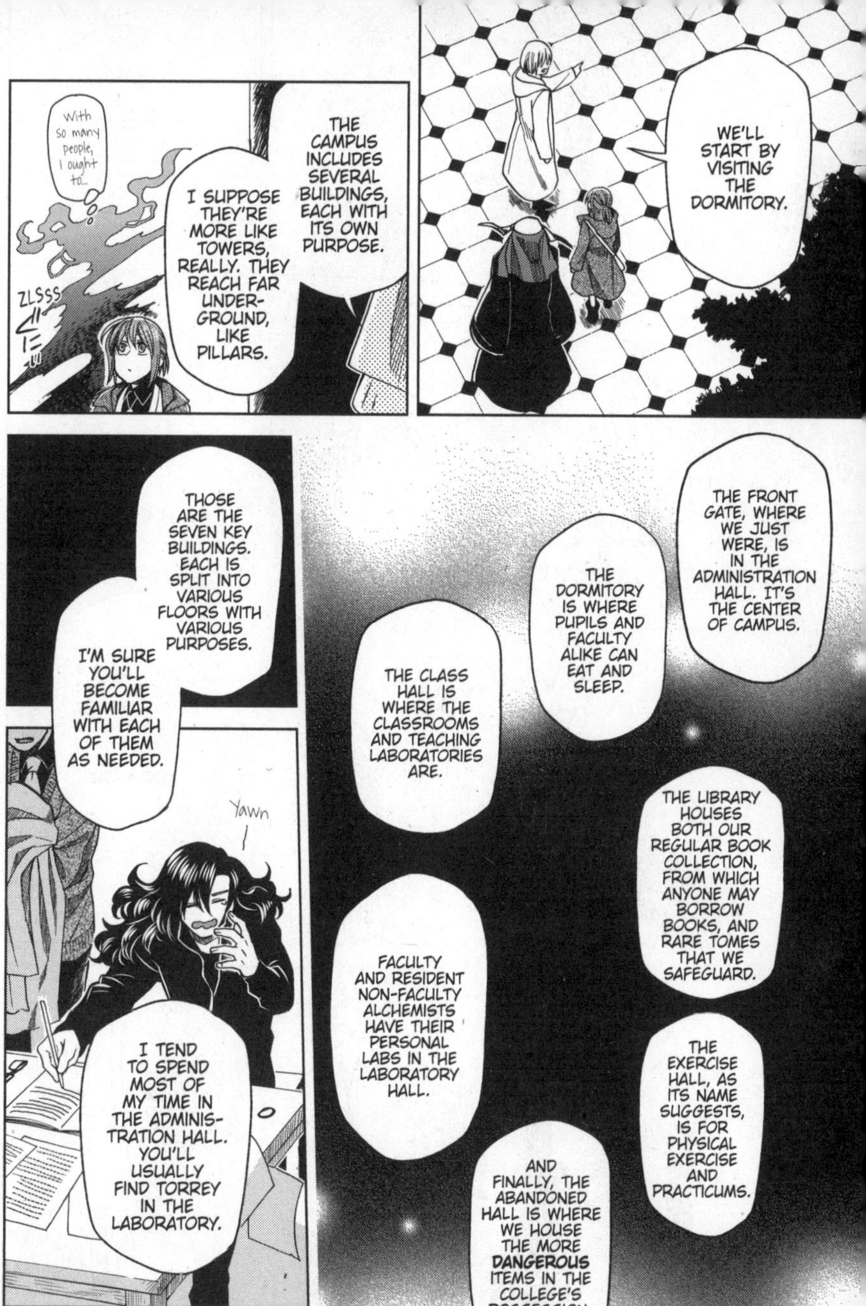
WE'LL START BY VISITING THE DORMITORY.
THE CAMPUS INCLUDES SEVERAL BUILDINGS, EACH WITH ITS OWN PURPOSE.
I SUPPOSE THEY'RE MORE LIKE TOWERS, REALLY. THEY REACH FAR UNDER-GROUND, LIKE PILLARS.
With so many people, I ought to...
ZLSSS
THE FRONT GATE, WHERE WE JUST WERE, IS IN THE ADMINISTRATION HALL. IT'S THE CENTER OF CAMPUS.
THE DORMITORY IS WHERE PUPILS AND FACULTY ALIKE CAN EAT AND SLEEP.
THE CLASS HALL IS WHERE THE CLASSROOMS AND TEACHING LABORATORIES ARE.
THE LIBRARY HOUSES BOTH OUR REGULAR BOOK COLLECTION, FROM WHICH ANYONE MAY BORROW BOOKS, AND RARE TOMES THAT WE SAFEGUARD.
FACULTY AND RESIDENT NON-FACULTY ALCHEMISTS HAVE THEIR PERSONAL LABS IN THE LABORATORY HALL.
THE EXERCISE HALL, AS ITS NAME SUGGESTS, IS FOR PHYSICAL EXERCISE AND PRACTICUMS.
AND FINALLY, THE ABANDONED HALL IS WHERE WE HOUSE THE MORE **DANGEROUS** ITEMS IN THE COLLEGE'S POSSESSION.
THOSE ARE THE SEVEN KEY BUILDINGS. EACH IS SPLIT INTO VARIOUS FLOORS WITH VARIOUS PURPOSES.
I'M SURE YOU'LL BECOME FAMILIAR WITH EACH OF THEM AS NEEDED.
Yawn
I TEND TO SPEND MOST OF MY TIME IN THE ADMINIS-TRATION HALL. YOU'LL USUALLY FIND TORREY IN THE LABORATORY.

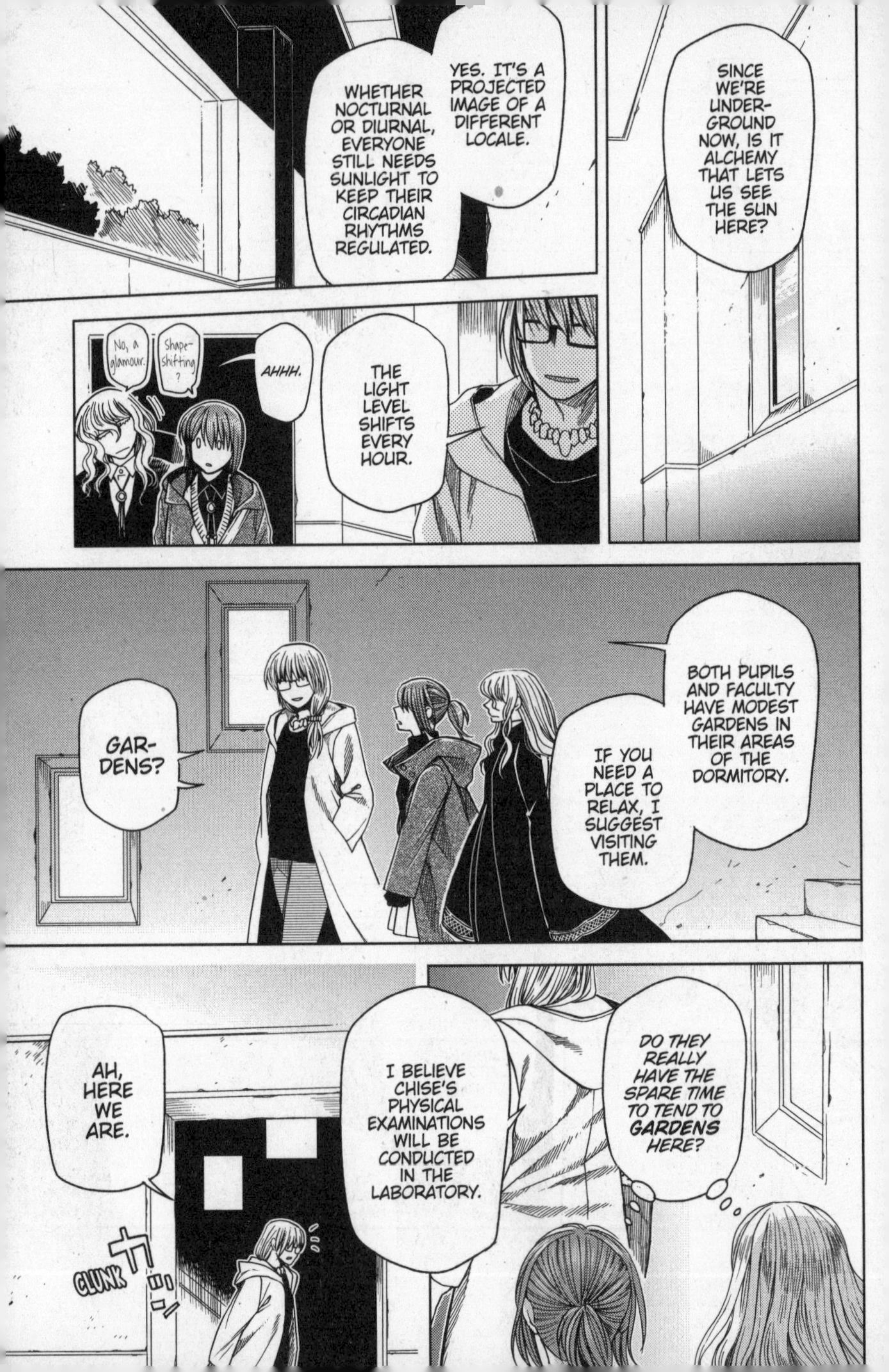

SINCE WE'RE UNDERGROUND NOW, IS IT ALCHEMY THAT LETS US SEE THE SUN HERE?
YES. IT'S A PROJECTED IMAGE OF A DIFFERENT LOCALE.
WHETHER NOCTURNAL OR DIURNAL, EVERYONE STILL NEEDS SUNLIGHT TO KEEP THEIR CIRCADIAN RHYTHMS REGULATED.
THE LIGHT LEVEL SHIFTS EVERY HOUR.
AHHH.
Shape-shifting?
No, a glamour.
BOTH PUPILS AND FACULTY HAVE MODEST GARDENS IN THEIR AREAS OF THE DORMITORY.
IF YOU NEED A PLACE TO RELAX, I SUGGEST VISITING THEM.
GARDENS?
DO THEY REALLY HAVE THE SPARE TIME TO TEND TO GARDENS HERE?
I BELIEVE CHISE'S PHYSICAL EXAMINATIONS WILL BE CONDUCTED IN THE LABORATORY.
AH, HERE WE ARE.
CLUNK

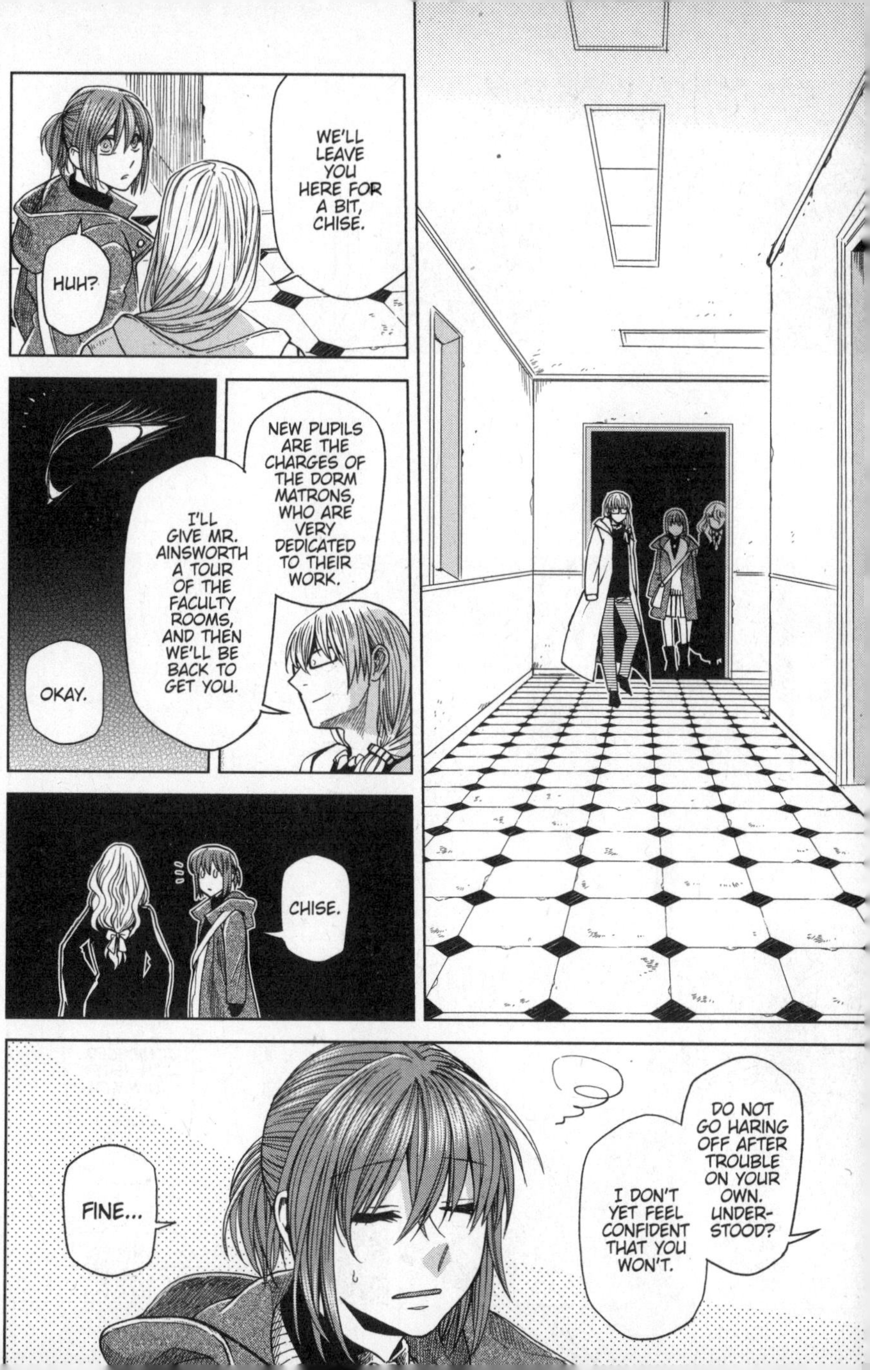
WE'LL LEAVE YOU HERE FOR A BIT, CHISE.
HUH?
NEW PUPILS ARE THE CHARGES OF THE DORM MATRONS, WHO ARE VERY DEDICATED TO THEIR WORK.
I'LL GIVE MR. AINSWORTH A TOUR OF THE FACULTY ROOMS, AND THEN WE'LL BE BACK TO GET YOU.
OKAY.
CHISE.
DO NOT GO HARING OFF AFTER TROUBLE ON YOUR OWN. UNDER-STOOD?
I DON'T YET FEEL CONFIDENT THAT YOU WON'T.
FINE...

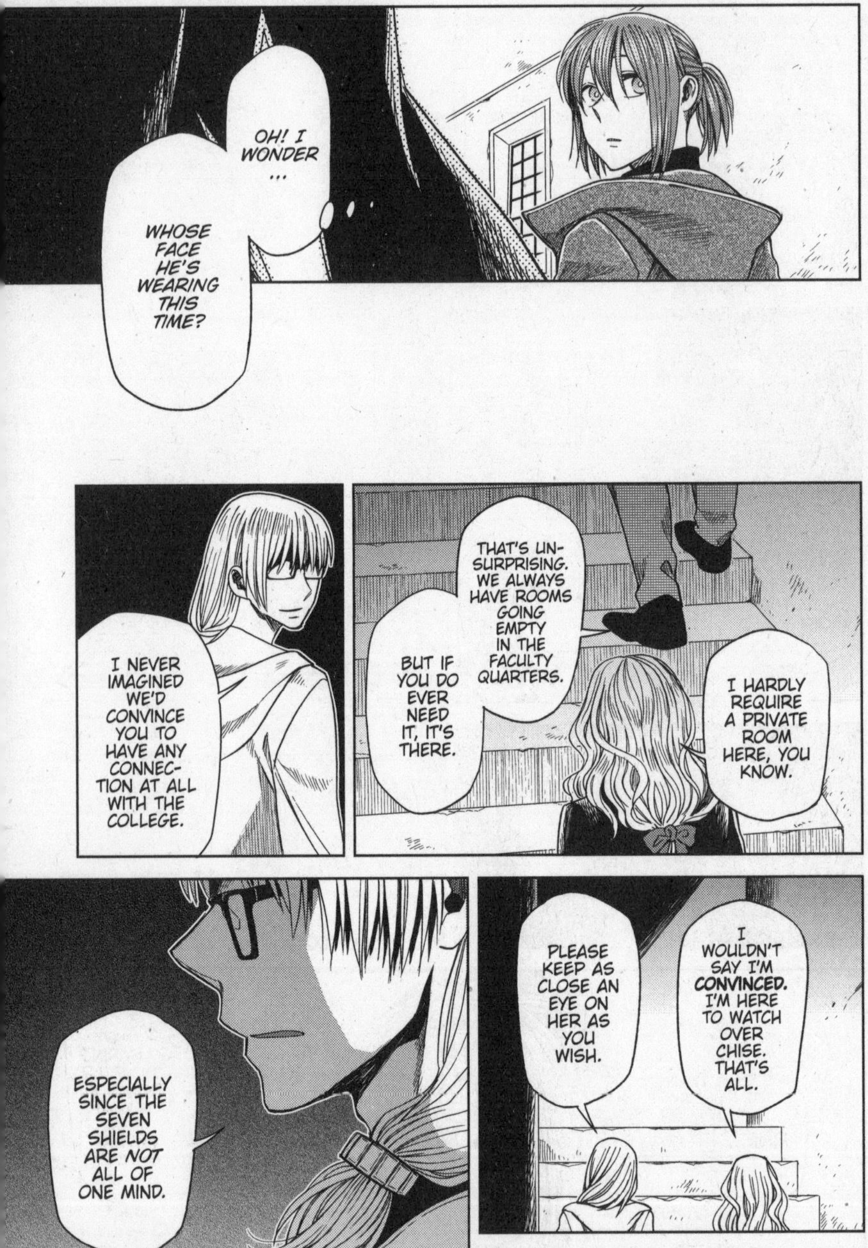
OH! I WONDER... WHOSE FACE HE'S WEARING THIS TIME?
I HARDLY REQUIRE A PRIVATE ROOM HERE, YOU KNOW.
THAT'S UNSURPRISING. WE ALWAYS HAVE ROOMS GOING EMPTY IN THE FACULTY QUARTERS.
BUT IF YOU DO EVER NEED IT, IT'S THERE.
I NEVER IMAGINED WE'D CONVINCE YOU TO HAVE ANY CONNECTION AT ALL WITH THE COLLEGE.
I WOULDN'T SAY I'M **CONVINCED.** I'M HERE TO WATCH OVER CHISE. THAT'S ALL.
PLEASE KEEP AS CLOSE AN EYE ON HER AS YOU WISH.
ESPECIALLY SINCE THE SEVEN SHIELDS ARE *NOT* ALL OF ONE MIND.

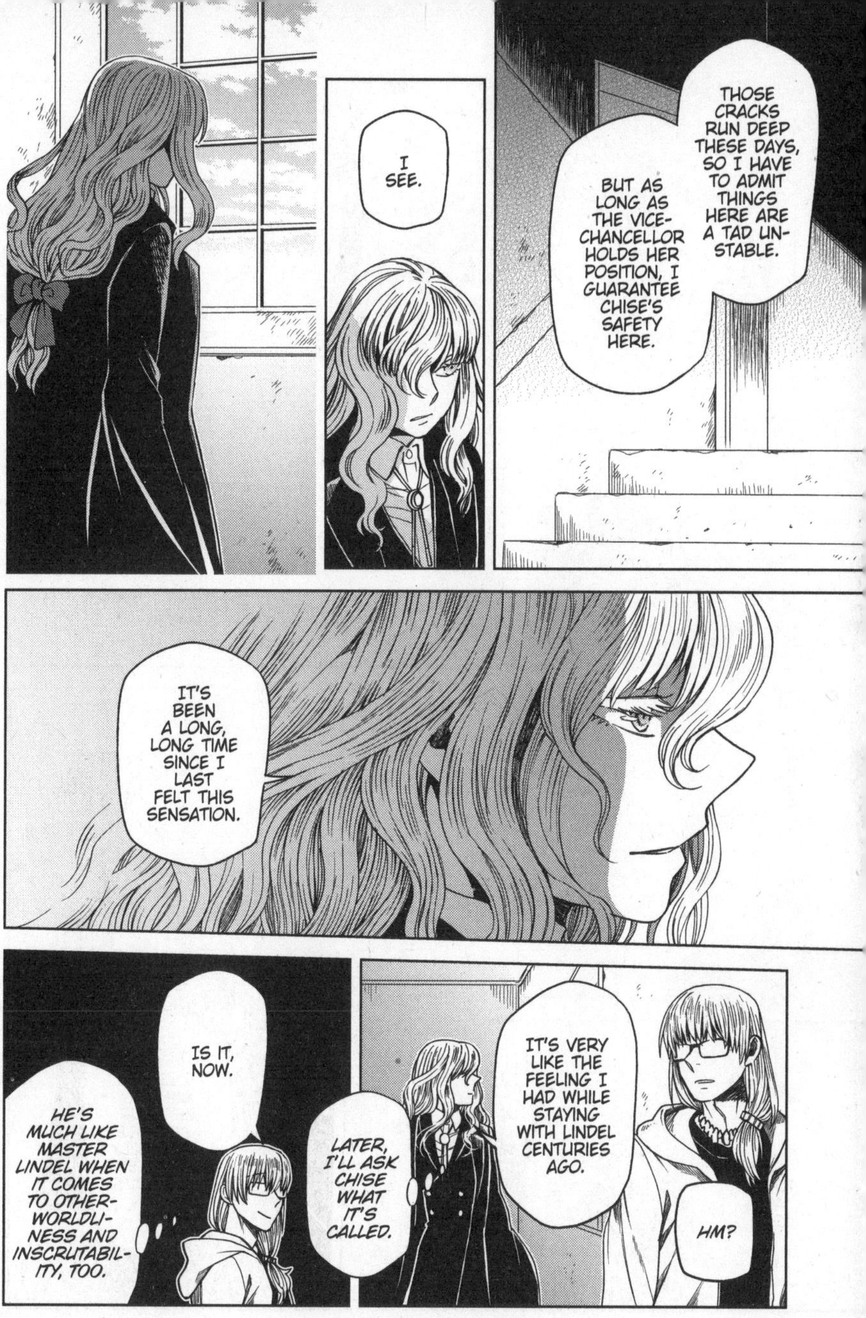
THOSE CRACKS RUN DEEP THESE DAYS, SO I HAVE TO ADMIT THINGS HERE ARE A TAD UNSTABLE.
BUT AS LONG AS THE VICE-CHANCELLOR HOLDS HER POSITION, I GUARANTEE CHISE'S SAFETY HERE.
I SEE.
IT'S BEEN A LONG, LONG TIME SINCE I LAST FELT THIS SENSATION.
IT'S VERY LIKE THE FEELING I HAD WHILE STAYING WITH LINDEL CENTURIES AGO.
HM?
LATER, I'LL ASK CHISE WHAT IT'S CALLED.
IS IT, NOW.
HE'S MUCH LIKE MASTER LINDEL WHEN IT COMES TO OTHERWORLDLINESS AND INSCRUTABILITY, TOO.

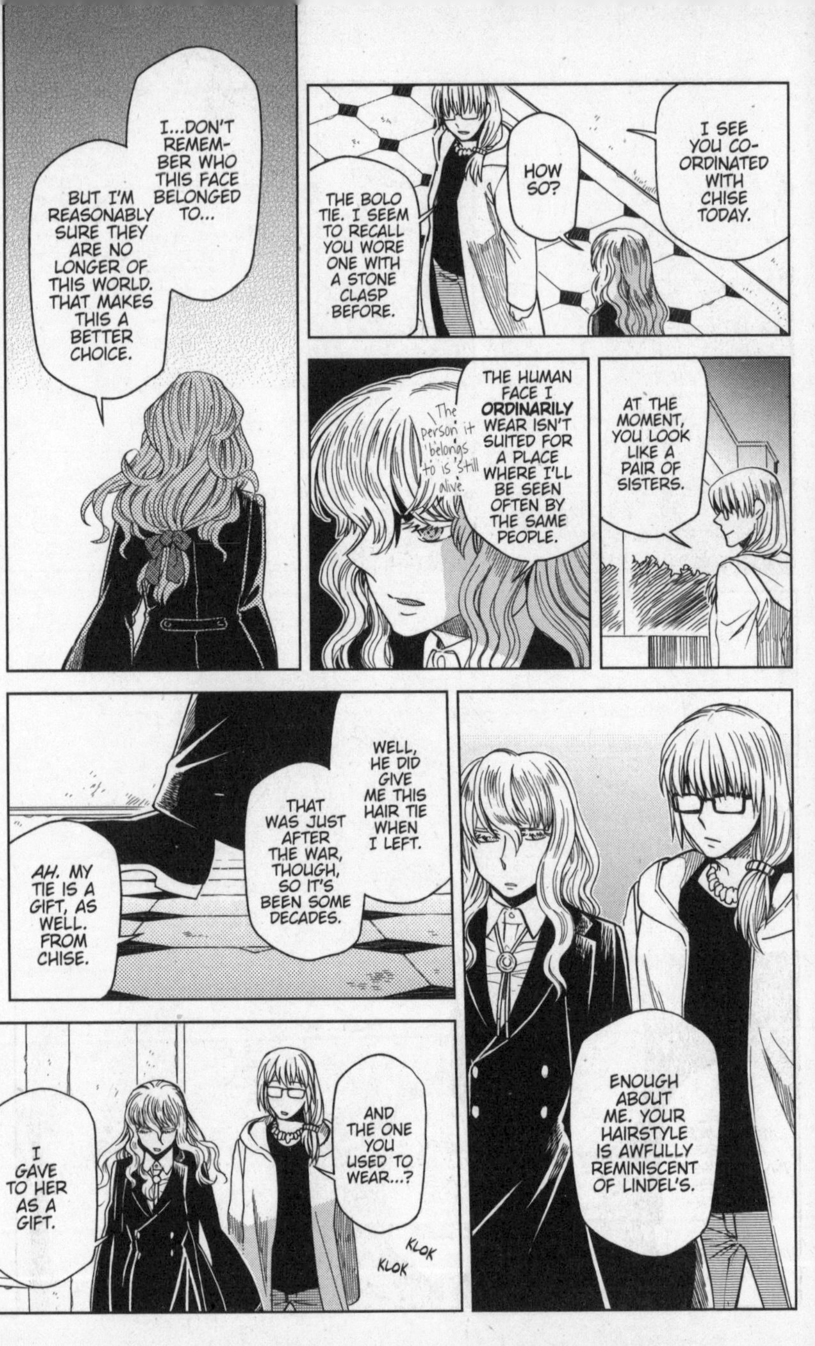
I SEE YOU CO-ORDINATED WITH CHISE TODAY.
HOW SO?
THE BOLO TIE. I SEEM TO RECALL YOU WORE ONE WITH A STONE CLASP BEFORE.
AT THE MOMENT, YOU LOOK LIKE A PAIR OF SISTERS.
THE HUMAN FACE I **ORDINARILY** WEAR ISN'T SUITED FOR A PLACE WHERE I'LL BE SEEN OFTEN BY THE SAME PEOPLE.
The person it belongs to is still alive.
I...DON'T REMEMBER WHO THIS FACE BELONGED TO...
BUT I'M REASONABLY SURE THEY ARE NO LONGER OF THIS WORLD. THAT MAKES THIS A BETTER CHOICE.
ENOUGH ABOUT ME. YOUR HAIRSTYLE IS AWFULLY REMINISCENT OF LINDEL'S.
WELL, HE DID GIVE ME THIS HAIR TIE WHEN I LEFT.
THAT WAS JUST AFTER THE WAR, THOUGH, SO IT'S BEEN SOME DECADES.
AH. MY TIE IS A GIFT, AS WELL. FROM CHISE.
AND THE ONE YOU USED TO WEAR...?
KLOK
KLOK
I GAVE TO HER AS A GIFT.

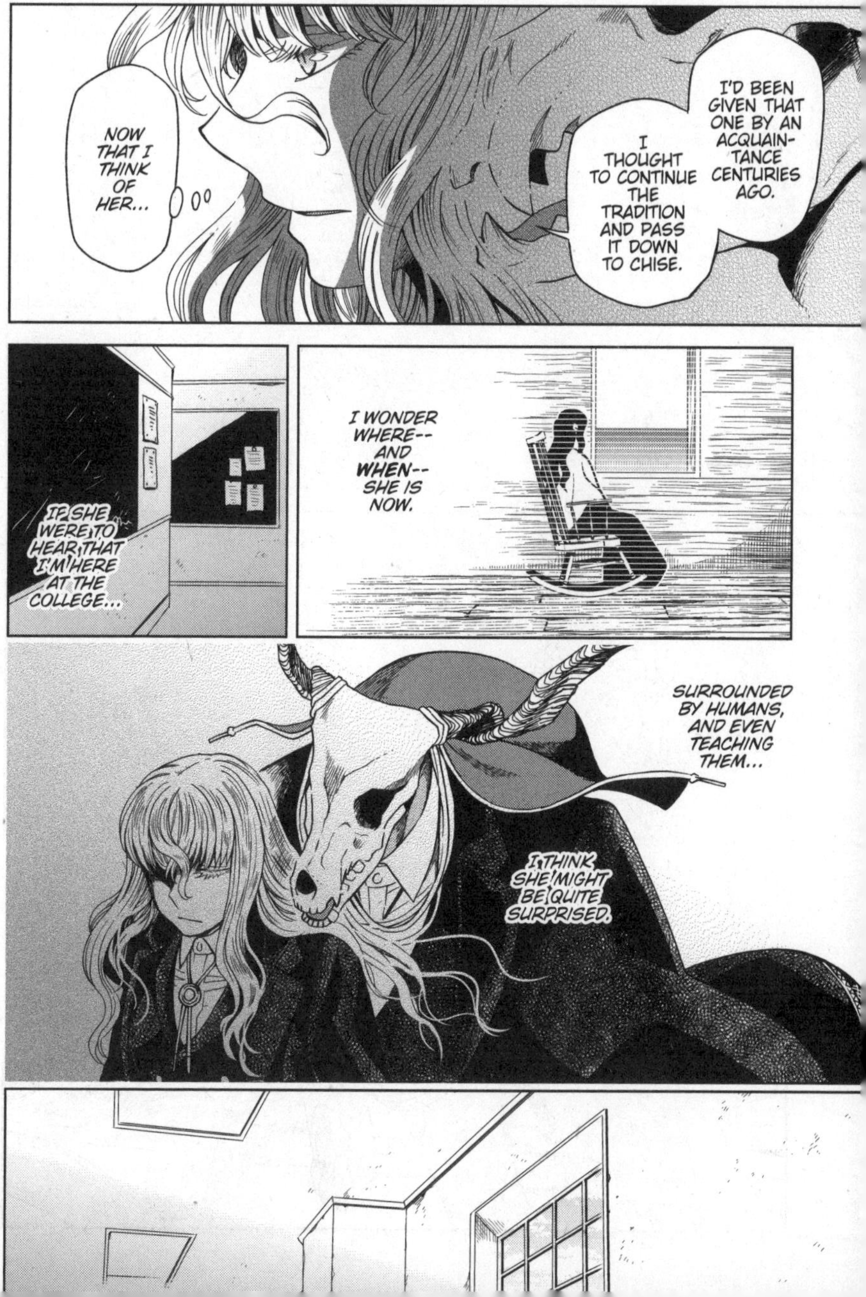
I'D BEEN GIVEN THAT ONE BY AN ACQUAIN-TANCE CENTURIES AGO.
I THOUGHT TO CONTINUE THE TRADITION AND PASS IT DOWN TO CHISE.
NOW THAT I THINK OF HER...
I WONDER WHERE--AND WHEN--SHE IS NOW.
IF SHE WERE TO HEAR THAT I'M HERE AT THE COLLEGE...
SURROUNDED BY HUMANS, AND EVEN TEACHING THEM...
I THINK SHE MIGHT BE QUITE SURPRISED.

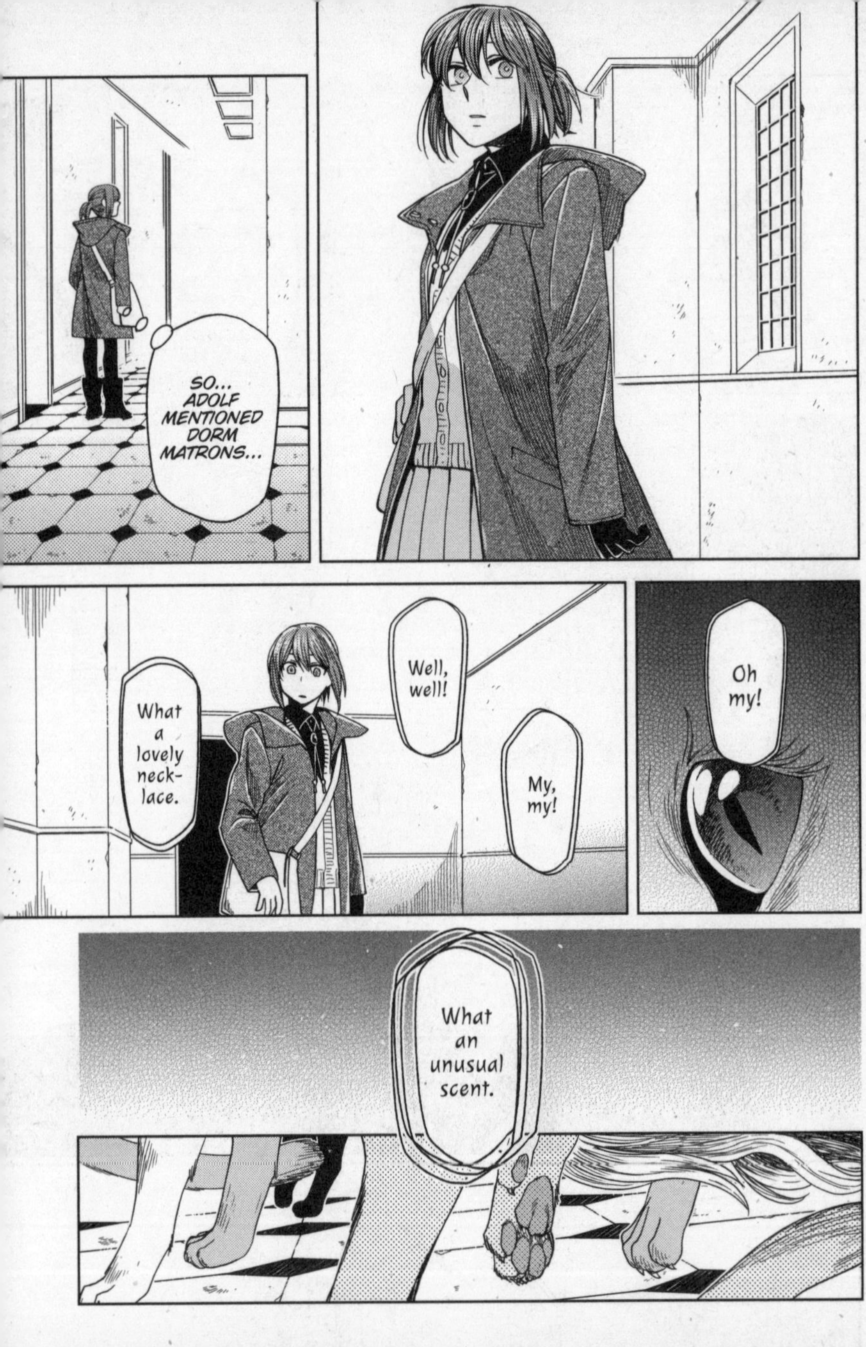
SO... ADOLF MENTIONED DORM MATRONS...
Oh my!
Well, well!
My, my!
What a lovely neck-lace.
What an unusual scent.

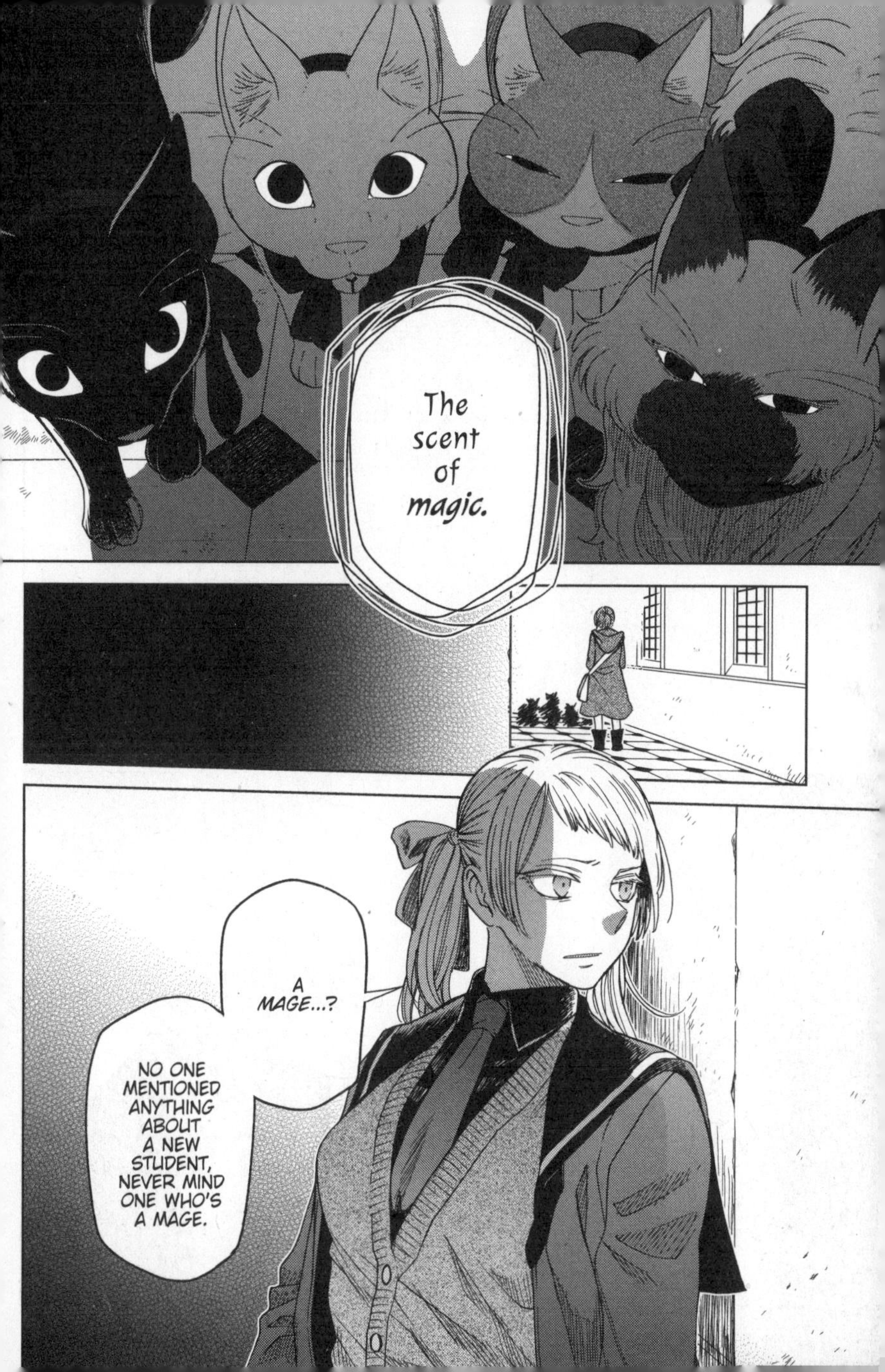

The scent of magic.
A MAGE...?
NO ONE MENTIONED ANYTHING ABOUT A NEW STUDENT, NEVER MIND ONE WHO'S A MAGE.

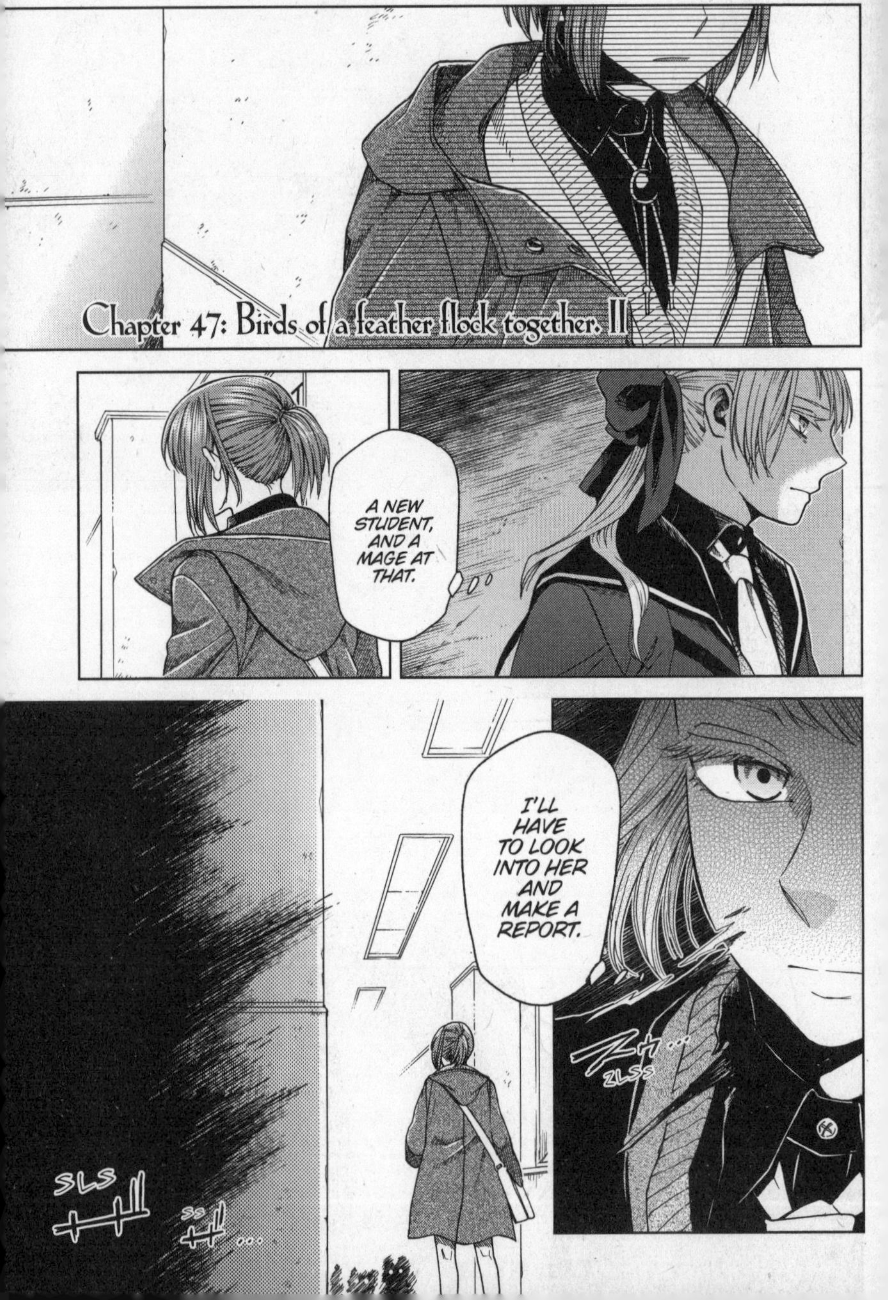
Chapter 47: Birds of a feather flock together. II
A NEW STUDENT, AND A MAGE AT THAT.
I'LL HAVE TO LOOK INTO HER AND MAKE A REPORT.
ZLSS
SLS
SS...

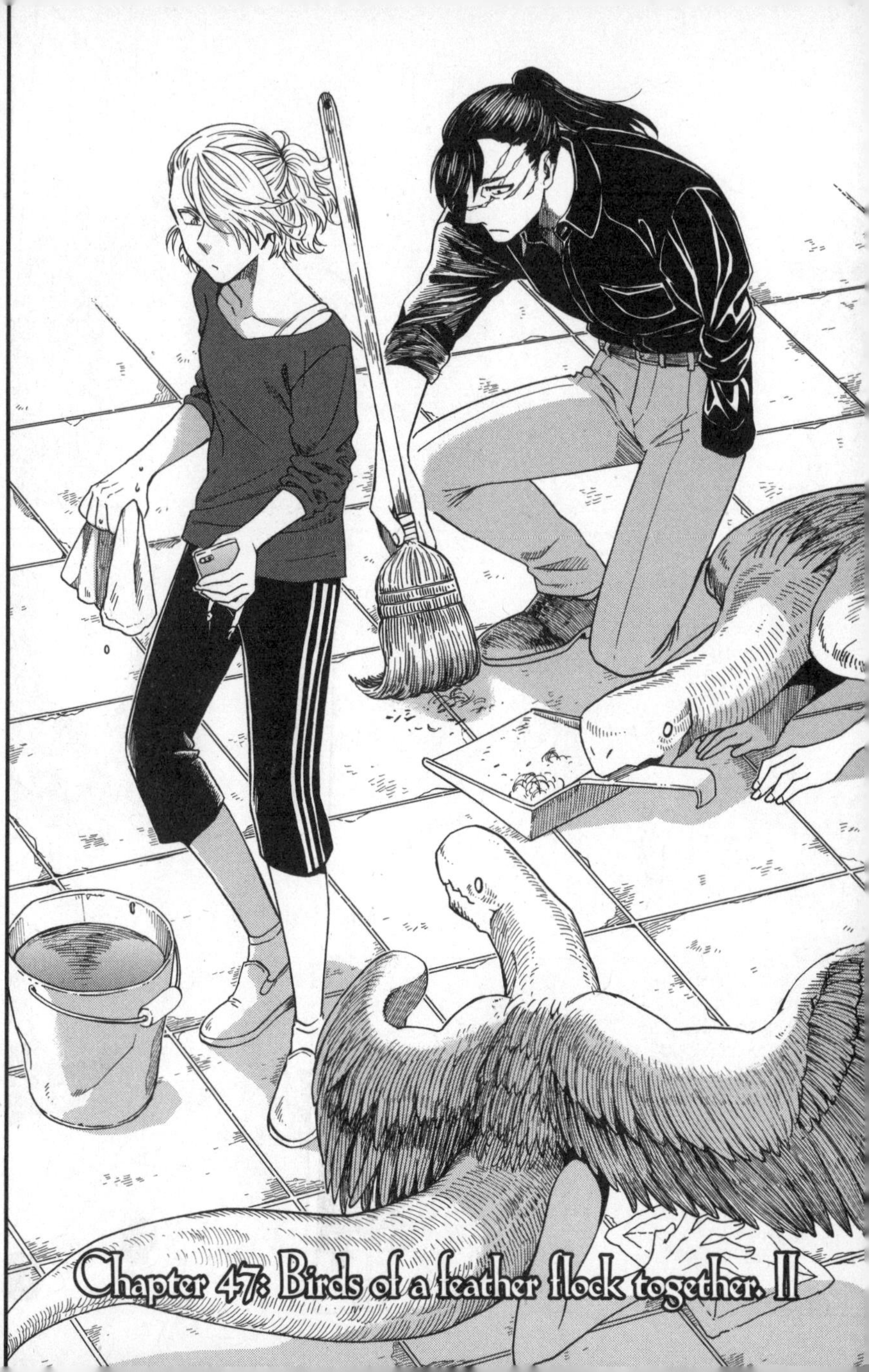
Chapter 47: Birds of a feather flock together. II

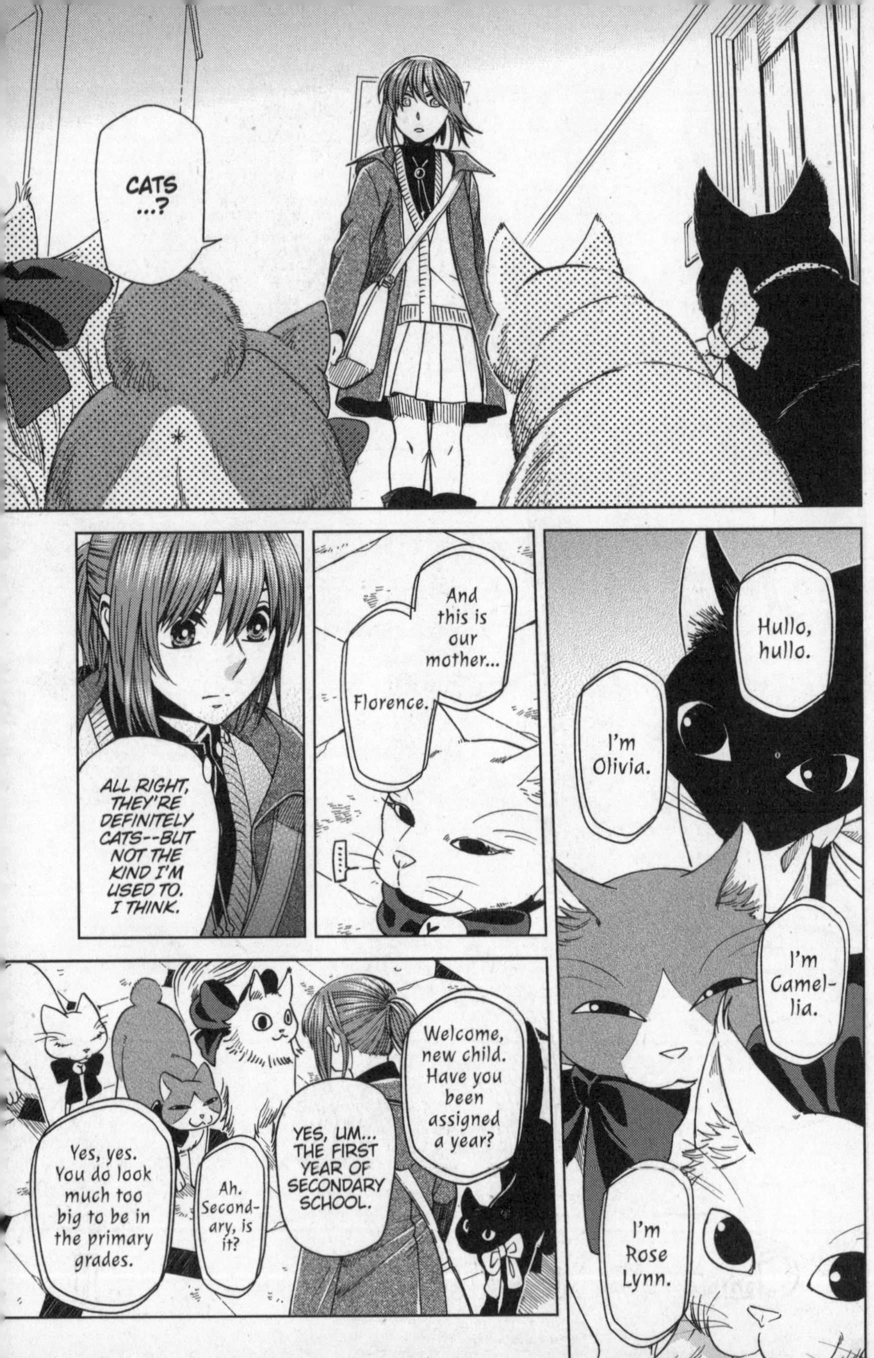
CATS ...?
Hullo, hullo.
I'm Olivia.
I'm Camellia.
I'm Rose Lynn.
And this is our mother...
Florence.
......
ALL RIGHT, THEY'RE DEFINITELY CATS--BUT NOT THE KIND I'M USED TO. I THINK.
Welcome, new child. Have you been assigned a year?
YES, UM... THE FIRST YEAR OF SECONDARY SCHOOL.
Ah. Secondary, is it?
Yes, yes. You do look much too big to be in the primary grades.

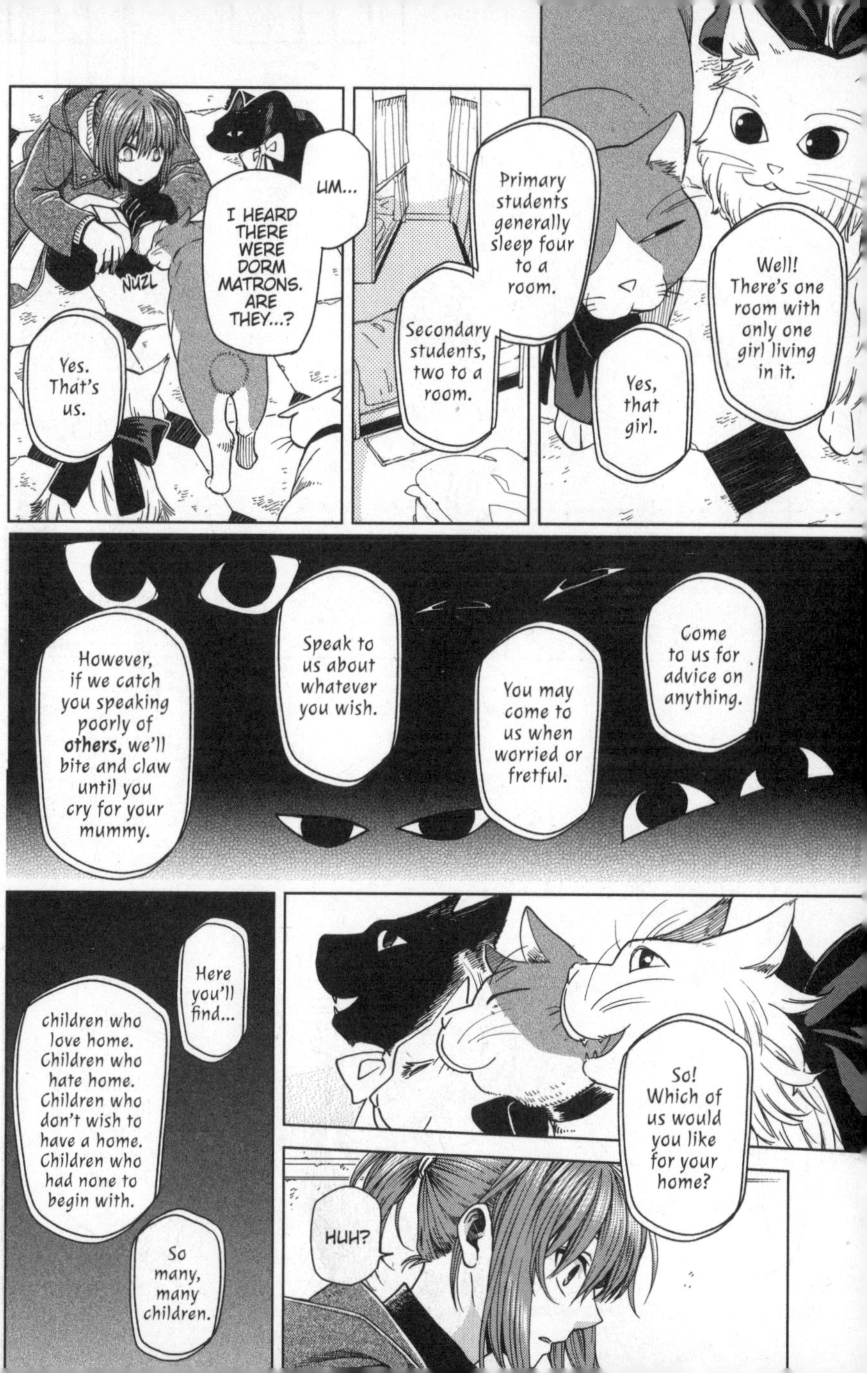
Well! There's one room with only one girl living in it.
Yes, that girl.
Primary students generally sleep four to a room.
Secondary students, two to a room.
UM...
I HEARD THERE WERE DORM MATRONS. ARE THEY...?
NUZL
Yes. That's us.
Come to us for advice on anything.
You may come to us when worried or fretful.
Speak to us about whatever you wish.
However, if we catch you speaking poorly of **others,** we'll bite and claw until you cry for your mummy.
So! Which of us would you like for your home?
.....
HUH?
Here you'll find...
children who love home. Children who hate home. Children who don't wish to have a home. Children who had none to begin with.
So many, many children.

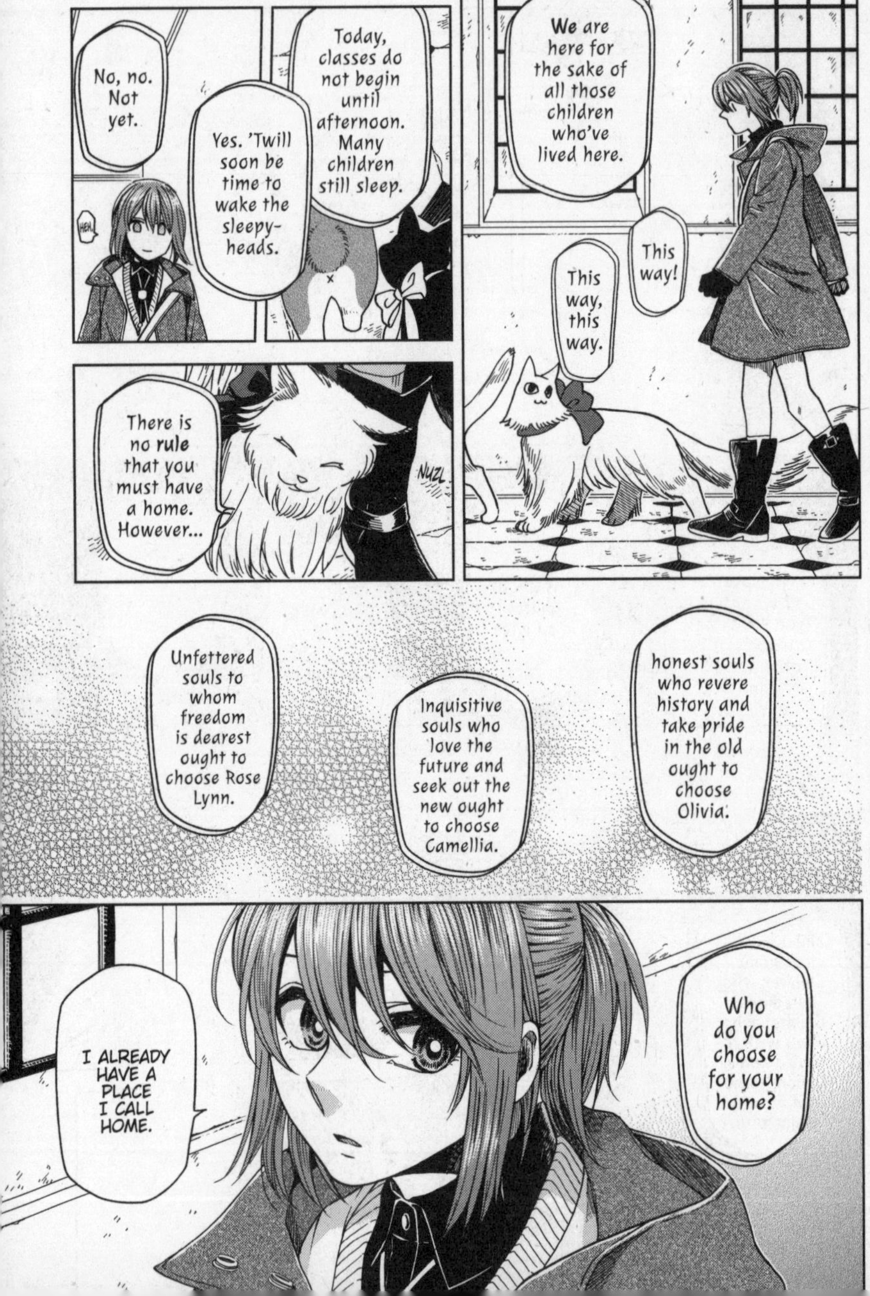
We are here for the sake of all those children who've lived here.
This way!
This way, this way.
Today, classes do not begin until afternoon. Many children still sleep.
Yes. 'Twill soon be time to wake the sleepy-heads.
No, no. Not yet.
HEH
There is no rule that you must have a home. However...
NUZL
honest souls who revere history and take pride in the old ought to choose Olivia.
Inquisitive souls who love the future and seek out the new ought to choose Camellia.
Unfettered souls to whom freedom is dearest ought to choose Rose Lynn.
Who do you choose for your home?
I ALREADY HAVE A PLACE I CALL HOME.

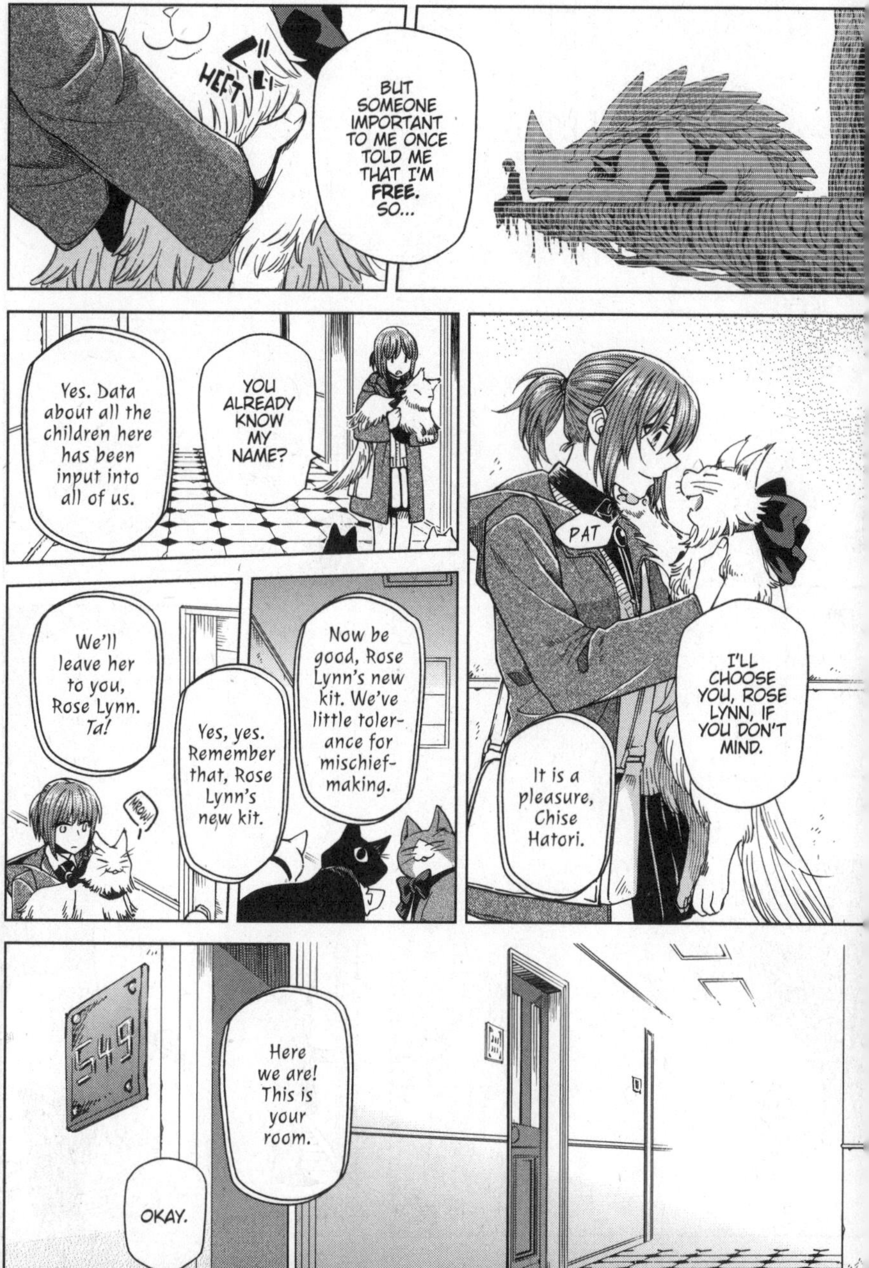
HEFT
BUT SOMEONE IMPORTANT TO ME ONCE TOLD ME THAT I'M FREE. SO...
PAT
I'LL CHOOSE YOU, ROSE LYNN, IF YOU DON'T MIND.
It is a pleasure, Chise Hatori.
YOU ALREADY KNOW MY NAME?
Yes. Data about all the children here has been input into all of us.
Now be good, Rose Lynn's new kit. We've little tolerance for mischief-making.
Yes, yes. Remember that, Rose Lynn's new kit.
We'll leave her to you, Rose Lynn. Ta!
MROW!
549
Here we are! This is your room.
OKAY.

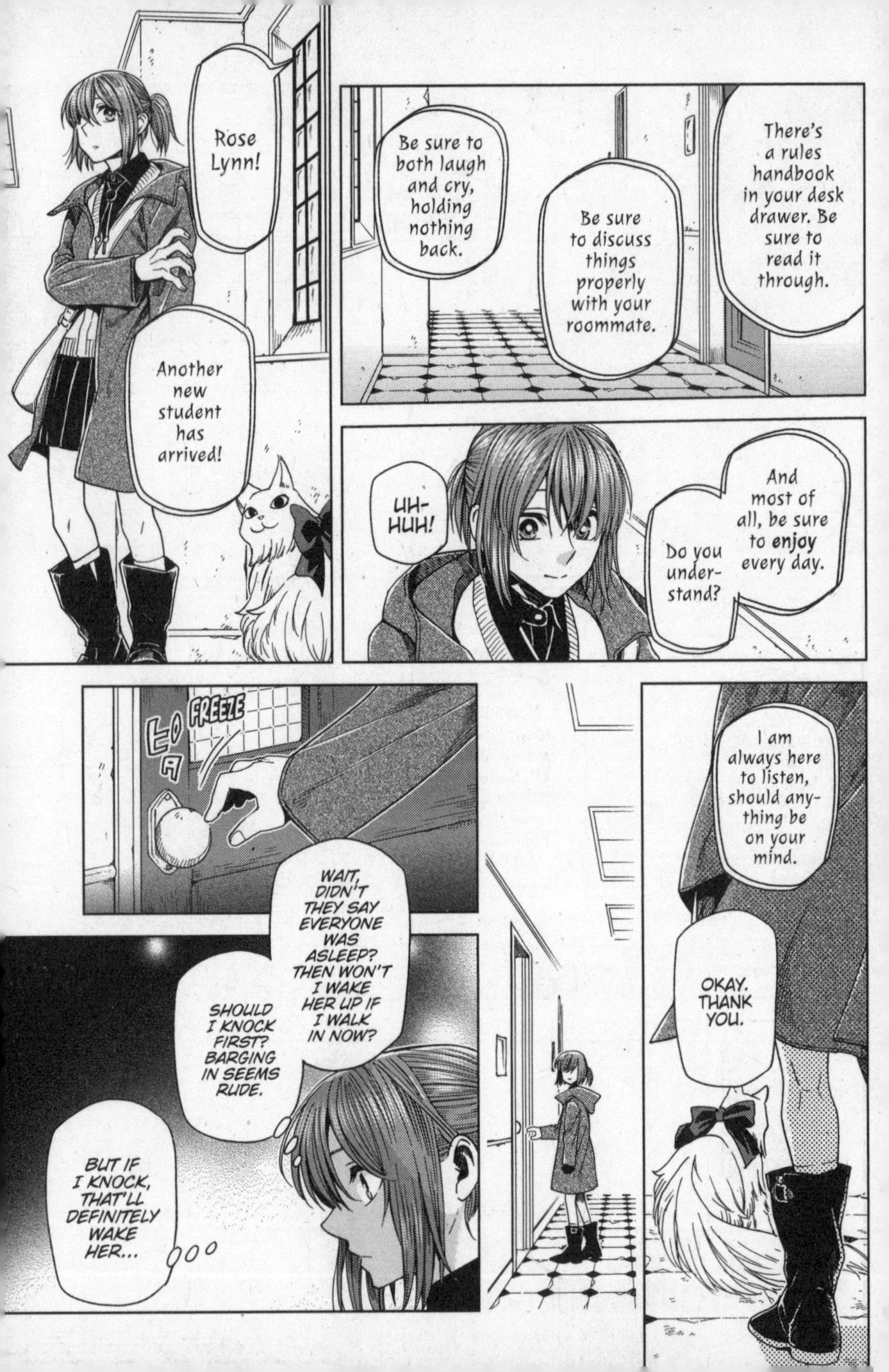

There's a rules handbook in your desk drawer. Be sure to read it through.
Be sure to discuss things properly with your roommate.
Be sure to both laugh and cry, holding nothing back.
And most of all, be sure to **enjoy** every day.
Do you understand?
UH-HUH!
Rose Lynn!
Another new student has arrived!
I am always here to listen, should anything be on your mind.
OKAY. THANK YOU.
FREEZE
WAIT, DIDN'T THEY SAY EVERYONE WAS ASLEEP? THEN WON'T I WAKE HER UP IF I WALK IN NOW?
SHOULD I KNOCK FIRST? BARGING IN SEEMS RUDE.
BUT IF I KNOCK, THAT'LL DEFINITELY WAKE HER...

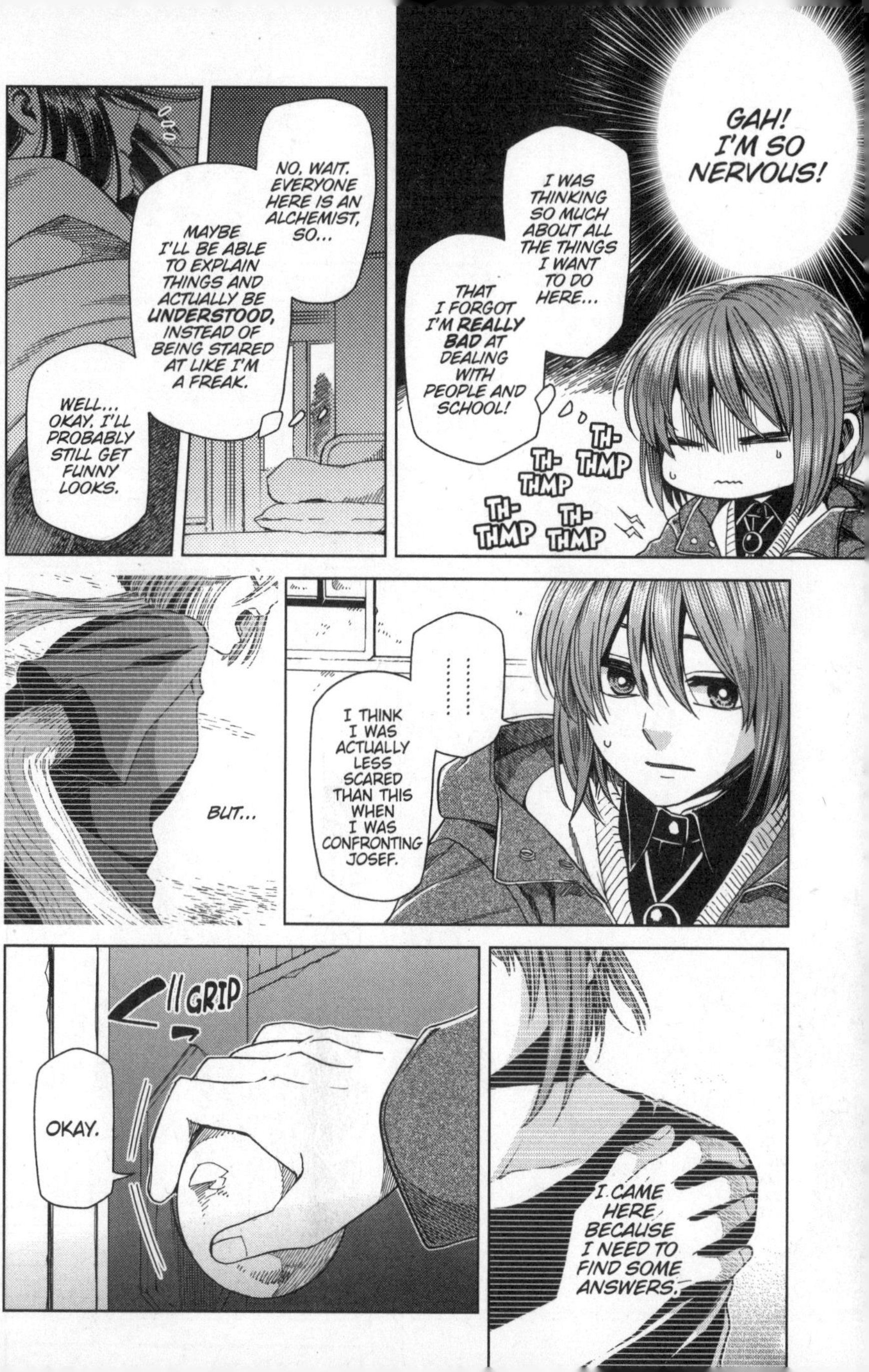
GAH! I'M SO NERVOUS!
I WAS THINKING SO MUCH ABOUT ALL THE THINGS I WANT TO DO HERE...
THAT I FORGOT I'M REALLY BAD AT DEALING WITH PEOPLE AND SCHOOL!
TH-THMP
TH-THMP
TH-THMP
TH-THMP
NO, WAIT. EVERYONE HERE IS AN ALCHEMIST, SO...
MAYBE I'LL BE ABLE TO EXPLAIN THINGS AND ACTUALLY BE UNDERSTOOD, INSTEAD OF BEING STARED AT LIKE I'M A FREAK.
WELL... OKAY, I'LL PROBABLY STILL GET FUNNY LOOKS.
......
I THINK I WAS ACTUALLY LESS SCARED THAN THIS WHEN I WAS CONFRONTING JOSEF.
BUT...
I CAME HERE BECAUSE I NEED TO FIND SOME ANSWERS.
GRIP
OKAY.

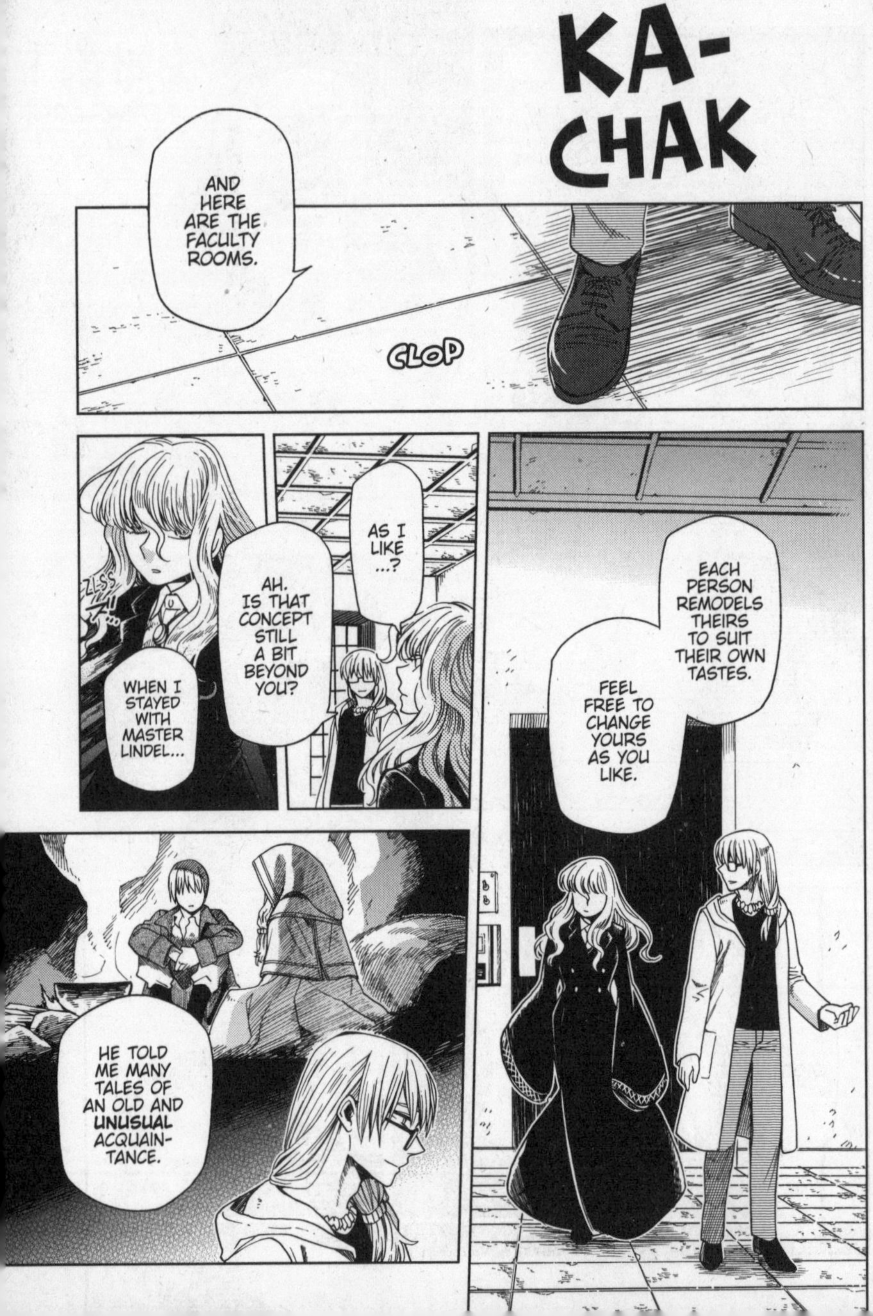
KA-CHAK
AND HERE ARE THE FACULTY ROOMS.
CLOP
EACH PERSON REMODELS THEIRS TO SUIT THEIR OWN TASTES.
FEEL FREE TO CHANGE YOURS AS YOU LIKE.
AS I LIKE ...?
AH. IS THAT CONCEPT STILL A BIT BEYOND YOU?
WHEN I STAYED WITH MASTER LINDEL...
HE TOLD ME MANY TALES OF AN OLD AND **UNUSUAL** ACQUAIN-TANCE.

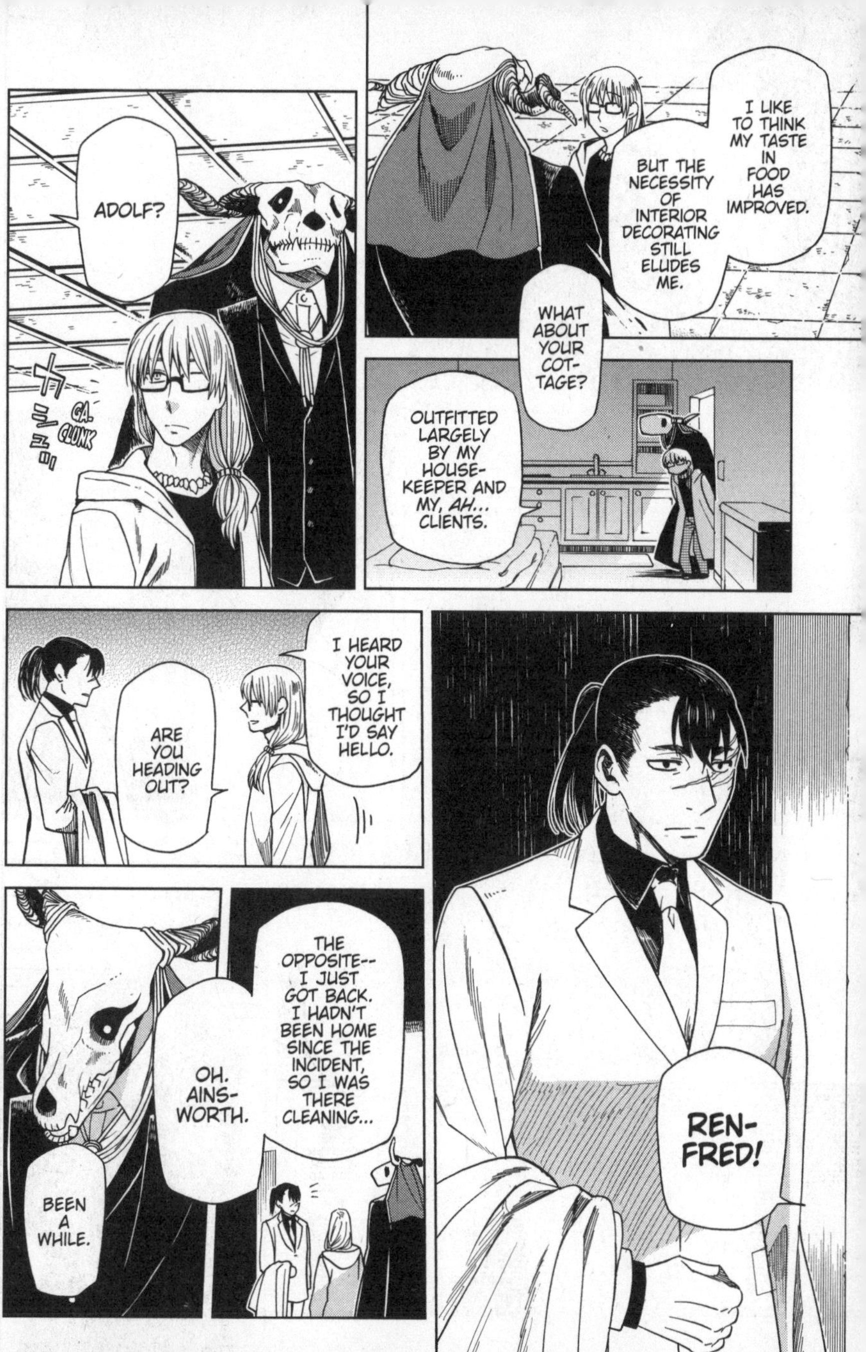
I LIKE TO THINK MY TASTE IN FOOD HAS IMPROVED.
BUT THE NECESSITY OF INTERIOR DECORATING STILL ELUDES ME.
WHAT ABOUT YOUR COT-TAGE?
OUTFITTED LARGELY BY MY HOUSE-KEEPER AND MY, *AH*... CLIENTS.
ADOLF?
GA-CLUNK
REN-FRED!
I HEARD YOUR VOICE, SO I THOUGHT I'D SAY HELLO.
ARE YOU HEADING OUT?
THE OPPOSITE-- I JUST GOT BACK. I HADN'T BEEN HOME SINCE THE INCIDENT, SO I WAS THERE CLEANING...
OH. AINS-WORTH.
BEEN A WHILE.

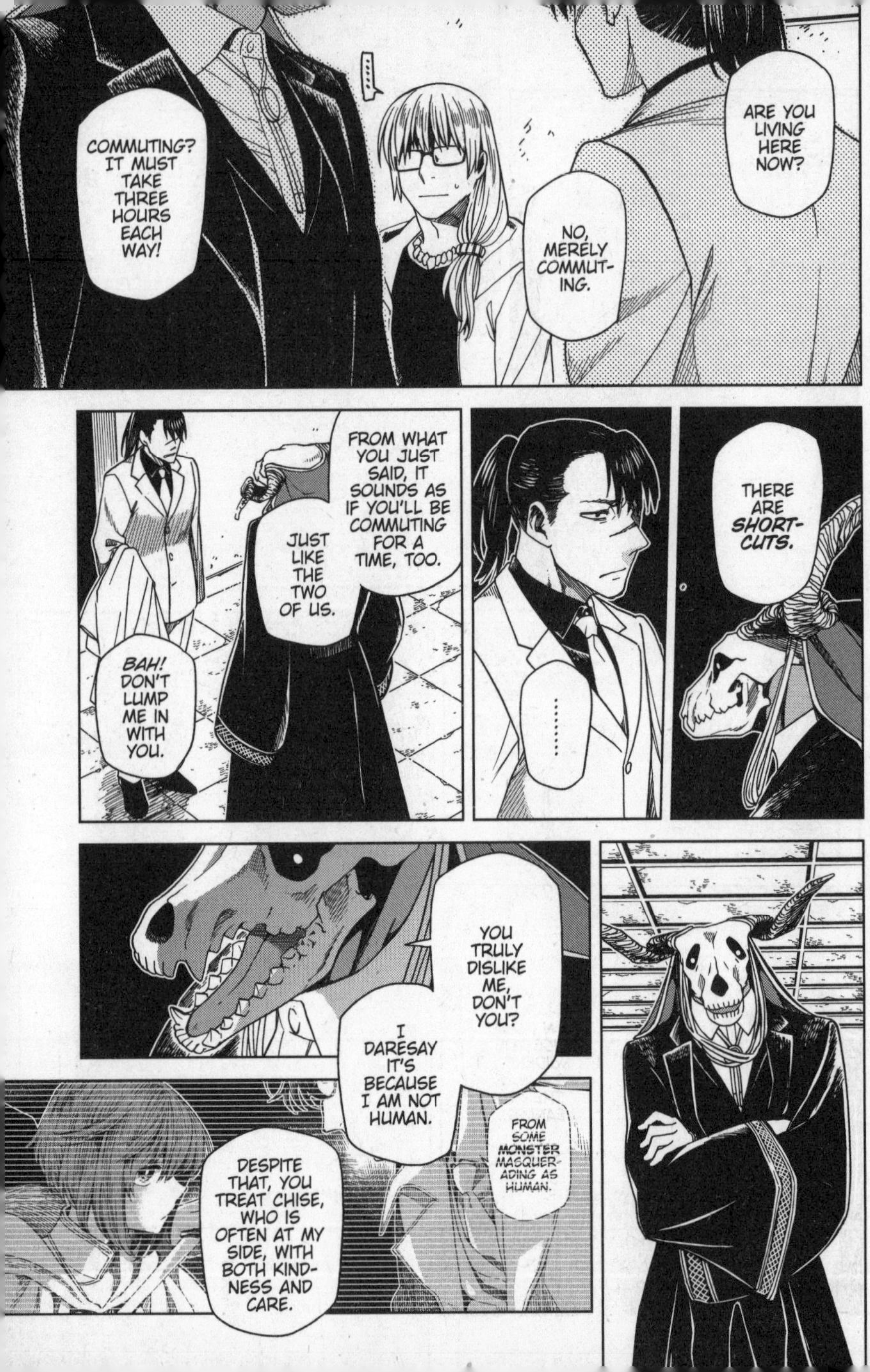
ARE YOU LIVING HERE NOW?
NO, MERELY COMMUT-ING.
.....
COMMUTING? IT MUST TAKE THREE HOURS EACH WAY!
THERE ARE SHORT-CUTS.
......
FROM WHAT YOU JUST SAID, IT SOUNDS AS IF YOU'LL BE COMMUTING FOR A TIME, TOO.
JUST LIKE THE TWO OF US.
BAH! DON'T LUMP ME IN WITH YOU.
YOU TRULY DISLIKE ME, DON'T YOU?
I DARESAY IT'S BECAUSE I AM NOT HUMAN.
FROM SOME MONSTER MASQUER-ADING AS HUMAN.
DESPITE THAT, YOU TREAT CHISE, WHO IS OFTEN AT MY SIDE, WITH BOTH KIND-NESS AND CARE.

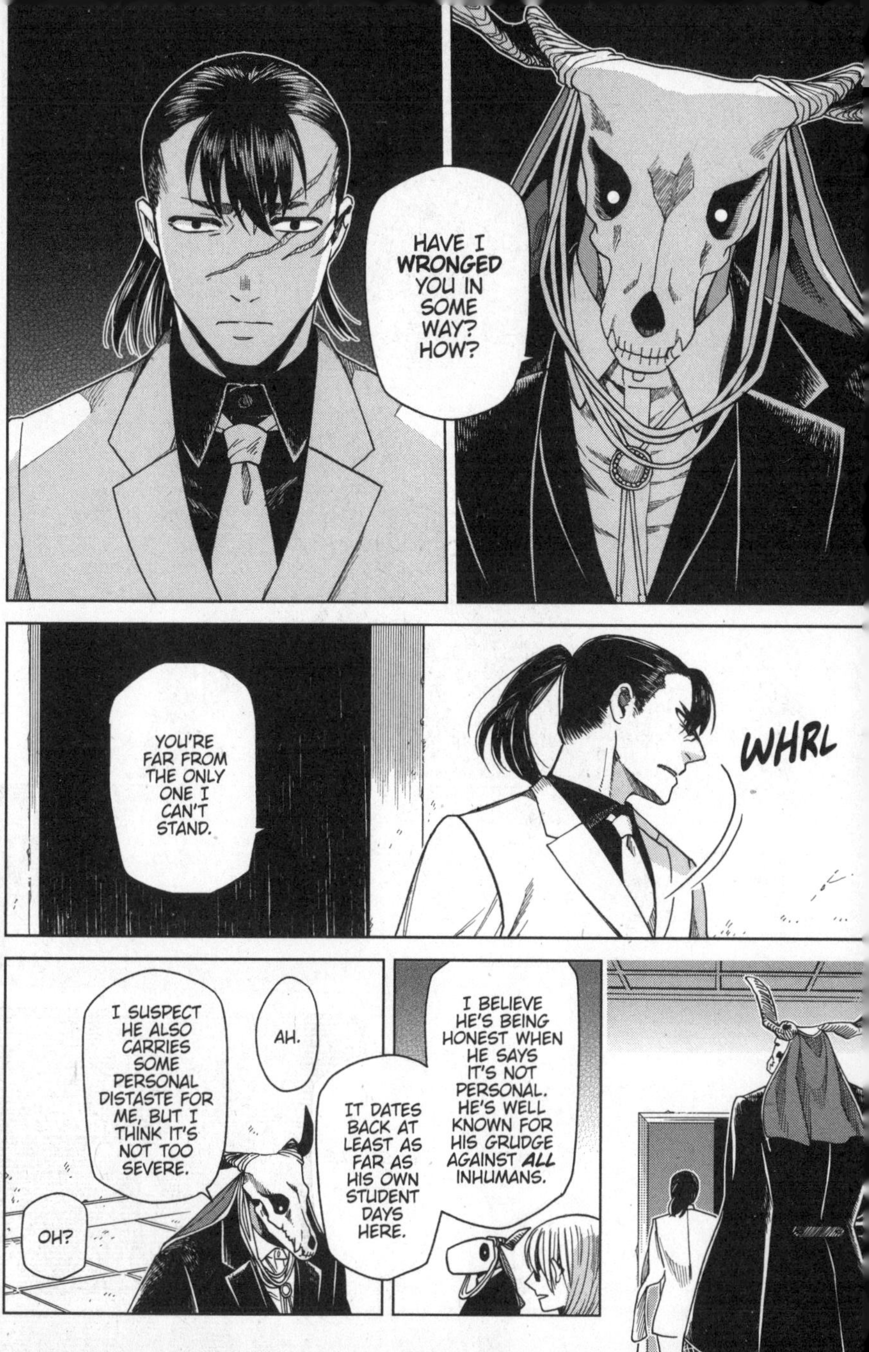
HAVE I **WRONGED** YOU IN SOME WAY? HOW?
WHRL
YOU'RE FAR FROM THE ONLY ONE I CAN'T STAND.
I BELIEVE HE'S BEING HONEST WHEN HE SAYS IT'S NOT PERSONAL. HE'S WELL KNOWN FOR HIS GRUDGE AGAINST ***ALL*** INHUMANS.
IT DATES BACK AT LEAST AS FAR AS HIS OWN STUDENT DAYS HERE.
AH.
I SUSPECT HE ALSO CARRIES SOME PERSONAL DISTASTE FOR ME, BUT I THINK IT'S NOT TOO SEVERE.
OH?

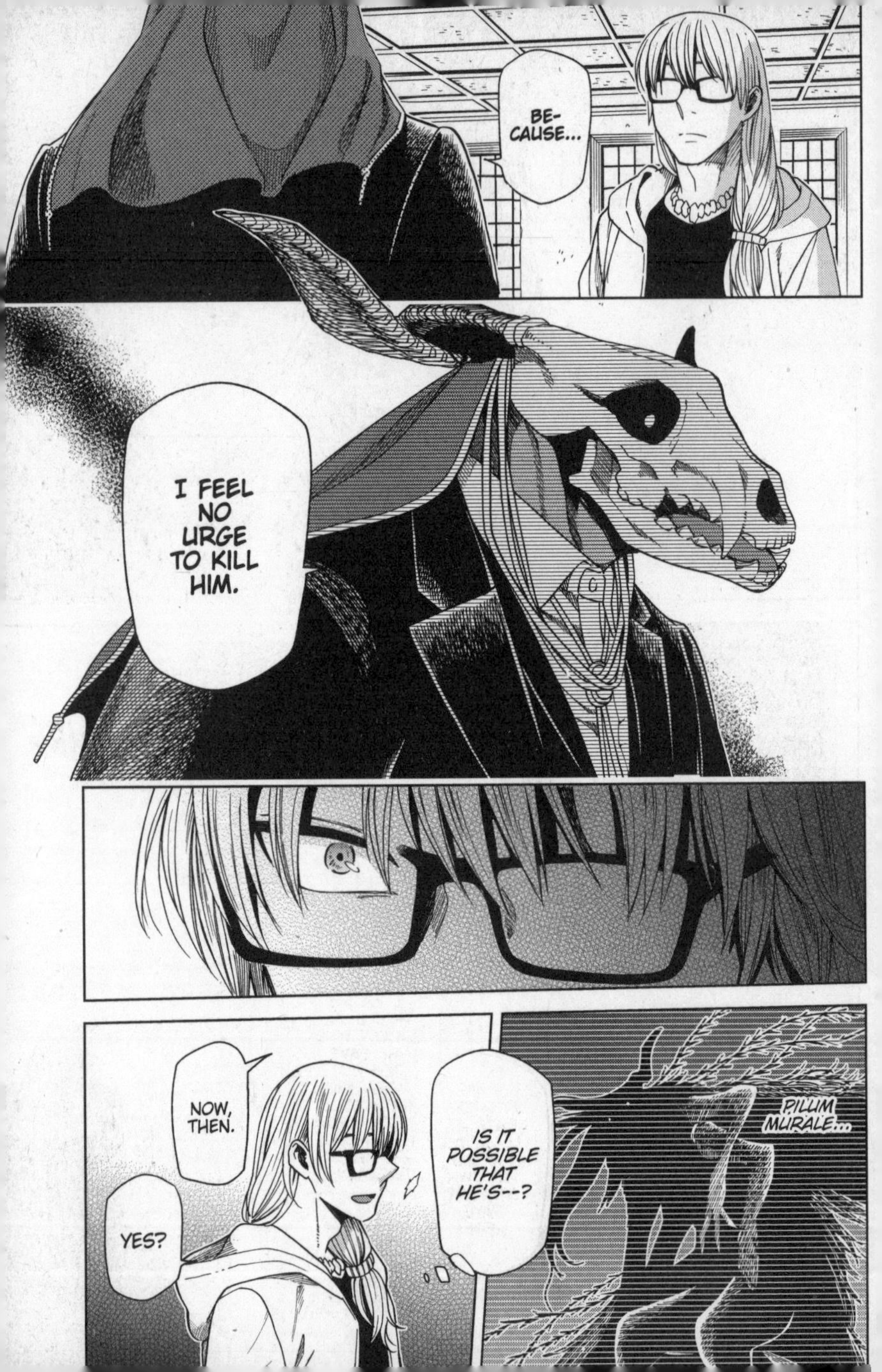
BE-CAUSE...
I FEEL NO URGE TO KILL HIM.
PILUM MURALE...
IS IT POSSIBLE THAT HE'S--?
NOW, THEN.
YES?

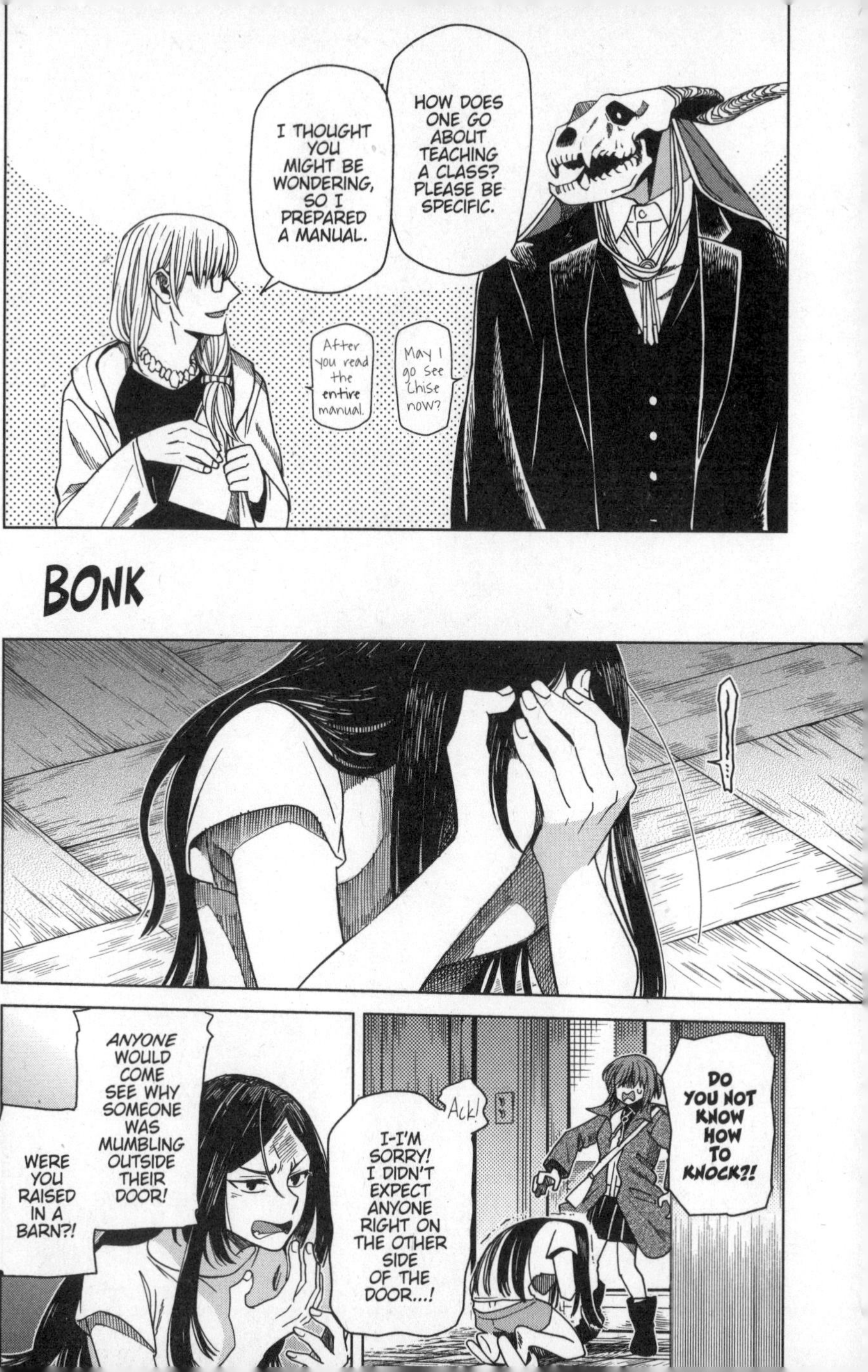
HOW DOES ONE GO ABOUT TEACHING A CLASS? PLEASE BE SPECIFIC.
I THOUGHT YOU MIGHT BE WONDERING, SO I PREPARED A MANUAL.
May I go see Chise now?
After you read the entire manual.
BONK
!
DO YOU NOT KNOW HOW TO KNOCK?!
Ack!
I-I'M SORRY! I DIDN'T EXPECT ANYONE RIGHT ON THE OTHER SIDE OF THE DOOR...!
ANYONE WOULD COME SEE WHY SOMEONE WAS MUMBLING OUTSIDE THEIR DOOR!
WERE YOU RAISED IN A BARN?!

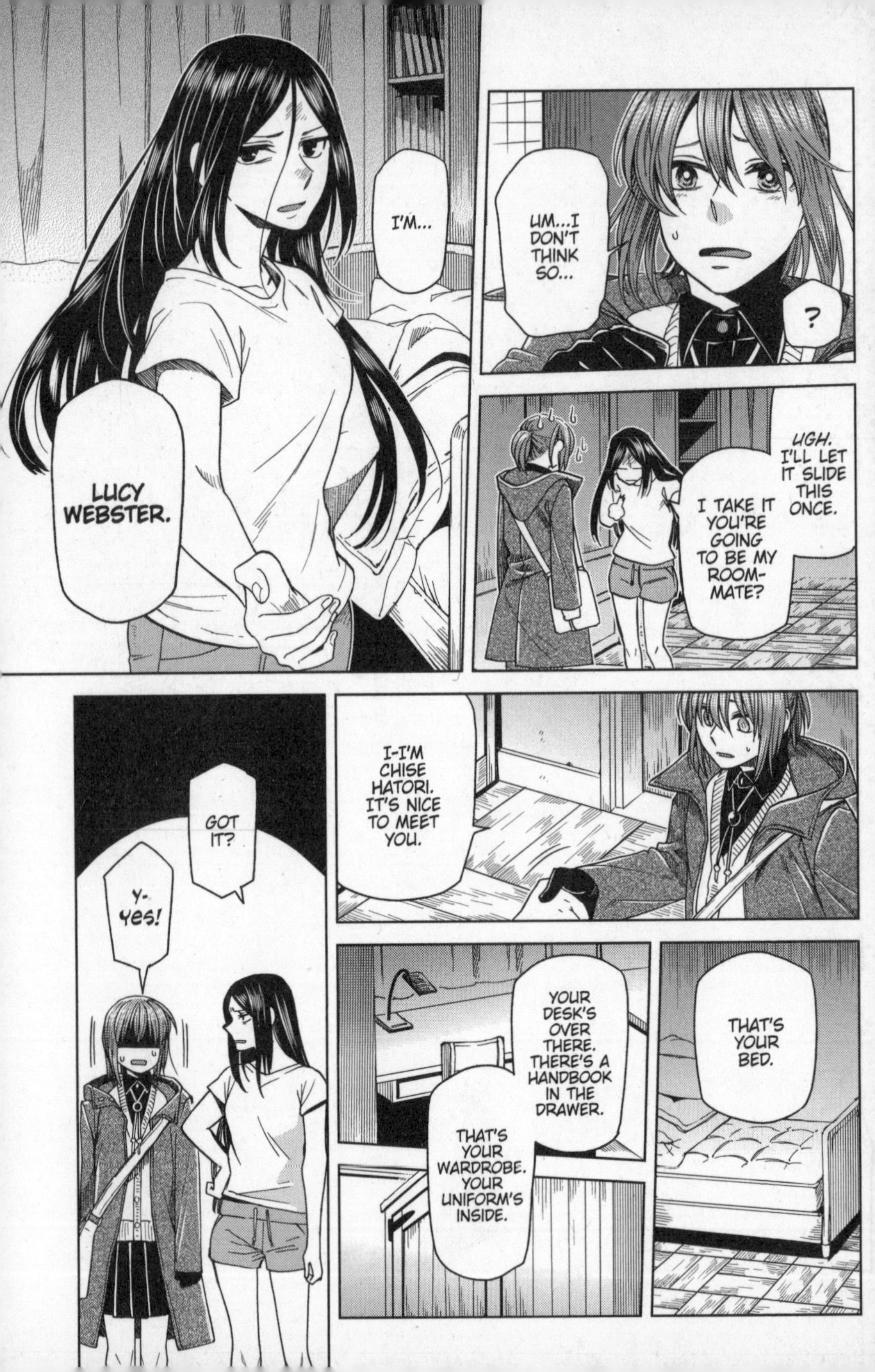
UM...I DON'T THINK SO...
?
UGH. I'LL LET IT SLIDE THIS ONCE.
I TAKE IT YOU'RE GOING TO BE MY ROOM-MATE?
I'M...
LUCY WEBSTER.
I-I'M CHISE HATORI. IT'S NICE TO MEET YOU.
THAT'S YOUR BED.
YOUR DESK'S OVER THERE. THERE'S A HANDBOOK IN THE DRAWER.
THAT'S YOUR WARDROBE. YOUR UNIFORM'S INSIDE.
GOT IT?
Y-YES!

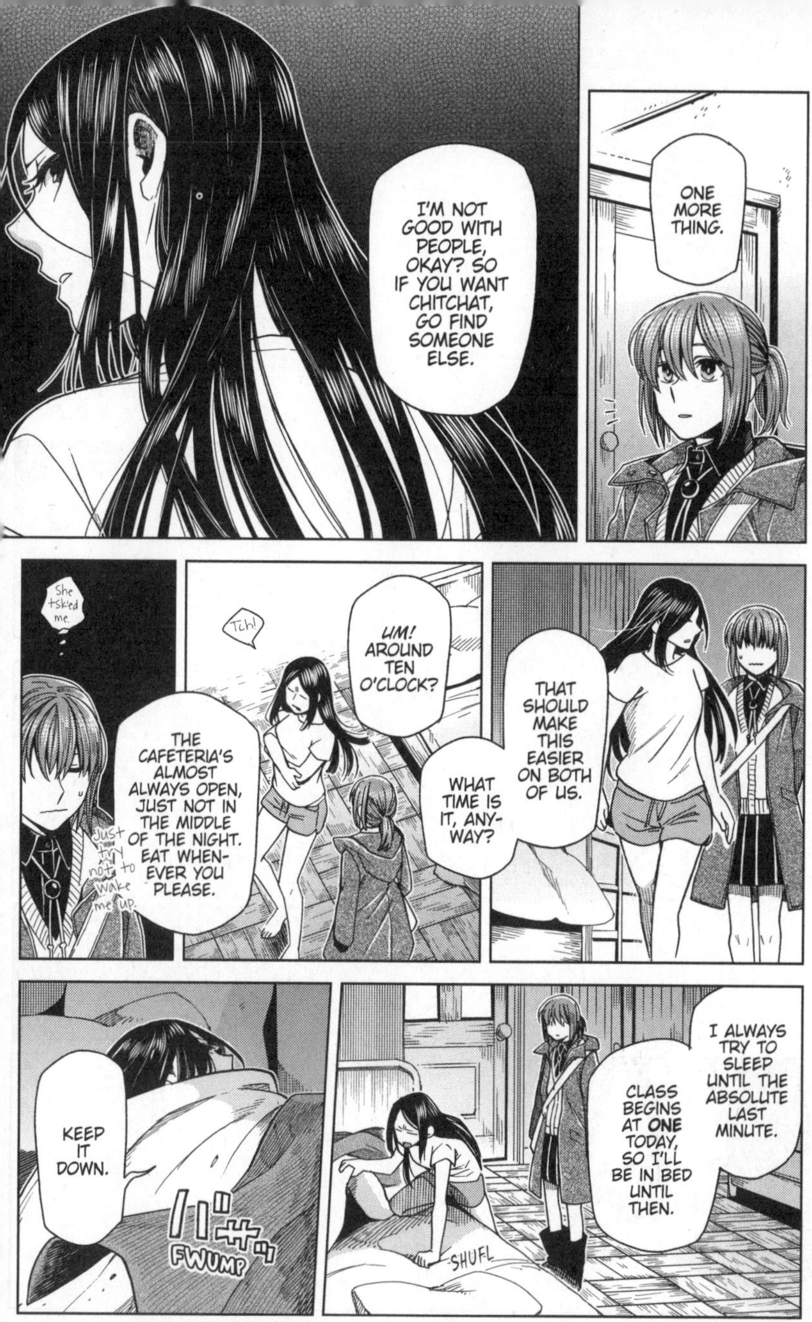
ONE MORE THING.
I'M NOT GOOD WITH PEOPLE, OKAY? SO IF YOU WANT CHITCHAT, GO FIND SOMEONE ELSE.
THAT SHOULD MAKE THIS EASIER ON BOTH OF US.
WHAT TIME IS IT, ANYWAY?
UM! AROUND TEN O'CLOCK?
Tch!
She tsk'ed me.
THE CAFETERIA'S ALMOST ALWAYS OPEN, JUST NOT IN THE MIDDLE OF THE NIGHT. EAT WHENEVER YOU PLEASE.
Just try not to wake me up.
I ALWAYS TRY TO SLEEP UNTIL THE ABSOLUTE LAST MINUTE.
CLASS BEGINS AT **ONE** TODAY, SO I'LL BE IN BED UNTIL THEN.
SHUFL
KEEP IT DOWN.
FWUMP

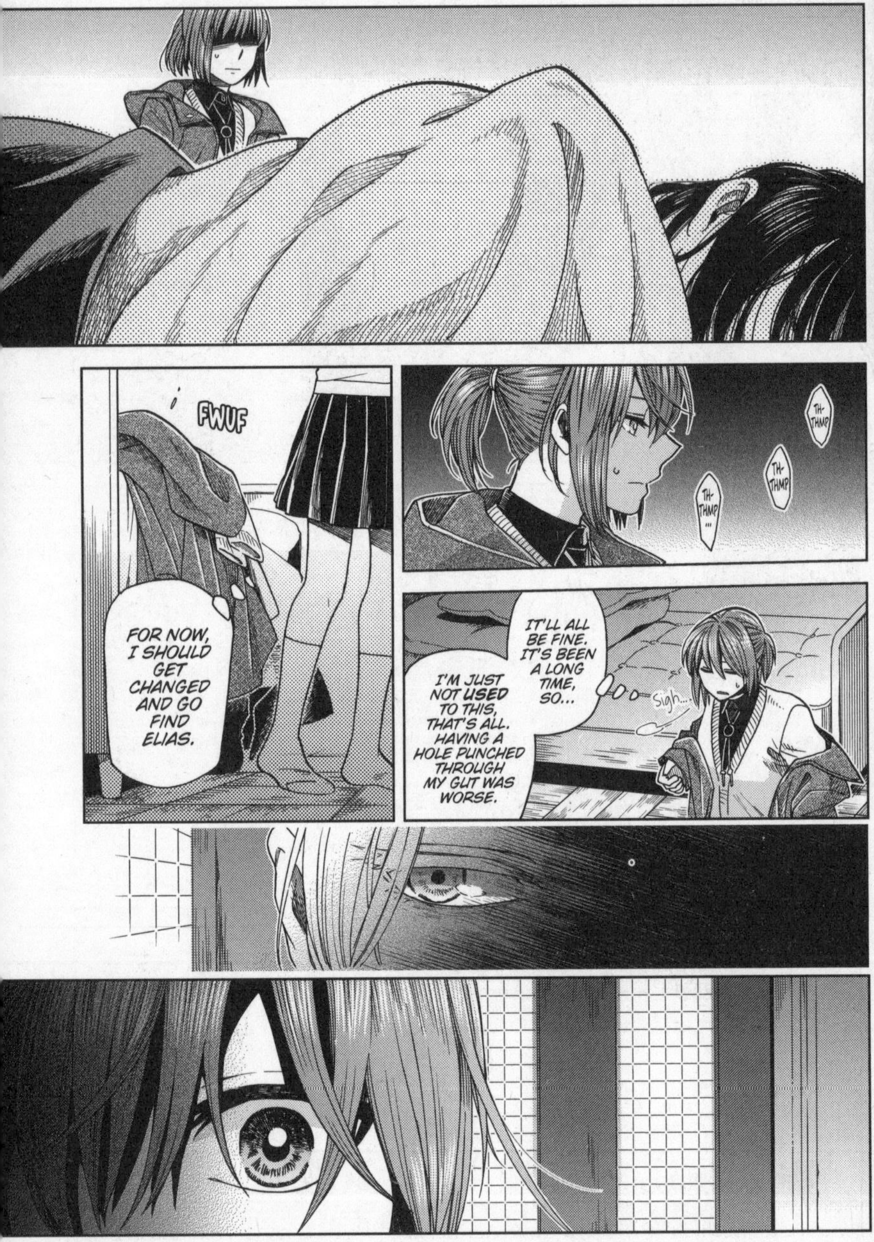
TH-THMP
TH-THMP
TH-THMP...
IT'LL ALL BE FINE. IT'S BEEN A LONG TIME, SO...
I'M JUST NOT USED TO THIS, THAT'S ALL. HAVING A HOLE PUNCHED THROUGH MY GUT WAS WORSE.
Sigh...
FWUF
FOR NOW, I SHOULD GET CHANGED AND GO FIND ELIAS.

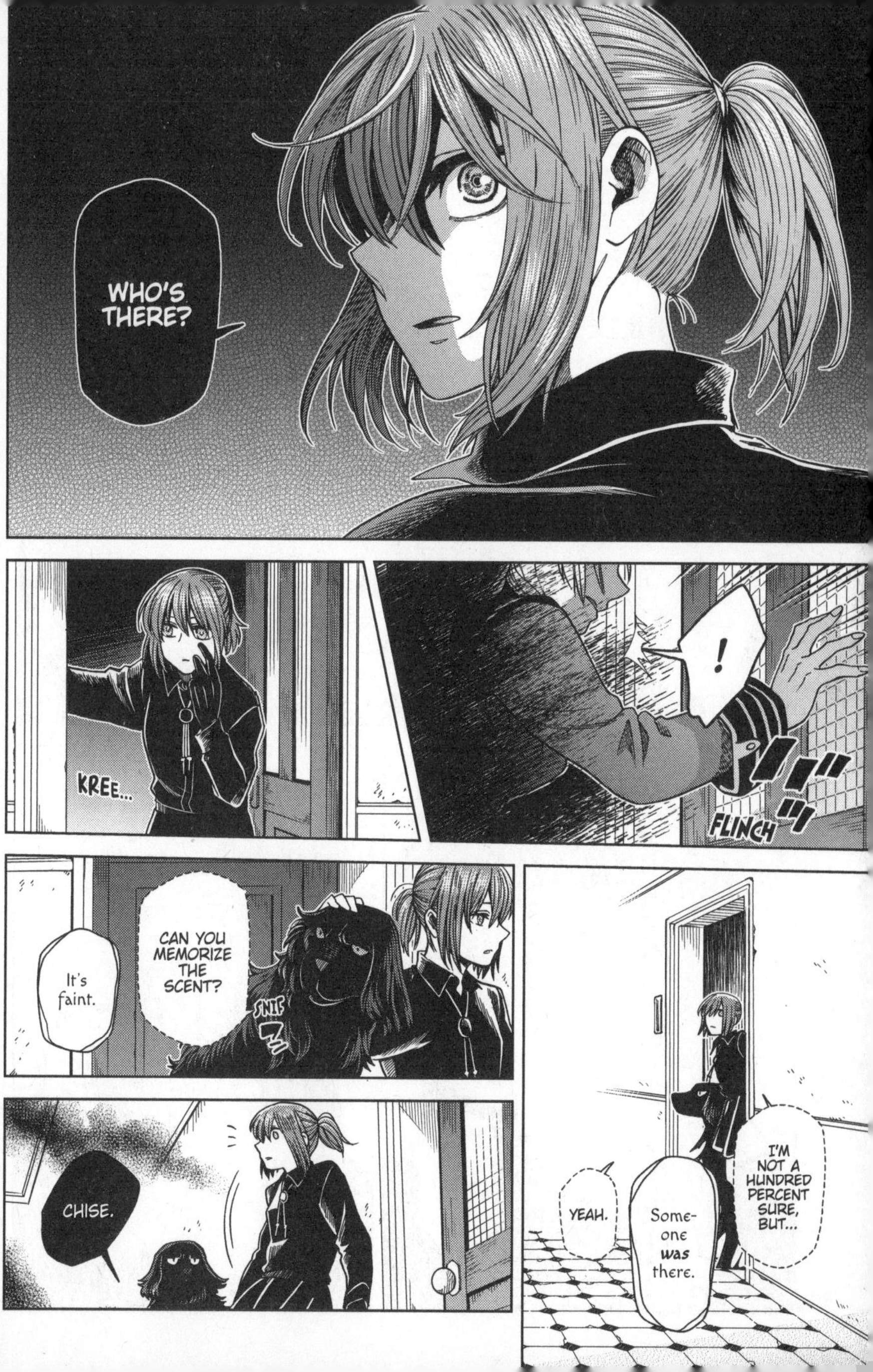
WHO'S THERE?
!
FLINCH
KREE...
I'M NOT A HUNDRED PERCENT SURE, BUT...
Someone was there.
YEAH.
CAN YOU MEMORIZE THE SCENT?
SNIF
It's faint.
CHISE.

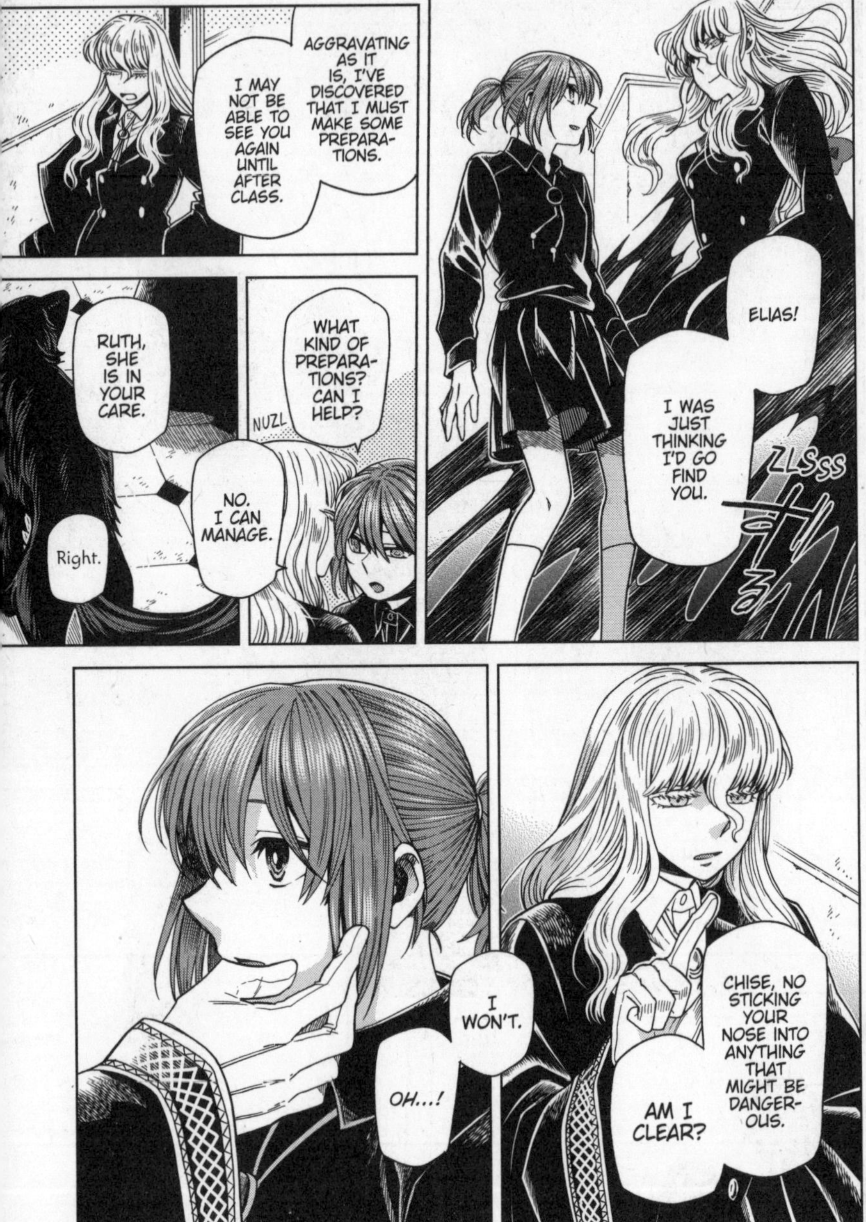
ELIAS!
I WAS JUST THINKING I'D GO FIND YOU.
ZLSSS
AGGRAVATING AS IT IS, I'VE DISCOVERED THAT I MUST MAKE SOME PREPARATIONS.
I MAY NOT BE ABLE TO SEE YOU AGAIN UNTIL AFTER CLASS.
NUZL
WHAT KIND OF PREPARATIONS? CAN I HELP?
NO. I CAN MANAGE.
RUTH, SHE IS IN YOUR CARE.
Right.
CHISE, NO STICKING YOUR NOSE INTO ANYTHING THAT MIGHT BE DANGEROUS.
AM I CLEAR?
I WON'T.
OH...!

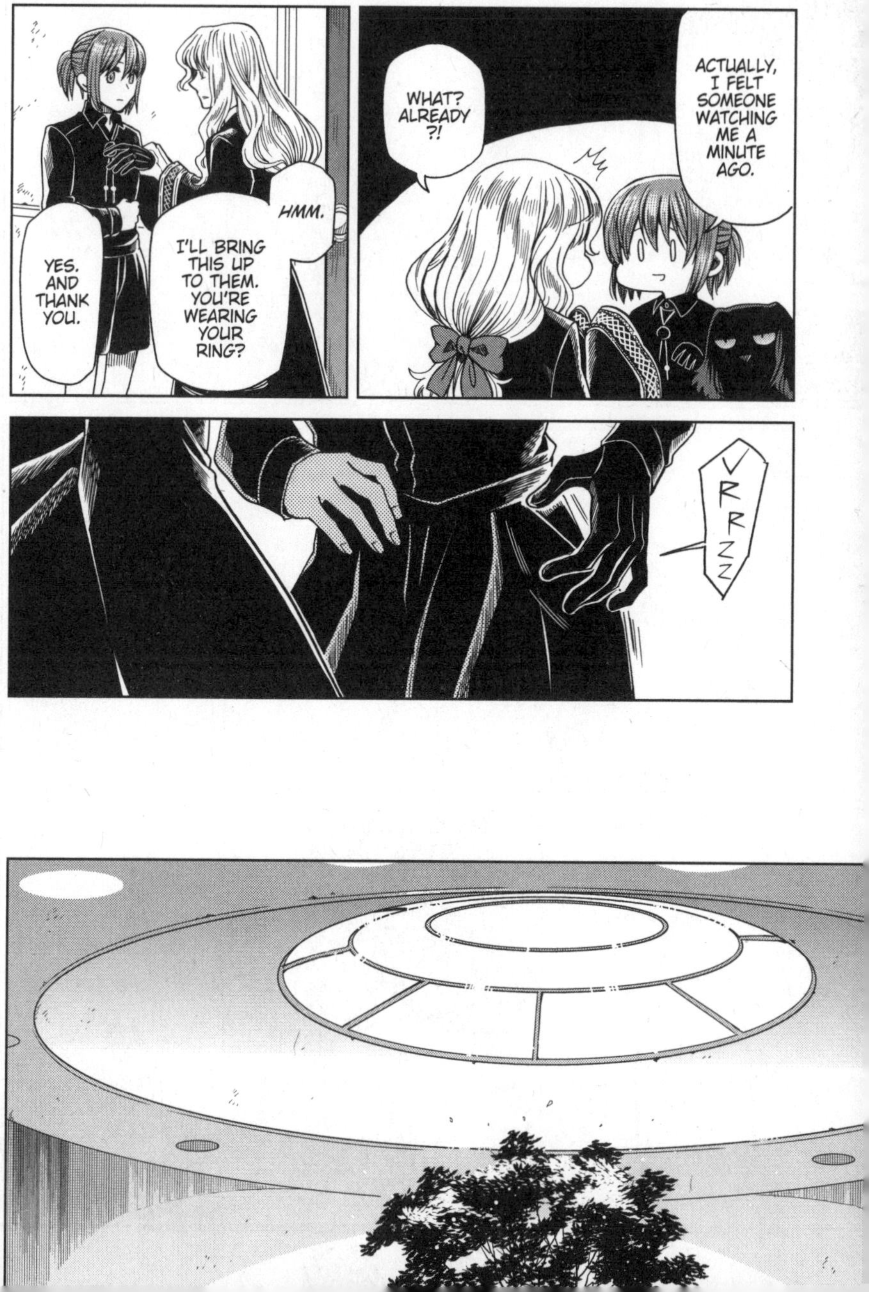
ACTUALLY, I FELT SOMEONE WATCHING ME A MINUTE AGO.
WHAT? ALREADY?!
HMM.
I'LL BRING THIS UP TO THEM. YOU'RE WEARING YOUR RING?
YES. AND THANK YOU.
VRRZZ

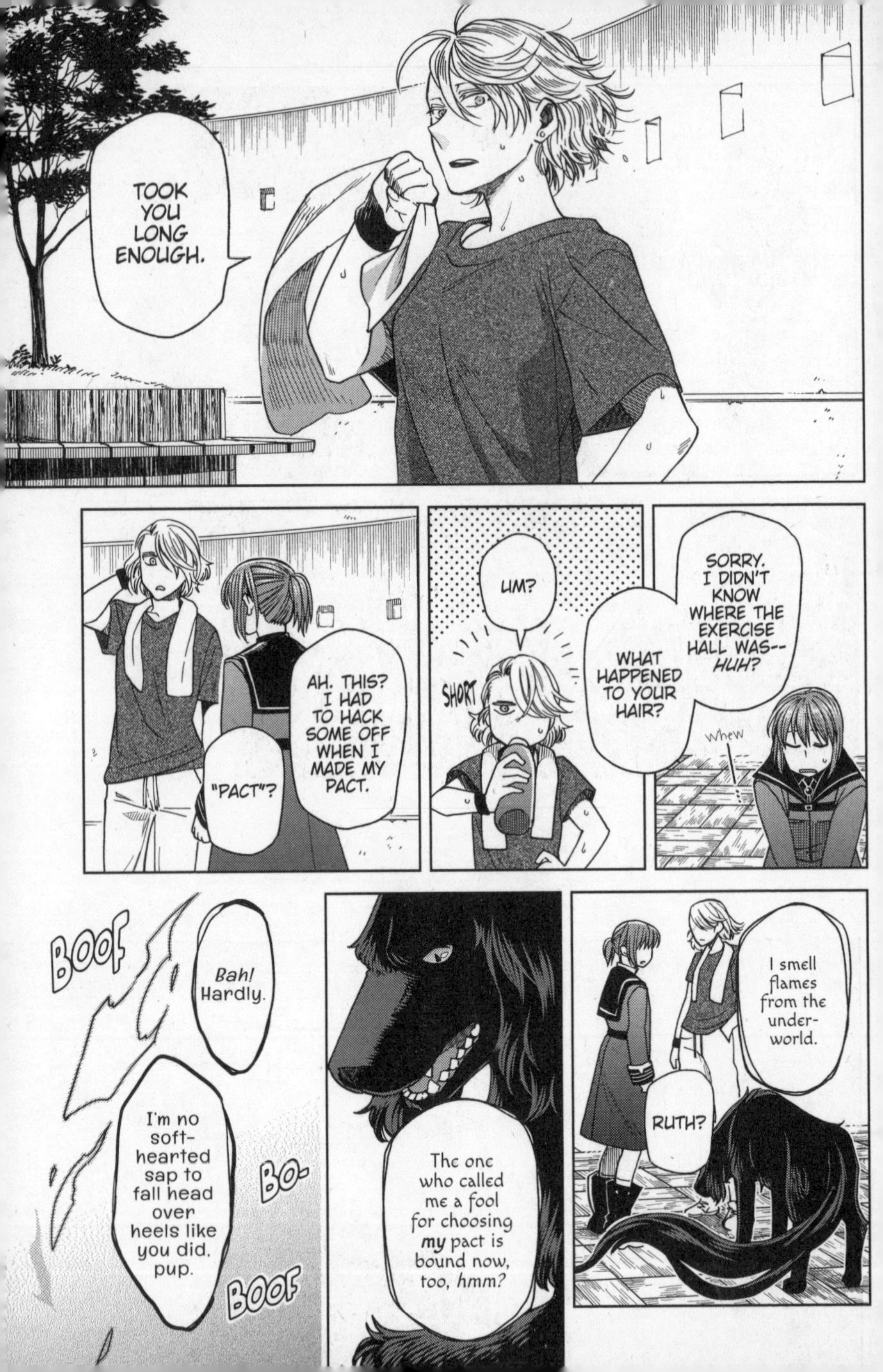
TOOK YOU LONG ENOUGH.
SORRY. I DIDN'T KNOW WHERE THE EXERCISE HALL WAS-- *HUH?*
Whew
UM?
WHAT HAPPENED TO YOUR HAIR?
SHORT
AH. THIS? I HAD TO HACK SOME OFF WHEN I MADE MY PACT.
"PACT"?
I smell flames from the under-world.
RUTH?
The one who called me a fool for choosing **my** pact is bound now, too, *hmm?*
BOOF
Bah! Hardly.
I'm no soft-hearted sap to fall head over heels like you did, pup.
BO-
BOOF

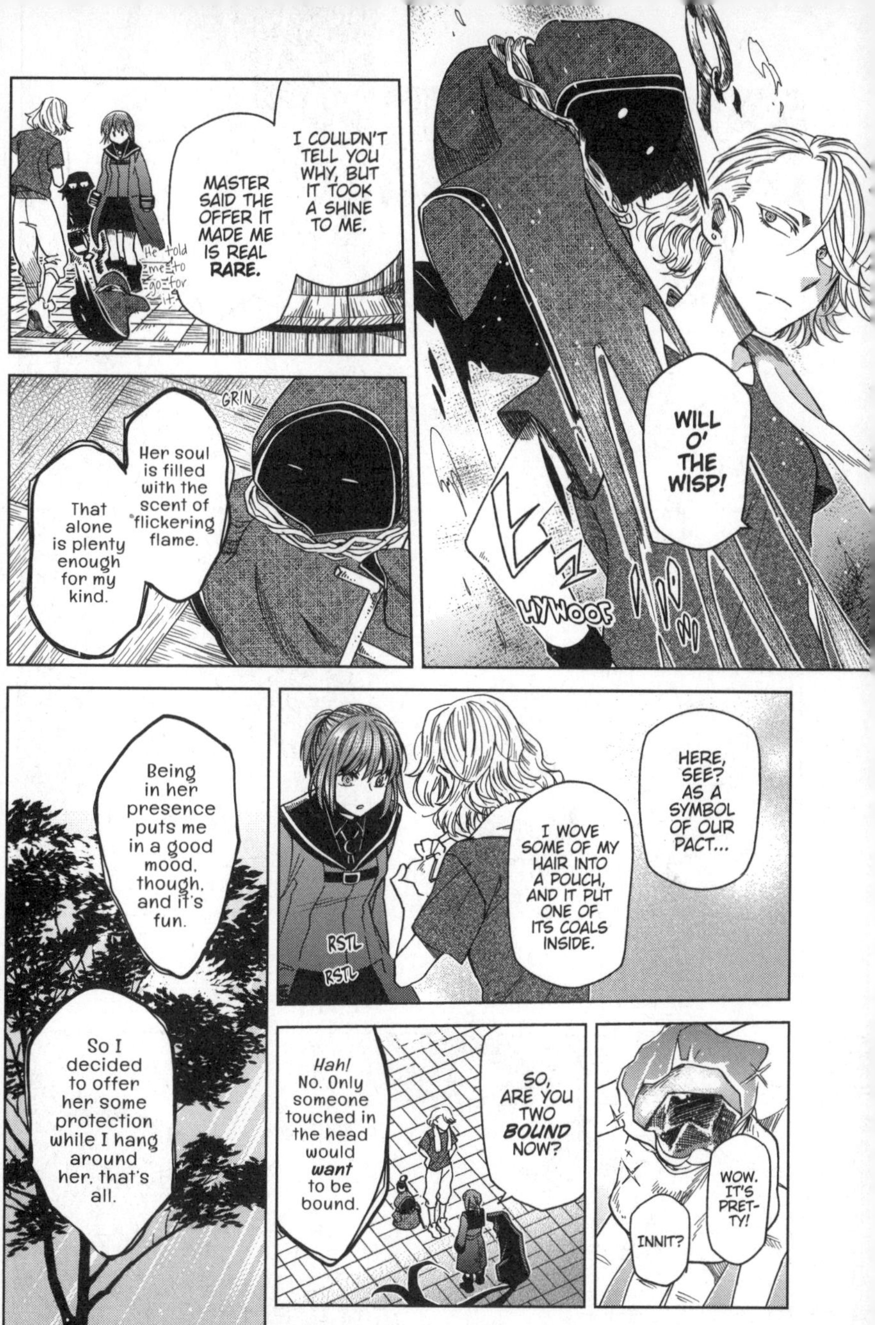
WILL O' THE WISP!
HYWOOF
I COULDN'T TELL YOU WHY, BUT IT TOOK A SHINE TO ME.
MASTER SAID THE OFFER IT MADE ME IS REAL **RARE.**
He told me to go for it.
GRIN
Her soul is filled with the scent of flickering flame.
That alone is plenty enough for my kind.
HERE, SEE? AS A SYMBOL OF OUR PACT...
I WOVE SOME OF MY HAIR INTO A POUCH, AND IT PUT ONE OF ITS COALS INSIDE.
RSTL
RSTL
WOW. IT'S PRETTY!
INNIT?
SO, ARE YOU TWO ***BOUND*** NOW?
Hah! No. Only someone touched in the head would ***want*** to be bound.
Being in her presence puts me in a good mood, though, and it's fun.
So I decided to offer her some protection while I hang around her, that's all.

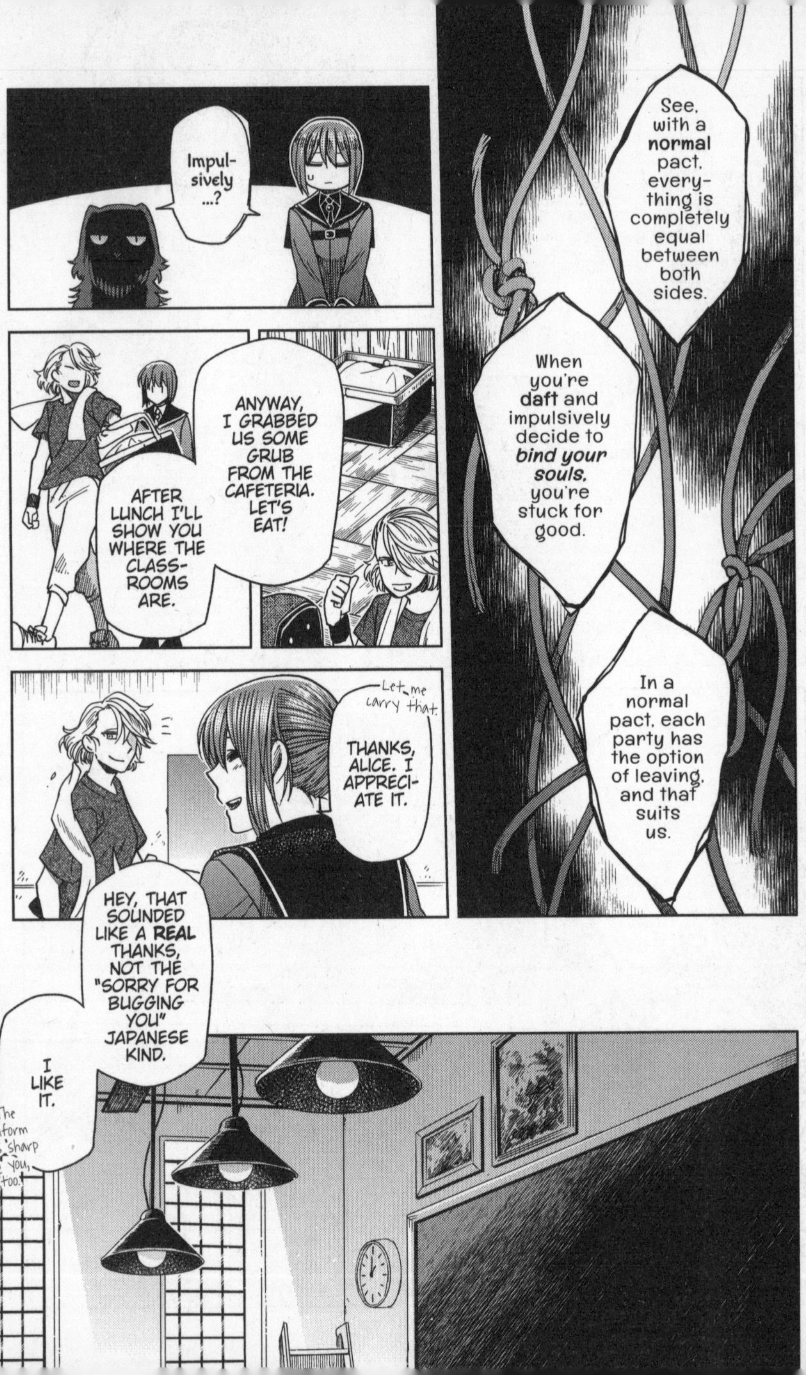
See, with a **normal** pact, everything is completely equal between both sides.
When you're **daft** and impulsively decide to ***bind your souls,*** you're stuck for good.
In a normal pact, each party has the option of leaving, and that suits us.
Impul-sively ...?
ANYWAY, I GRABBED US SOME GRUB FROM THE CAFETERIA. LET'S EAT!
AFTER LUNCH I'LL SHOW YOU WHERE THE CLASS-ROOMS ARE.
Let me carry that.
THANKS, ALICE. I APPRECI-ATE IT.
HEY, THAT SOUNDED LIKE A **REAL** THANKS, NOT THE "SORRY FOR BUGGING YOU" JAPANESE KIND.
I LIKE IT.
The uniform looks sharp on you, too.

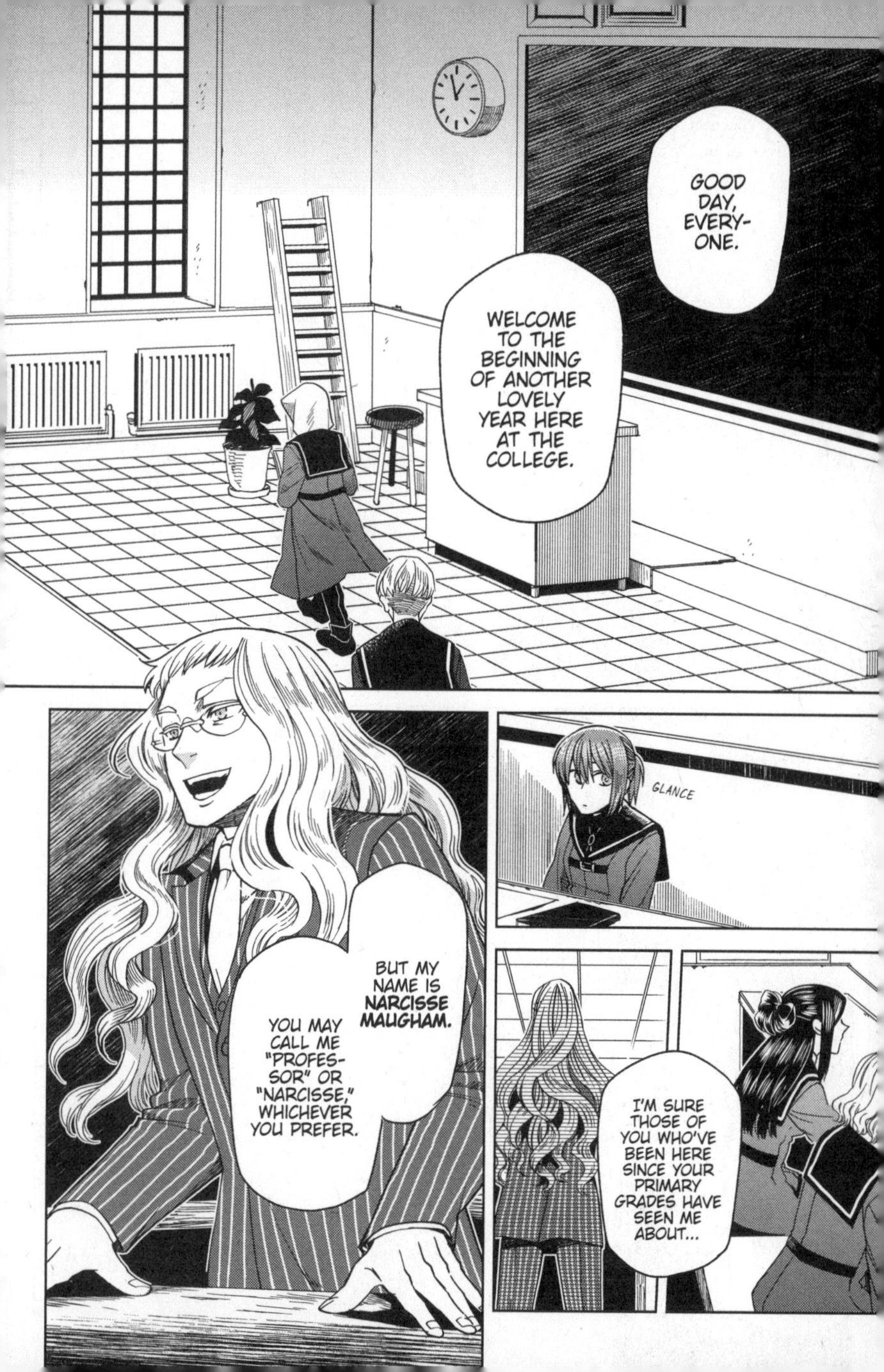
GOOD DAY, EVERYONE.
WELCOME TO THE BEGINNING OF ANOTHER LOVELY YEAR HERE AT THE COLLEGE.
GLANCE
I'M SURE THOSE OF YOU WHO'VE BEEN HERE SINCE YOUR PRIMARY GRADES HAVE SEEN ME ABOUT...
BUT MY NAME IS **NARCISSE MAUGHAM.**
YOU MAY CALL ME "PROFESSOR" OR "NARCISSE," WHICHEVER YOU PREFER.

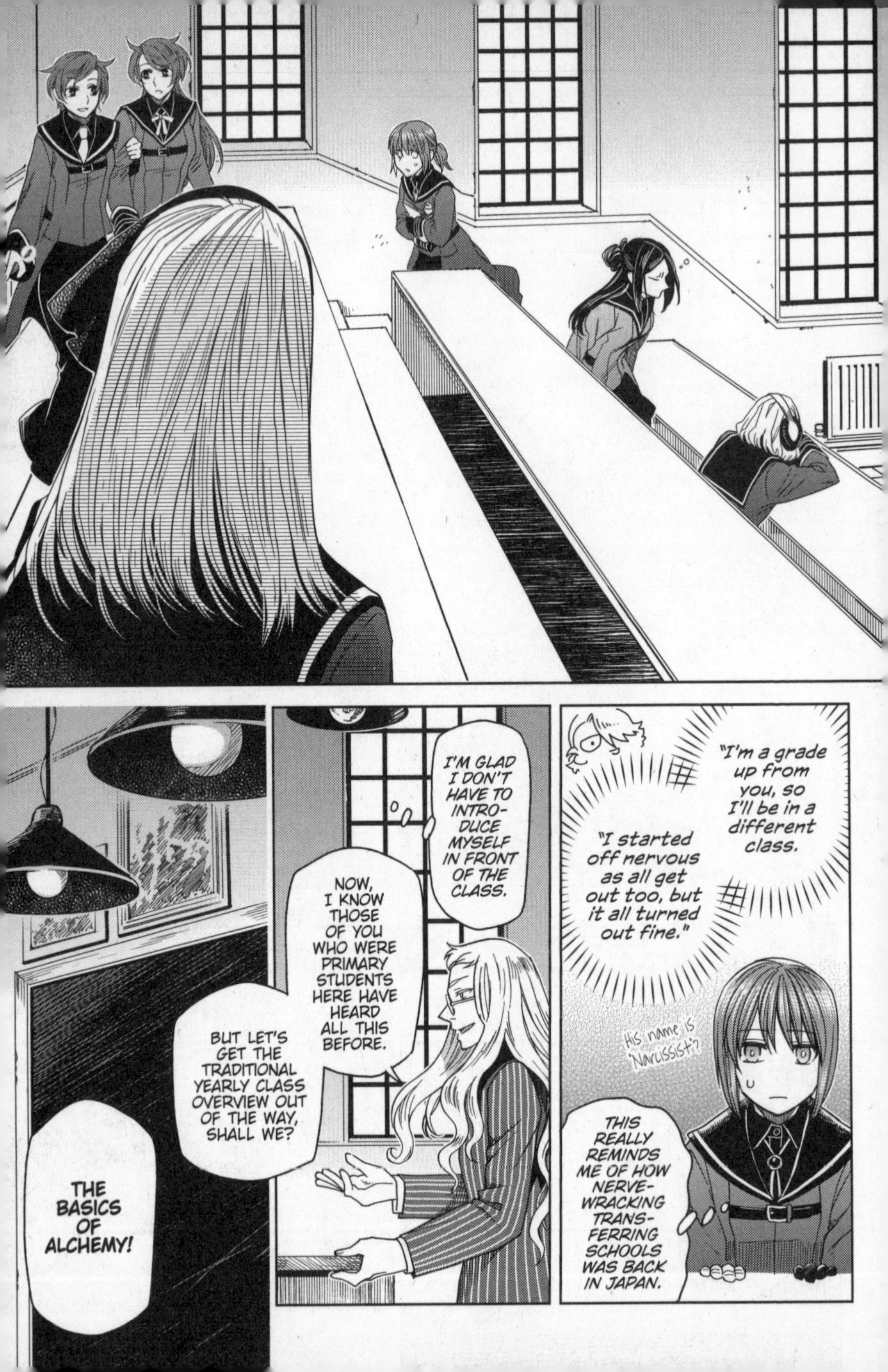
"I'm a grade up from you, so I'll be in a different class.
"I started off nervous as all get out too, but it all turned out fine."
His name is "Narcissist"?
THIS REALLY REMINDS ME OF HOW NERVE-WRACKING TRANS-FERRING SCHOOLS WAS BACK IN JAPAN.
I'M GLAD I DON'T HAVE TO INTRO-DUCE MYSELF IN FRONT OF THE CLASS.
NOW, I KNOW THOSE OF YOU WHO WERE PRIMARY STUDENTS HERE HAVE HEARD ALL THIS BEFORE.
BUT LET'S GET THE TRADITIONAL YEARLY CLASS OVERVIEW OUT OF THE WAY, SHALL WE?
THE BASICS OF ALCHEMY!

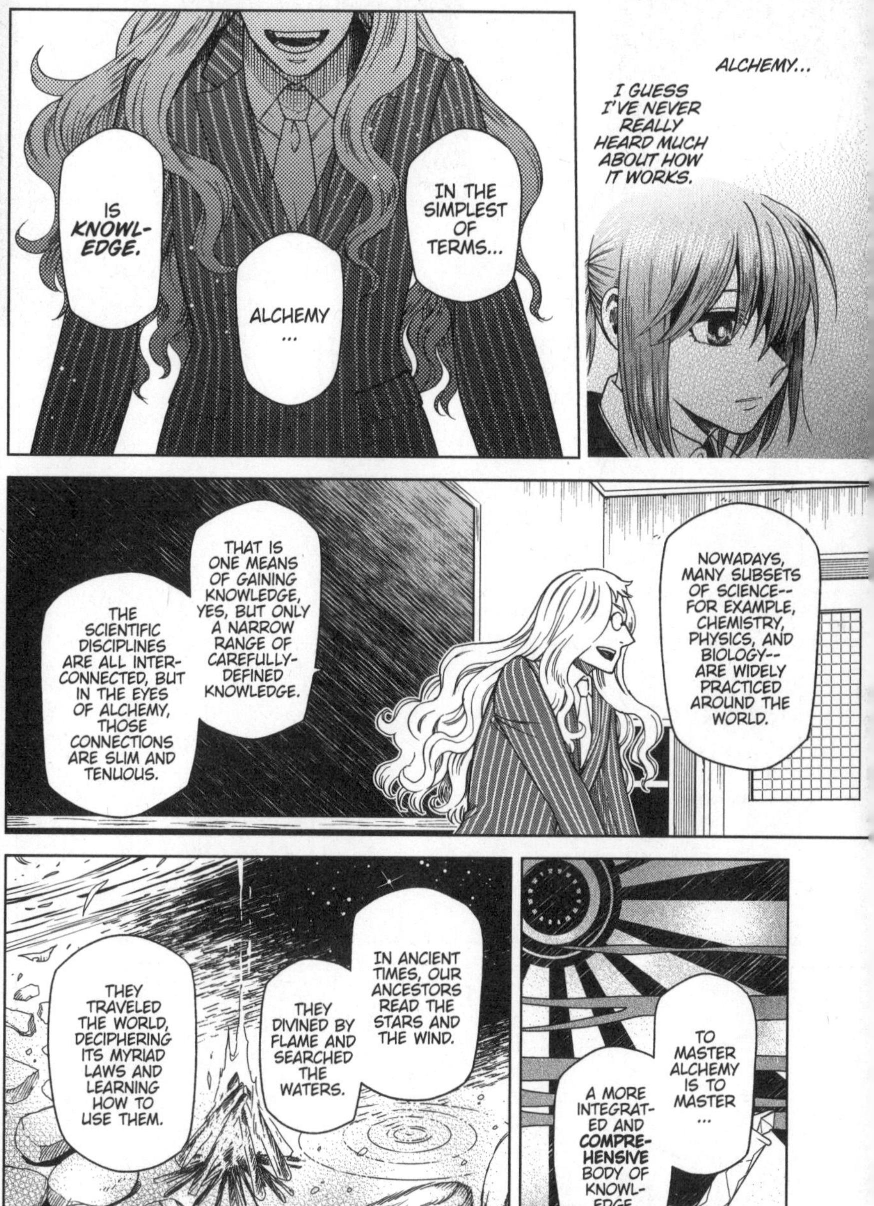
ALCHEMY...
I GUESS I'VE NEVER REALLY HEARD MUCH ABOUT HOW IT WORKS.
IN THE SIMPLEST OF TERMS...
ALCHEMY ...
IS KNOWL-EDGE.
NOWADAYS, MANY SUBSETS OF SCIENCE--FOR EXAMPLE, CHEMISTRY, PHYSICS, AND BIOLOGY--ARE WIDELY PRACTICED AROUND THE WORLD.
THAT IS ONE MEANS OF GAINING KNOWLEDGE, YES, BUT ONLY A NARROW RANGE OF CAREFULLY-DEFINED KNOWLEDGE.
THE SCIENTIFIC DISCIPLINES ARE ALL INTER-CONNECTED, BUT IN THE EYES OF ALCHEMY, THOSE CONNECTIONS ARE SLIM AND TENUOUS.
TO MASTER ALCHEMY IS TO MASTER ...
A MORE INTEGRAT-ED AND COMPRE-HENSIVE BODY OF KNOWL-EDGE.
IN ANCIENT TIMES, OUR ANCESTORS READ THE STARS AND THE WIND.
THEY DIVINED BY FLAME AND SEARCHED THE WATERS.
THEY TRAVELED THE WORLD, DECIPHERING ITS MYRIAD LAWS AND LEARNING HOW TO USE THEM.

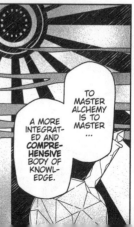

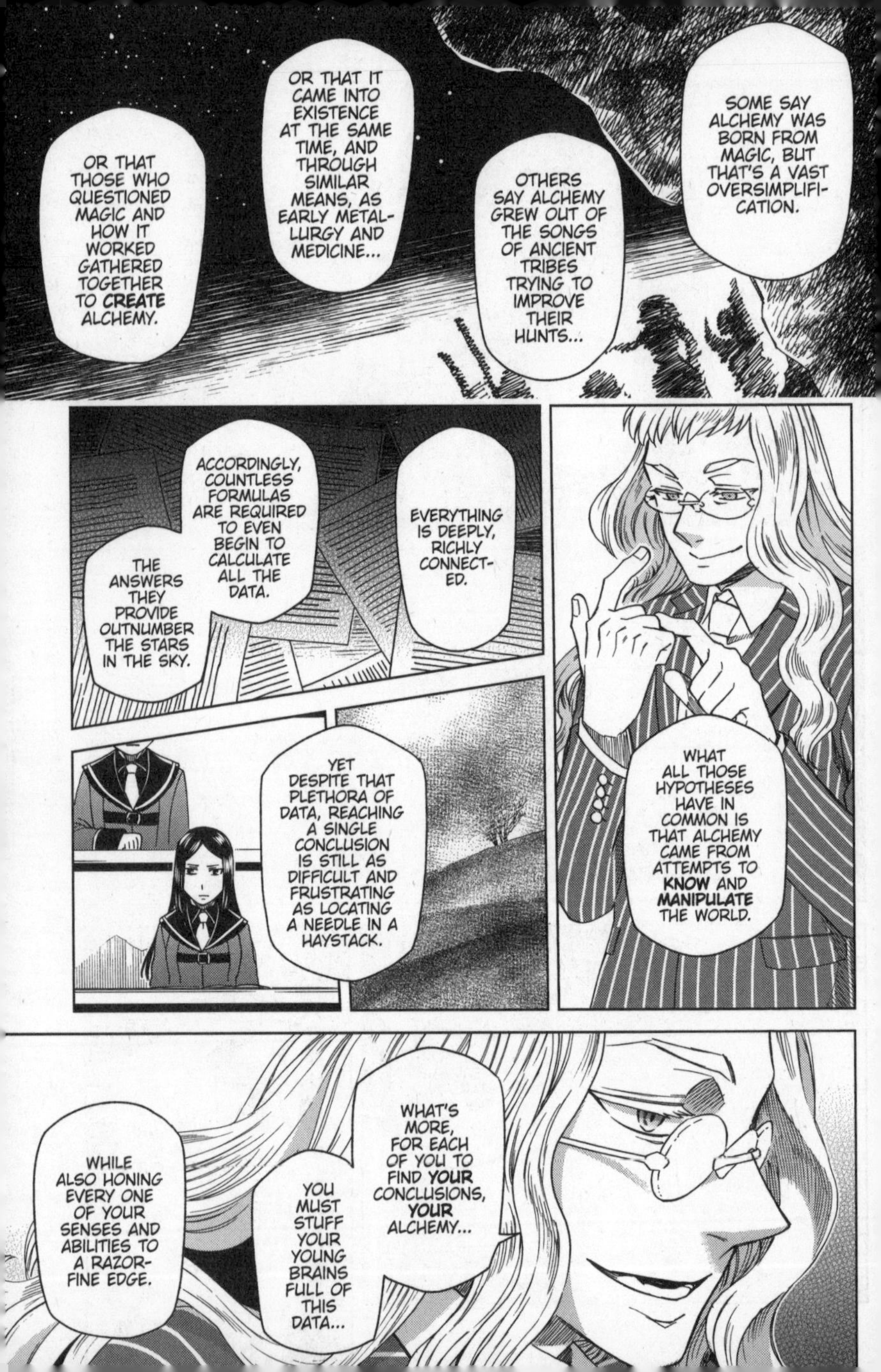
SOME SAY ALCHEMY WAS BORN FROM MAGIC, BUT THAT'S A VAST OVERSIMPLIFICATION.
OTHERS SAY ALCHEMY GREW OUT OF THE SONGS OF ANCIENT TRIBES TRYING TO IMPROVE THEIR HUNTS...
OR THAT IT CAME INTO EXISTENCE AT THE SAME TIME, AND THROUGH SIMILAR MEANS, AS EARLY METALLURGY AND MEDICINE...
OR THAT THOSE WHO QUESTIONED MAGIC AND HOW IT WORKED GATHERED TOGETHER TO **CREATE** ALCHEMY.
WHAT ALL THOSE HYPOTHESES HAVE IN COMMON IS THAT ALCHEMY CAME FROM ATTEMPTS TO **KNOW** AND **MANIPULATE** THE WORLD.
EVERYTHING IS DEEPLY, RICHLY CONNECTED.
ACCORDINGLY, COUNTLESS FORMULAS ARE REQUIRED TO EVEN BEGIN TO CALCULATE ALL THE DATA.
THE ANSWERS THEY PROVIDE OUTNUMBER THE STARS IN THE SKY.
YET DESPITE THAT PLETHORA OF DATA, REACHING A SINGLE CONCLUSION IS STILL AS DIFFICULT AND FRUSTRATING AS LOCATING A NEEDLE IN A HAYSTACK.
WHAT'S MORE, FOR EACH OF YOU TO FIND **YOUR** CONCLUSIONS, **YOUR** ALCHEMY...
YOU MUST STUFF YOUR YOUNG BRAINS FULL OF THIS DATA...
WHILE ALSO HONING EVERY ONE OF YOUR SENSES AND ABILITIES TO A RAZOR-FINE EDGE.

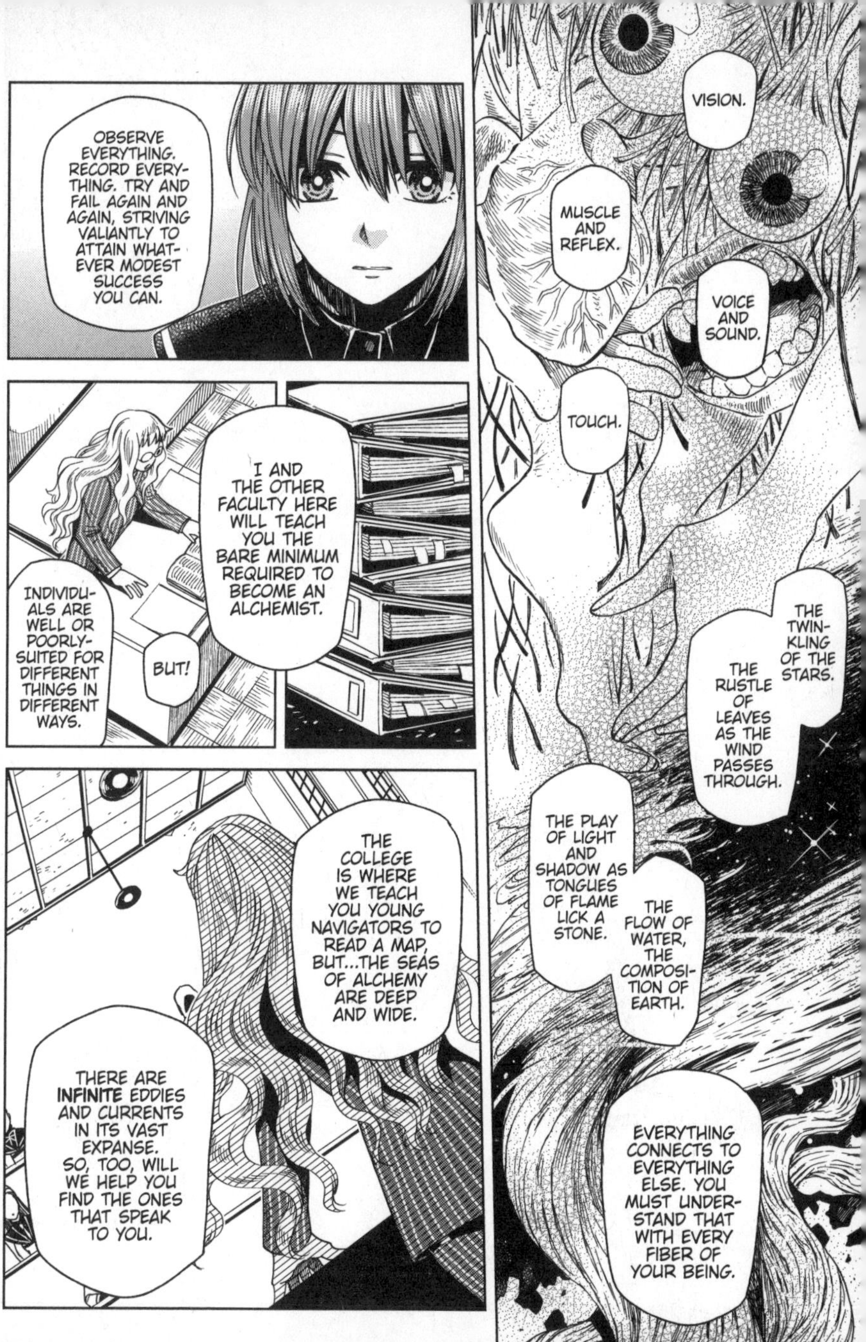
VISION.
MUSCLE AND REFLEX.
VOICE AND SOUND.
TOUCH.
THE TWINKLING OF THE STARS.
THE RUSTLE OF LEAVES AS THE WIND PASSES THROUGH.
THE FLOW OF WATER, THE COMPOSITION OF EARTH.
THE PLAY OF LIGHT AND SHADOW AS TONGUES OF FLAME LICK A STONE.
EVERYTHING CONNECTS TO EVERYTHING ELSE. YOU MUST UNDERSTAND THAT WITH EVERY FIBER OF YOUR BEING.
OBSERVE EVERYTHING. RECORD EVERYTHING. TRY AND FAIL AGAIN AND AGAIN, STRIVING VALIANTLY TO ATTAIN WHATEVER MODEST SUCCESS YOU CAN.
I AND THE OTHER FACULTY HERE WILL TEACH YOU THE BARE MINIMUM REQUIRED TO BECOME AN ALCHEMIST.
BUT!
INDIVIDUALS ARE WELL OR POORLY-SUITED FOR DIFFERENT THINGS IN DIFFERENT WAYS.
THE COLLEGE IS WHERE WE TEACH YOU YOUNG NAVIGATORS TO READ A MAP, BUT...THE SEAS OF ALCHEMY ARE DEEP AND WIDE.
THERE ARE **INFINITE** EDDIES AND CURRENTS IN ITS VAST EXPANSE. SO, TOO, WILL WE HELP YOU FIND THE ONES THAT SPEAK TO YOU.

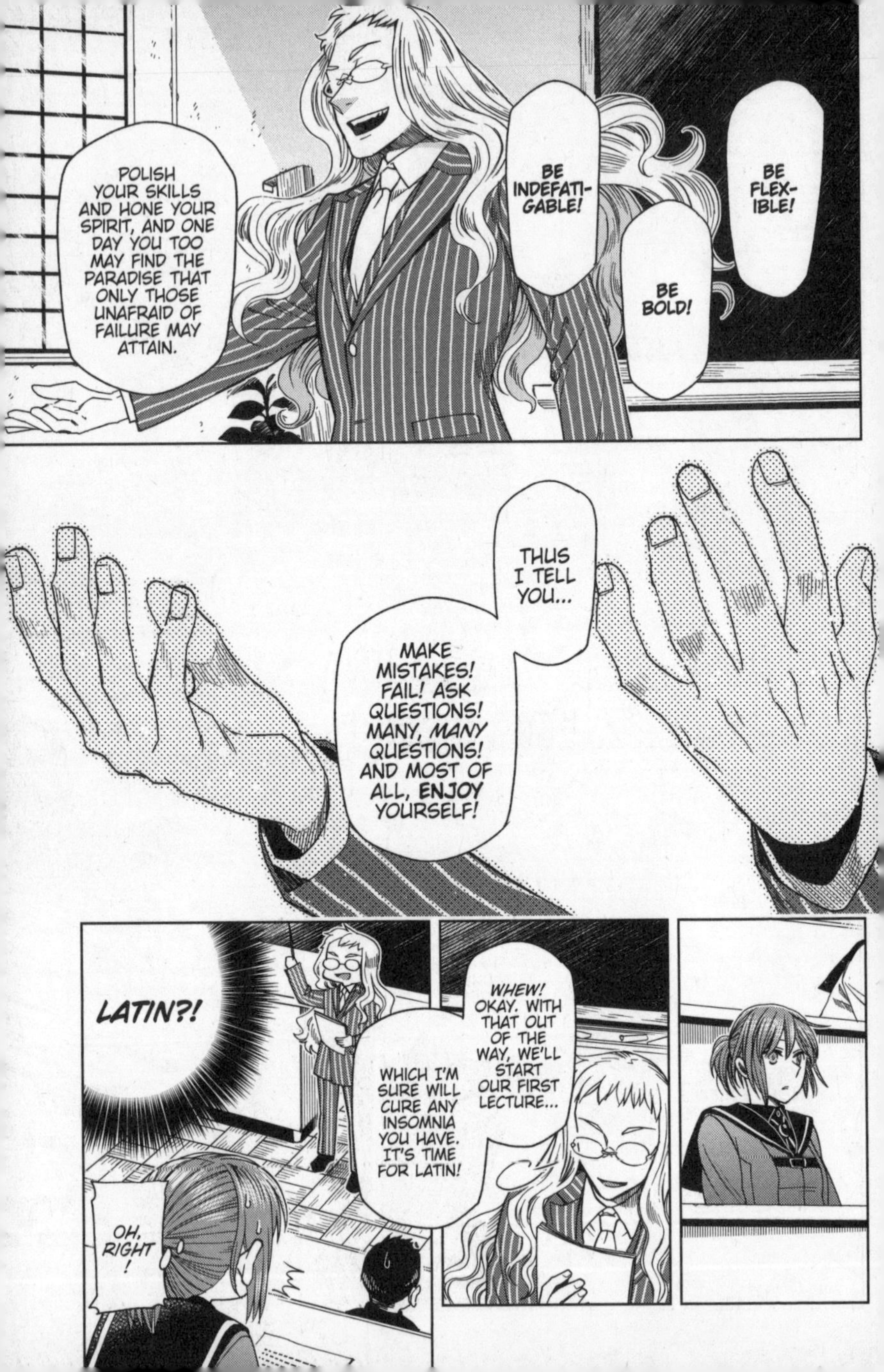
BE FLEXIBLE!
BE BOLD!
BE INDEFATIGABLE!
POLISH YOUR SKILLS AND HONE YOUR SPIRIT, AND ONE DAY YOU TOO MAY FIND THE PARADISE THAT ONLY THOSE UNAFRAID OF FAILURE MAY ATTAIN.
THUS I TELL YOU...
MAKE MISTAKES! FAIL! ASK QUESTIONS! MANY, *MANY* QUESTIONS! AND MOST OF ALL, **ENJOY** YOURSELF!
WHEW! OKAY. WITH THAT OUT OF THE WAY, WE'LL START OUR FIRST LECTURE...
WHICH I'M SURE WILL CURE ANY INSOMNIA YOU HAVE. IT'S TIME FOR LATIN!
LATIN?!
OH, RIGHT!

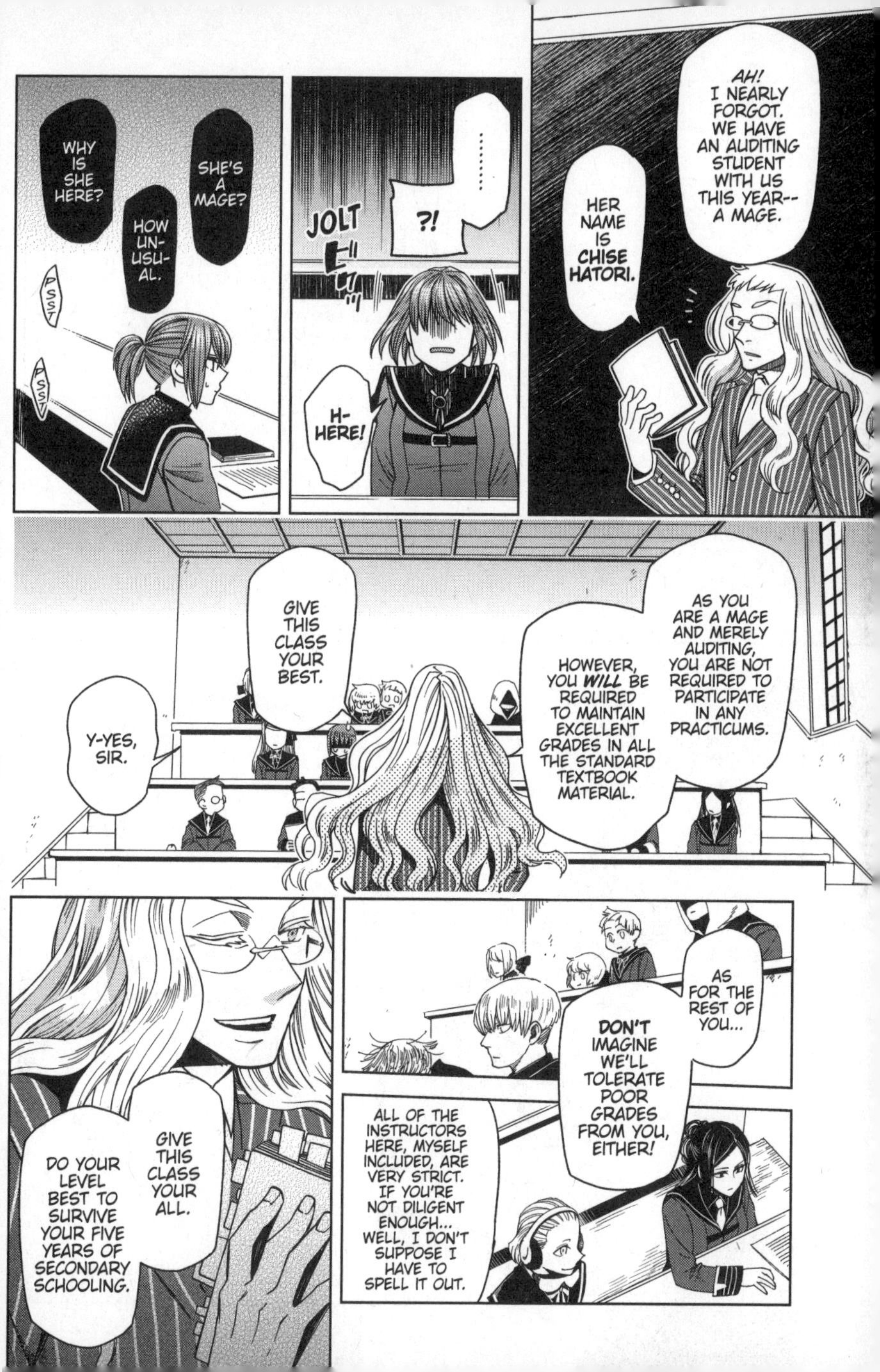
AH! I NEARLY FORGOT. WE HAVE AN AUDITING STUDENT WITH US THIS YEAR-- A MAGE.
HER NAME IS **CHISE HATORI.**
......
?!
JOLT
H- HERE!
SHE'S A MAGE?
WHY IS SHE HERE?
HOW UN- USU- AL.
PSST
PSST
AS YOU ARE A MAGE AND MERELY AUDITING, YOU ARE NOT REQUIRED TO PARTICIPATE IN ANY PRACTICUMS.
HOWEVER, YOU ***WILL*** BE REQUIRED TO MAINTAIN EXCELLENT GRADES IN ALL THE STANDARD TEXTBOOK MATERIAL.
GIVE THIS CLASS YOUR BEST.
Y-YES, SIR.
AS FOR THE REST OF YOU...
DON'T IMAGINE WE'LL TOLERATE POOR GRADES FROM YOU, EITHER!
ALL OF THE INSTRUCTORS HERE, MYSELF INCLUDED, ARE VERY STRICT. IF YOU'RE NOT DILIGENT ENOUGH... WELL, I DON'T SUPPOSE I HAVE TO SPELL IT OUT.
GIVE THIS CLASS YOUR ALL.
DO YOUR LEVEL BEST TO SURVIVE YOUR FIVE YEARS OF SECONDARY SCHOOLING.

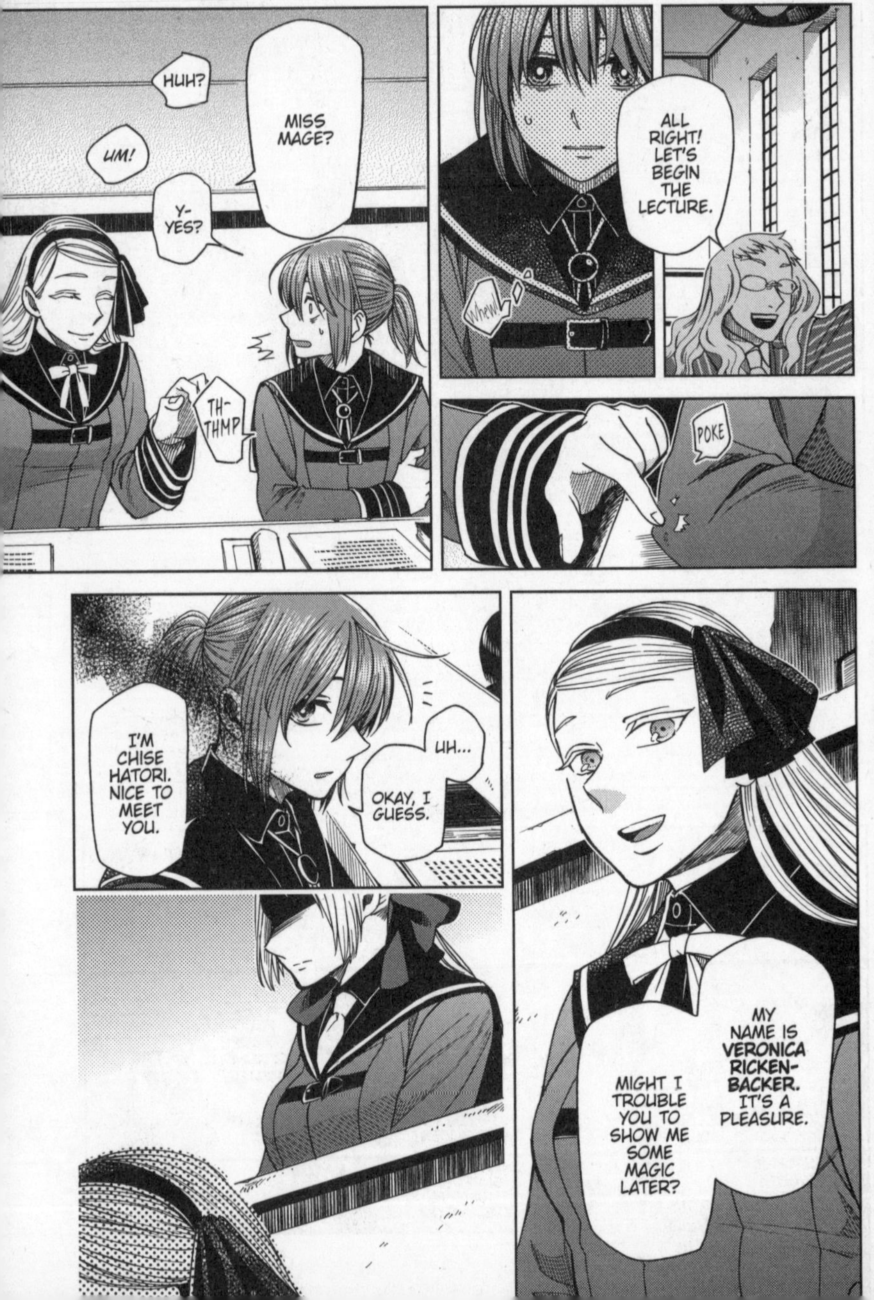
ALL RIGHT! LET'S BEGIN THE LECTURE.
Whew
POKE
MISS MAGE?
HUH?
UM!
Y-YES?
TH-THMP
MY NAME IS VERONICA RICKEN-BACKER. IT'S A PLEASURE.
MIGHT I TROUBLE YOU TO SHOW ME SOME MAGIC LATER?
UH...
OKAY, I GUESS.
I'M CHISE HATORI. NICE TO MEET YOU.

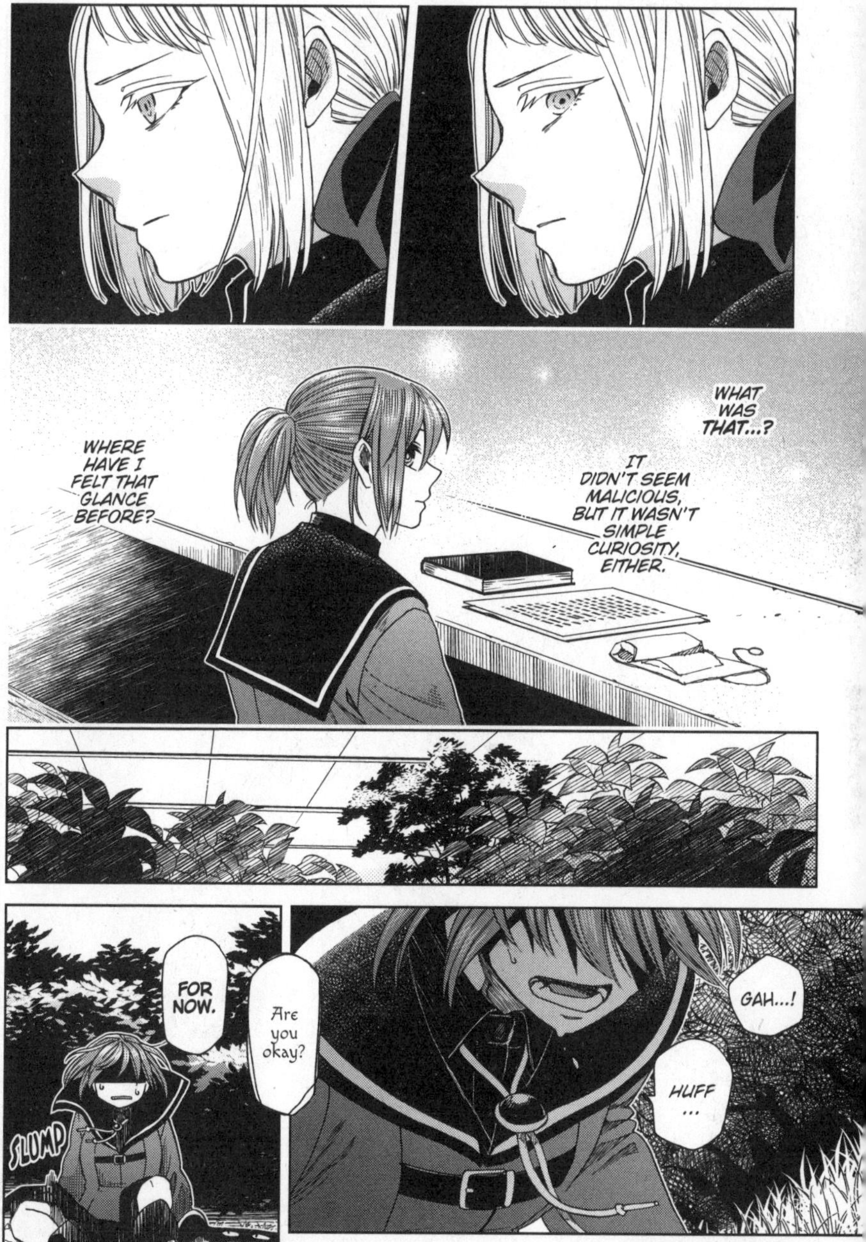
WHAT WAS THAT...?
IT DIDN'T SEEM MALICIOUS, BUT IT WASN'T SIMPLE CURIOSITY, EITHER.
WHERE HAVE I FELT THAT GLANCE BEFORE?
GAH...!
HUFF...
Are you okay?
FOR NOW.
SLUMP

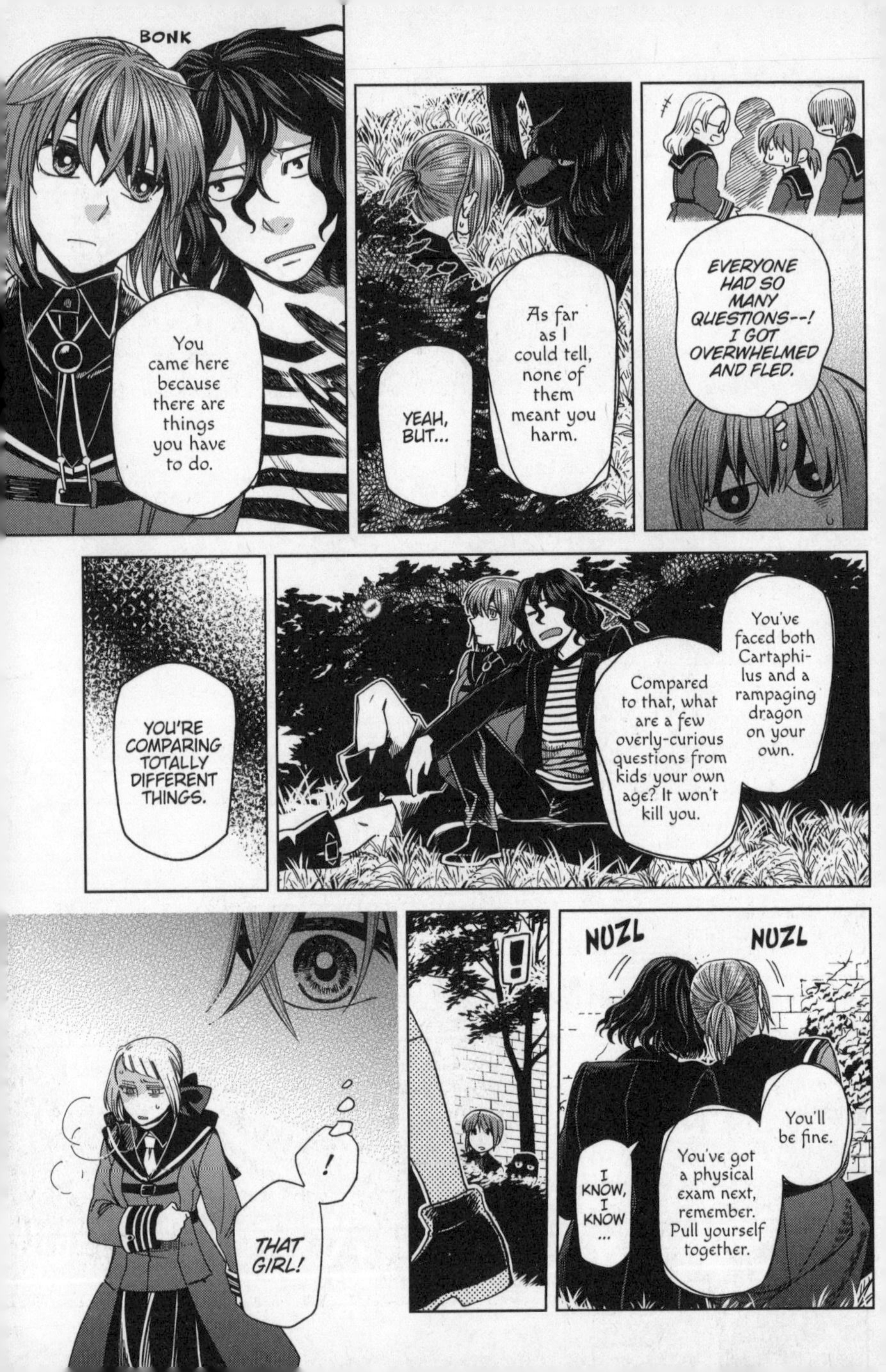
EVERYONE HAD SO MANY QUESTIONS--! I GOT OVERWHELMED AND FLED.
As far as I could tell, none of them meant you harm.
YEAH, BUT...
BONK
You came here because there are things you have to do.
You've faced both Cartaphilus and a rampaging dragon on your own.
Compared to that, what are a few overly-curious questions from kids your own age? It won't kill you.
YOU'RE COMPARING TOTALLY DIFFERENT THINGS.
NUZL
NUZL
You'll be fine.
You've got a physical exam next, remember. Pull yourself together.
I KNOW, I KNOW...
!
!
THAT GIRL!

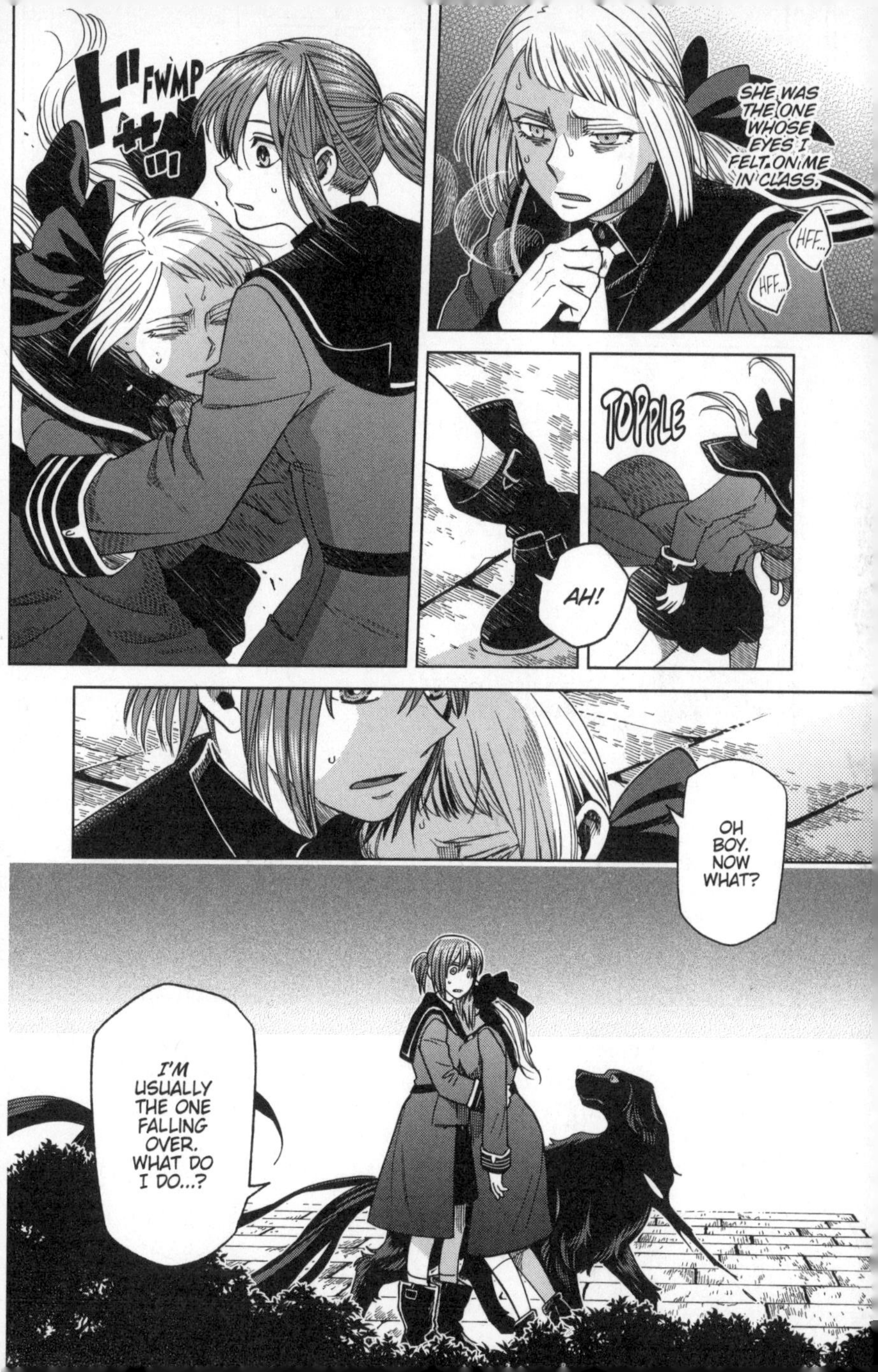
SHE WAS THE ONE WHOSE EYES I FELT ON ME IN CLASS.
HFF...
HFF...
TOPPLE
AH!
FWMP
OH BOY. NOW WHAT?
I'M USUALLY THE ONE FALLING OVER. WHAT DO I DO...?

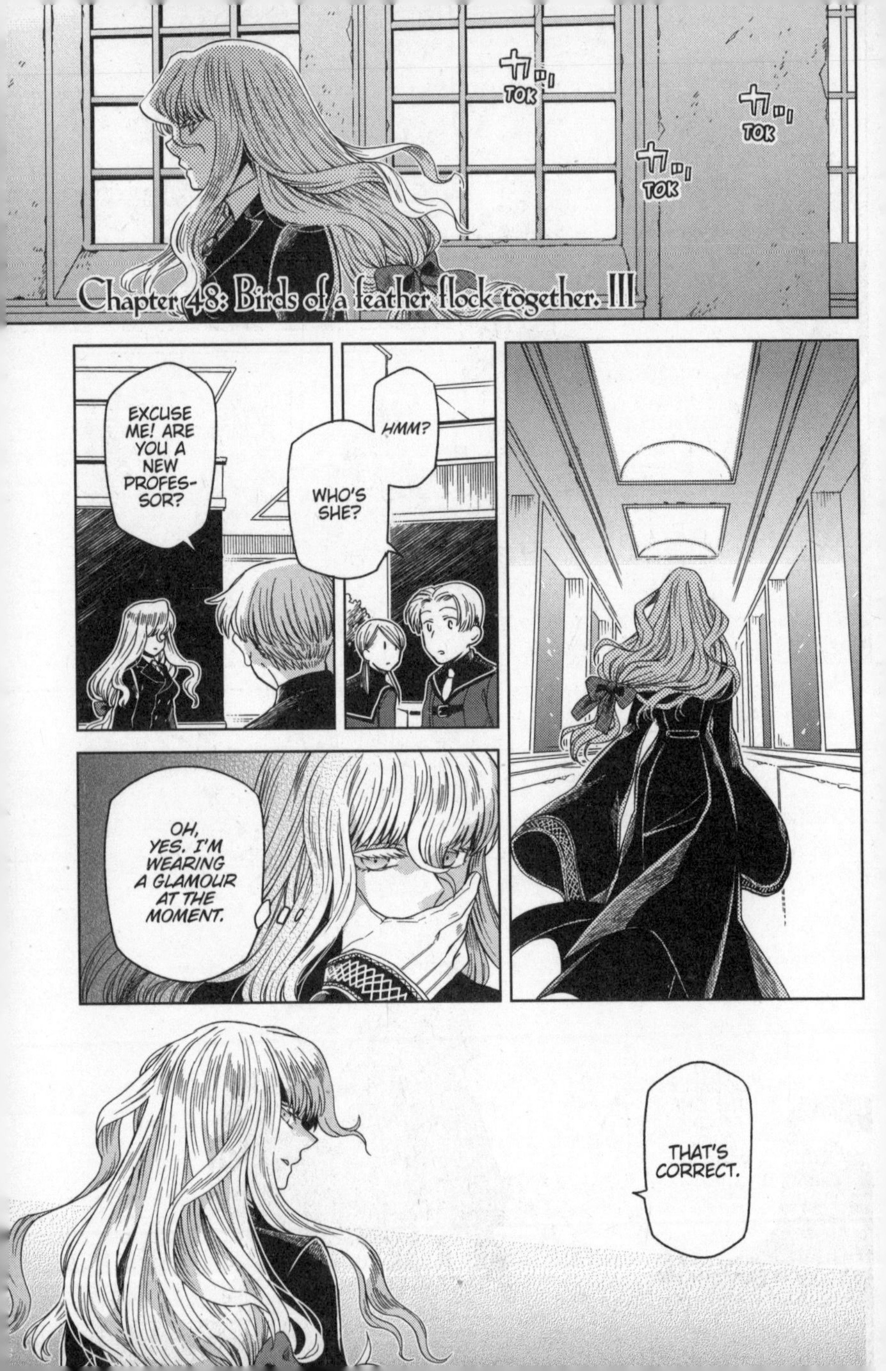
カッ
TOK
カッ
TOK
カッ
TOK
Chapter 48: Birds of a feather flock together. III
HMM?
WHO'S SHE?
EXCUSE ME! ARE YOU A NEW PROFES-SOR?
OH, YES. I'M WEARING A GLAMOUR AT THE MOMENT.
THAT'S CORRECT.

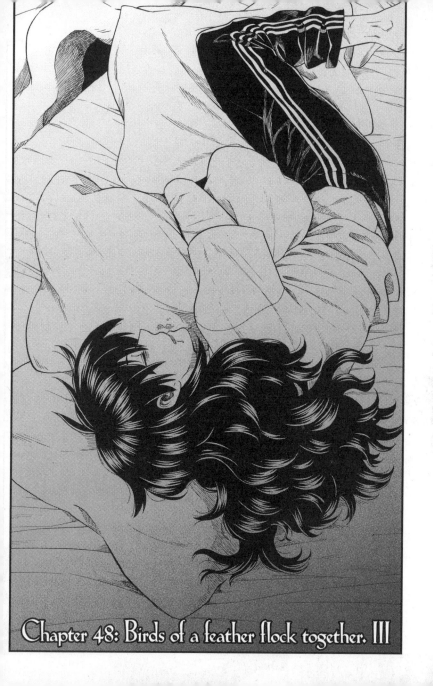

Chapter 48: Birds of a feather flock together. III

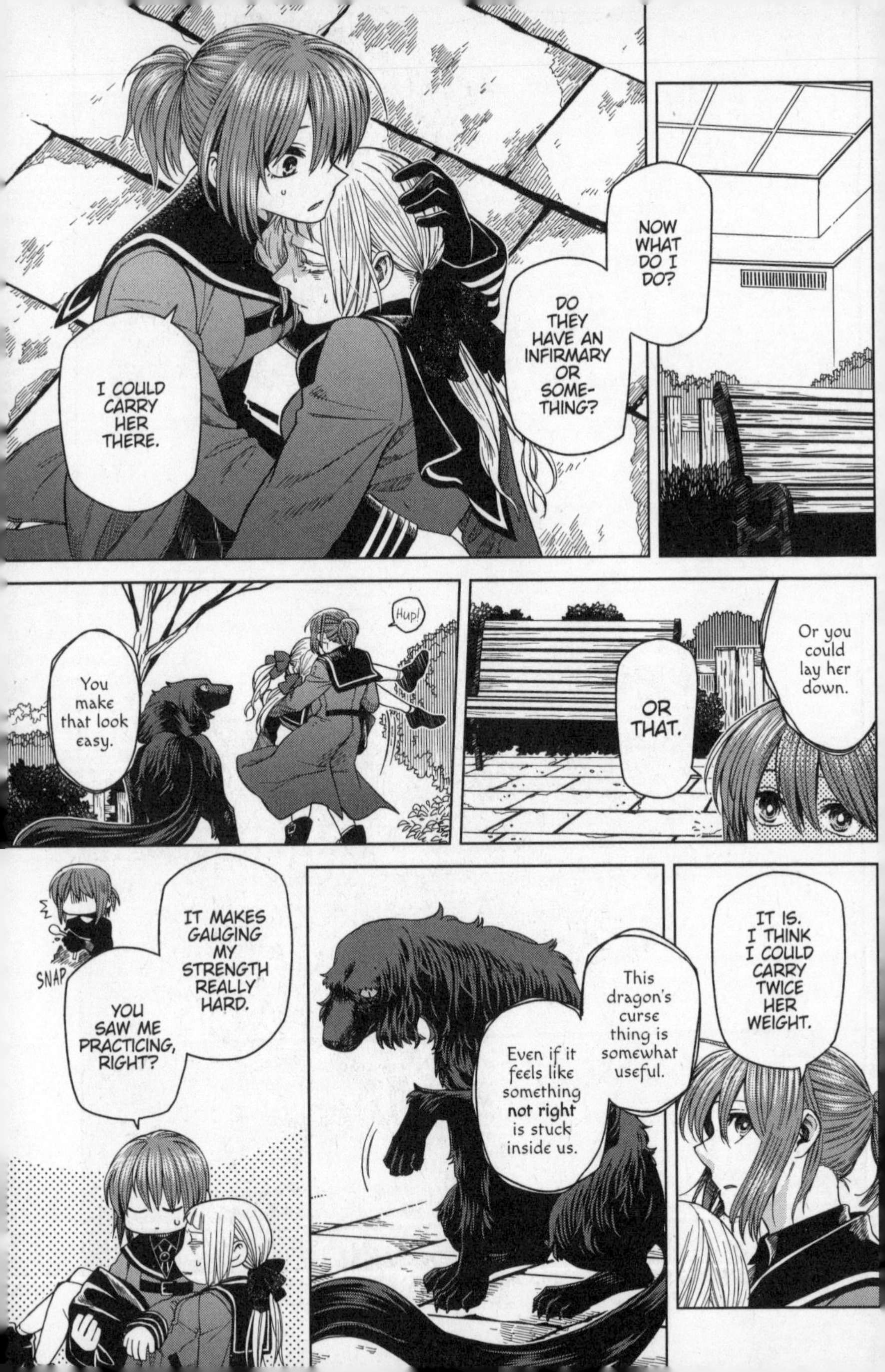
NOW WHAT DO I DO?
DO THEY HAVE AN INFIRMARY OR SOMETHING?
I COULD CARRY HER THERE.
Or you could lay her down.
OR THAT.
Hup!
You make that look easy.
IT IS. I THINK I COULD CARRY TWICE HER WEIGHT.
This dragon's curse thing is somewhat useful.
Even if it feels like something **not right** is stuck inside us.
IT MAKES GAUGING MY STRENGTH REALLY HARD.
SNAP
YOU SAW ME PRACTICING, RIGHT?

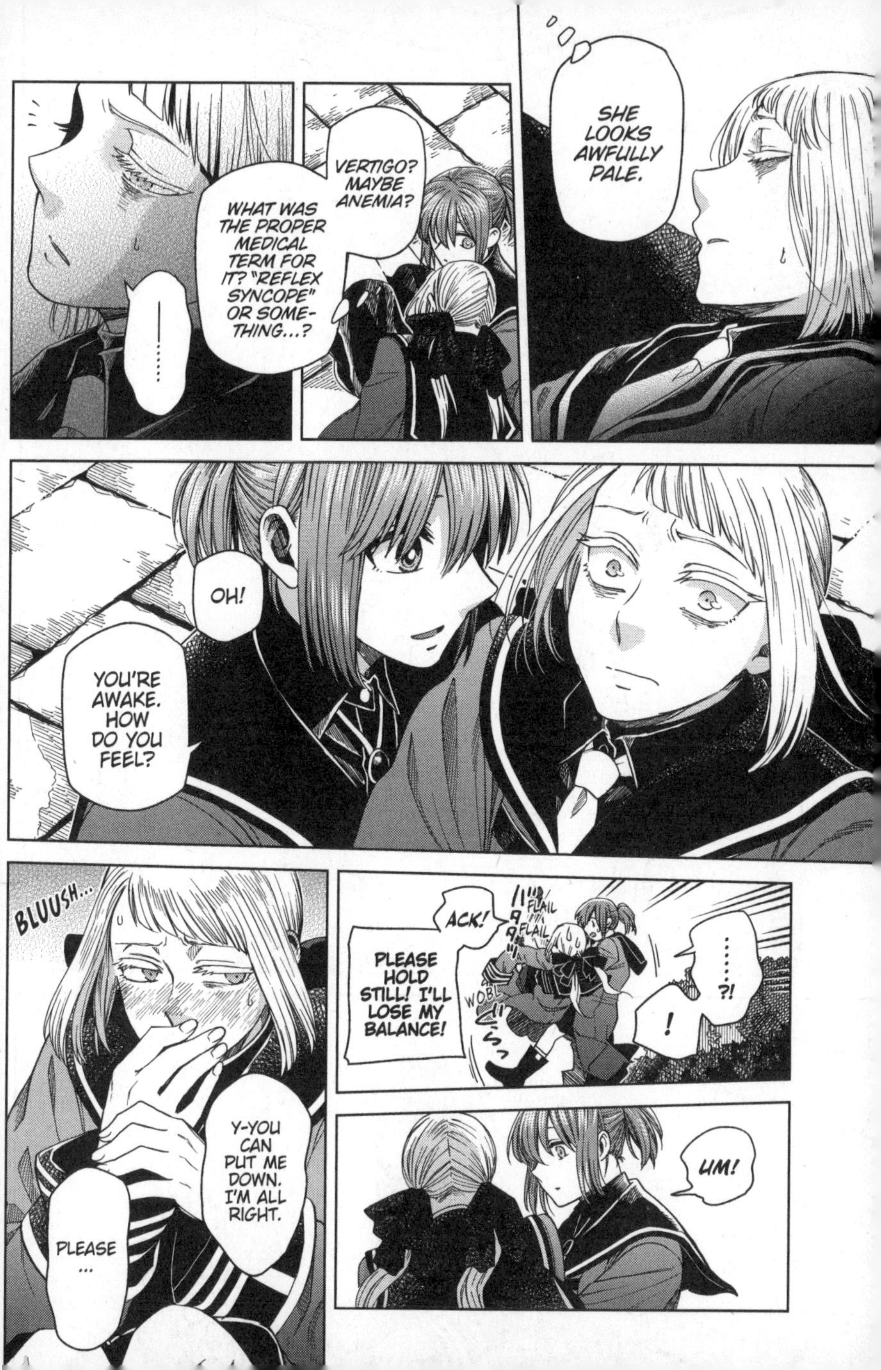
SHE LOOKS AWFULLY PALE.
VERTIGO? MAYBE ANEMIA?
WHAT WAS THE PROPER MEDICAL TERM FOR IT? "REFLEX SYNCOPE" OR SOMETHING...?
......
OH!
YOU'RE AWAKE. HOW DO YOU FEEL?
......?!
!
FLAIL FLAIL
ACK!
PLEASE HOLD STILL! I'LL LOSE MY BALANCE!
UM!
BLUUSH...
Y-YOU CAN PUT ME DOWN. I'M ALL RIGHT.
PLEASE...

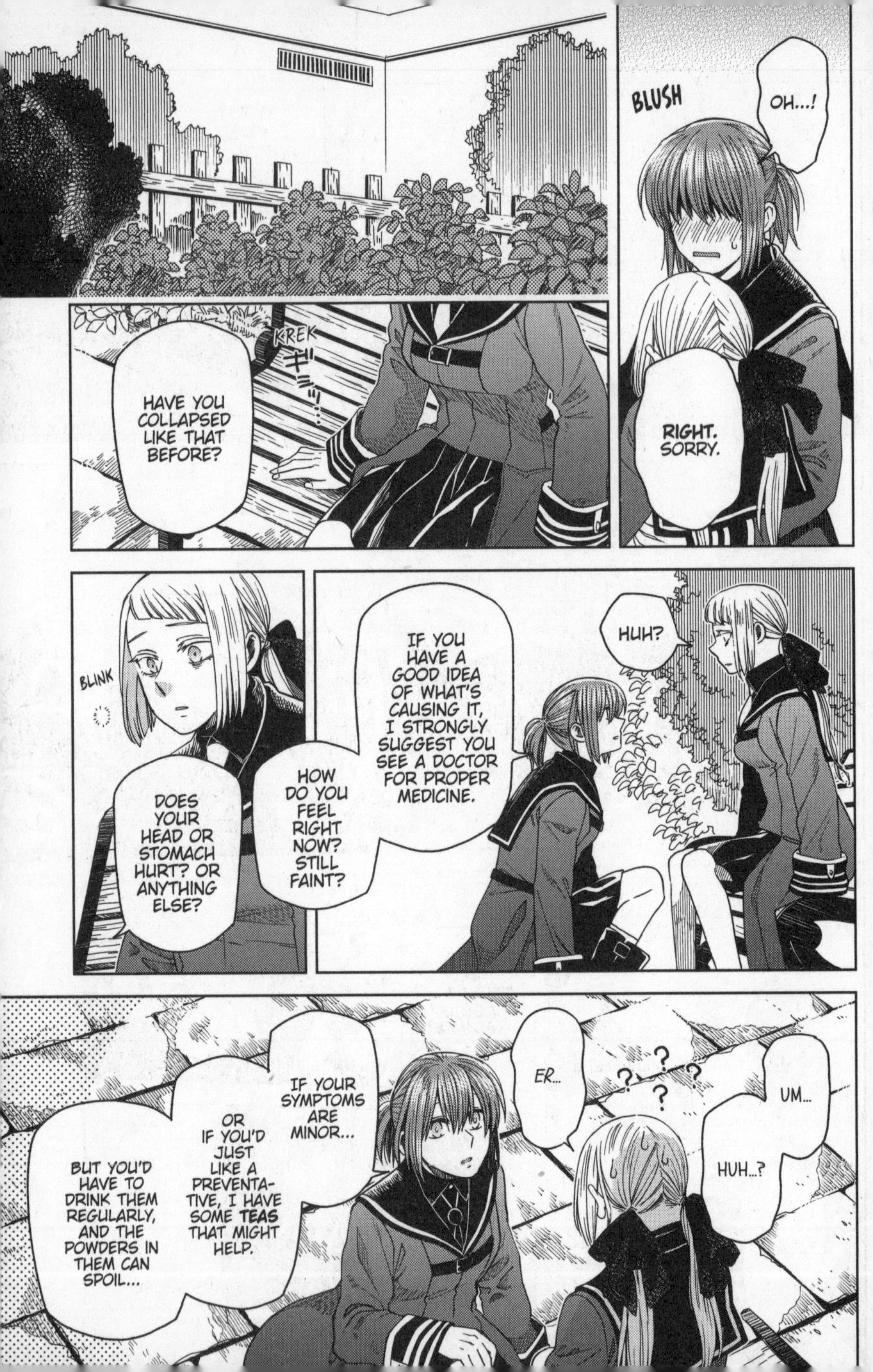
BLUSH
OH...!
RIGHT. SORRY.
KREK
HAVE YOU COLLAPSED LIKE THAT BEFORE?
HUH?
IF YOU HAVE A GOOD IDEA OF WHAT'S CAUSING IT, I STRONGLY SUGGEST YOU SEE A DOCTOR FOR PROPER MEDICINE.
HOW DO YOU FEEL RIGHT NOW? STILL FAINT?
BLINK
DOES YOUR HEAD OR STOMACH HURT? OR ANYTHING ELSE?
UM...
HUH...?
ER...
IF YOUR SYMPTOMS ARE MINOR...
OR IF YOU'D JUST LIKE A PREVENTA-TIVE, I HAVE SOME **TEAS** THAT MIGHT HELP.
BUT YOU'D HAVE TO DRINK THEM REGULARLY, AND THE POWDERS IN THEM CAN SPOIL...

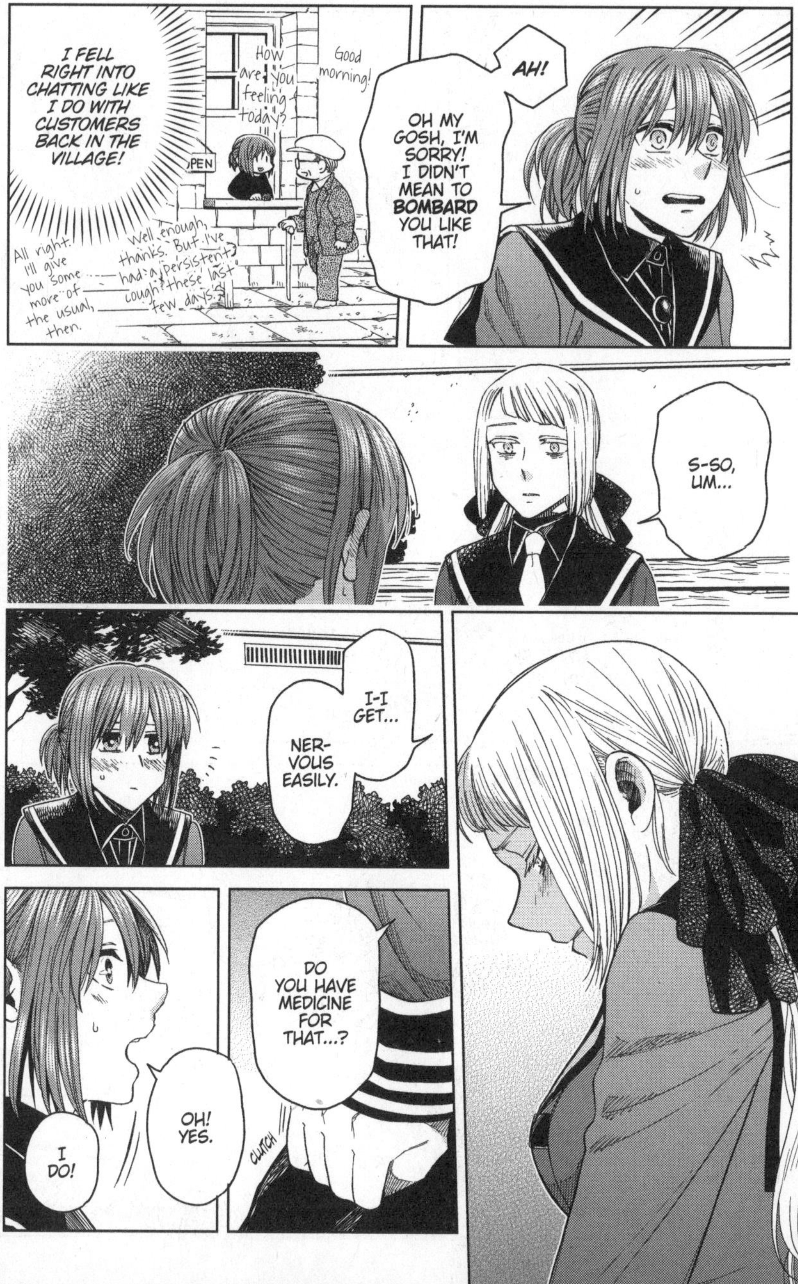
AH!
OH MY GOSH, I'M SORRY! I DIDN'T MEAN TO BOMBARD YOU LIKE THAT!
I FELL RIGHT INTO CHATTING LIKE I DO WITH CUSTOMERS BACK IN THE VILLAGE!
Good morning!
How are you feeling today?
Well enough, thanks. But I've had a persistent cough these last few days.
All right. I'll give you some more of the usual, then.
S-SO, UM...
I-I GET...
NER-VOUS EASILY.
DO YOU HAVE MEDICINE FOR THAT...?
CLUTCH
OH! YES.
I DO!

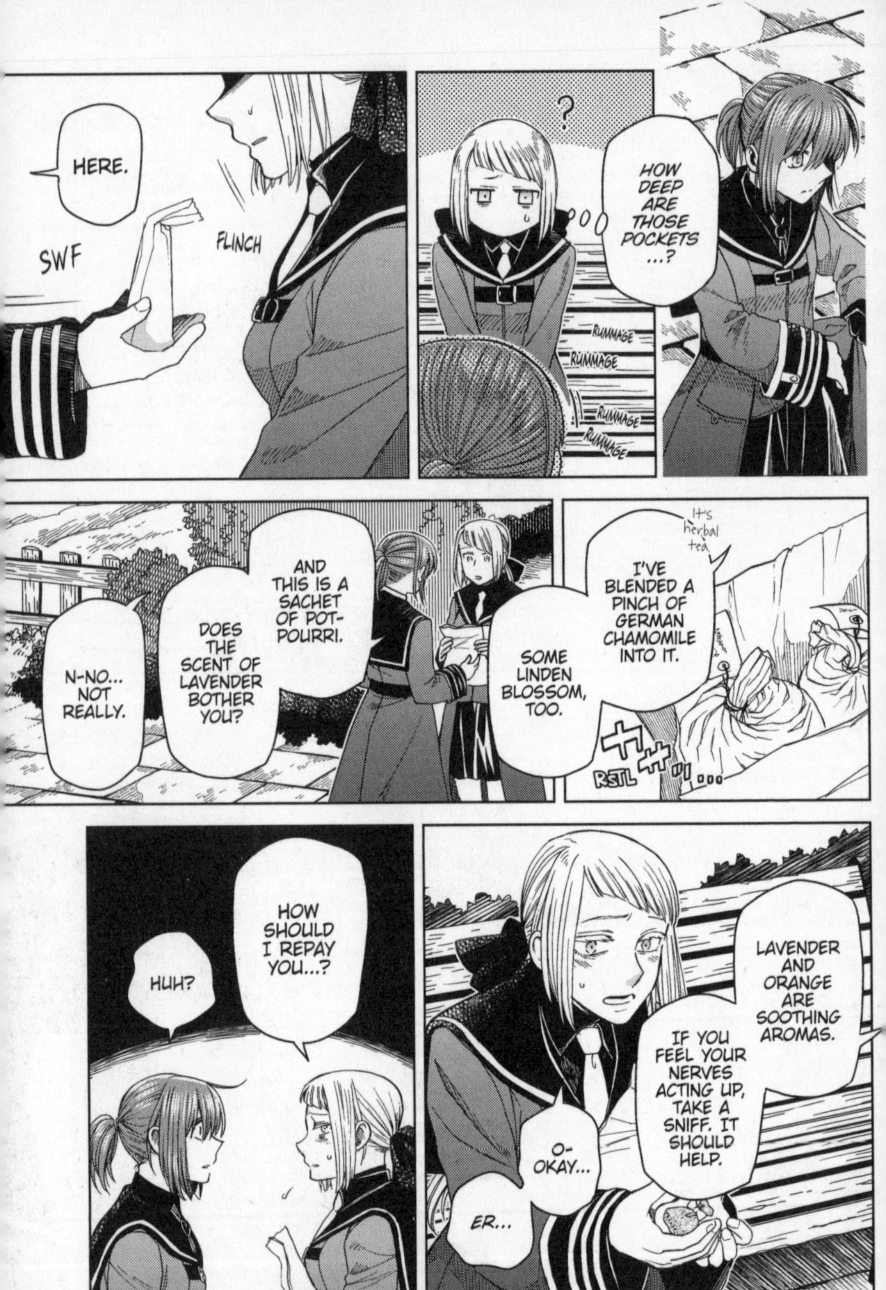
?
HOW DEEP ARE THOSE POCKETS ...?
RUMMAGE
RUMMAGE
RUMMAGE
RUMMAGE
HERE.
SWF
FLINCH
It's herbal tea
I'VE BLENDED A PINCH OF GERMAN CHAMOMILE INTO IT.
SOME LINDEN BLOSSOM, TOO.
RSTL
AND THIS IS A SACHET OF POT-POURRI.
DOES THE SCENT OF LAVENDER BOTHER YOU?
N-NO... NOT REALLY.
LAVENDER AND ORANGE ARE SOOTHING AROMAS.
IF YOU FEEL YOUR NERVES ACTING UP, TAKE A SNIFF. IT SHOULD HELP.
O-OKAY...
ER...
HOW SHOULD I REPAY YOU...?
HUH?

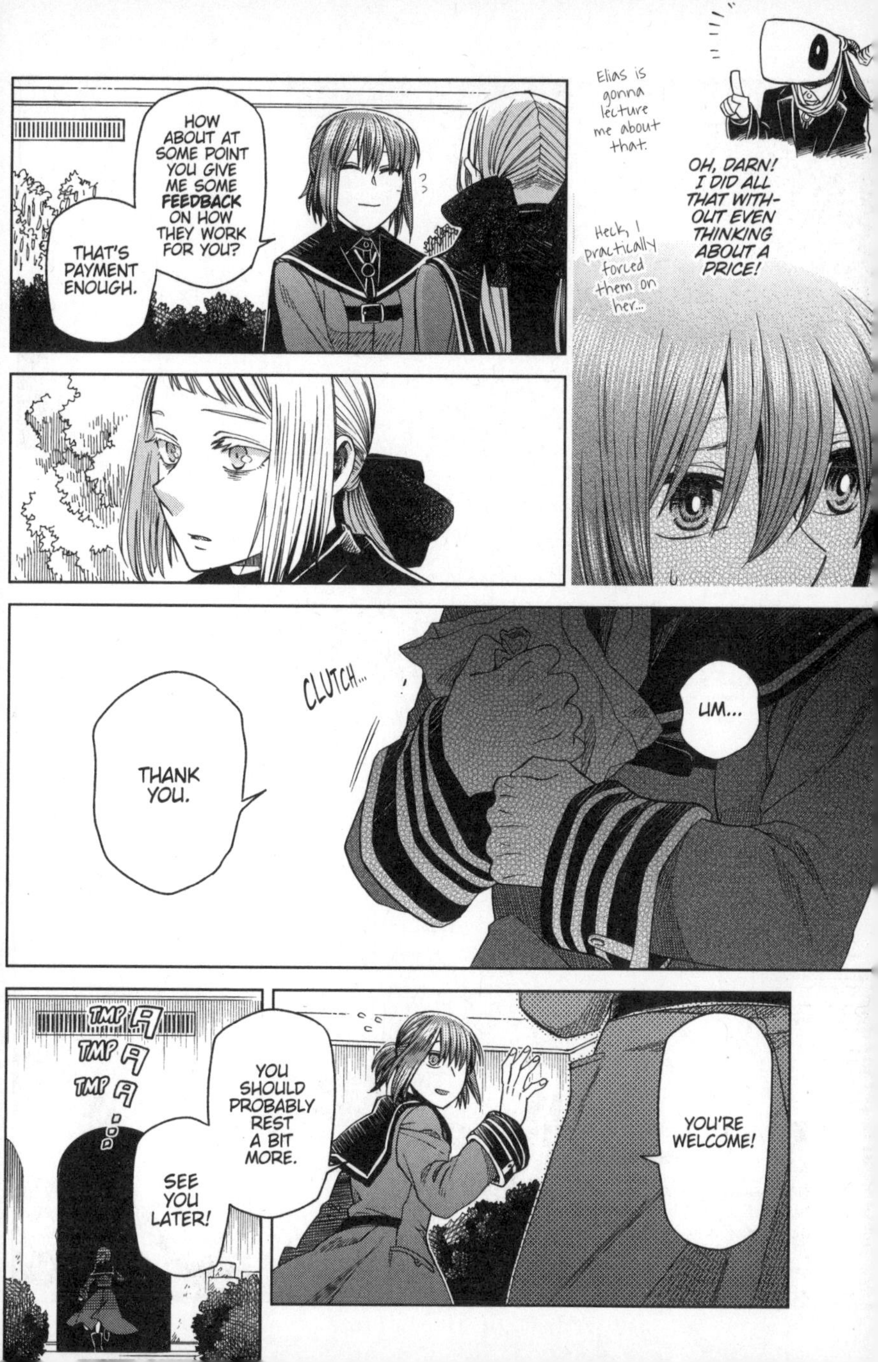
Elias is gonna lecture me about that.
OH, DARN! I DID ALL THAT WITHOUT EVEN THINKING ABOUT A PRICE!
Heck, I practically forced them on her...
HOW ABOUT AT SOME POINT YOU GIVE ME SOME **FEEDBACK** ON HOW THEY WORK FOR YOU?
THAT'S PAYMENT ENOUGH.
UM...
CLUTCH...
THANK YOU.
YOU'RE WELCOME!
YOU SHOULD PROBABLY REST A BIT MORE.
SEE YOU LATER!
TMP
TMP
TMP

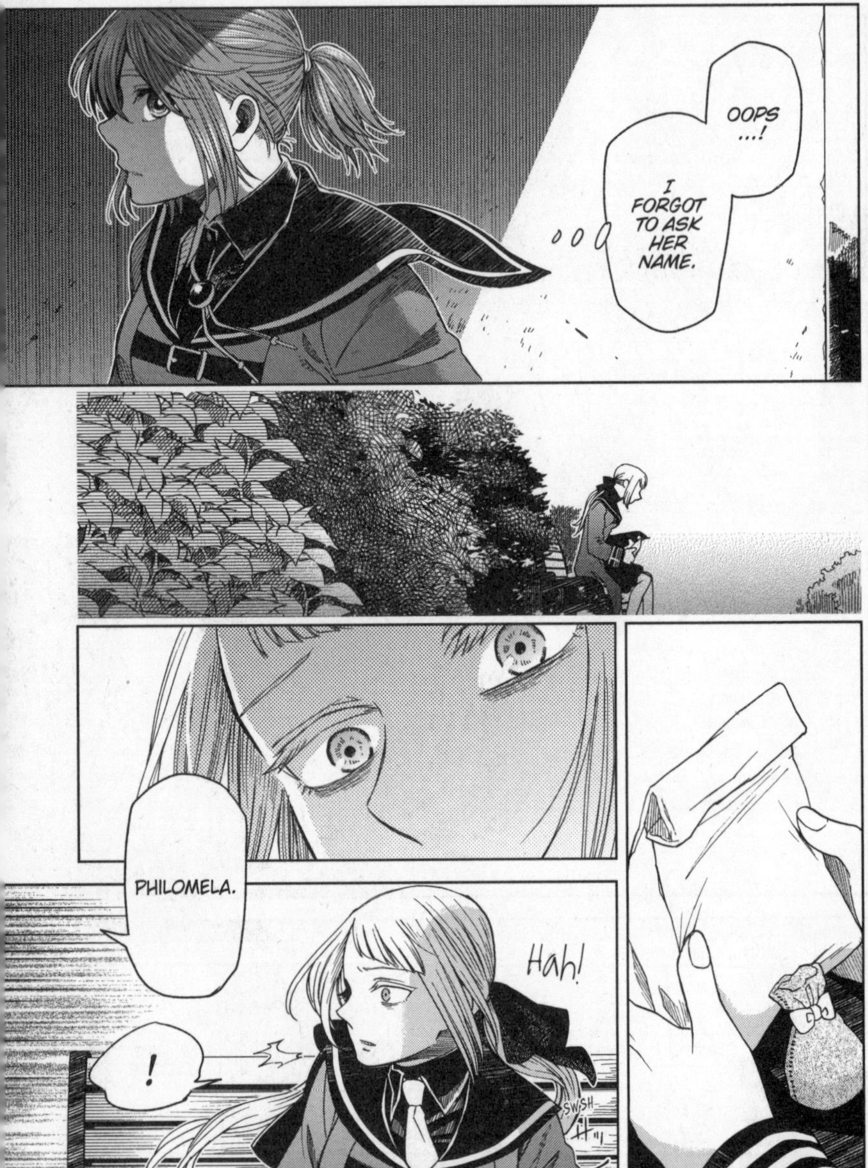
OOPS ...!
I FORGOT TO ASK HER NAME.
PHILOMELA.
Hah!
!
SWISH

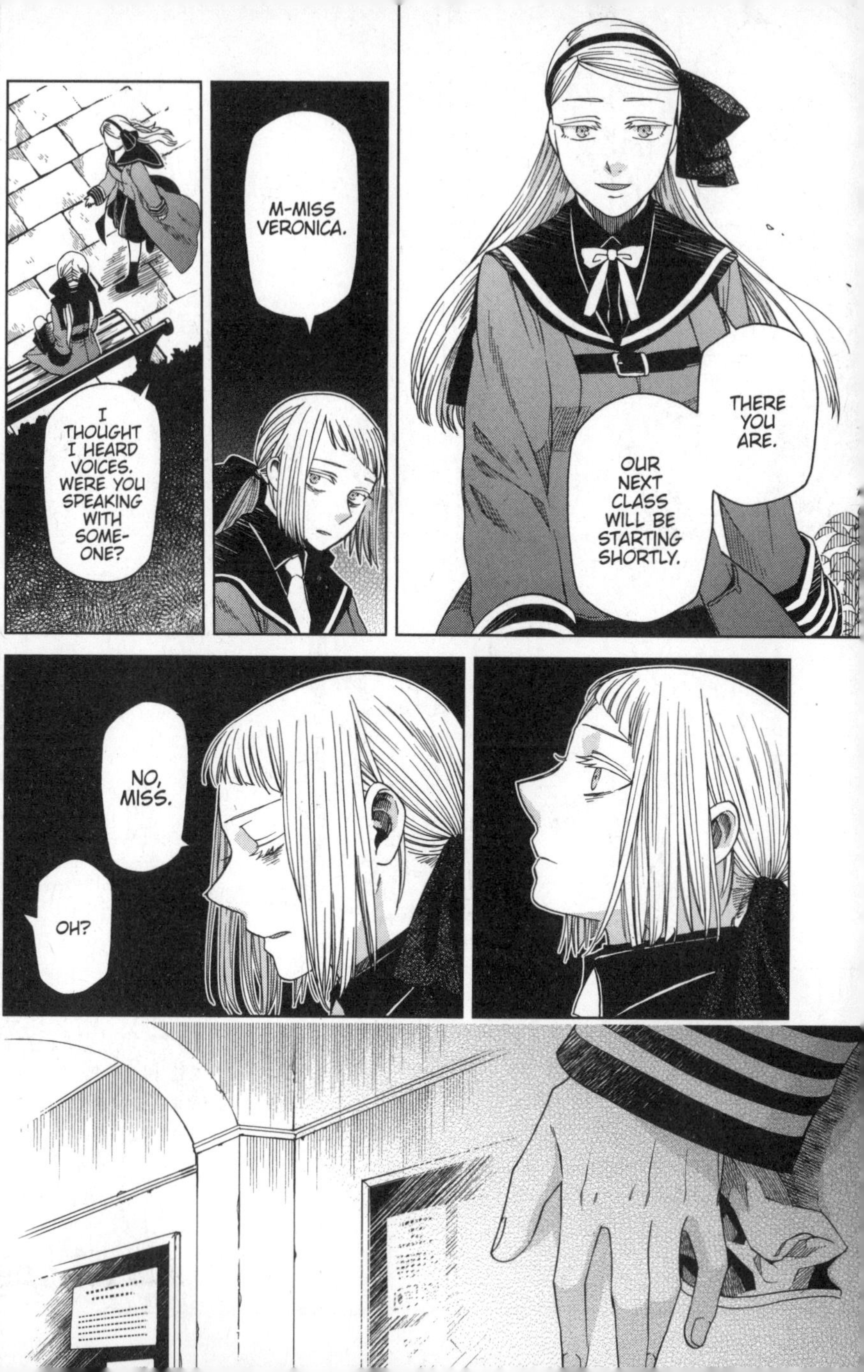
THERE YOU ARE.
OUR NEXT CLASS WILL BE STARTING SHORTLY.
M-MISS VERONICA.
I THOUGHT I HEARD VOICES. WERE YOU SPEAKING WITH SOME-ONE?
NO, MISS.
OH?

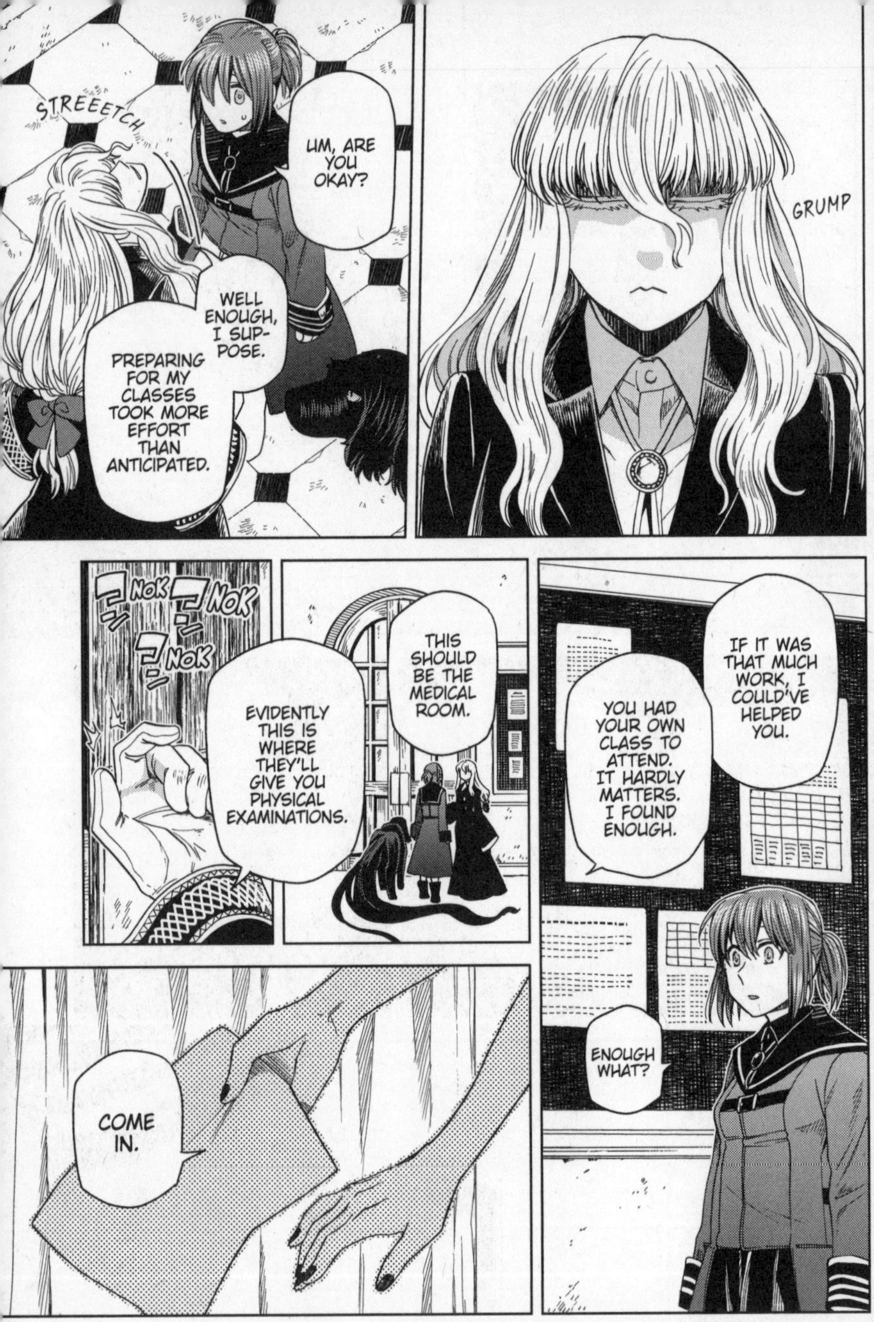
GRUMP
UM, ARE YOU OKAY?
STREEETCH
WELL ENOUGH, I SUPPOSE.
PREPARING FOR MY CLASSES TOOK MORE EFFORT THAN ANTICIPATED.
IF IT WAS THAT MUCH WORK, I COULD'VE HELPED YOU.
YOU HAD YOUR OWN CLASS TO ATTEND. IT HARDLY MATTERS. I FOUND ENOUGH.
ENOUGH WHAT?
THIS SHOULD BE THE MEDICAL ROOM.
EVIDENTLY THIS IS WHERE THEY'LL GIVE YOU PHYSICAL EXAMINATIONS.
NOK NOK NOK
COME IN.

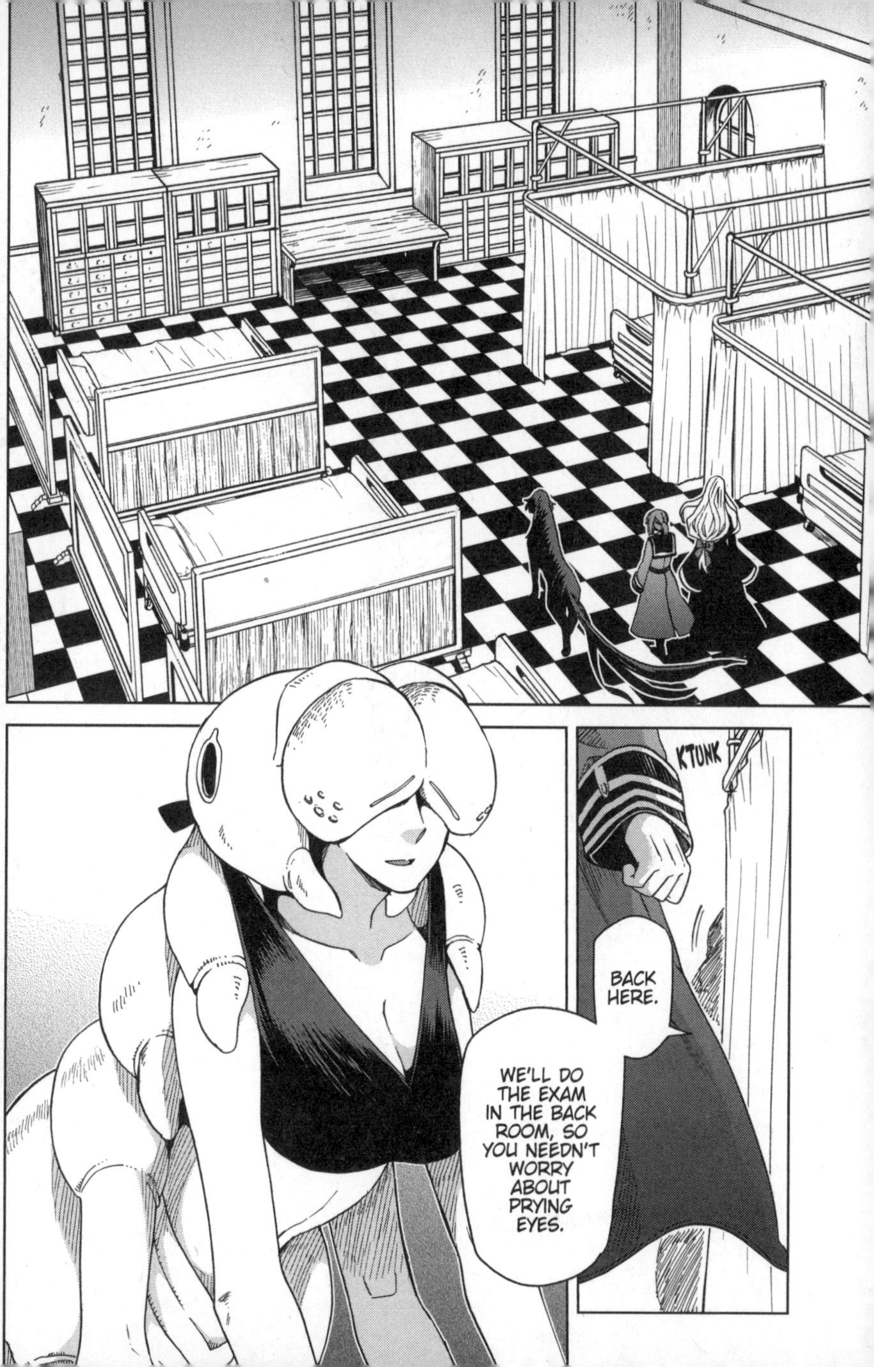
KTUNK
BACK HERE.
WE'LL DO THE EXAM IN THE BACK ROOM, SO YOU NEEDN'T WORRY ABOUT PRYING EYES.

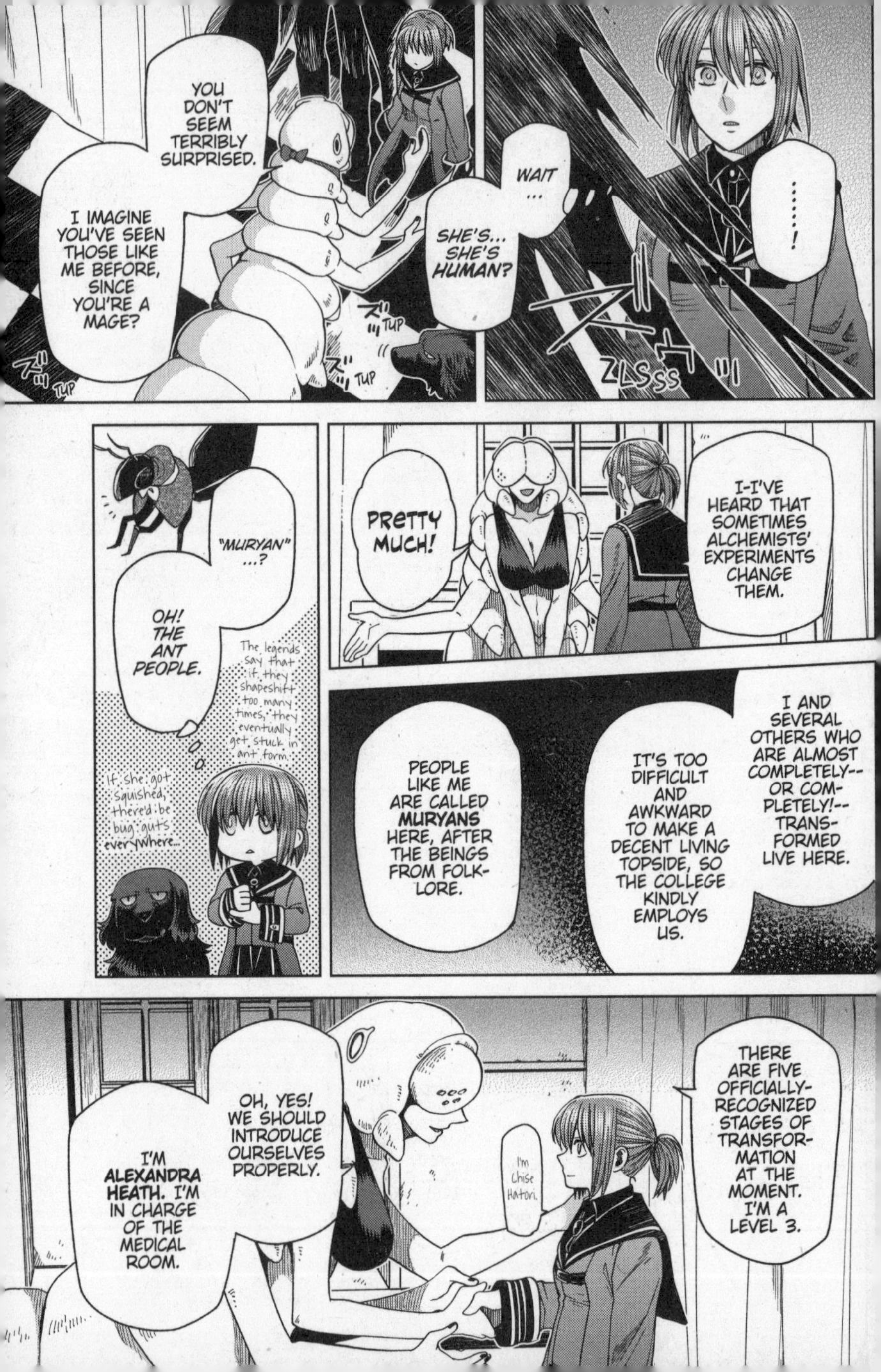
......!
ZLSSS
WAIT... SHE'S... SHE'S HUMAN?
YOU DON'T SEEM TERRIBLY SURPRISED.
I IMAGINE YOU'VE SEEN THOSE LIKE ME BEFORE, SINCE YOU'RE A MAGE?
TUP
TUP
TUP
I-I'VE HEARD THAT SOMETIMES ALCHEMISTS' EXPERIMENTS CHANGE THEM.
PRETTY MUCH!
I AND SEVERAL OTHERS WHO ARE ALMOST COMPLETELY-- OR COMPLETELY!-- TRANSFORMED LIVE HERE.
IT'S TOO DIFFICULT AND AWKWARD TO MAKE A DECENT LIVING TOPSIDE, SO THE COLLEGE KINDLY EMPLOYS US.
PEOPLE LIKE ME ARE CALLED **MURYANS** HERE, AFTER THE BEINGS FROM FOLKLORE.
"MURYAN" ...?
OH! THE ANT PEOPLE.
The legends say that if they shapeshift too many times, they eventually get stuck in ant form.
If she got squished, there'd be bug guts everywhere...
THERE ARE FIVE OFFICIALLY-RECOGNIZED STAGES OF TRANSFORMATION AT THE MOMENT. I'M A LEVEL 3.
I'm Chise Hatori.
OH, YES! WE SHOULD INTRODUCE OURSELVES PROPERLY.
I'M **ALEXANDRA HEATH**. I'M IN CHARGE OF THE MEDICAL ROOM.

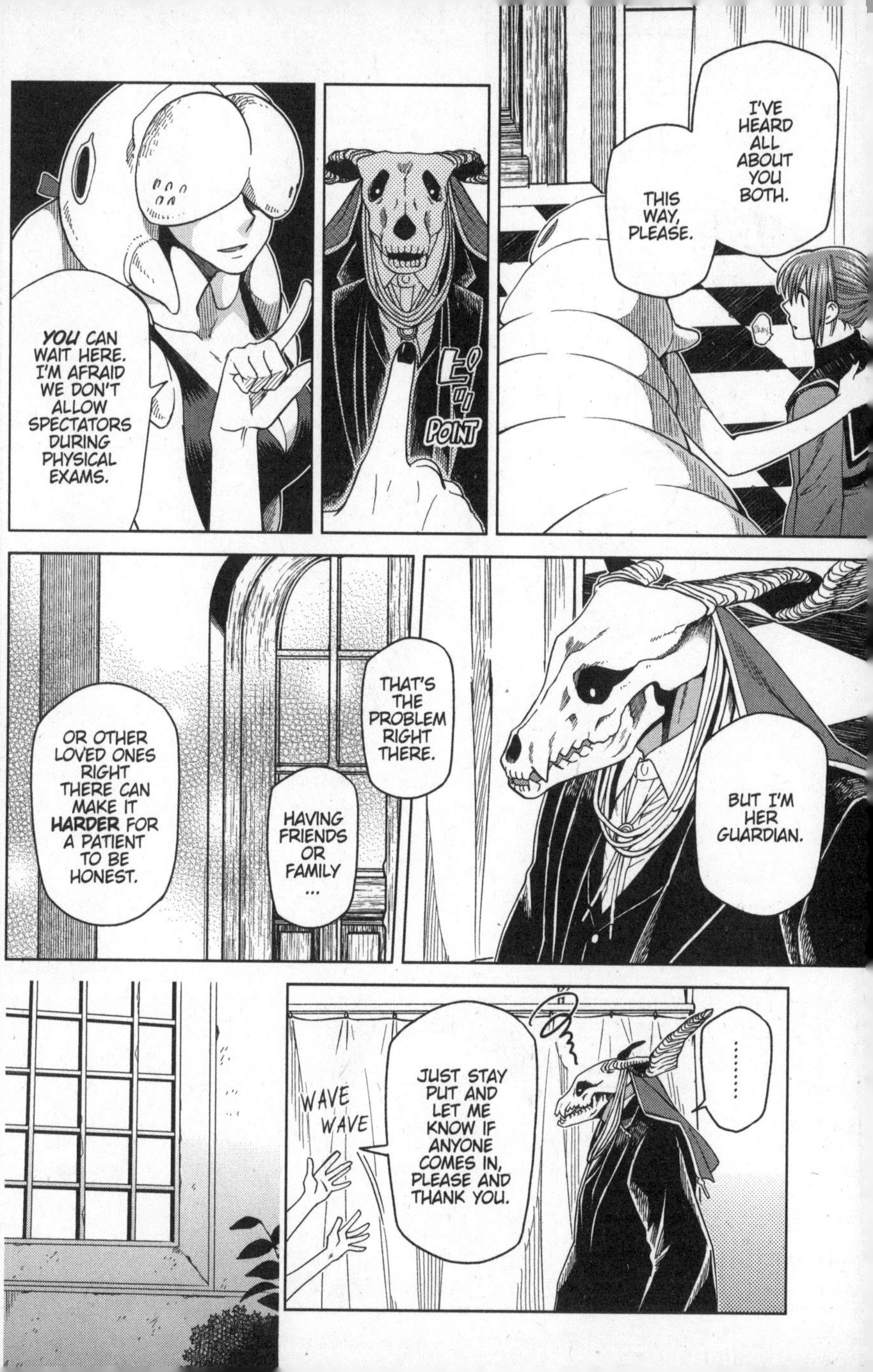
I'VE HEARD ALL ABOUT YOU BOTH.
THIS WAY, PLEASE.
POINT
YOU CAN WAIT HERE. I'M AFRAID WE DON'T ALLOW SPECTATORS DURING PHYSICAL EXAMS.
BUT I'M HER GUARDIAN.
THAT'S THE PROBLEM RIGHT THERE.
HAVING FRIENDS OR FAMILY ...
OR OTHER LOVED ONES RIGHT THERE CAN MAKE IT HARDER FOR A PATIENT TO BE HONEST.
......
JUST STAY PUT AND LET ME KNOW IF ANYONE COMES IN, PLEASE AND THANK YOU.
WAVE WAVE

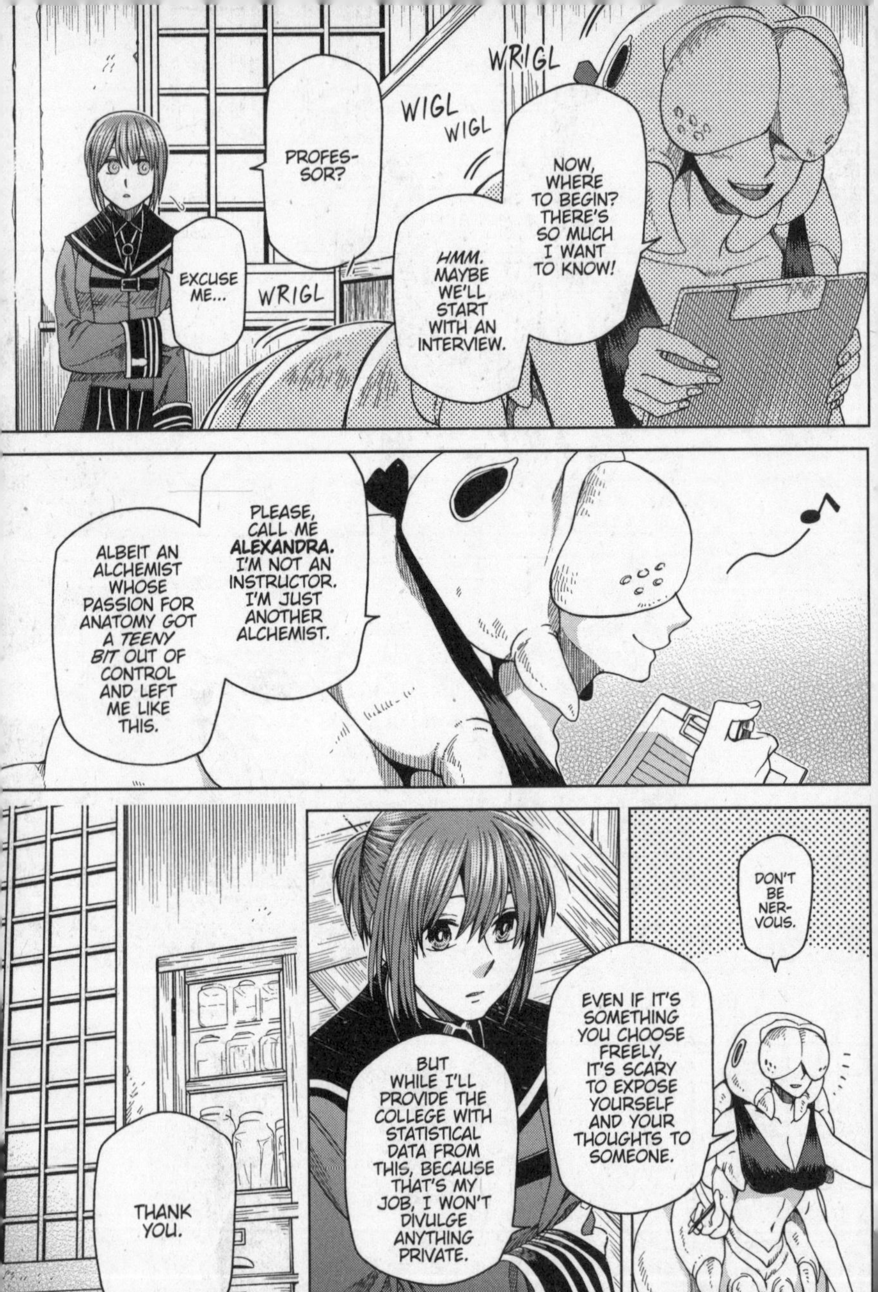

WRIGL
NOW, WHERE TO BEGIN? THERE'S SO MUCH I WANT TO KNOW!
WIGL WIGL
HMM. MAYBE WE'LL START WITH AN INTERVIEW.
PROFES-SOR?
WRIGL
EXCUSE ME...
PLEASE, CALL ME ALEXANDRA. I'M NOT AN INSTRUCTOR. I'M JUST ANOTHER ALCHEMIST.
ALBEIT AN ALCHEMIST WHOSE PASSION FOR ANATOMY GOT A TEENY BIT OUT OF CONTROL AND LEFT ME LIKE THIS.
DON'T BE NER-VOUS.
EVEN IF IT'S SOMETHING YOU CHOOSE FREELY, IT'S SCARY TO EXPOSE YOURSELF AND YOUR THOUGHTS TO SOMEONE.
BUT WHILE I'LL PROVIDE THE COLLEGE WITH STATISTICAL DATA FROM THIS, BECAUSE THAT'S MY JOB, I WON'T DIVULGE ANYTHING PRIVATE.
THANK YOU.

Well, this is a change.

Before, you would have hidden in the shadows to keep an eye on her. What happened?

LET ME THINK OF HOW TO SAY THIS.

HMM...

"WHAT HAP-PENED?"

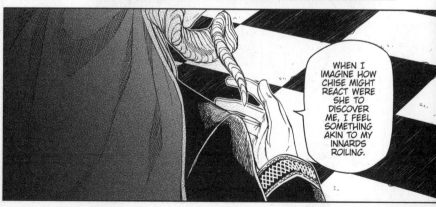

WHEN I IMAGINE HOW CHISE MIGHT REACT WERE SHE TO DISCOVER ME, I FEEL SOMETHING AKIN TO MY INNARDS ROILING.

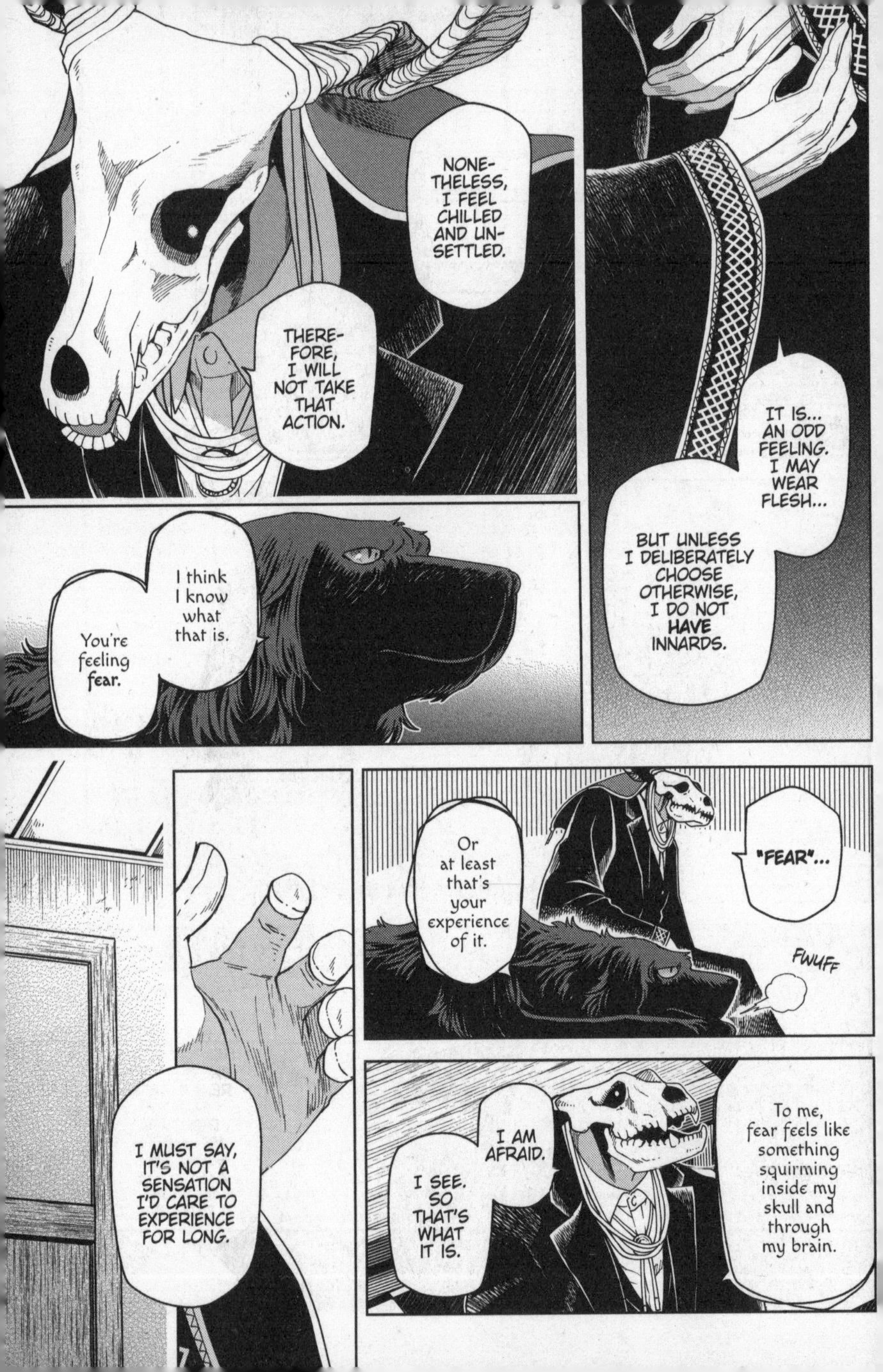
IT IS... AN ODD FEELING. I MAY WEAR FLESH...
BUT UNLESS I DELIBERATELY CHOOSE OTHERWISE, I DO NOT HAVE INNARDS.
NONE-THELESS, I FEEL CHILLED AND UN-SETTLED.
THERE-FORE, I WILL NOT TAKE THAT ACTION.
I think I know what that is.
You're feeling fear.
"FEAR"...
FWUFF
Or at least that's your experience of it.
To me, fear feels like something squirming inside my skull and through my brain.
I AM AFRAID.
I SEE. SO THAT'S WHAT IT IS.
I MUST SAY, IT'S NOT A SENSATION I'D CARE TO EXPERIENCE FOR LONG.

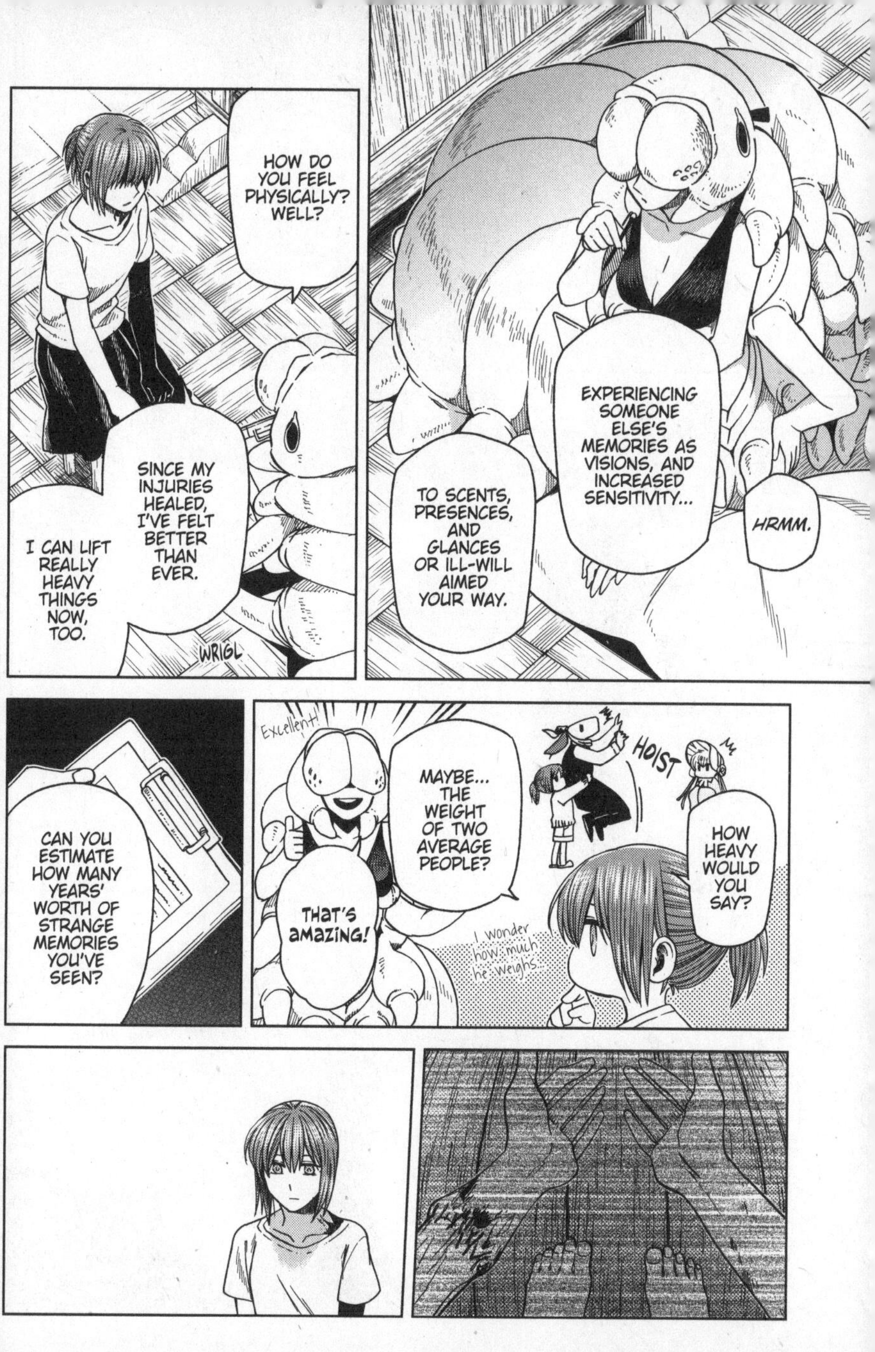
EXPERIENCING SOMEONE ELSE'S MEMORIES AS VISIONS, AND INCREASED SENSITIVITY...
TO SCENTS, PRESENCES, AND GLANCES OR ILL-WILL AIMED YOUR WAY.
HRMM.
HOW DO YOU FEEL PHYSICALLY? WELL?
SINCE MY INJURIES HEALED, I'VE FELT BETTER THAN EVER.
I CAN LIFT REALLY HEAVY THINGS NOW, TOO.
WRIGL
HOW HEAVY WOULD YOU SAY?
HOIST
MAYBE... THE WEIGHT OF TWO AVERAGE PEOPLE?
Excellent!
THAT'S amazing!
I wonder how much he weighs...
CAN YOU ESTIMATE HOW MANY YEARS' WORTH OF STRANGE MEMORIES YOU'VE SEEN?

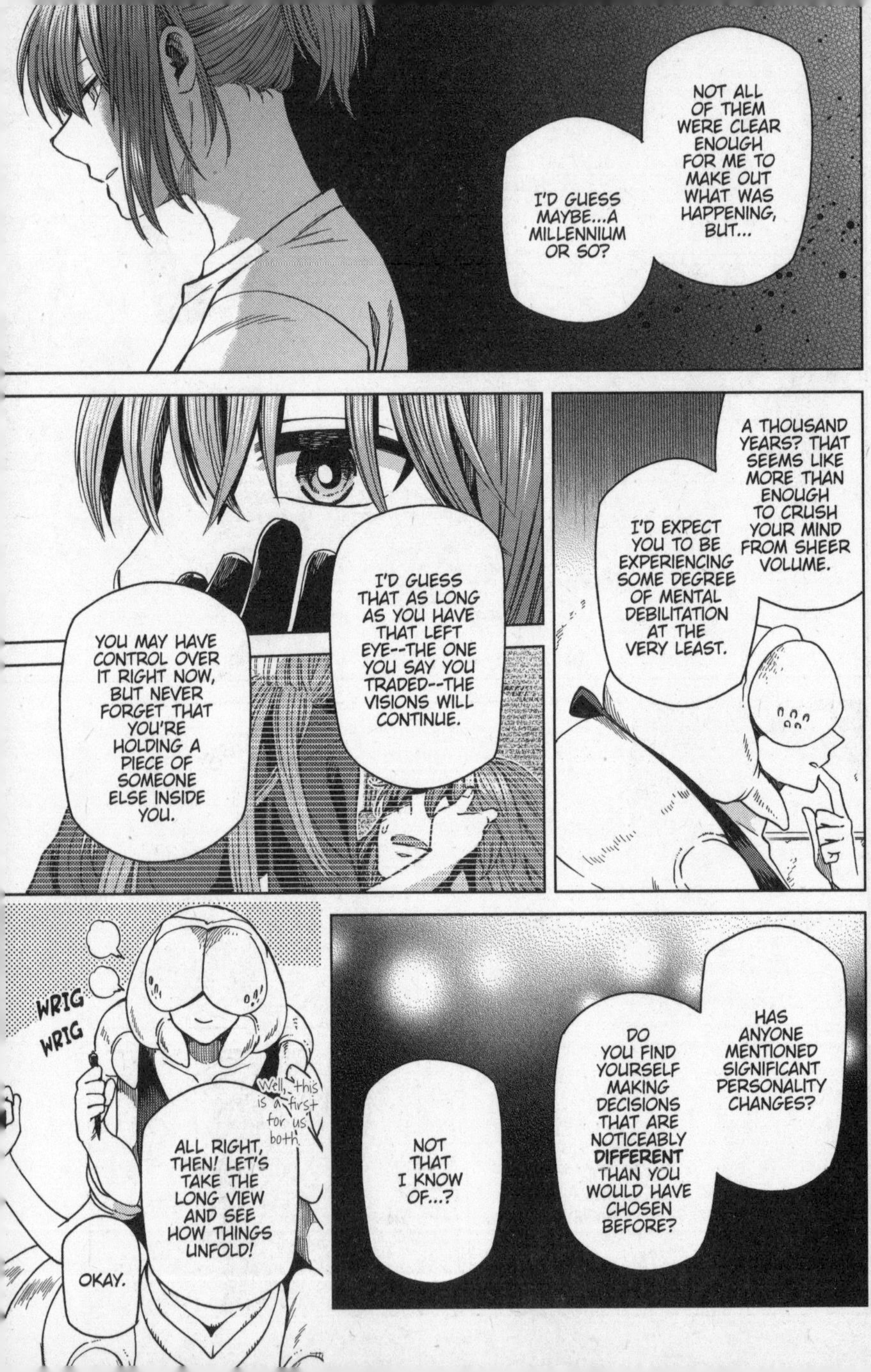
NOT ALL OF THEM WERE CLEAR ENOUGH FOR ME TO MAKE OUT WHAT WAS HAPPENING, BUT...
I'D GUESS MAYBE...A MILLENNIUM OR SO?
A THOUSAND YEARS? THAT SEEMS LIKE MORE THAN ENOUGH TO CRUSH YOUR MIND FROM SHEER VOLUME.
I'D EXPECT YOU TO BE EXPERIENCING SOME DEGREE OF MENTAL DEBILITATION AT THE VERY LEAST.
I'D GUESS THAT AS LONG AS YOU HAVE THAT LEFT EYE--THE ONE YOU SAY YOU TRADED--THE VISIONS WILL CONTINUE.
YOU MAY HAVE CONTROL OVER IT RIGHT NOW, BUT NEVER FORGET THAT YOU'RE HOLDING A PIECE OF SOMEONE ELSE INSIDE YOU.
HAS ANYONE MENTIONED SIGNIFICANT PERSONALITY CHANGES?
DO YOU FIND YOURSELF MAKING DECISIONS THAT ARE NOTICEABLY **DIFFERENT** THAN YOU WOULD HAVE CHOSEN BEFORE?
NOT THAT I KNOW OF...?
Well, this is a first for us both.
ALL RIGHT, THEN! LET'S TAKE THE LONG VIEW AND SEE HOW THINGS UNFOLD!
WRIG WRIG
OKAY.

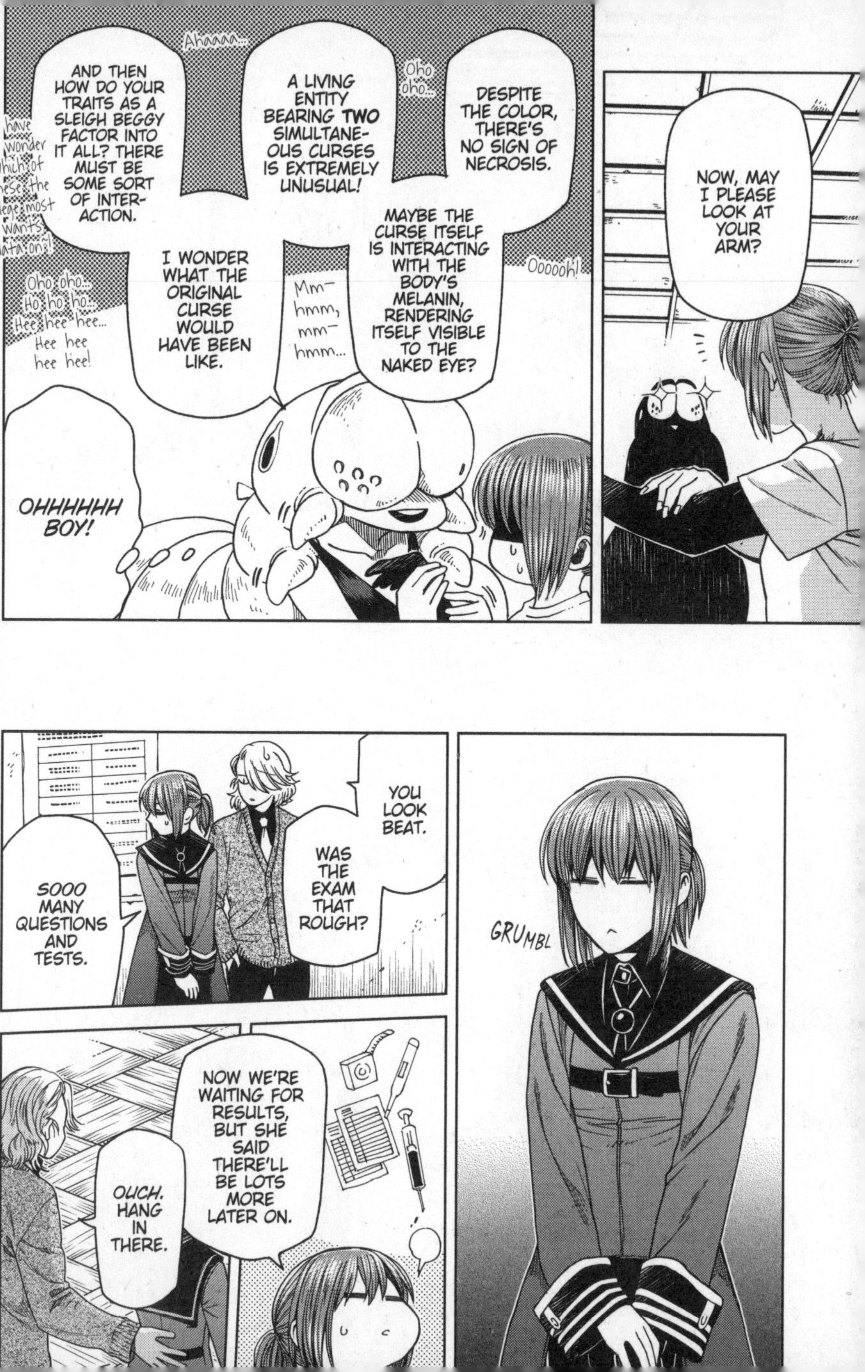
NOW, MAY I PLEASE LOOK AT YOUR ARM?
Oooooh!
DESPITE THE COLOR, THERE'S NO SIGN OF NECROSIS.
Oho oho...
A LIVING ENTITY BEARING **TWO** SIMULTANE-OUS CURSES IS EXTREMELY UNUSUAL!
Ahaaaa...
AND THEN HOW DO YOUR TRAITS AS A SLEIGH BEGGY FACTOR INTO IT ALL? THERE MUST BE SOME SORT OF INTER-ACTION.
I have to wonder which of these the college most wants data on~!
MAYBE THE CURSE ITSELF IS INTERACTING WITH THE BODY'S MELANIN, RENDERING ITSELF VISIBLE TO THE NAKED EYE?
Mm-hmm, mm-hmm...
I WONDER WHAT THE ORIGINAL CURSE WOULD HAVE BEEN LIKE.
Oho oho... Ho ho ho... Hee hee hee... Hee hee hee hee!
OHHHHHH BOY!
GRUMBL
YOU LOOK BEAT.
WAS THE EXAM THAT ROUGH?
SOOO MANY QUESTIONS AND TESTS.
NOW WE'RE WAITING FOR RESULTS, BUT SHE SAID THERE'LL BE LOTS MORE LATER ON.
OUCH. HANG IN THERE.

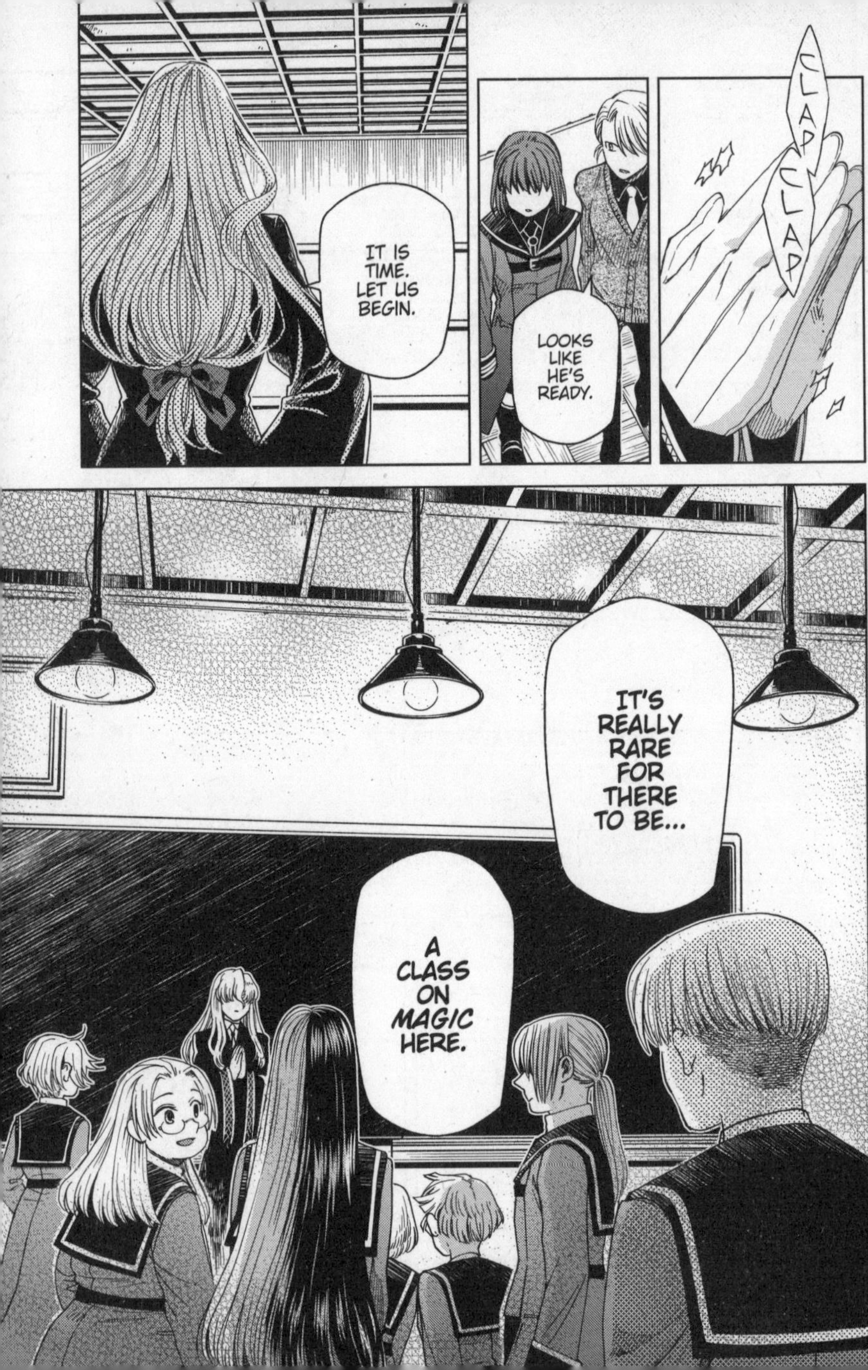
CLAP CLAP CLAP
LOOKS LIKE HE'S READY.
IT IS TIME. LET US BEGIN.
IT'S REALLY RARE FOR THERE TO BE...
A CLASS ON *MAGIC* HERE.

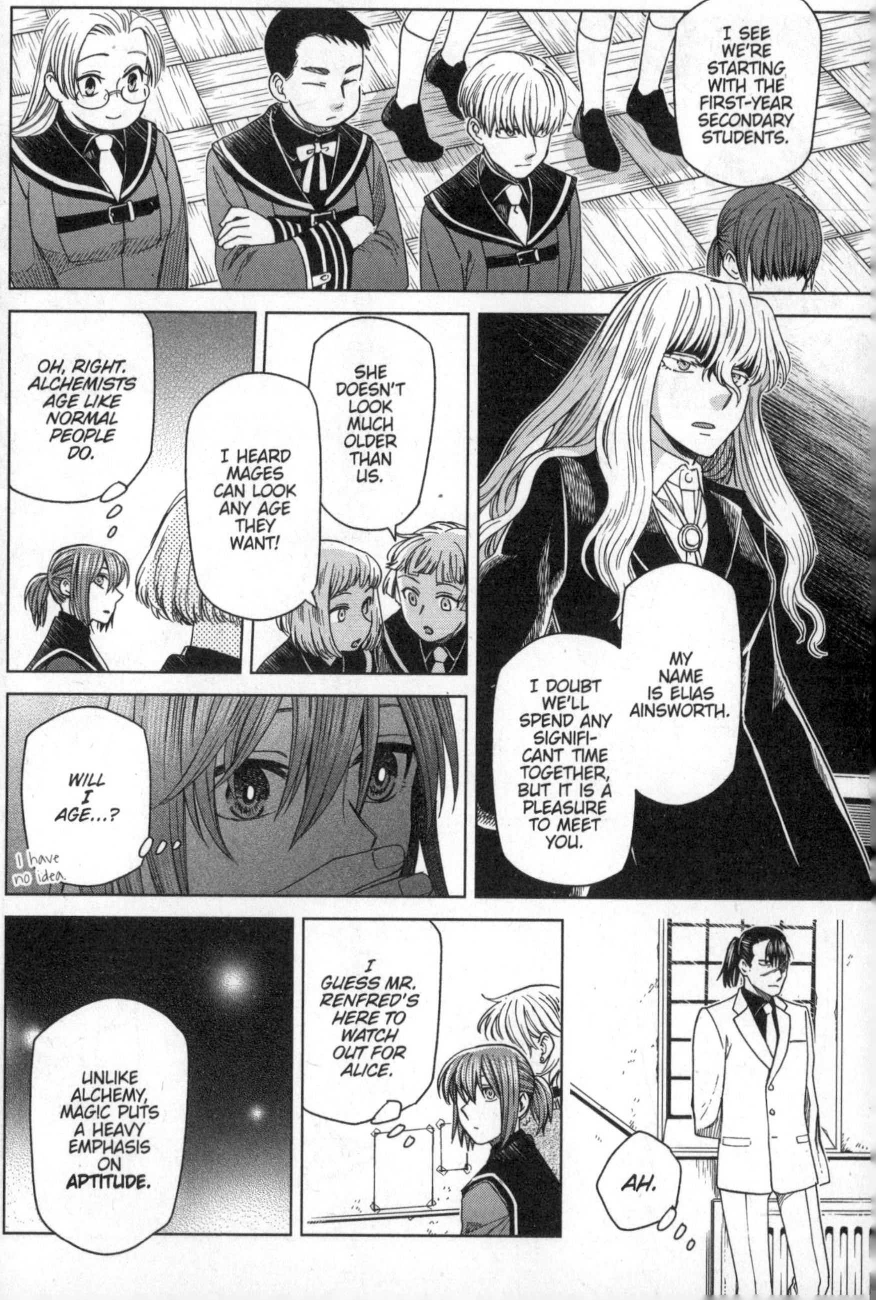
I SEE WE'RE STARTING WITH THE FIRST-YEAR SECONDARY STUDENTS.
MY NAME IS ELIAS AINSWORTH.
I DOUBT WE'LL SPEND ANY SIGNIFI-CANT TIME TOGETHER, BUT IT IS A PLEASURE TO MEET YOU.
SHE DOESN'T LOOK MUCH OLDER THAN US.
I HEARD MAGES CAN LOOK ANY AGE THEY WANT!
OH, RIGHT. ALCHEMISTS AGE LIKE NORMAL PEOPLE DO.
WILL I AGE...?
I have no idea.
AH.
I GUESS MR. RENFRED'S HERE TO WATCH OUT FOR ALICE.
UNLIKE ALCHEMY, MAGIC PUTS A HEAVY EMPHASIS ON APTITUDE.

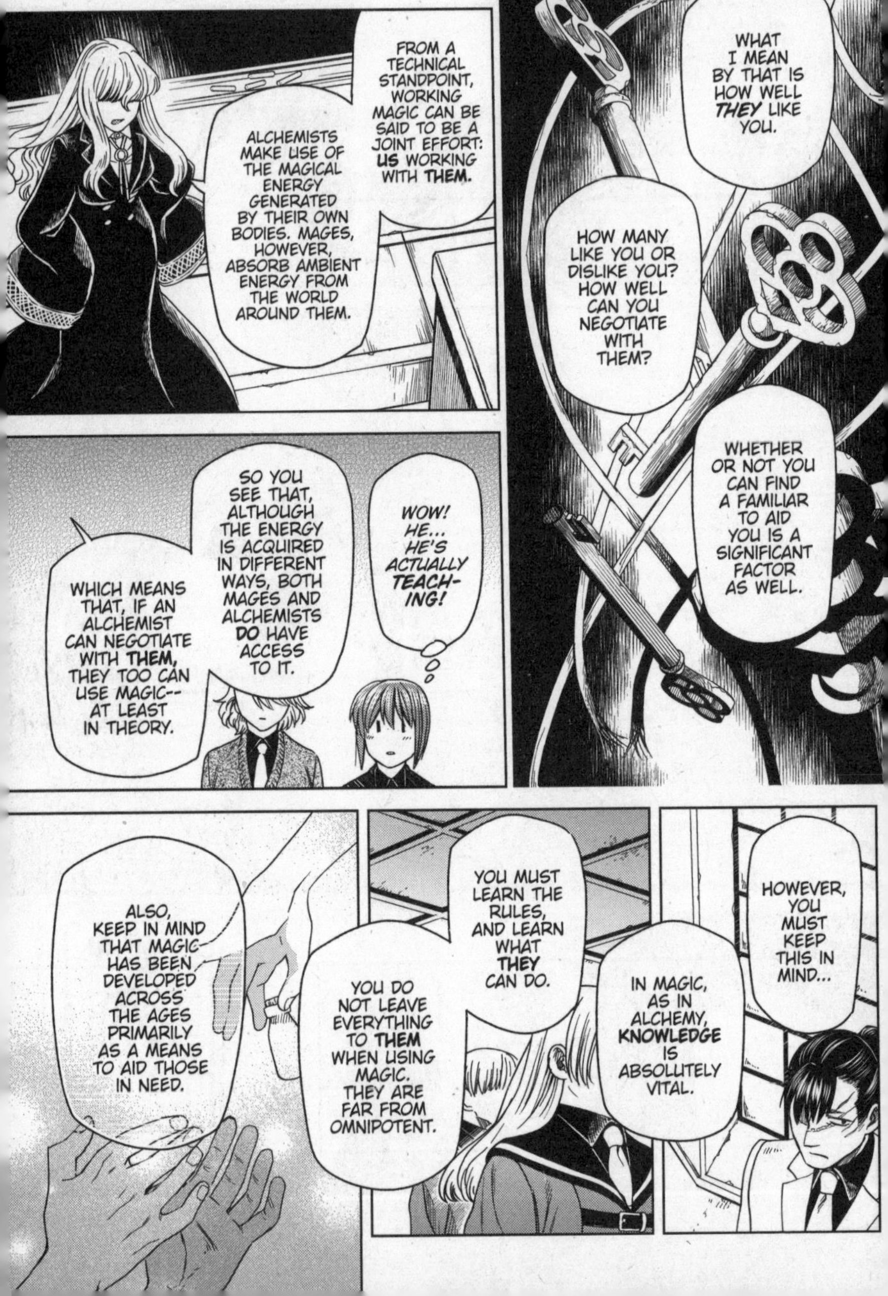
WHAT I MEAN BY THAT IS HOW WELL THEY LIKE YOU.
HOW MANY LIKE YOU OR DISLIKE YOU? HOW WELL CAN YOU NEGOTIATE WITH THEM?
WHETHER OR NOT YOU CAN FIND A FAMILIAR TO AID YOU IS A SIGNIFICANT FACTOR AS WELL.
FROM A TECHNICAL STANDPOINT, WORKING MAGIC CAN BE SAID TO BE A JOINT EFFORT: US WORKING WITH THEM.
ALCHEMISTS MAKE USE OF THE MAGICAL ENERGY GENERATED BY THEIR OWN BODIES. MAGES, HOWEVER, ABSORB AMBIENT ENERGY FROM THE WORLD AROUND THEM.
WOW! HE... HE'S ACTUALLY TEACHING!
SO YOU SEE THAT, ALTHOUGH THE ENERGY IS ACQUIRED IN DIFFERENT WAYS, BOTH MAGES AND ALCHEMISTS DO HAVE ACCESS TO IT.
WHICH MEANS THAT, IF AN ALCHEMIST CAN NEGOTIATE WITH THEM, THEY TOO CAN USE MAGIC--AT LEAST IN THEORY.
HOWEVER, YOU MUST KEEP THIS IN MIND...
IN MAGIC, AS IN ALCHEMY, KNOWLEDGE IS ABSOLUTELY VITAL.
YOU MUST LEARN THE RULES, AND LEARN WHAT THEY CAN DO.
YOU DO NOT LEAVE EVERYTHING TO THEM WHEN USING MAGIC. THEY ARE FAR FROM OMNIPOTENT.
ALSO, KEEP IN MIND THAT MAGIC HAS BEEN DEVELOPED ACROSS THE AGES PRIMARILY AS A MEANS TO AID THOSE IN NEED.

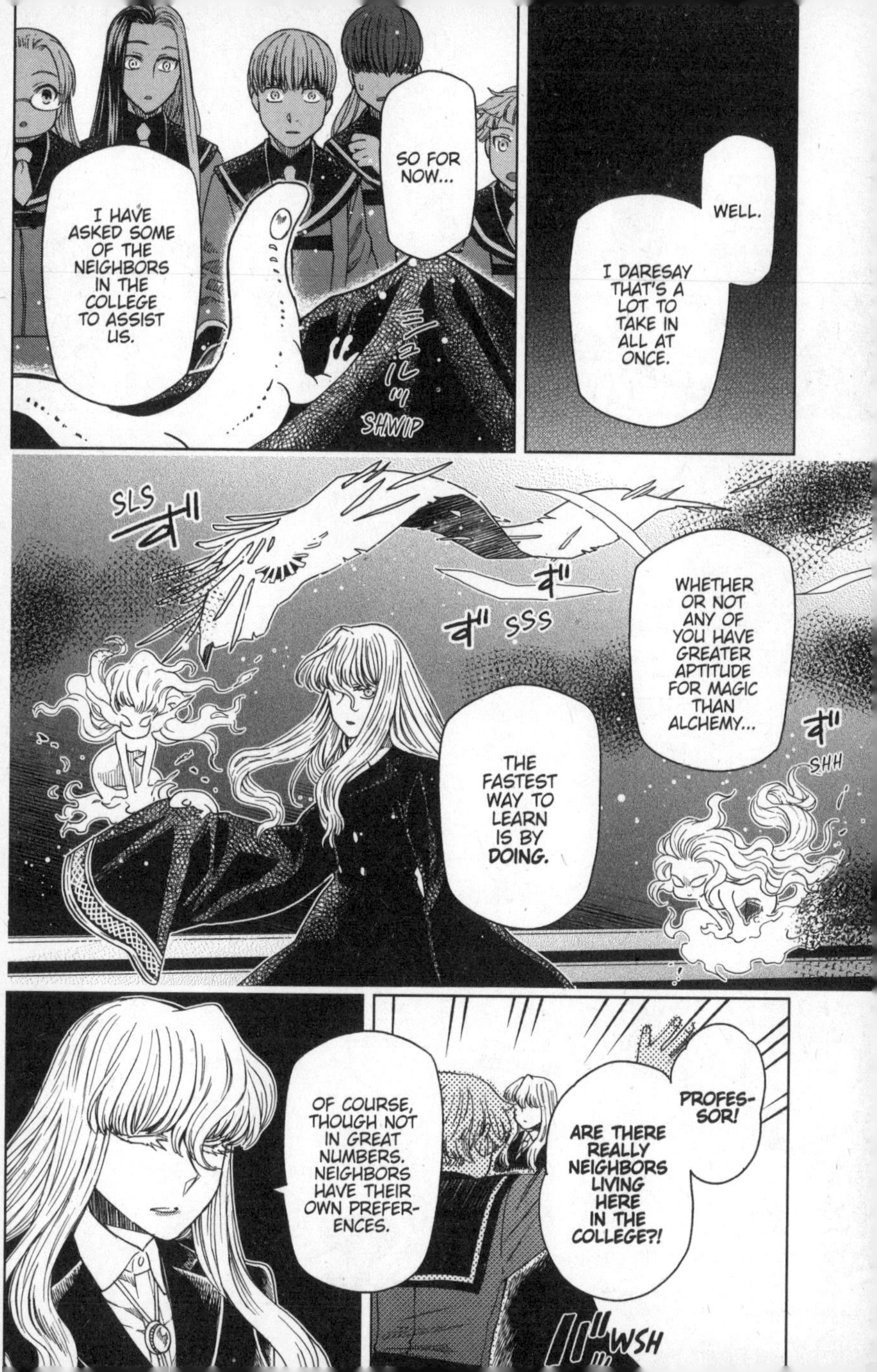
WELL.
I DARESAY THAT'S A LOT TO TAKE IN ALL AT ONCE.
SO FOR NOW...
シュルッ
SHWIP
I HAVE ASKED SOME OF THE NEIGHBORS IN THE COLLEGE TO ASSIST US.
ず
SHH
WHETHER OR NOT ANY OF YOU HAVE GREATER APTITUDE FOR MAGIC THAN ALCHEMY...
ず
ず SSS
SLS ず
THE FASTEST WAY TO LEARN IS BY DOING.
PROFES-SOR!
ARE THERE REALLY NEIGHBORS LIVING HERE IN THE COLLEGE?!
WSH
OF COURSE, THOUGH NOT IN GREAT NUMBERS. NEIGHBORS HAVE THEIR OWN PREFER-ENCES.

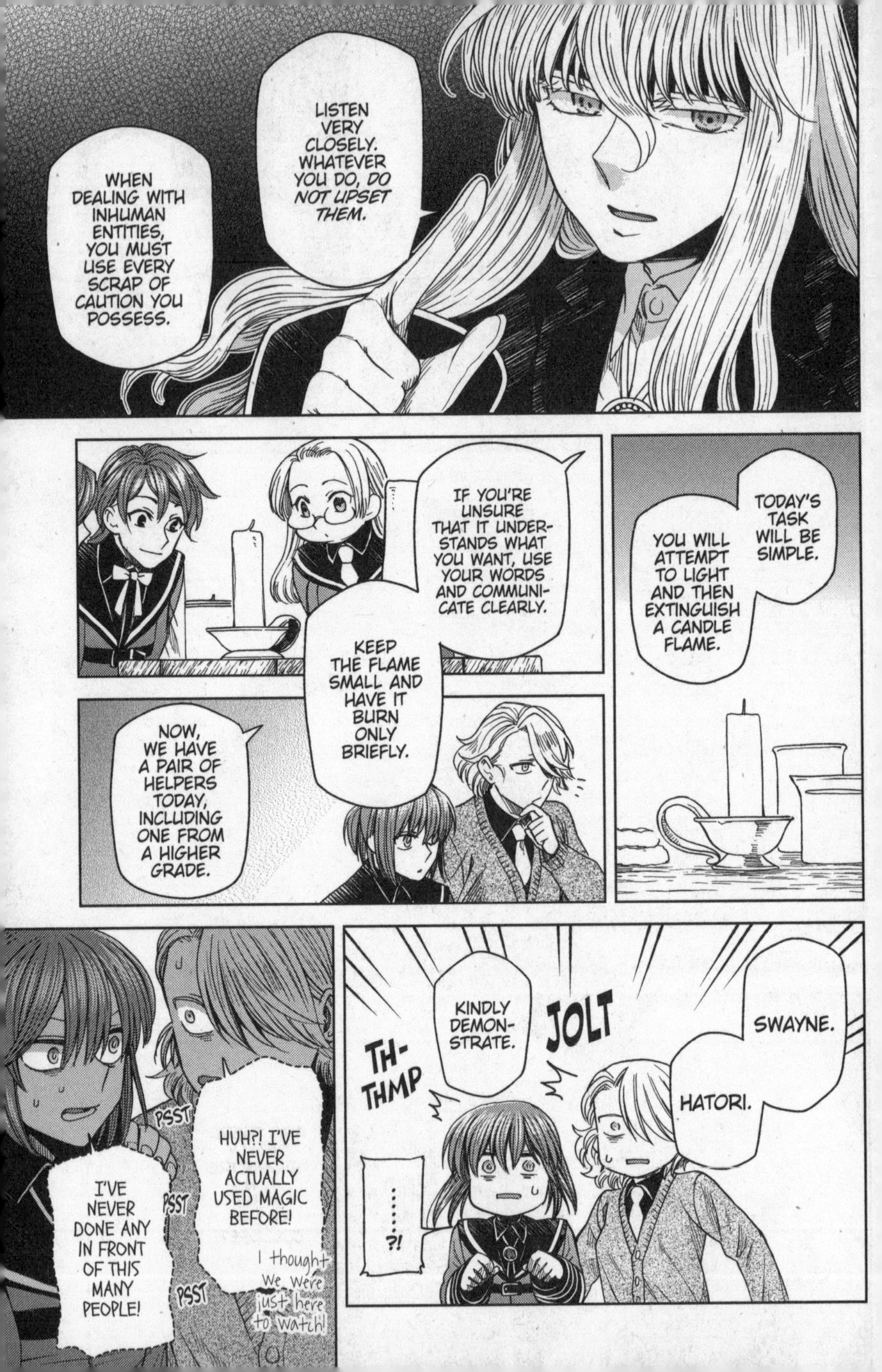
LISTEN VERY CLOSELY. WHATEVER YOU DO, DO NOT UPSET THEM.
WHEN DEALING WITH INHUMAN ENTITIES, YOU MUST USE EVERY SCRAP OF CAUTION YOU POSSESS.
TODAY'S TASK WILL BE SIMPLE.
YOU WILL ATTEMPT TO LIGHT AND THEN EXTINGUISH A CANDLE FLAME.
IF YOU'RE UNSURE THAT IT UNDER-STANDS WHAT YOU WANT, USE YOUR WORDS AND COMMUNI-CATE CLEARLY.
......
KEEP THE FLAME SMALL AND HAVE IT BURN ONLY BRIEFLY.
NOW, WE HAVE A PAIR OF HELPERS TODAY, INCLUDING ONE FROM A HIGHER GRADE.
SWAYNE.
HATORI.
JOLT
KINDLY DEMON-STRATE.
TH-THMP
......?!
HUH?! I'VE NEVER ACTUALLY USED MAGIC BEFORE!
PSST
PSST
PSST
I'VE NEVER DONE ANY IN FRONT OF THIS MANY PEOPLE!
I thought we were just here to watch!

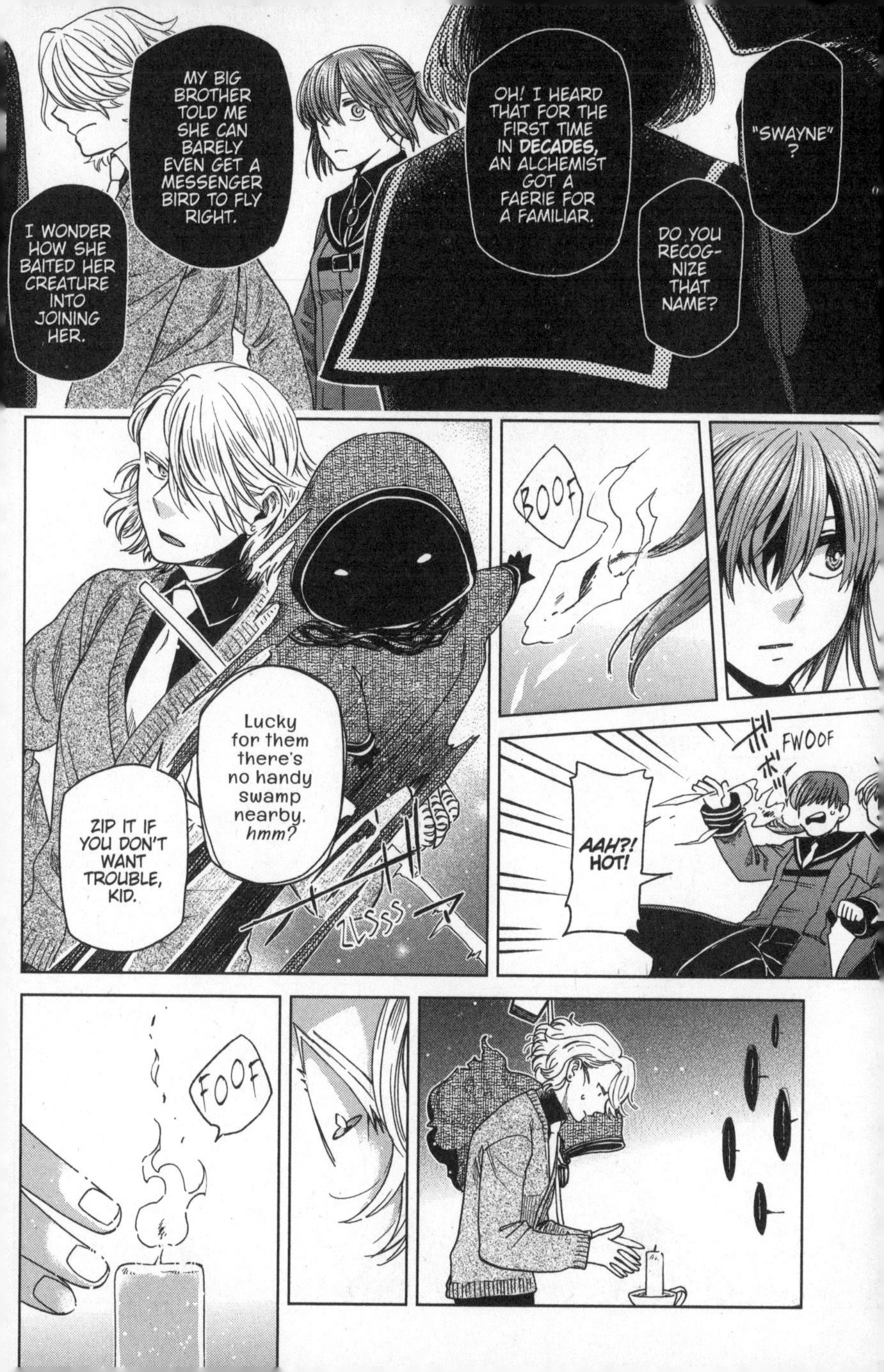
"SWAYNE"?
DO YOU RECOGNIZE THAT NAME?
OH! I HEARD THAT FOR THE FIRST TIME IN **DECADES,** AN ALCHEMIST GOT A FAERIE FOR A FAMILIAR.
MY BIG BROTHER TOLD ME SHE CAN BARELY EVEN GET A MESSENGER BIRD TO FLY RIGHT.
I WONDER HOW SHE BAITED HER CREATURE INTO JOINING HER.
BOOF
FWOOF
AAH?! HOT!
Lucky for them there's no handy swamp nearby. *hmm?*
ZIP IT IF YOU DON'T WANT TROUBLE, KID.
ZZSSS
FOOF

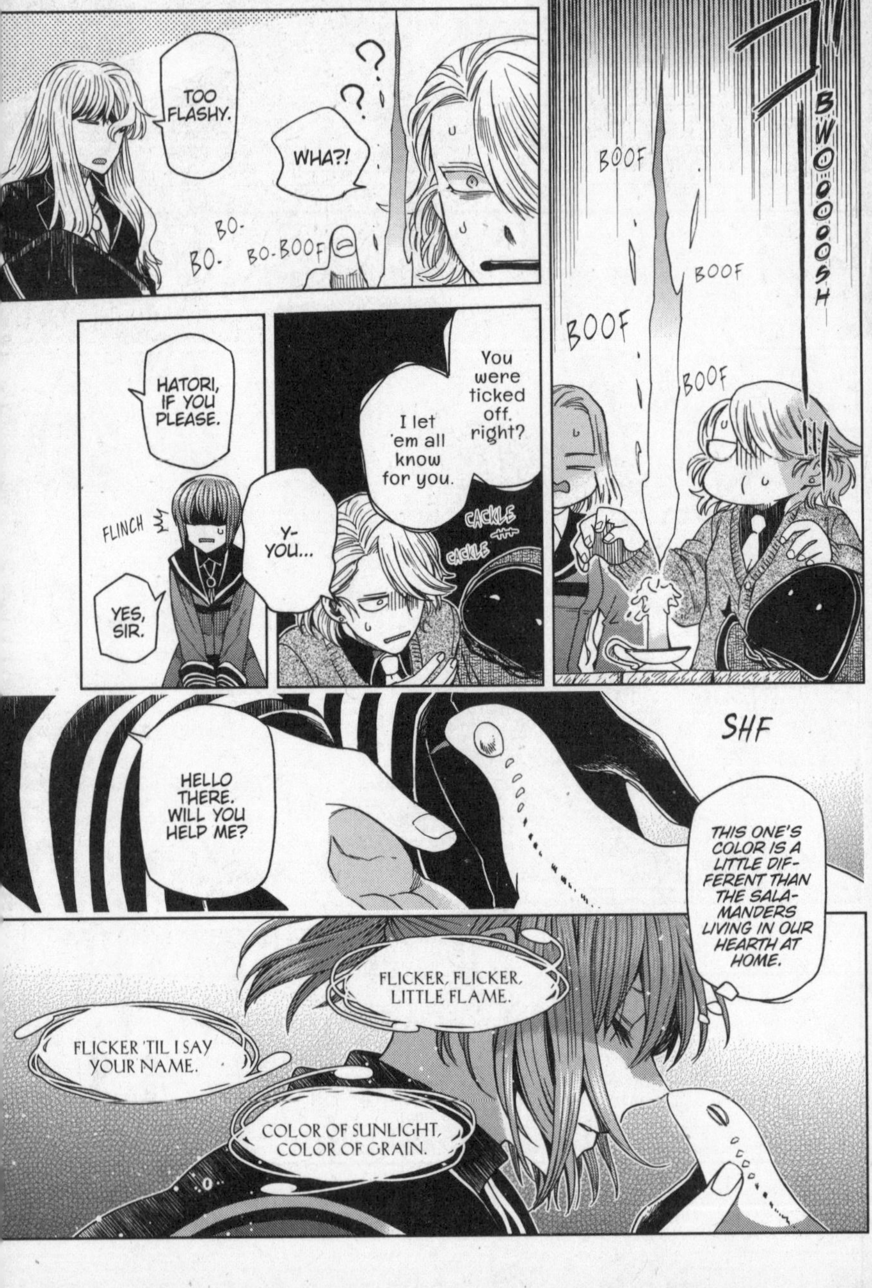
BWOOOOOSH
BOOF
BOOF
BOOF
BOOF
?
?
WHA?!
BO-
BO-
BO-BOOF
TOO FLASHY.
You were ticked off, right?
I let 'em all know for you.
Y-YOU...
CACKLE
CACKLE
HATORI, IF YOU PLEASE.
FLINCH
YES, SIR.
SHF
THIS ONE'S COLOR IS A LITTLE DIF-FERENT THAN THE SALA-MANDERS LIVING IN OUR HEARTH AT HOME.
HELLO THERE. WILL YOU HELP ME?
FLICKER, FLICKER, LITTLE FLAME.
FLICKER 'TIL I SAY YOUR NAME.
COLOR OF SUNLIGHT, COLOR OF GRAIN.

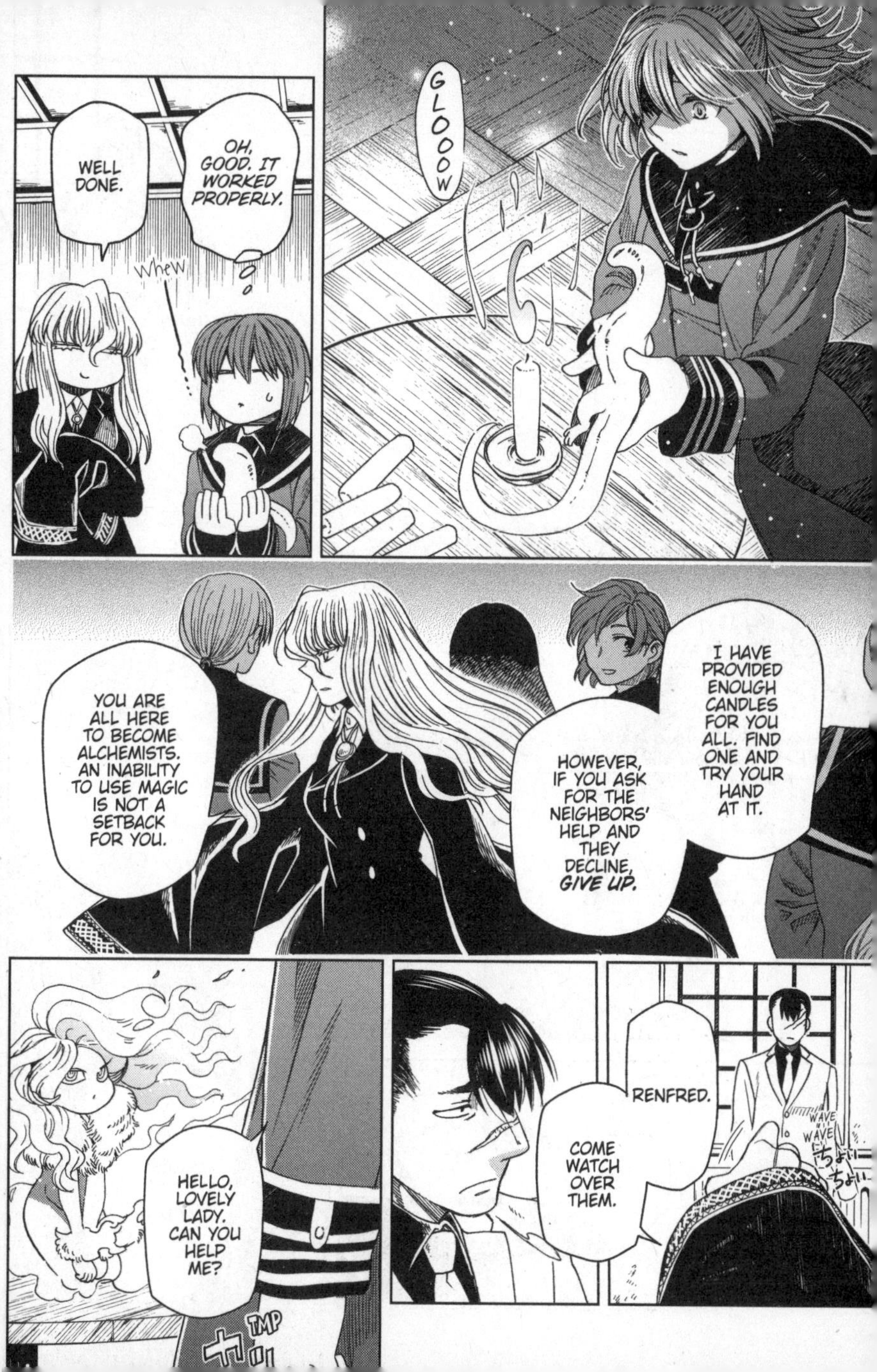
GLOOOW
OH, GOOD. IT WORKED PROPERLY.
WELL DONE.
Whew
I HAVE PROVIDED ENOUGH CANDLES FOR YOU ALL. FIND ONE AND TRY YOUR HAND AT IT.
HOWEVER, IF YOU ASK FOR THE NEIGHBORS' HELP AND THEY DECLINE, GIVE UP.
YOU ARE ALL HERE TO BECOME ALCHEMISTS. AN INABILITY TO USE MAGIC IS NOT A SETBACK FOR YOU.
RENFRED.
WAVE WAVE
ちょい ちょい
COME WATCH OVER THEM.
HELLO, LOVELY LADY. CAN YOU HELP ME?
TMP

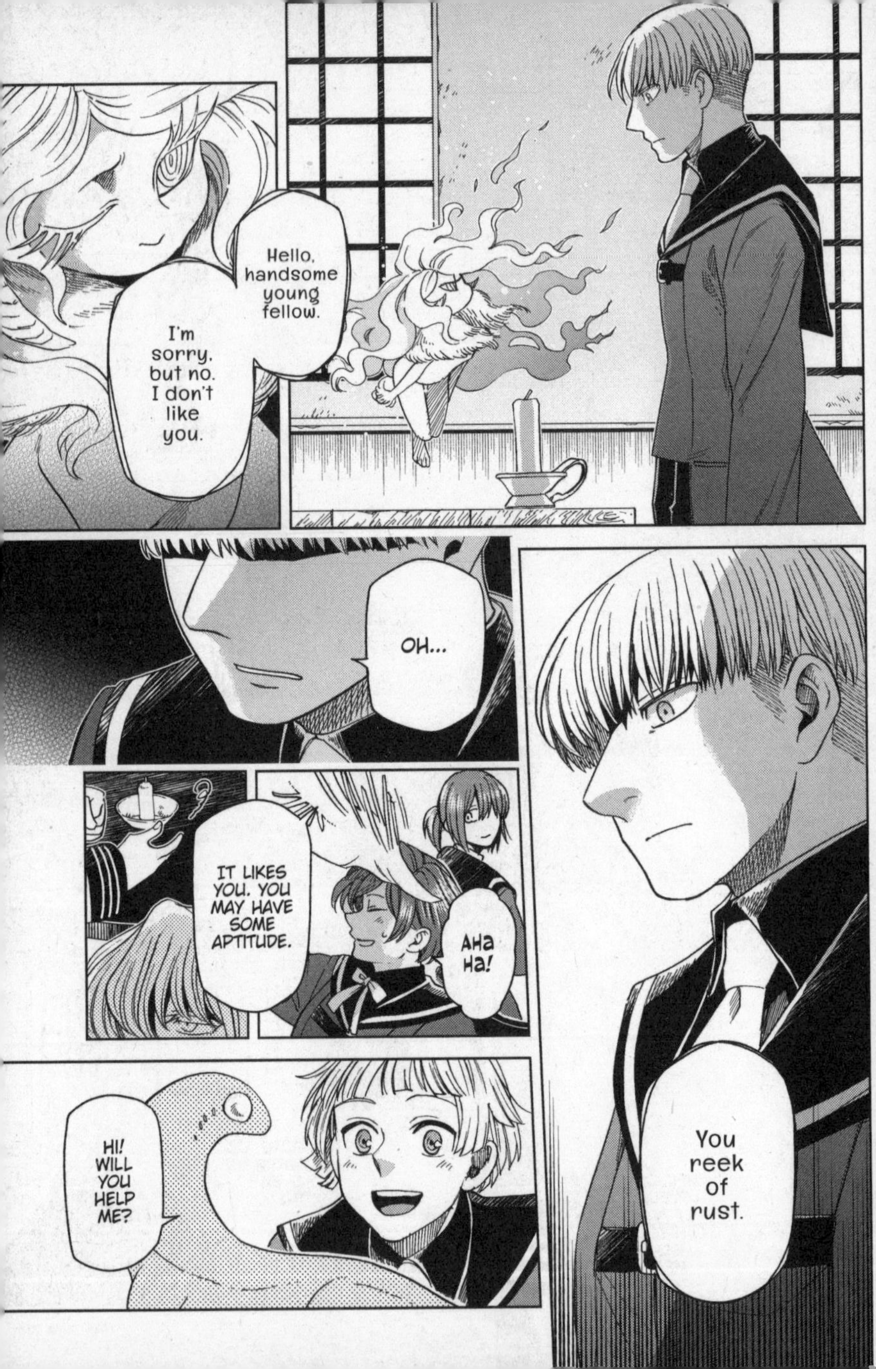
Hello, handsome young fellow.
I'm sorry, but no. I don't like you.
You reek of rust.
OH...
AHA HA!
IT LIKES YOU. YOU MAY HAVE SOME APTITUDE.
HI! WILL YOU HELP ME?

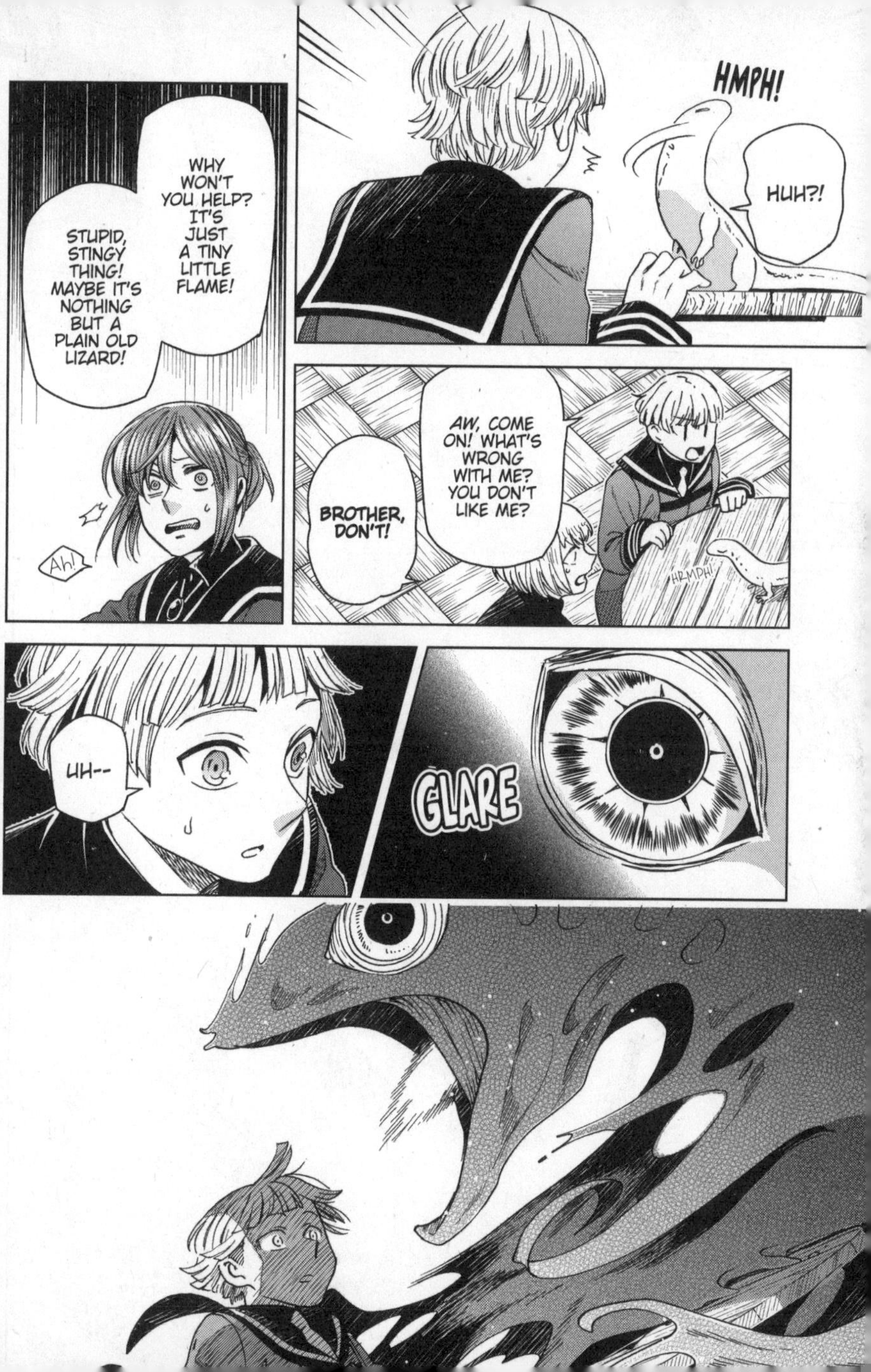
HMPH!
HUH?!
AW, COME ON! WHAT'S WRONG WITH ME? YOU DON'T LIKE ME?
BROTHER, DON'T!
HRMPH!
WHY WON'T YOU HELP? IT'S JUST A TINY LITTLE FLAME!
STUPID, STINGY THING! MAYBE IT'S NOTHING BUT A PLAIN OLD LIZARD!
Ah!
GLARE
UH--

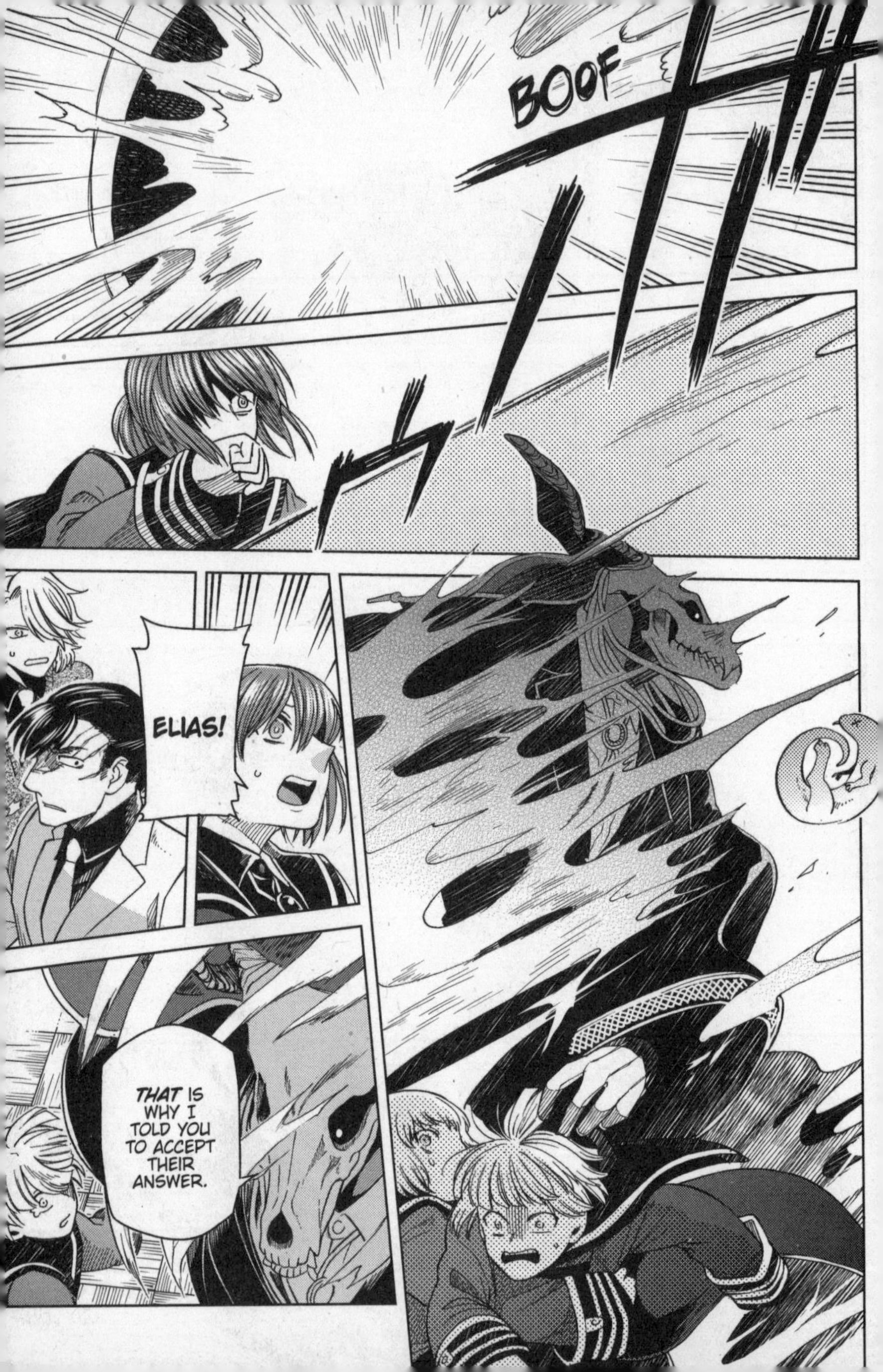
BOOF
ELIAS!
THAT IS WHY I TOLD YOU TO ACCEPT THEIR ANSWER.

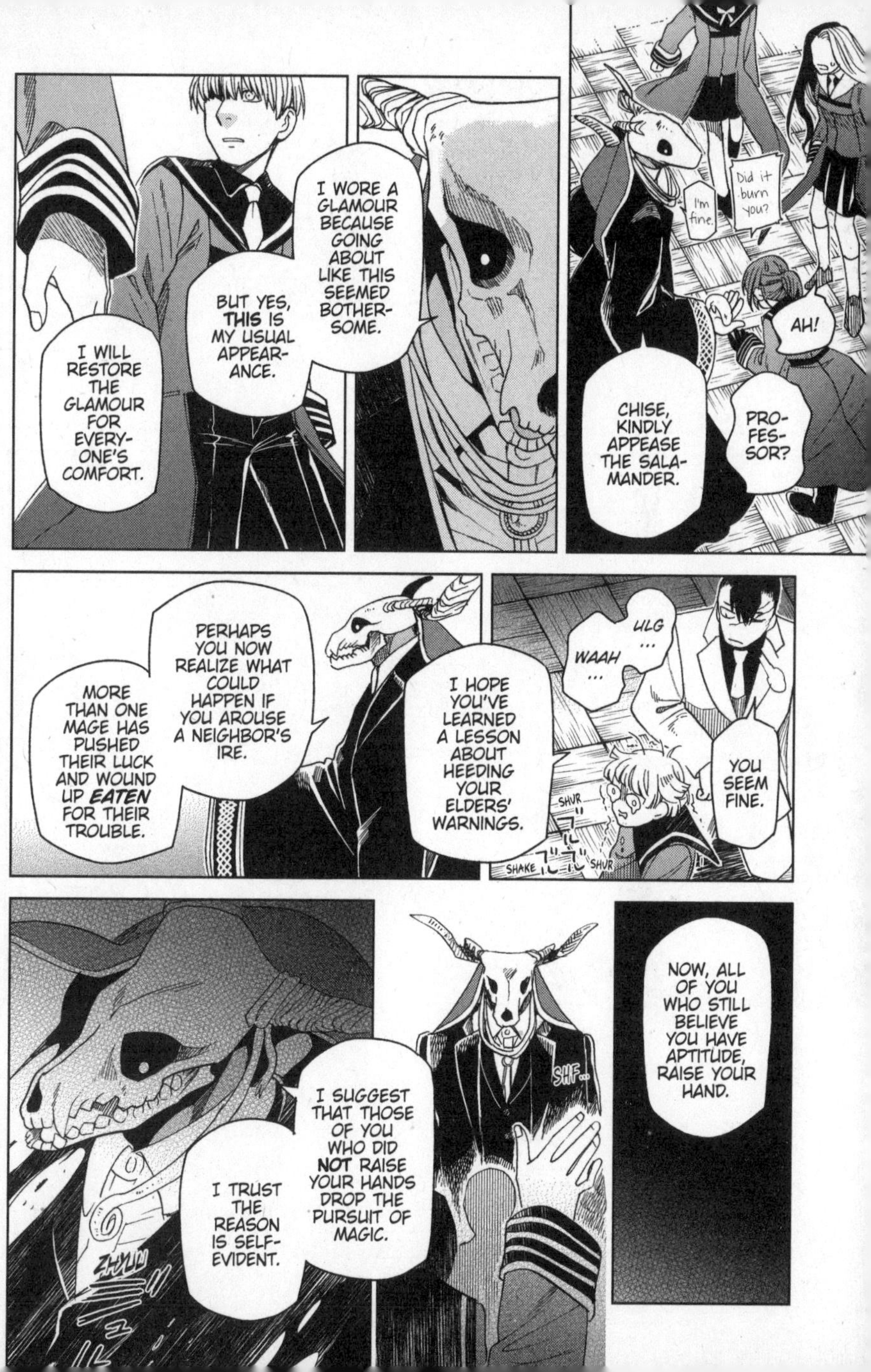
Did it burn you?
I'm fine.
AH!
PRO-FES-SOR?
CHISE, KINDLY APPEASE THE SALAMANDER.
I WORE A GLAMOUR BECAUSE GOING ABOUT LIKE THIS SEEMED BOTHER-SOME.
BUT YES, **THIS** IS MY USUAL APPEAR-ANCE.
I WILL RESTORE THE GLAMOUR FOR EVERY-ONE'S COMFORT.
ULG...
WAAH...
YOU SEEM FINE.
SHUR
SHAKE
SHUR
I HOPE YOU'VE LEARNED A LESSON ABOUT HEEDING YOUR ELDERS' WARNINGS.
PERHAPS YOU NOW REALIZE WHAT COULD HAPPEN IF YOU AROUSE A NEIGHBOR'S IRE.
MORE THAN ONE MAGE HAS PUSHED THEIR LUCK AND WOUND UP ***EATEN*** FOR THEIR TROUBLE.
NOW, ALL OF YOU WHO STILL BELIEVE YOU HAVE APTITUDE, RAISE YOUR HAND.
SHF...
I SUGGEST THAT THOSE OF YOU WHO DID **NOT** RAISE YOUR HANDS DROP THE PURSUIT OF MAGIC.
I TRUST THE REASON IS SELF-EVIDENT.
ZHYUU

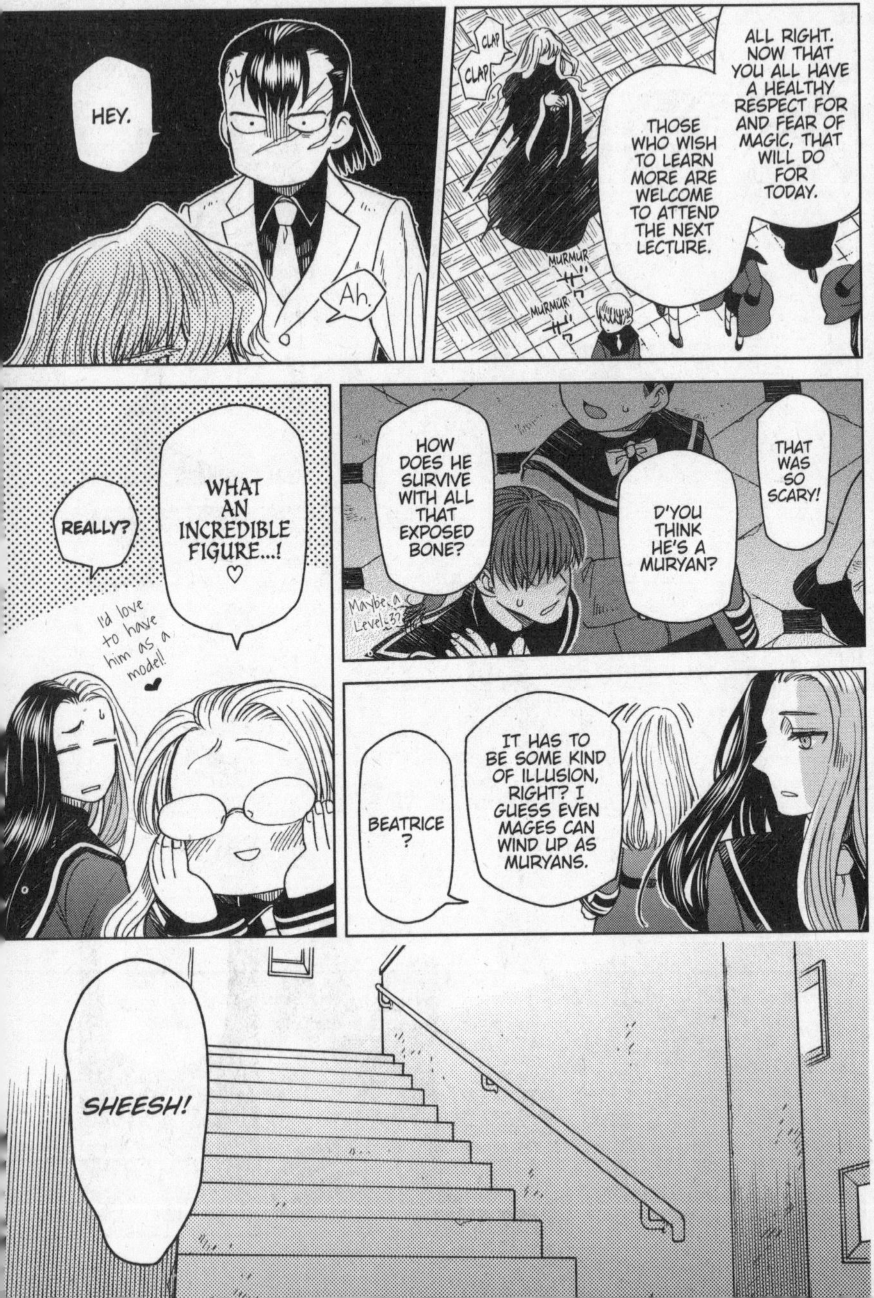

ALL RIGHT. NOW THAT YOU ALL HAVE A HEALTHY RESPECT FOR AND FEAR OF MAGIC, THAT WILL DO FOR TODAY.
THOSE WHO WISH TO LEARN MORE ARE WELCOME TO ATTEND THE NEXT LECTURE.
CLAP
CLAP
MURMUR
MURMUR
HEY.
Ah.
THAT WAS SO SCARY!
D'YOU THINK HE'S A MURYAN?
HOW DOES HE SURVIVE WITH ALL THAT EXPOSED BONE?
Maybe a Level 3?
IT HAS TO BE SOME KIND OF ILLUSION, RIGHT? I GUESS EVEN MAGES CAN WIND UP AS MURYANS.
BEATRICE?
WHAT AN INCREDIBLE FIGURE...! ♡
REALLY?
I'd love to have him as a model! ♥
SHEESH!

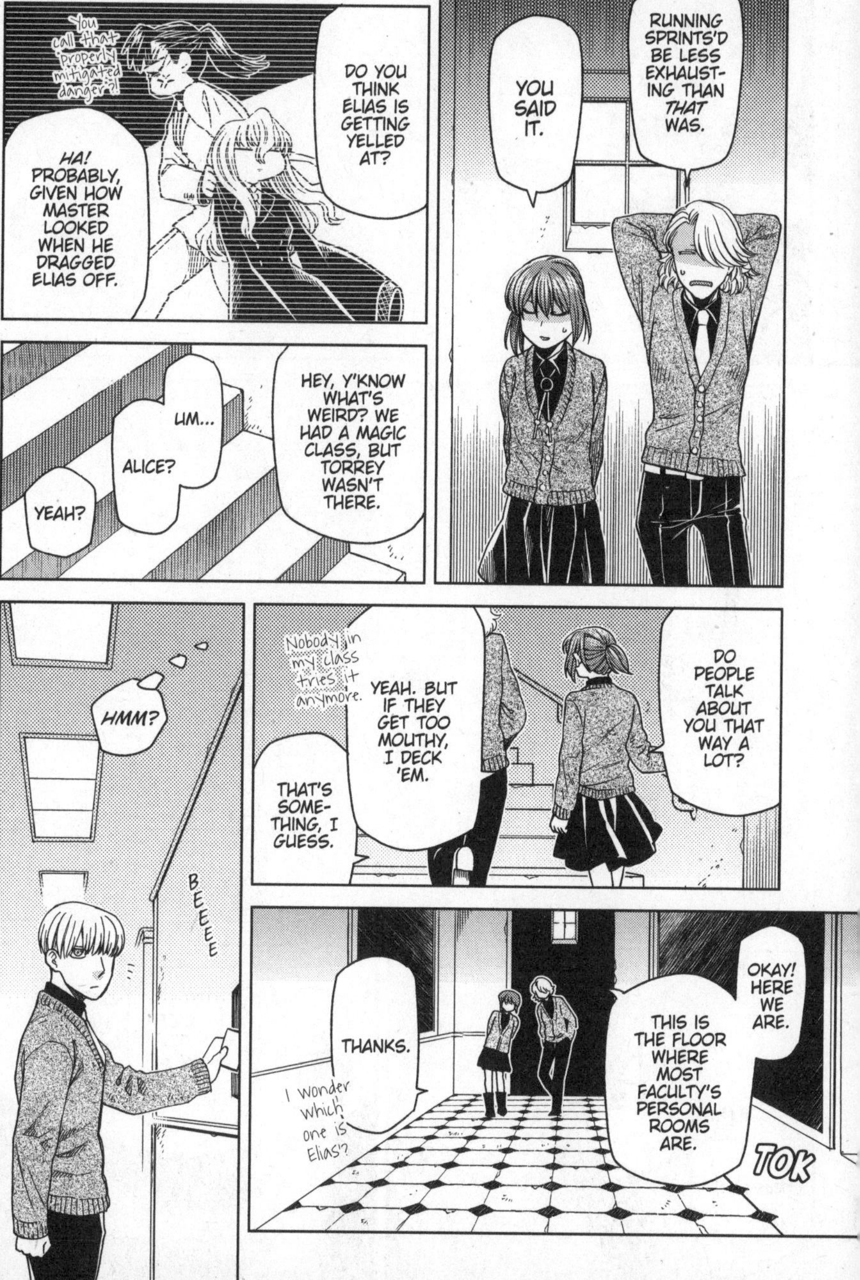
RUNNING SPRINTS'D BE LESS EXHAUST-ING THAN *THAT* WAS.
YOU SAID IT.
DO YOU THINK ELIAS IS GETTING YELLED AT?
HA! PROBABLY, GIVEN HOW MASTER LOOKED WHEN HE DRAGGED ELIAS OFF.
You call that properly mitigated danger?!
HEY, Y'KNOW WHAT'S WEIRD? WE HAD A MAGIC CLASS, BUT TORREY WASN'T THERE.
UM...
ALICE?
YEAH?
DO PEOPLE TALK ABOUT YOU THAT WAY A LOT?
YEAH. BUT IF THEY GET TOO MOUTHY, I DECK 'EM.
Nobody in my class tries it anymore.
THAT'S SOME-THING, I GUESS.
OKAY! HERE WE ARE.
THIS IS THE FLOOR WHERE MOST FACULTY'S PERSONAL ROOMS ARE.
TOK
THANKS.
I wonder which one is Elias'?
HMM?
BEEEEE

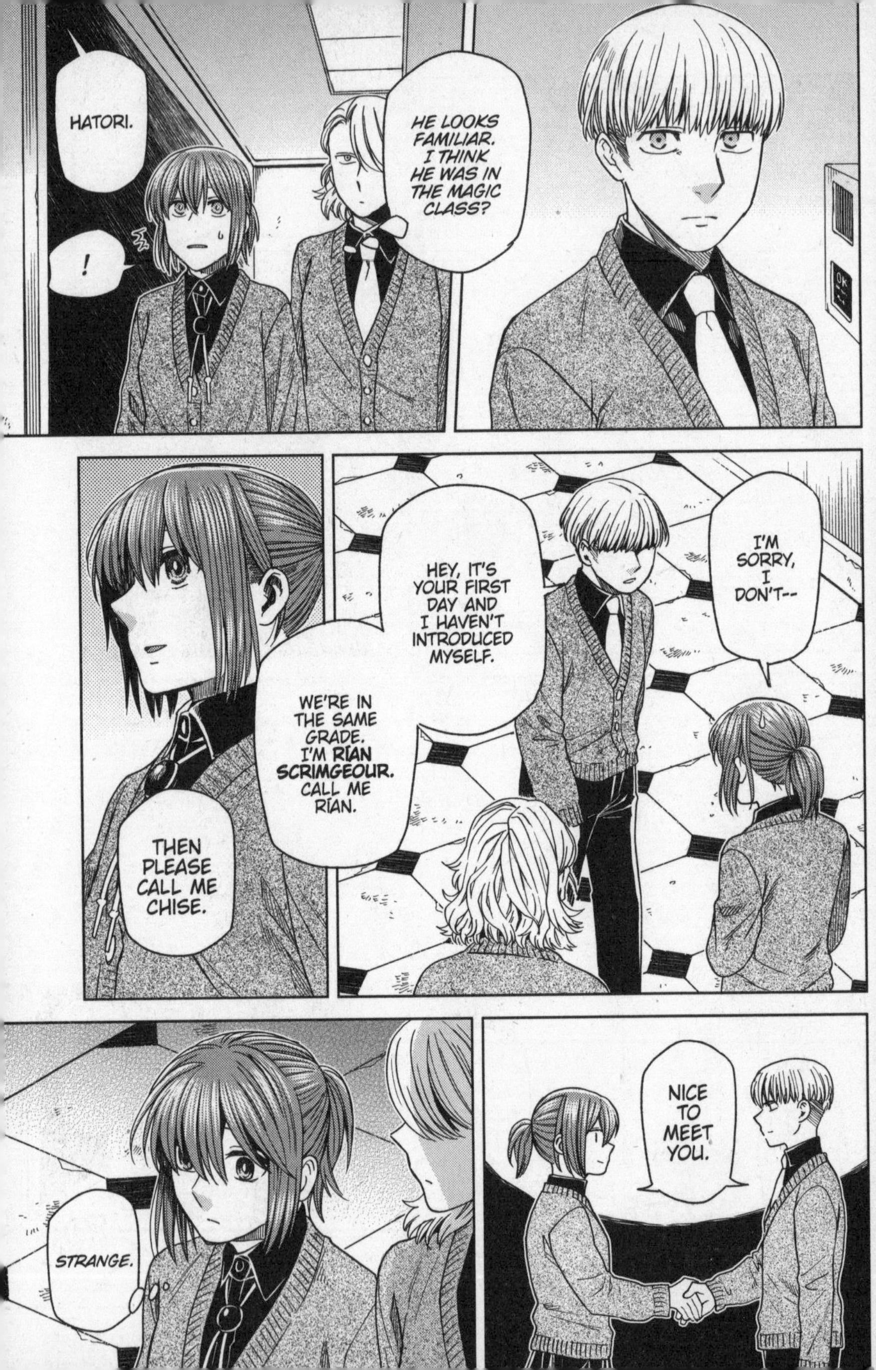
HE LOOKS FAMILIAR. I THINK HE WAS IN THE MAGIC CLASS?
HATORI.
!
I'M SORRY, I DON'T--
HEY, IT'S YOUR FIRST DAY AND I HAVEN'T INTRODUCED MYSELF.
WE'RE IN THE SAME GRADE. I'M RÍAN SCRIMGEOUR. CALL ME RÍAN.
THEN PLEASE CALL ME CHISE.
NICE TO MEET YOU.
STRANGE.

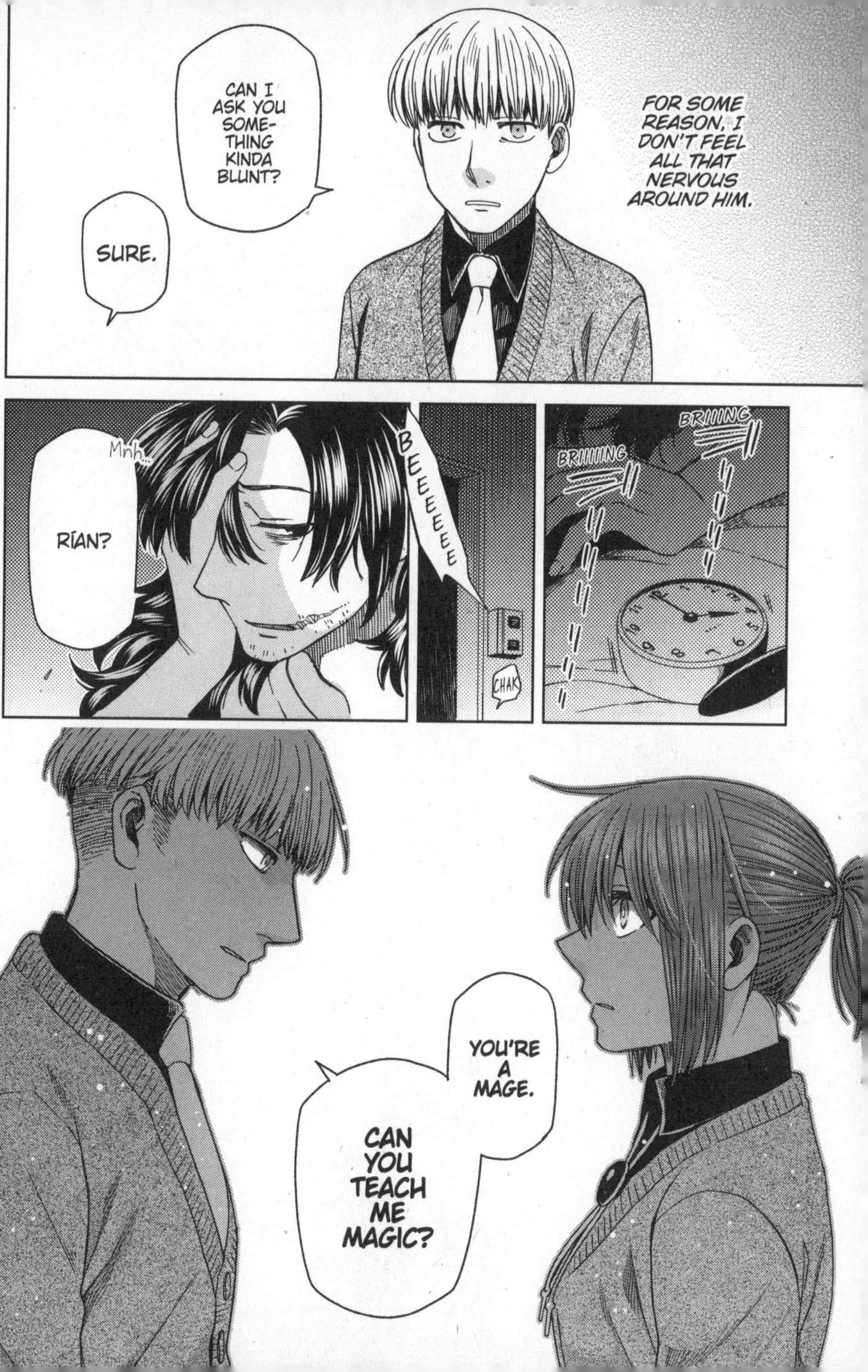
FOR SOME REASON, I DON'T FEEL ALL THAT NERVOUS AROUND HIM.
CAN I ASK YOU SOME-THING KINDA BLUNT?
SURE.
BRIIING
BRIIIIING
BEEEEEEE
CHAK
Mnh...
RÍAN?
YOU'RE A MAGE.
CAN YOU TEACH ME MAGIC?

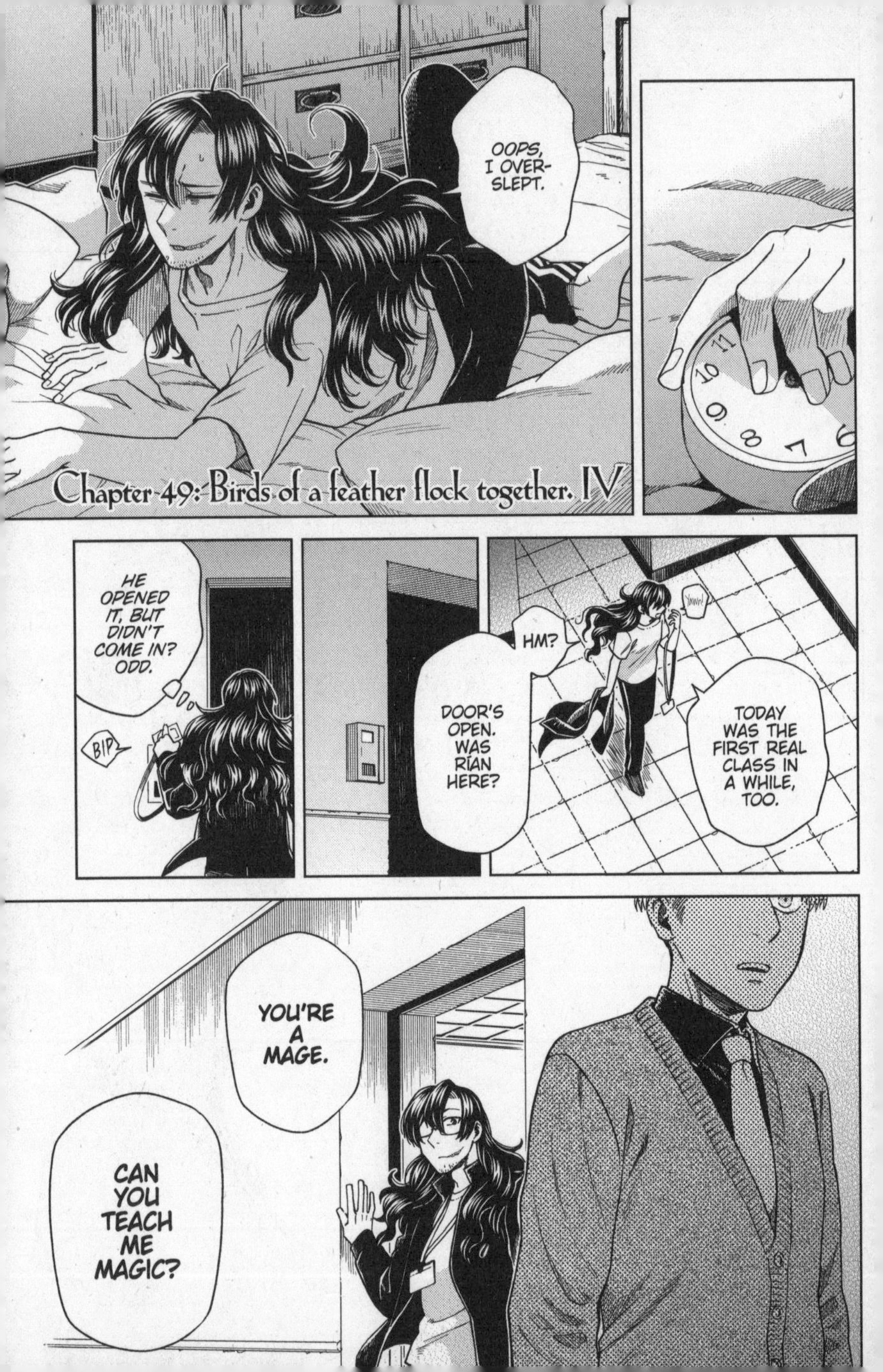
OOPS, I OVER-SLEPT.
Chapter 49: Birds of a feather flock together. IV
Yawn
HM?
TODAY WAS THE FIRST REAL CLASS IN A WHILE, TOO.
DOOR'S OPEN. WAS RÍAN HERE?
HE OPENED IT, BUT DIDN'T COME IN? ODD.
BIP
YOU'RE A MAGE.
CAN YOU TEACH ME MAGIC?

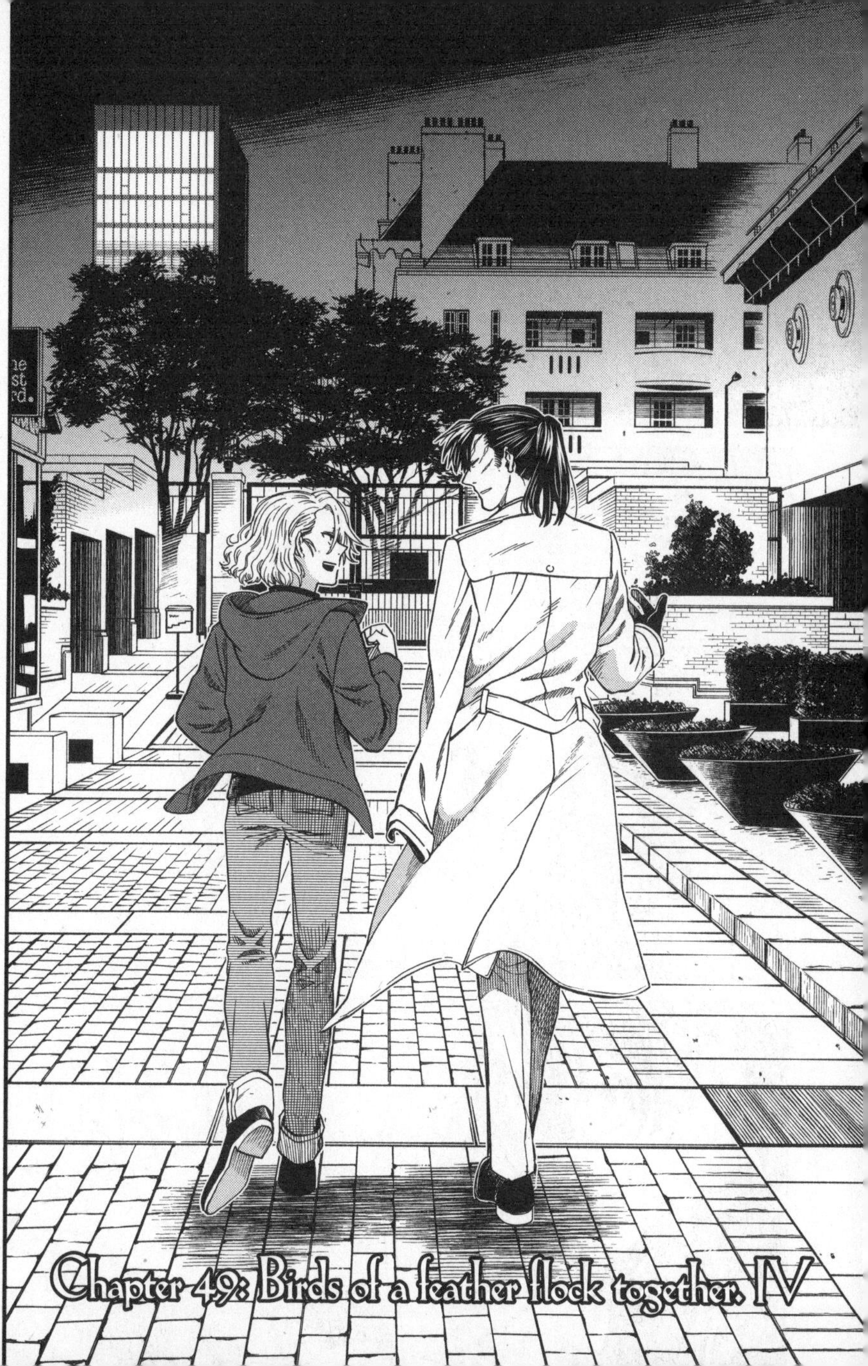

Chapter 49: Birds of a feather flock together. IV

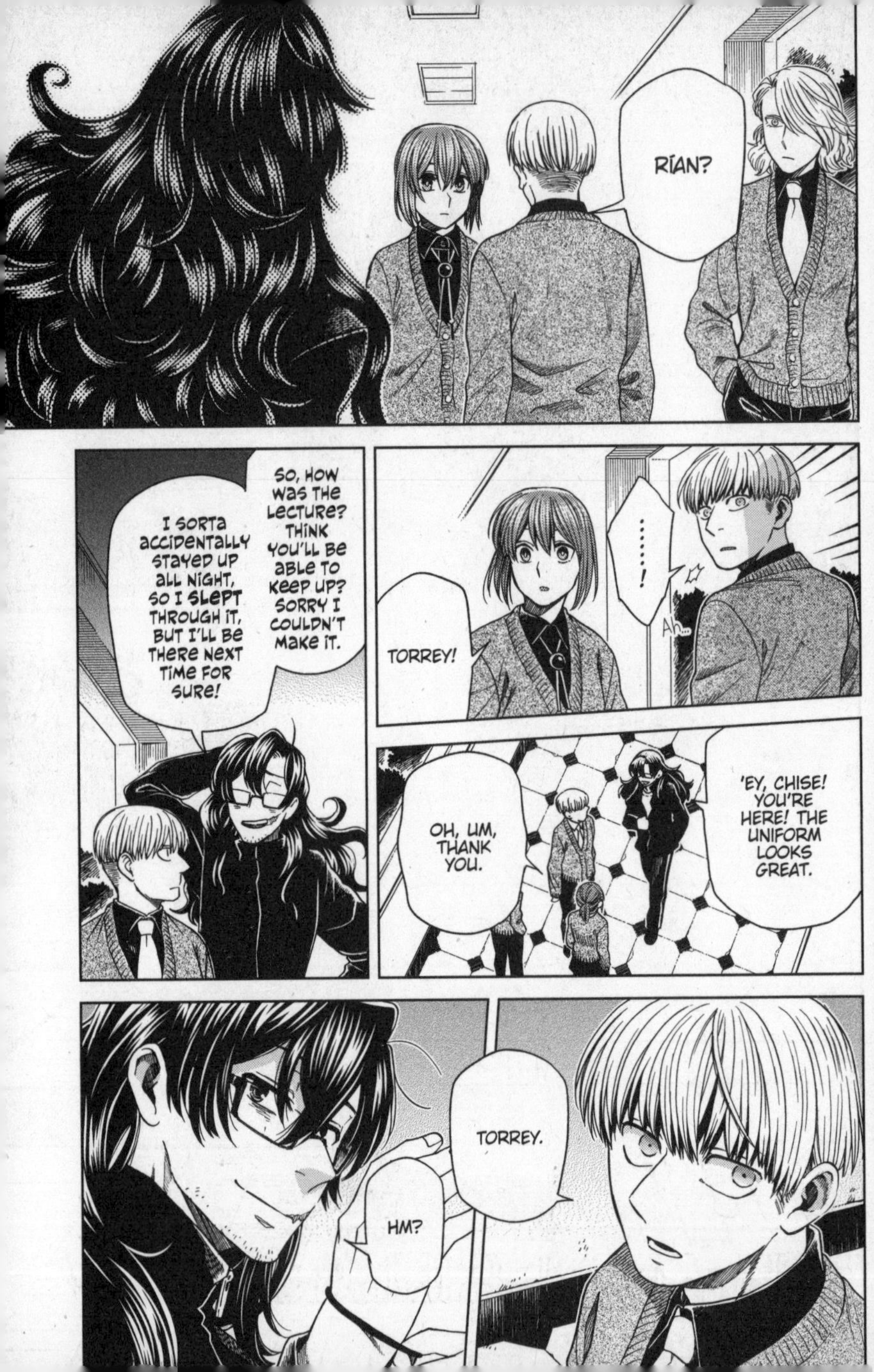
RĪAN?
......!
Ah...
TORREY!
'EY, CHISE! YOU'RE HERE! THE UNIFORM LOOKS GREAT.
OH, UM, THANK YOU.
SO, HOW WAS THE LECTURE? THINK YOU'LL BE ABLE TO KEEP UP? SORRY I COULDN'T MAKE IT.
I SORTA ACCIDENTALLY STAYED UP ALL NIGHT, SO I SLEPT THROUGH IT, BUT I'LL BE THERE NEXT TIME FOR SURE!
TORREY.
HM?

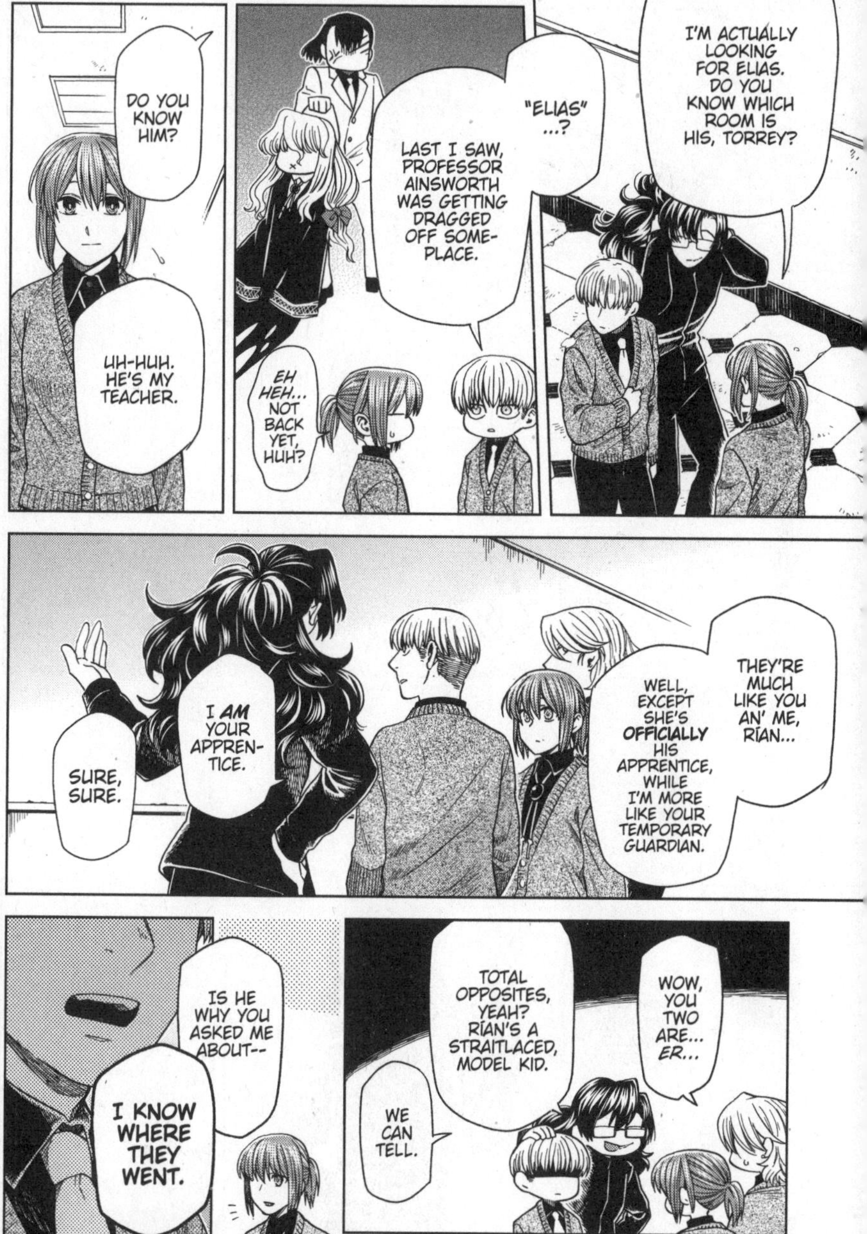
I'M ACTUALLY LOOKING FOR ELIAS. DO YOU KNOW WHICH ROOM IS HIS, TORREY?
"ELIAS" ...?
LAST I SAW, PROFESSOR AINSWORTH WAS GETTING DRAGGED OFF SOME-PLACE.
EH HEH... NOT BACK YET, HUH?
DO YOU KNOW HIM?
UH-HUH. HE'S MY TEACHER.
THEY'RE MUCH LIKE YOU AN' ME, RÍAN...
WELL, EXCEPT SHE'S **OFFICIALLY** HIS APPRENTICE, WHILE I'M MORE LIKE YOUR TEMPORARY GUARDIAN.
I ***AM*** YOUR APPREN-TICE.
SURE, SURE.
WOW, YOU TWO ARE... *ER...*
TOTAL OPPOSITES, YEAH? RÍAN'S A STRAITLACED, MODEL KID.
WE CAN TELL.
IS HE WHY YOU ASKED ME ABOUT--
I KNOW WHERE THEY WENT.

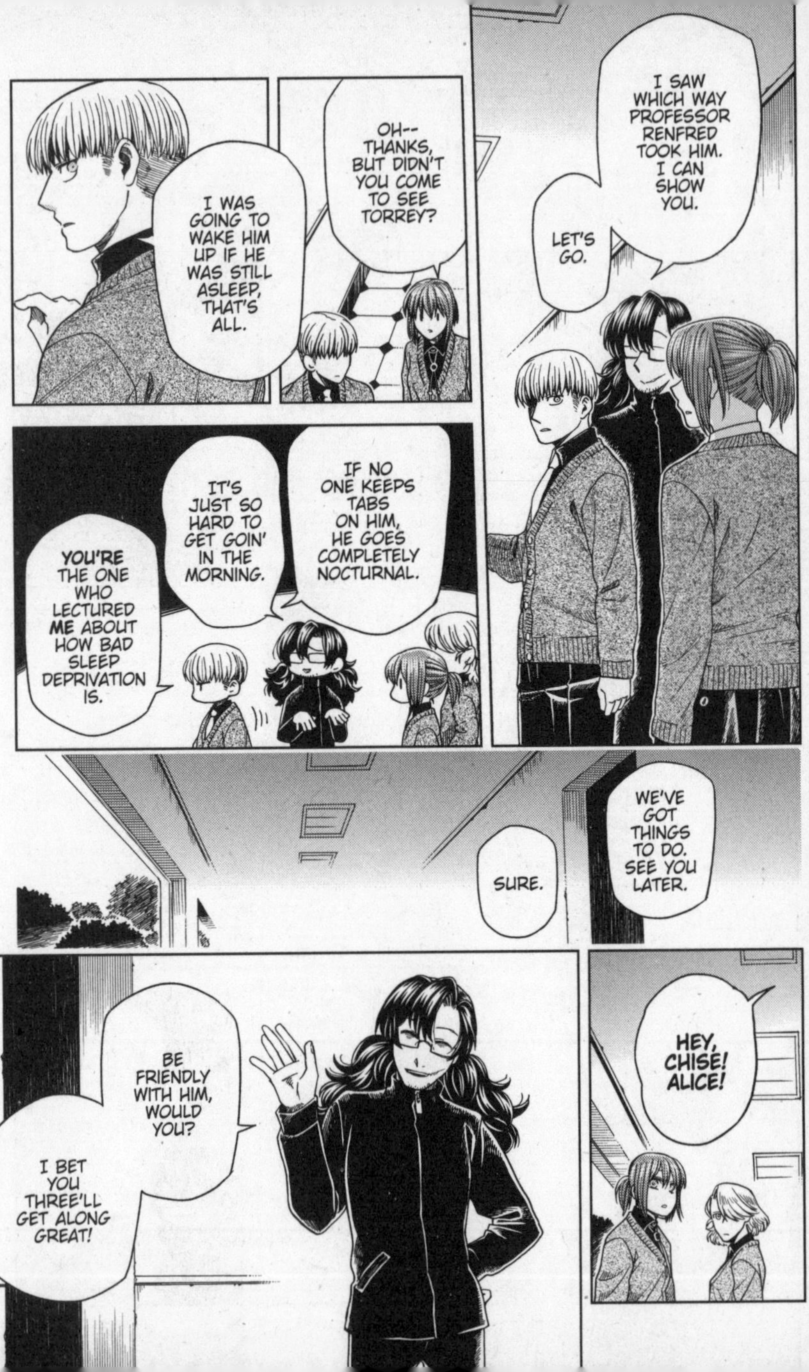
I SAW WHICH WAY PROFESSOR RENFRED TOOK HIM. I CAN SHOW YOU.
LET'S GO.
OH-- THANKS, BUT DIDN'T YOU COME TO SEE TORREY?
I WAS GOING TO WAKE HIM UP IF HE WAS STILL ASLEEP, THAT'S ALL.
IF NO ONE KEEPS TABS ON HIM, HE GOES COMPLETELY NOCTURNAL.
IT'S JUST SO HARD TO GET GOIN' IN THE MORNING.
YOU'RE THE ONE WHO LECTURED **ME** ABOUT HOW BAD SLEEP DEPRIVATION IS.
WE'VE GOT THINGS TO DO. SEE YOU LATER.
SURE.
HEY, CHISE! ALICE!
BE FRIENDLY WITH HIM, WOULD YOU?
I BET YOU THREE'LL GET ALONG GREAT!

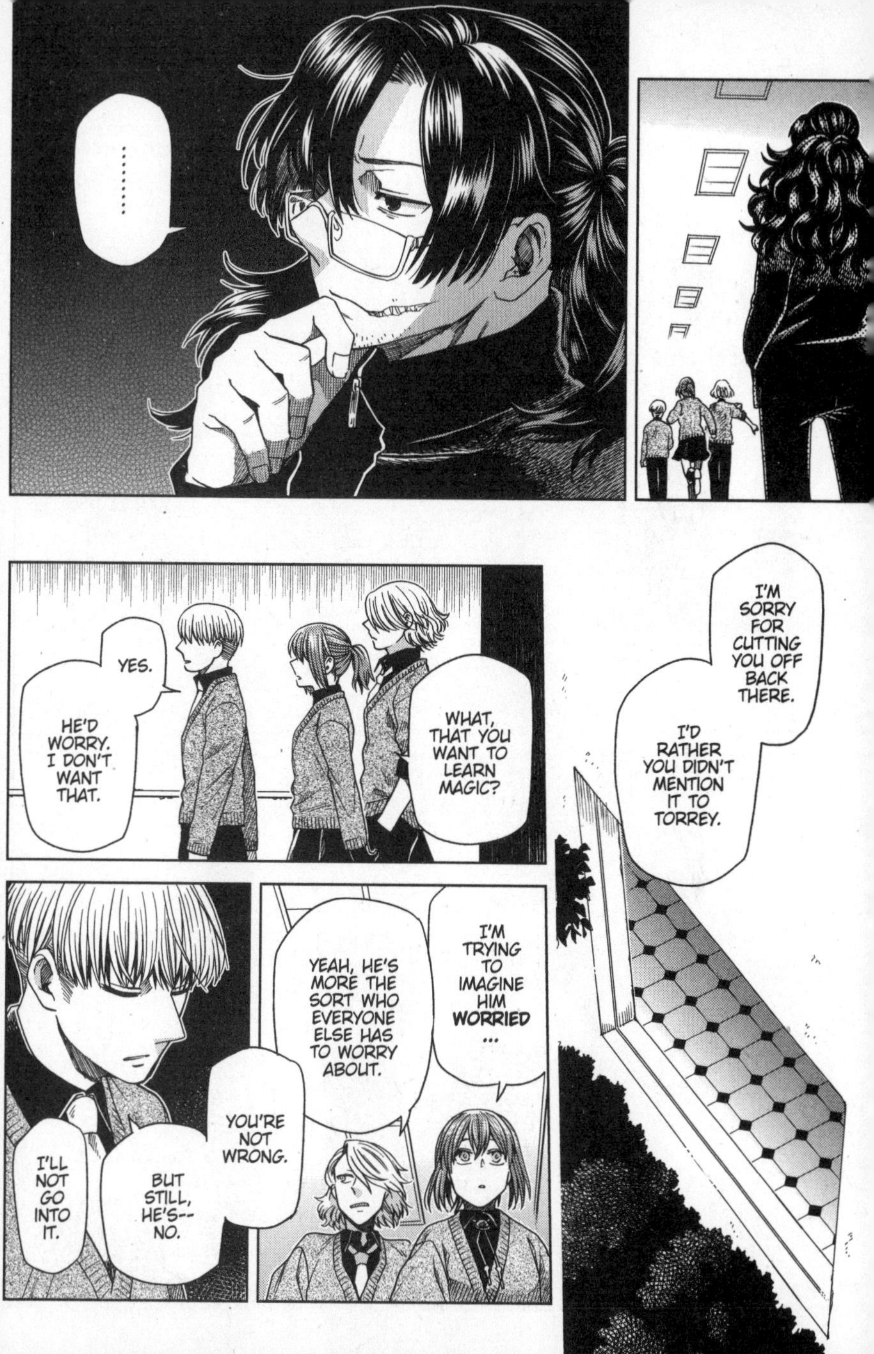
……
I'M SORRY FOR CUTTING YOU OFF BACK THERE.
I'D RATHER YOU DIDN'T MENTION IT TO TORREY.
WHAT, THAT YOU WANT TO LEARN MAGIC?
YES.
HE'D WORRY. I DON'T WANT THAT.
I'M TRYING TO IMAGINE HIM **WORRIED**...
YEAH, HE'S MORE THE SORT WHO EVERYONE ELSE HAS TO WORRY ABOUT.
YOU'RE NOT WRONG.
BUT STILL, HE'S-- NO.
I'LL NOT GO INTO IT.

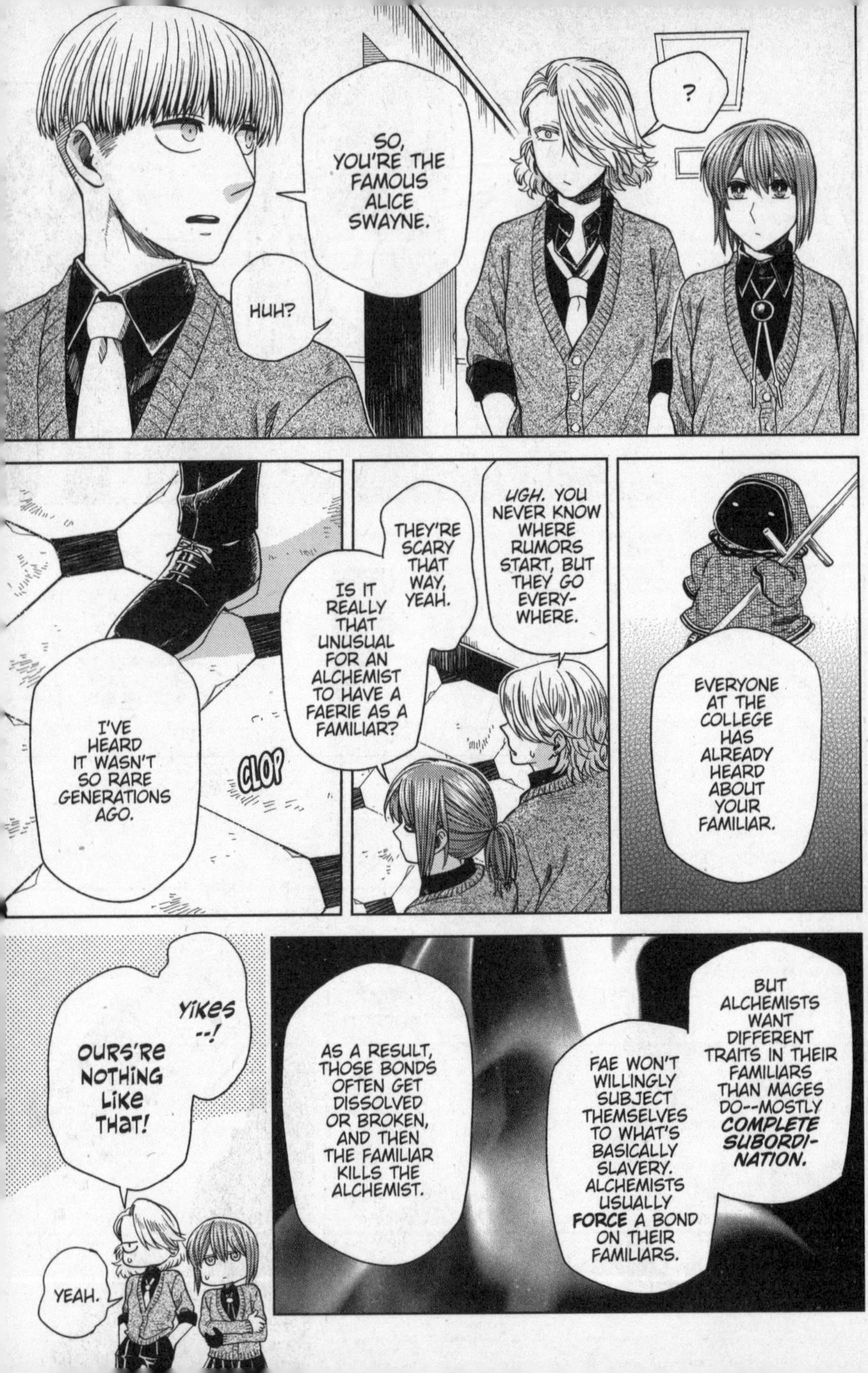
?
SO, YOU'RE THE FAMOUS ALICE SWAYNE.
HUH?
EVERYONE AT THE COLLEGE HAS ALREADY HEARD ABOUT YOUR FAMILIAR.
UGH. YOU NEVER KNOW WHERE RUMORS START, BUT THEY GO EVERY-WHERE.
THEY'RE SCARY THAT WAY, YEAH.
IS IT REALLY THAT UNUSUAL FOR AN ALCHEMIST TO HAVE A FAERIE AS A FAMILIAR?
CLOP
I'VE HEARD IT WASN'T SO RARE GENERATIONS AGO.
BUT ALCHEMISTS WANT DIFFERENT TRAITS IN THEIR FAMILIARS THAN MAGES DO--MOSTLY COMPLETE SUBORDI-NATION.
FAE WON'T WILLINGLY SUBJECT THEMSELVES TO WHAT'S BASICALLY SLAVERY. ALCHEMISTS USUALLY FORCE A BOND ON THEIR FAMILIARS.
AS A RESULT, THOSE BONDS OFTEN GET DISSOLVED OR BROKEN, AND THEN THE FAMILIAR KILLS THE ALCHEMIST.
YIKES--!
OURS'RE NOTHING LIKE THAT!
YEAH.

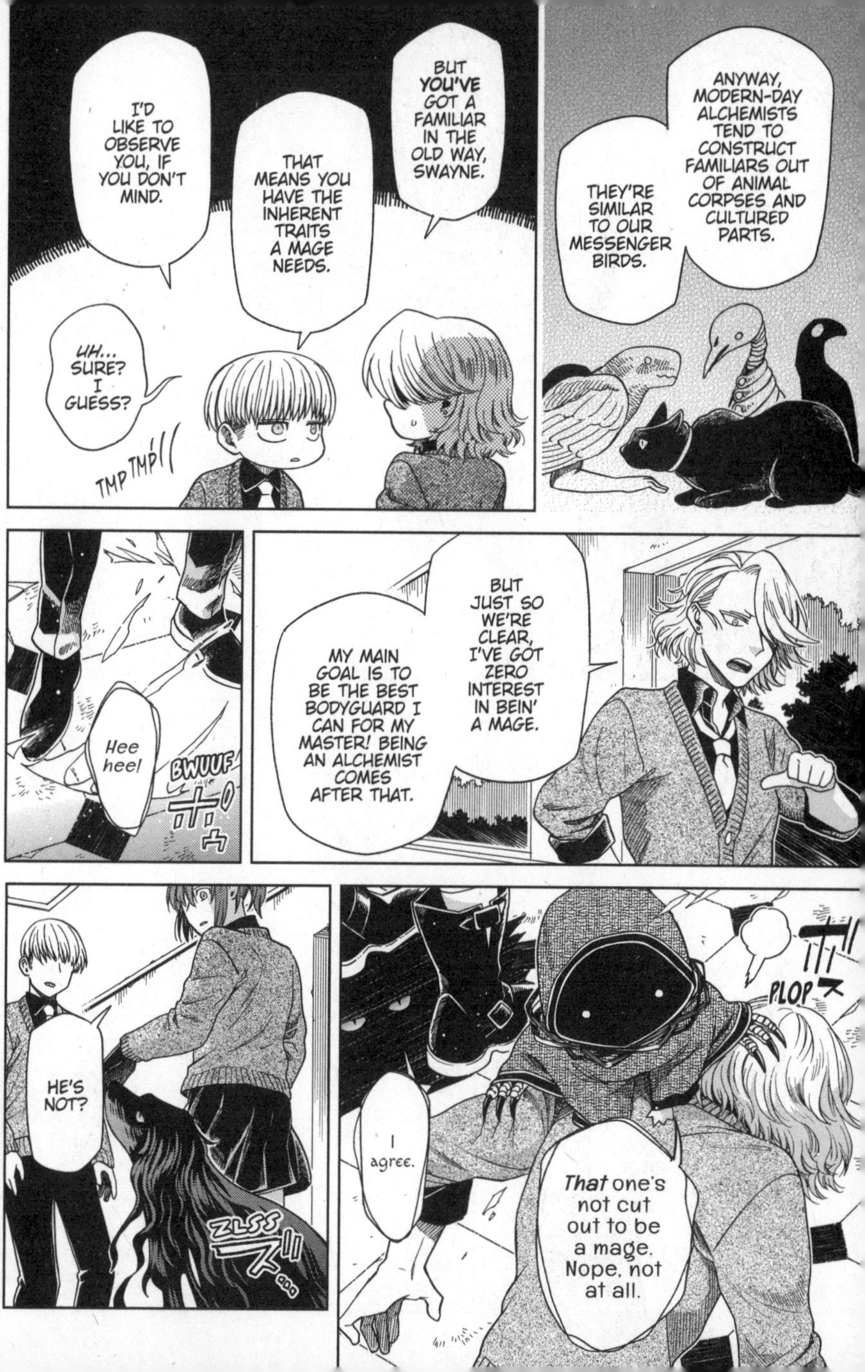
ANYWAY, MODERN-DAY ALCHEMISTS TEND TO CONSTRUCT FAMILIARS OUT OF ANIMAL CORPSES AND CULTURED PARTS.
THEY'RE SIMILAR TO OUR MESSENGER BIRDS.
BUT YOU'VE GOT A FAMILIAR IN THE OLD WAY, SWAYNE.
THAT MEANS YOU HAVE THE INHERENT TRAITS A MAGE NEEDS.
I'D LIKE TO OBSERVE YOU, IF YOU DON'T MIND.
UH... SURE? I GUESS?
TMP TMP
BUT JUST SO WE'RE CLEAR, I'VE GOT ZERO INTEREST IN BEIN' A MAGE.
MY MAIN GOAL IS TO BE THE BEST BODYGUARD I CAN FOR MY MASTER! BEING AN ALCHEMIST COMES AFTER THAT.
BWUUF
Hee hee!
PLOP
That one's not cut out to be a mage. Nope, not at all.
I agree.
HE'S NOT?
ZLSS

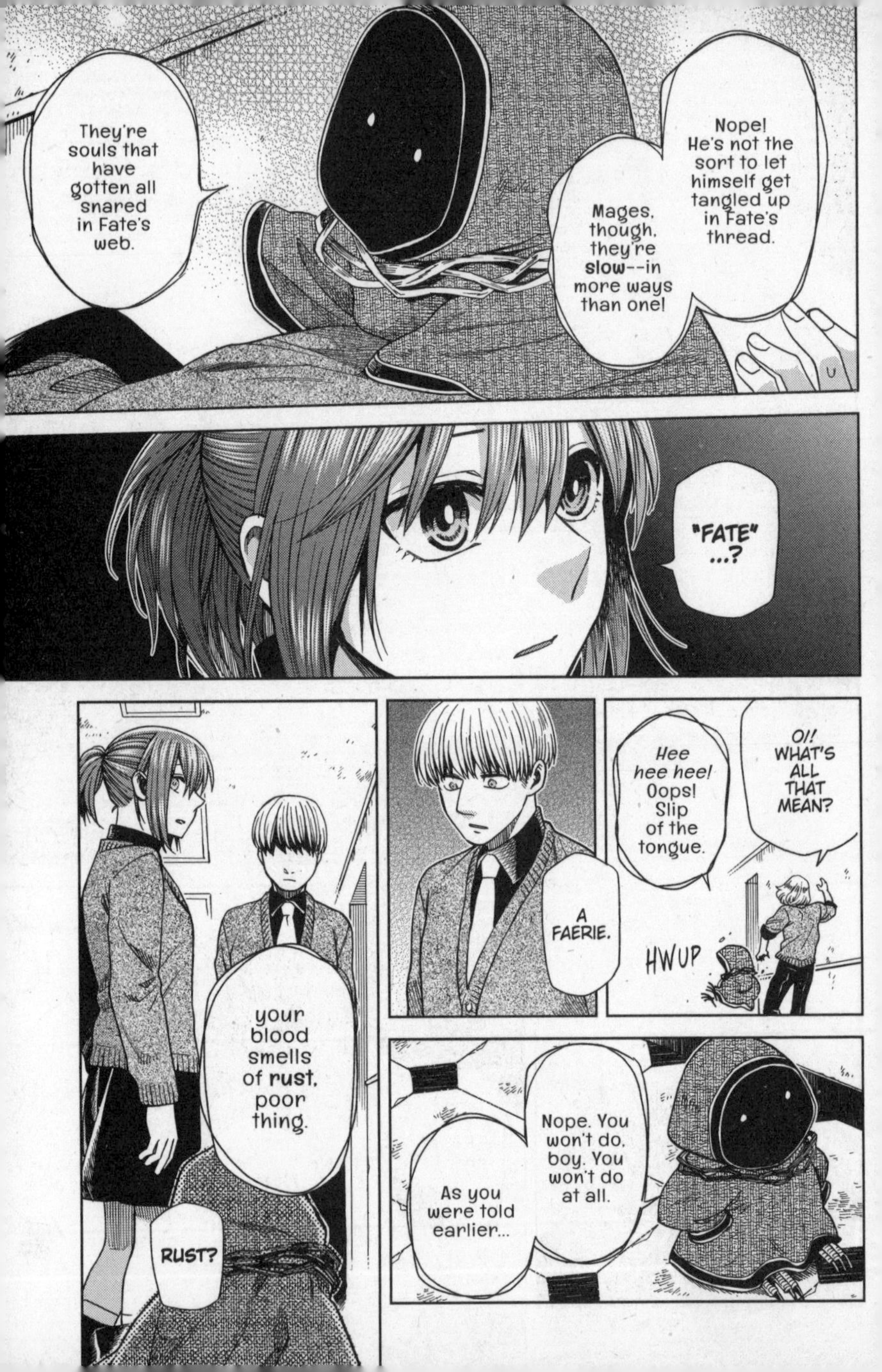
Nope! He's not the sort to let himself get tangled up in Fate's thread.
Mages, though, they're **slow**--in more ways than one!
They're souls that have gotten all snared in Fate's web.
"FATE" ...?
OI! WHAT'S ALL THAT MEAN?
Hee hee hee! Oops! Slip of the tongue.
HWUP
A FAERIE.
Nope. You won't do, boy. You won't do at all.
As you were told earlier...
your blood smells of **rust**, poor thing.
RUST?

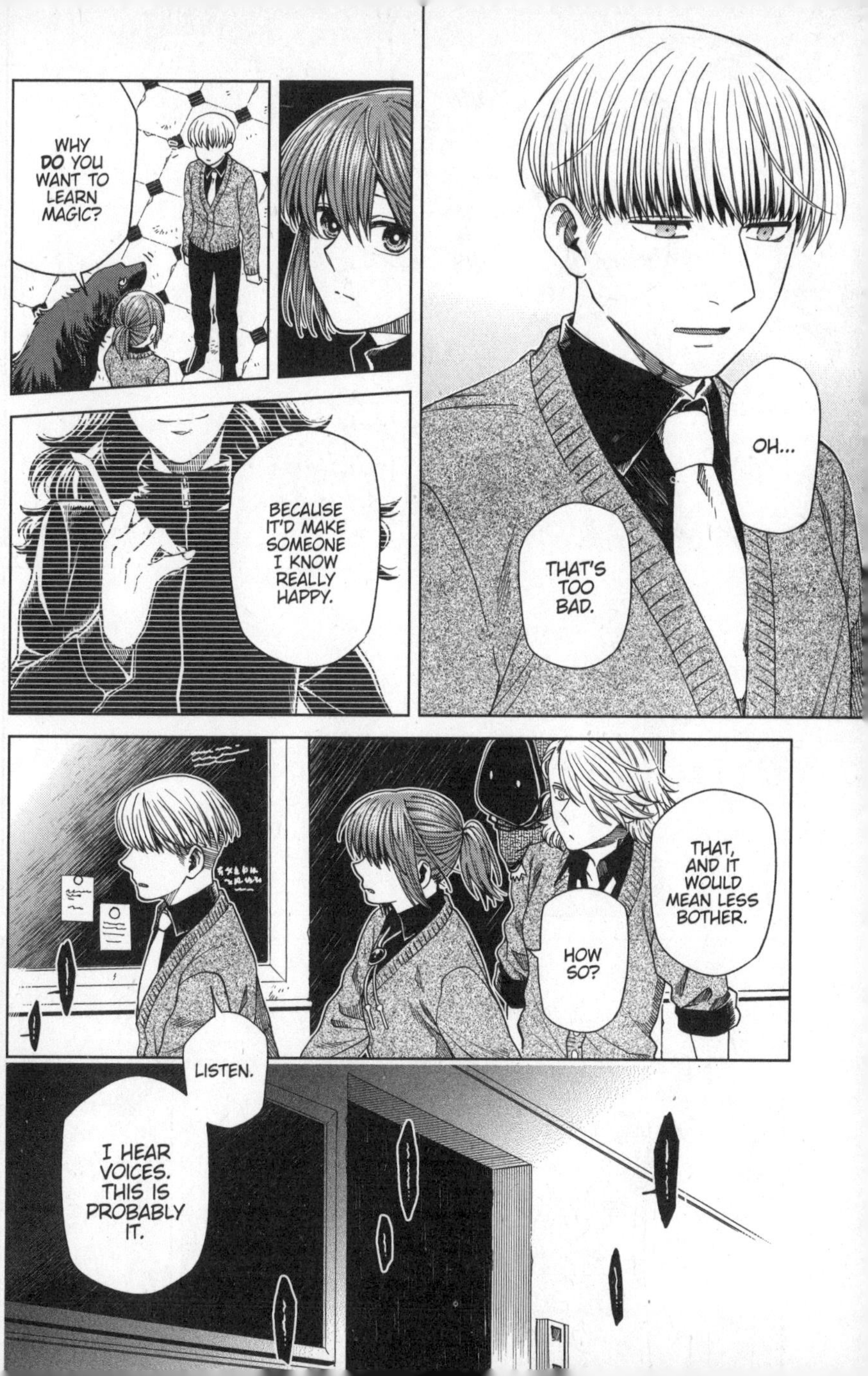
OH...
THAT'S TOO BAD.
WHY DO YOU WANT TO LEARN MAGIC?
BECAUSE IT'D MAKE SOMEONE I KNOW REALLY HAPPY.
THAT, AND IT WOULD MEAN LESS BOTHER.
HOW SO?
LISTEN.
I HEAR VOICES. THIS IS PROBABLY IT.

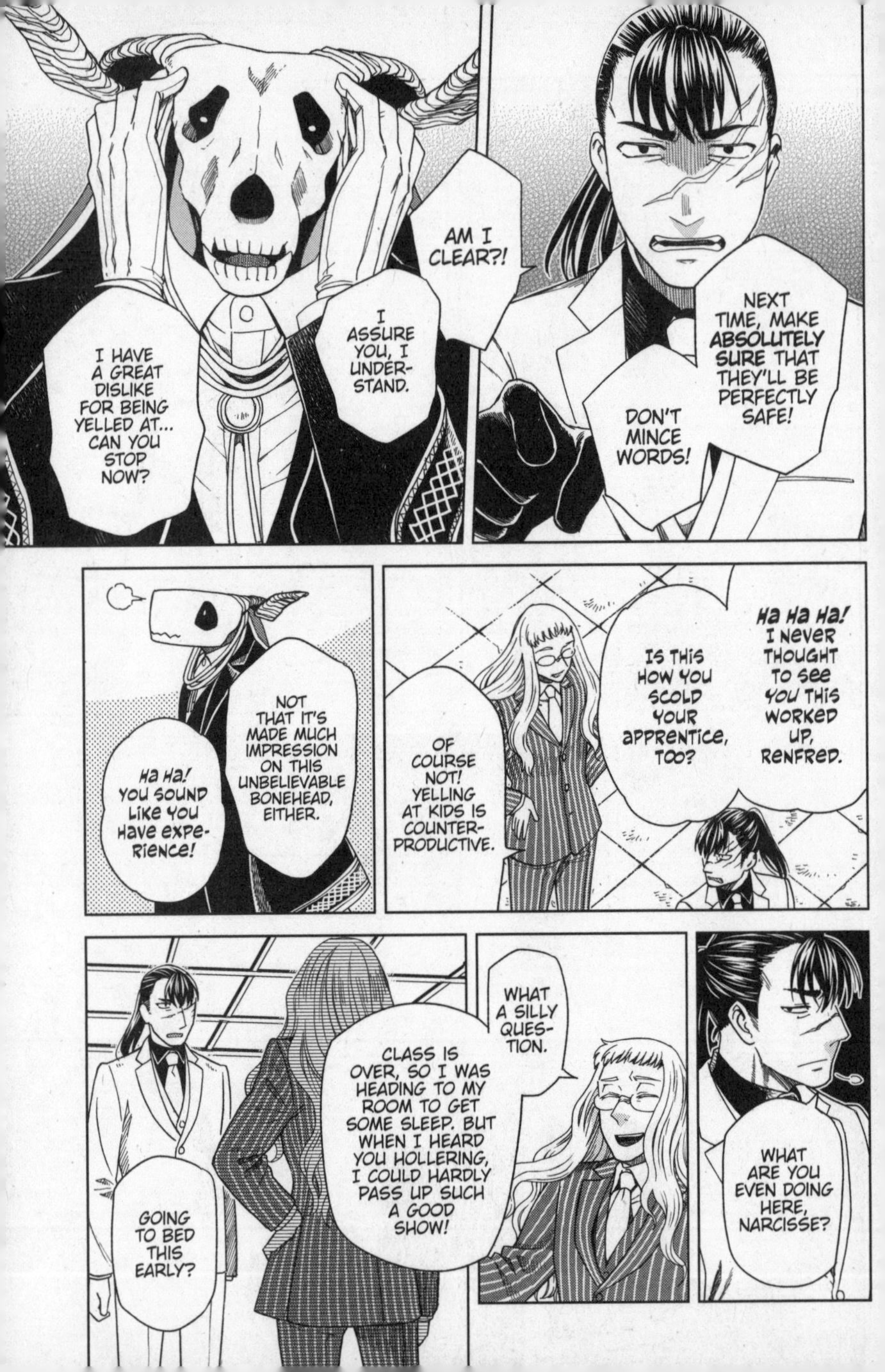
NEXT TIME, MAKE ABSOLUTELY SURE THAT THEY'LL BE PERFECTLY SAFE!
DON'T MINCE WORDS!
AM I CLEAR?!
I ASSURE YOU, I UNDER-STAND.
I HAVE A GREAT DISLIKE FOR BEING YELLED AT... CAN YOU STOP NOW?
HA HA HA! I NEVER THOUGHT TO SEE YOU THIS WORKED UP, RENFRED.
IS THIS HOW YOU SCOLD YOUR APPRENTICE, TOO?
OF COURSE NOT! YELLING AT KIDS IS COUNTER-PRODUCTIVE.
NOT THAT IT'S MADE MUCH IMPRESSION ON THIS UNBELIEVABLE BONEHEAD, EITHER.
HA HA! YOU SOUND LIKE YOU HAVE EXPE-RIENCE!
WHAT ARE YOU EVEN DOING HERE, NARCISSE?
WHAT A SILLY QUES-TION.
CLASS IS OVER, SO I WAS HEADING TO MY ROOM TO GET SOME SLEEP. BUT WHEN I HEARD YOU HOLLERING, I COULD HARDLY PASS UP SUCH A GOOD SHOW!
GOING TO BED THIS EARLY?

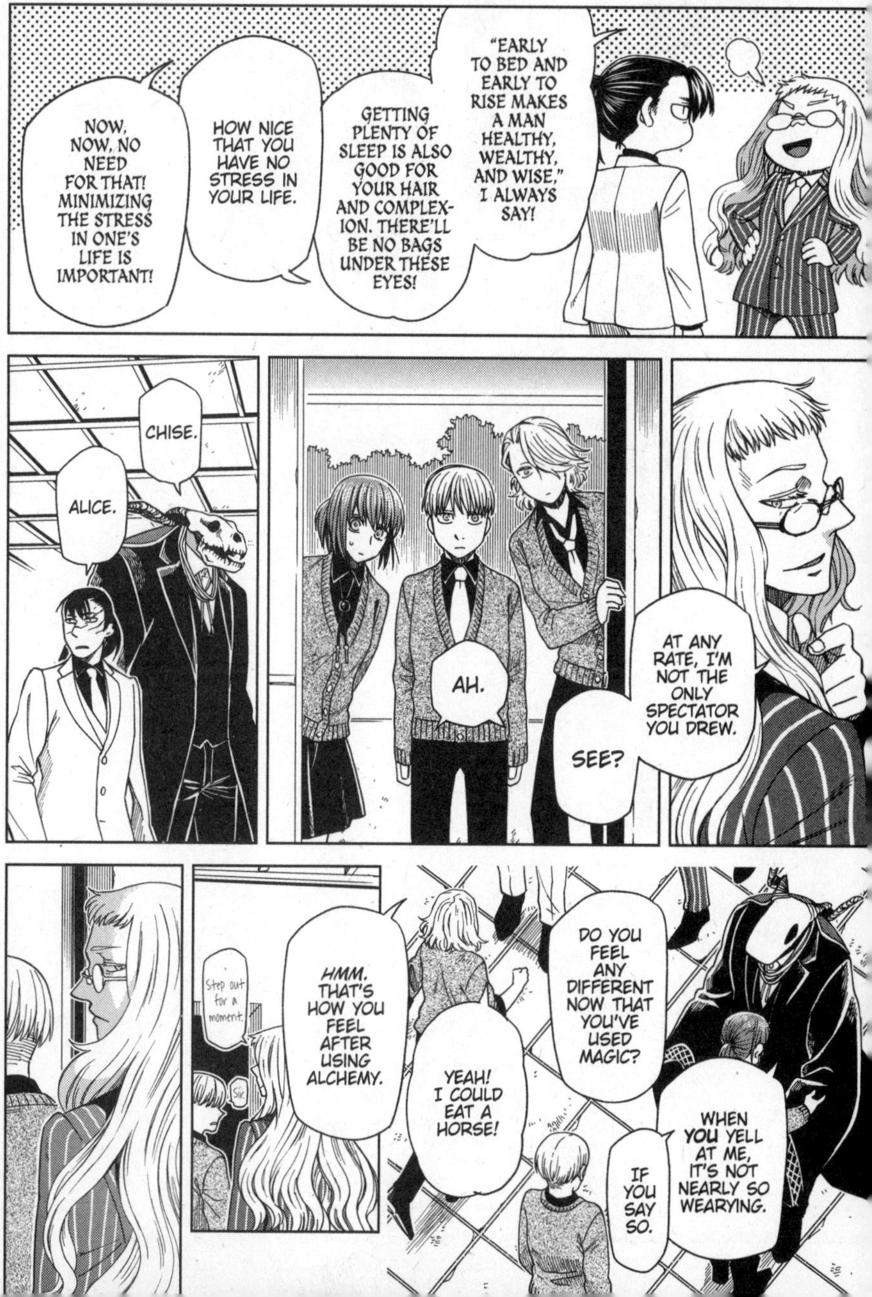
"EARLY TO BED AND EARLY TO RISE MAKES A MAN HEALTHY, WEALTHY, AND WISE," I ALWAYS SAY!
GETTING PLENTY OF SLEEP IS ALSO GOOD FOR YOUR HAIR AND COMPLEXION. THERE'LL BE NO BAGS UNDER THESE EYES!
HOW NICE THAT YOU HAVE NO STRESS IN YOUR LIFE.
NOW, NOW, NO NEED FOR THAT! MINIMIZING THE STRESS IN ONE'S LIFE IS IMPORTANT!
AT ANY RATE, I'M NOT THE ONLY SPECTATOR YOU DREW.
SEE?
AH.
CHISE.
ALICE.
DO YOU FEEL ANY DIFFERENT NOW THAT YOU'VE USED MAGIC?
WHEN YOU YELL AT ME, IT'S NOT NEARLY SO WEARYING.
IF YOU SAY SO.
HMM. THAT'S HOW YOU FEEL AFTER USING ALCHEMY.
YEAH! I COULD EAT A HORSE!
Step out for a moment.
Sir.

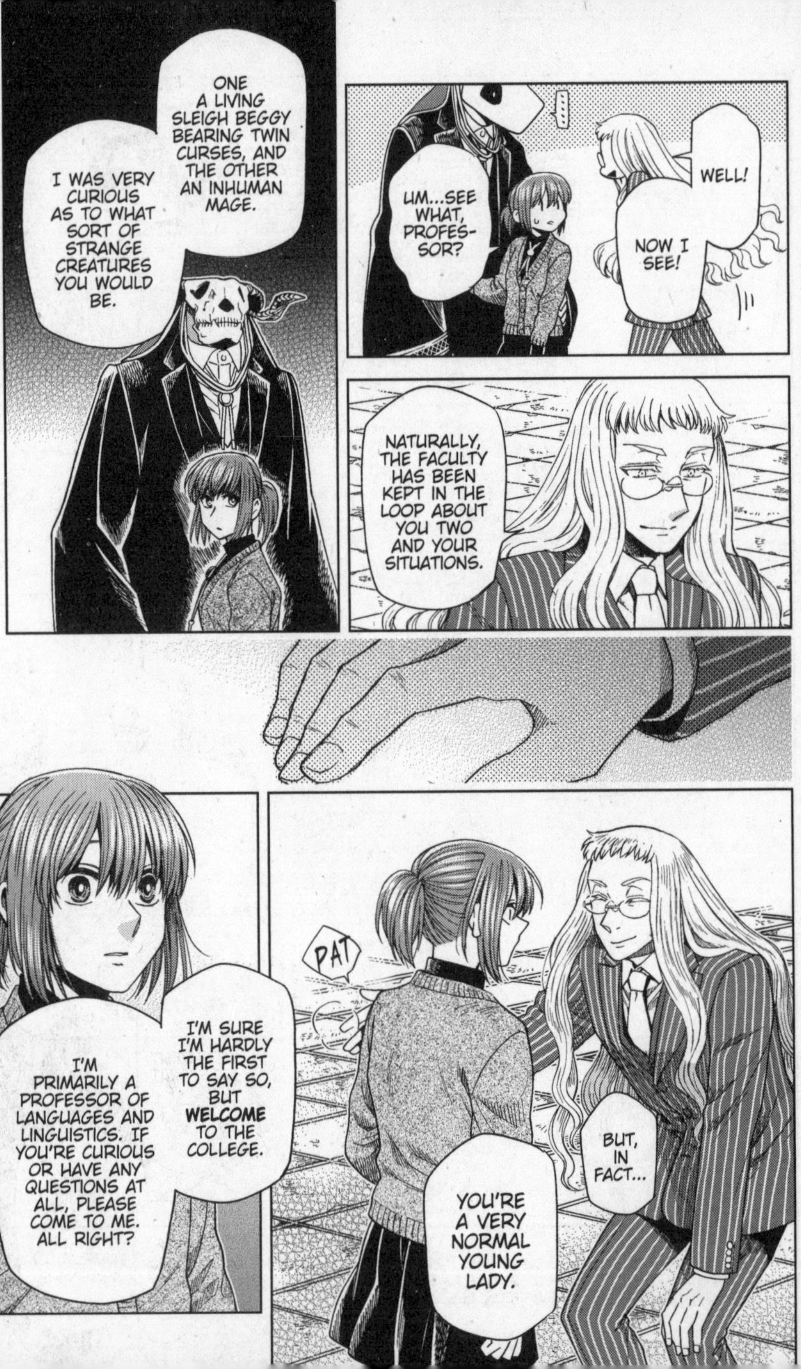
WELL!
NOW I SEE!
UM...SEE WHAT, PROFESSOR?
NATURALLY, THE FACULTY HAS BEEN KEPT IN THE LOOP ABOUT YOU TWO AND YOUR SITUATIONS.
ONE A LIVING SLEIGH BEGGY BEARING TWIN CURSES, AND THE OTHER AN INHUMAN MAGE.
I WAS VERY CURIOUS AS TO WHAT SORT OF STRANGE CREATURES YOU WOULD BE.
PAT
BUT, IN FACT...
YOU'RE A VERY NORMAL YOUNG LADY.
I'M SURE I'M HARDLY THE FIRST TO SAY SO, BUT **WELCOME** TO THE COLLEGE.
I'M PRIMARILY A PROFESSOR OF LANGUAGES AND LINGUISTICS. IF YOU'RE CURIOUS OR HAVE ANY QUESTIONS AT ALL, PLEASE COME TO ME. ALL RIGHT?

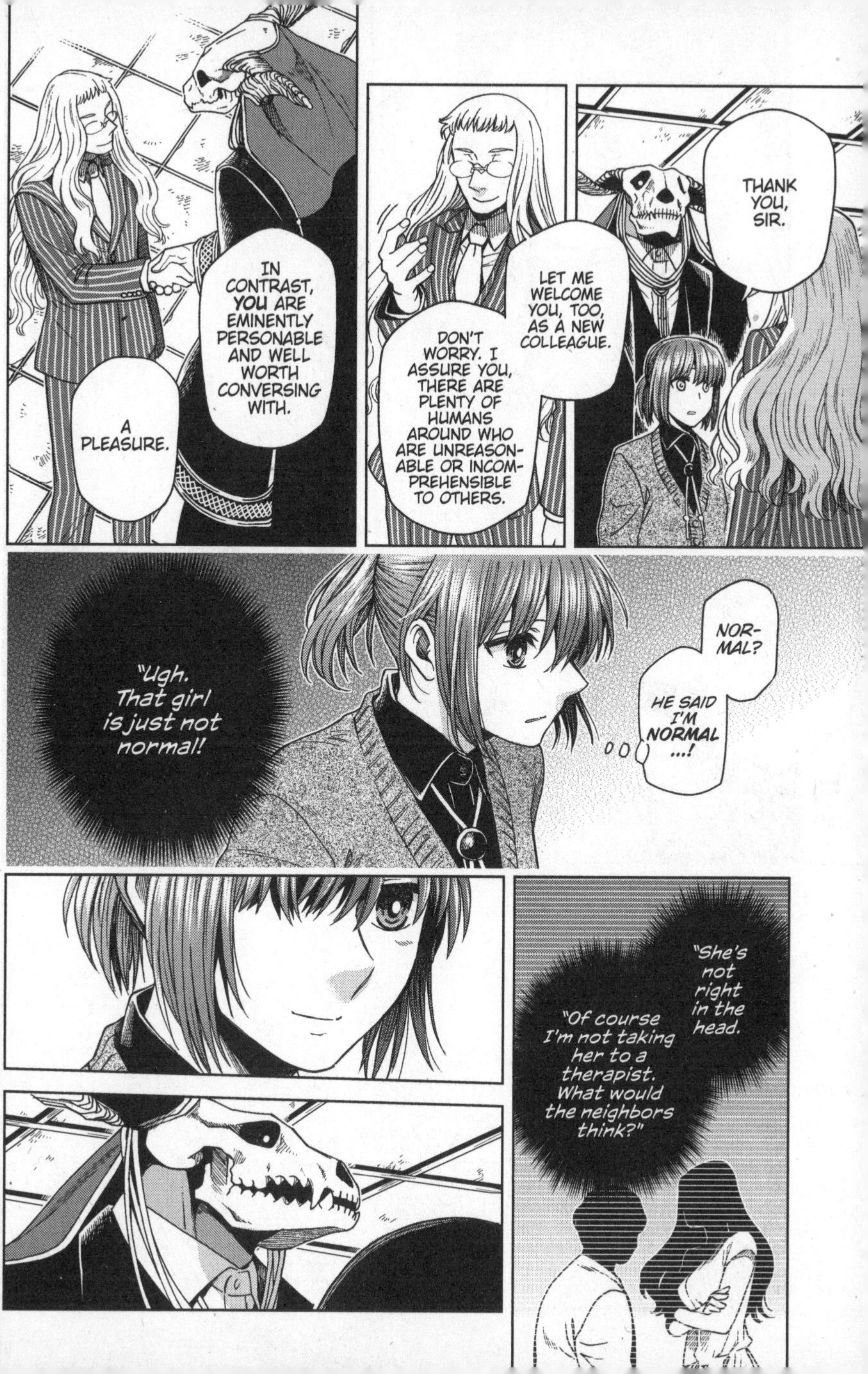
THANK YOU, SIR.
LET ME WELCOME YOU, TOO, AS A NEW COLLEAGUE.
DON'T WORRY. I ASSURE YOU, THERE ARE PLENTY OF HUMANS AROUND WHO ARE UNREASON-ABLE OR INCOM-PREHENSIBLE TO OTHERS.
IN CONTRAST, **YOU** ARE EMINENTLY PERSONABLE AND WELL WORTH CONVERSING WITH.
A PLEASURE.
NOR-MAL?
HE SAID I'M **NORMAL** ...!
"Ugh. That girl is just not normal!
"She's not right in the head.
"Of course I'm not taking her to a therapist. What would the neighbors think?"

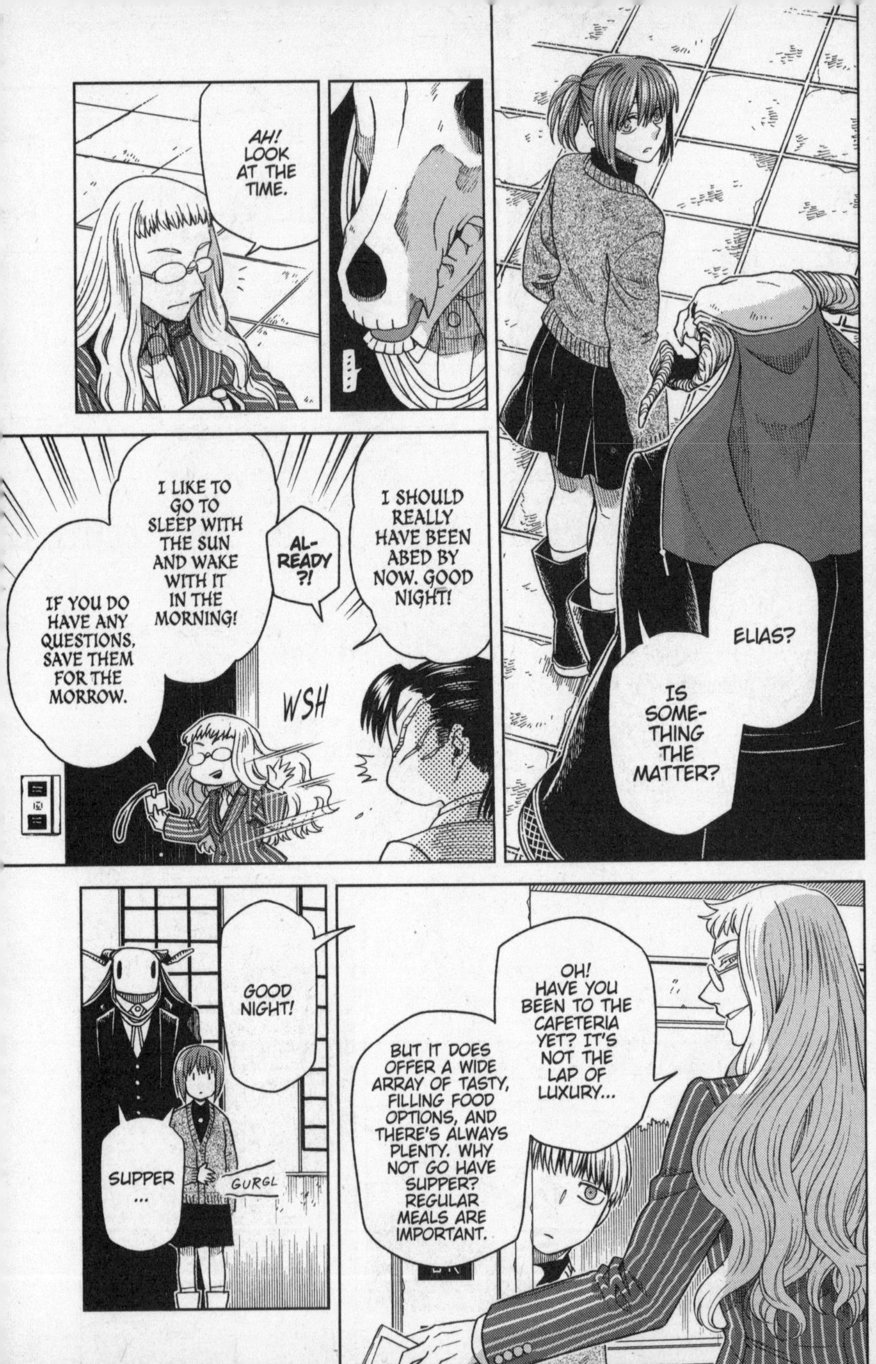
ELIAS?
IS SOMETHING THE MATTER?
AH! LOOK AT THE TIME.
I SHOULD REALLY HAVE BEEN ABED BY NOW. GOOD NIGHT!
AL-READY?!
I LIKE TO GO TO SLEEP WITH THE SUN AND WAKE WITH IT IN THE MORNING!
IF YOU DO HAVE ANY QUESTIONS, SAVE THEM FOR THE MORROW.
WSH
OH! HAVE YOU BEEN TO THE CAFETERIA YET? IT'S NOT THE LAP OF LUXURY...
BUT IT DOES OFFER A WIDE ARRAY OF TASTY, FILLING FOOD OPTIONS, AND THERE'S ALWAYS PLENTY. WHY NOT GO HAVE SUPPER? REGULAR MEALS ARE IMPORTANT.
GOOD NIGHT!
GURGL
SUPPER ...

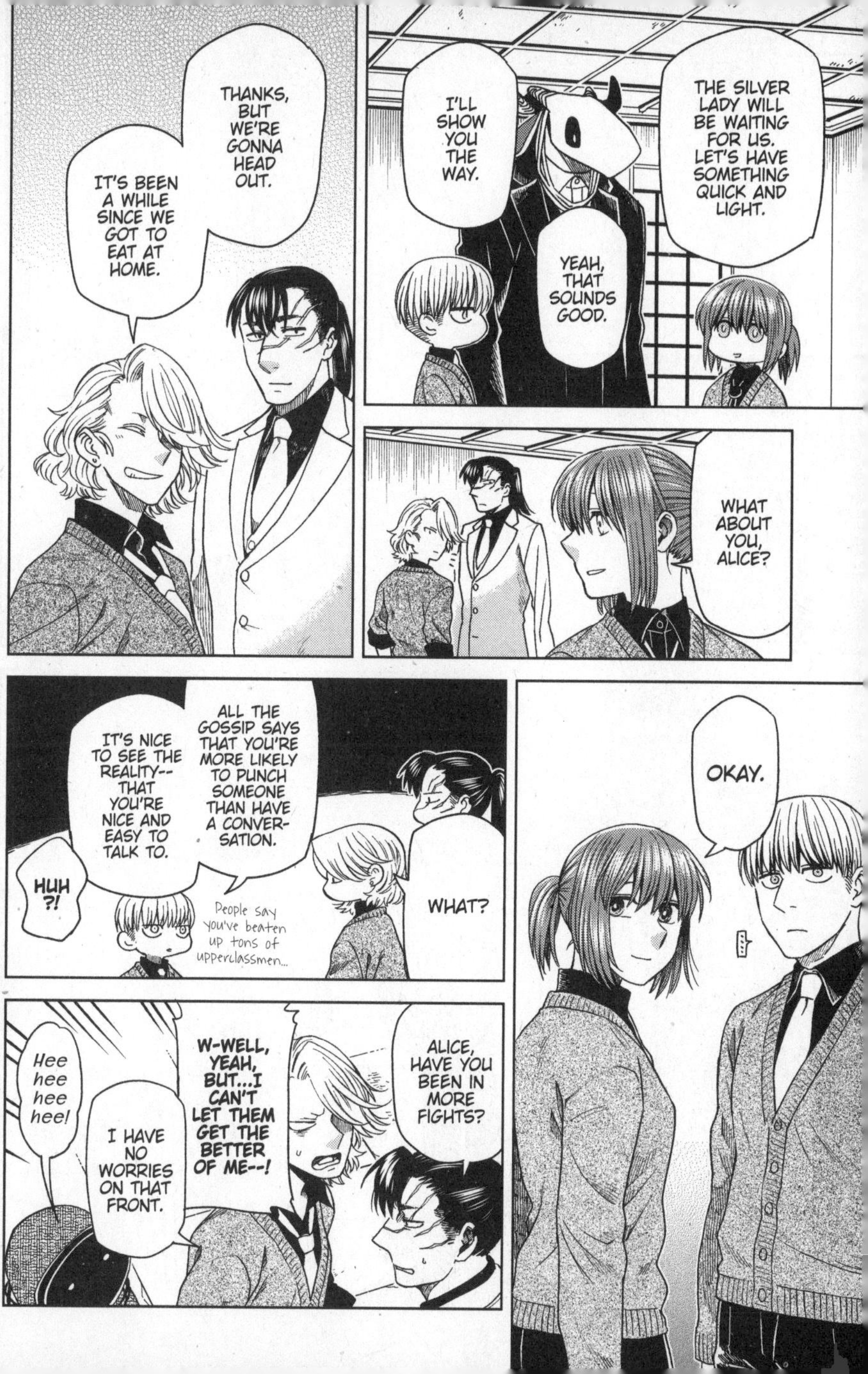
THE SILVER LADY WILL BE WAITING FOR US. LET'S HAVE SOMETHING QUICK AND LIGHT.
I'LL SHOW YOU THE WAY.
YEAH, THAT SOUNDS GOOD.
WHAT ABOUT YOU, ALICE?
THANKS, BUT WE'RE GONNA HEAD OUT.
IT'S BEEN A WHILE SINCE WE GOT TO EAT AT HOME.
OKAY.
ALL THE GOSSIP SAYS THAT YOU'RE MORE LIKELY TO PUNCH SOMEONE THAN HAVE A CONVER-SATION.
IT'S NICE TO SEE THE REALITY--THAT YOU'RE NICE AND EASY TO TALK TO.
WHAT?
People say you've beaten up tons of upperclassmen...
HUH?!
ALICE, HAVE YOU BEEN IN MORE FIGHTS?
W-WELL, YEAH, BUT...I CAN'T LET THEM GET THE BETTER OF ME--!
I HAVE NO WORRIES ON THAT FRONT.
Hee hee hee hee!

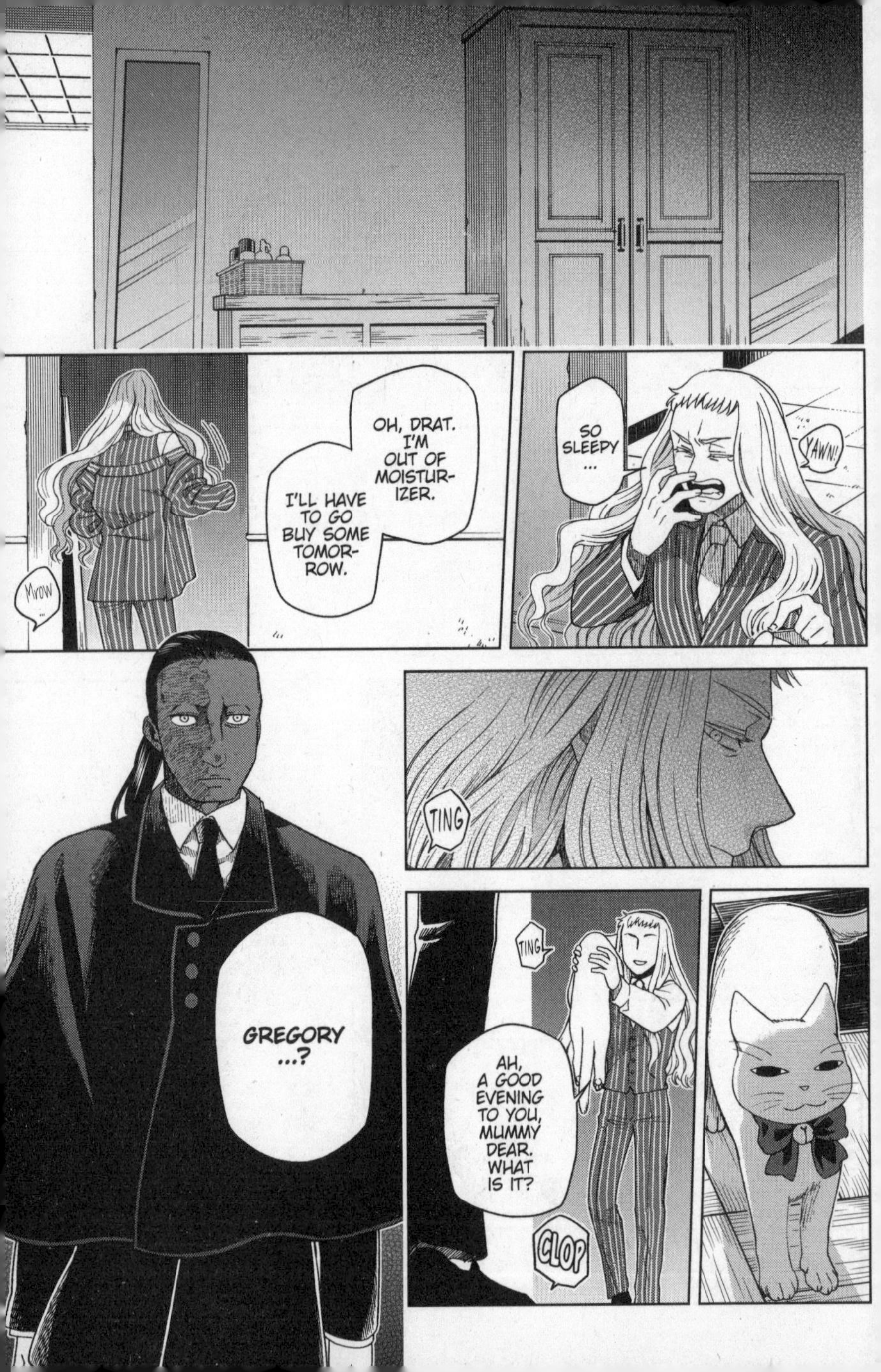
SO SLEEPY ...
YAWN!
OH, DRAT. I'M OUT OF MOISTUR-IZER.
I'LL HAVE TO GO BUY SOME TOMOR-ROW.
Mrow ...
TING
TING
AH, A GOOD EVENING TO YOU, MUMMY DEAR. WHAT IS IT?
CLOP
GREGORY ...?

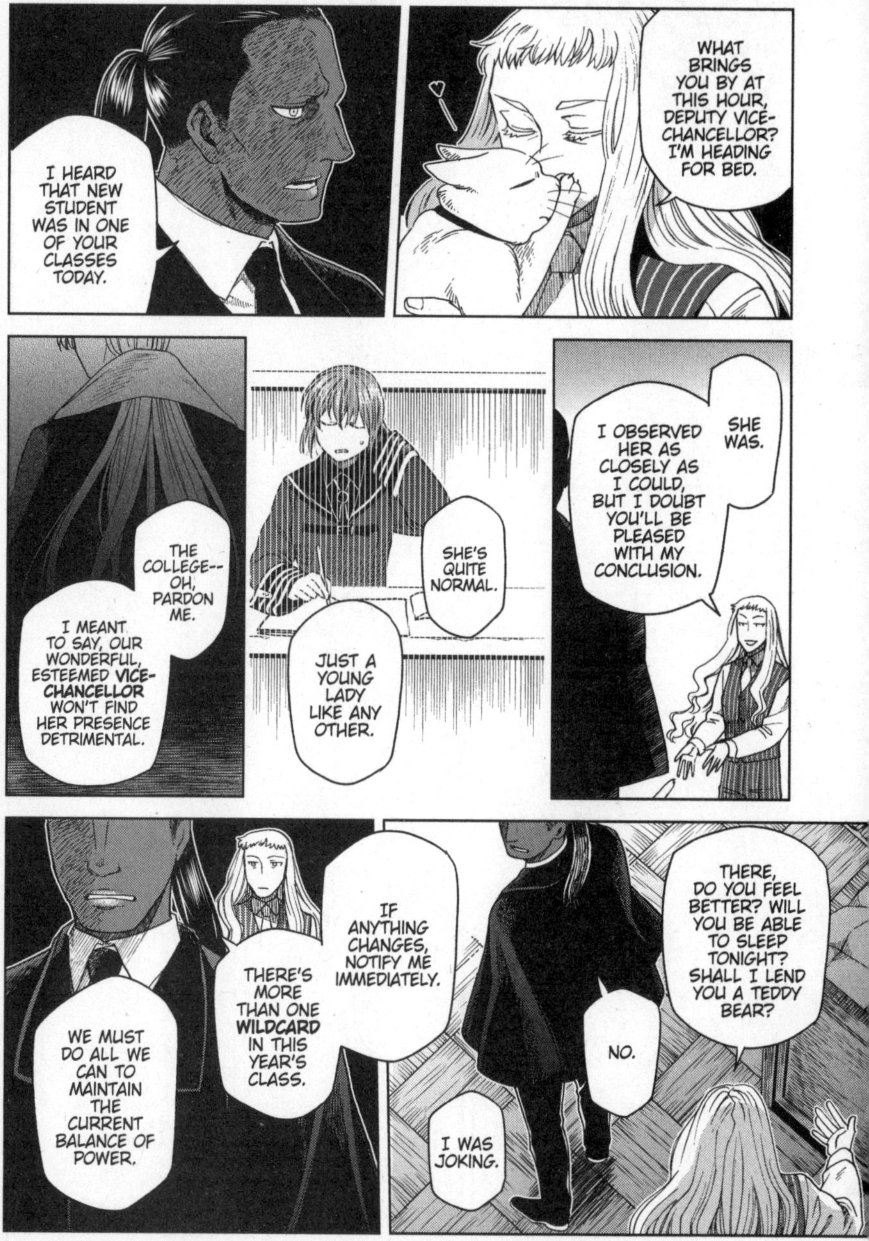
WHAT BRINGS YOU BY AT THIS HOUR, DEPUTY VICE-CHANCELLOR? I'M HEADING FOR BED.
I HEARD THAT NEW STUDENT WAS IN ONE OF YOUR CLASSES TODAY.
SHE WAS.
I OBSERVED HER AS CLOSELY AS I COULD, BUT I DOUBT YOU'LL BE PLEASED WITH MY CONCLUSION.
SHE'S QUITE NORMAL.
JUST A YOUNG LADY LIKE ANY OTHER.
THE COLLEGE--OH, PARDON ME.
I MEANT TO SAY, OUR WONDERFUL, ESTEEMED **VICE-CHANCELLOR** WON'T FIND HER PRESENCE DETRIMENTAL.
THERE, DO YOU FEEL BETTER? WILL YOU BE ABLE TO SLEEP TONIGHT? SHALL I LEND YOU A TEDDY BEAR?
NO.
I WAS JOKING.
IF ANYTHING CHANGES, NOTIFY ME IMMEDIATELY.
THERE'S MORE THAN ONE **WILDCARD** IN THIS YEAR'S CLASS.
WE MUST DO ALL WE CAN TO MAINTAIN THE CURRENT BALANCE OF POWER.

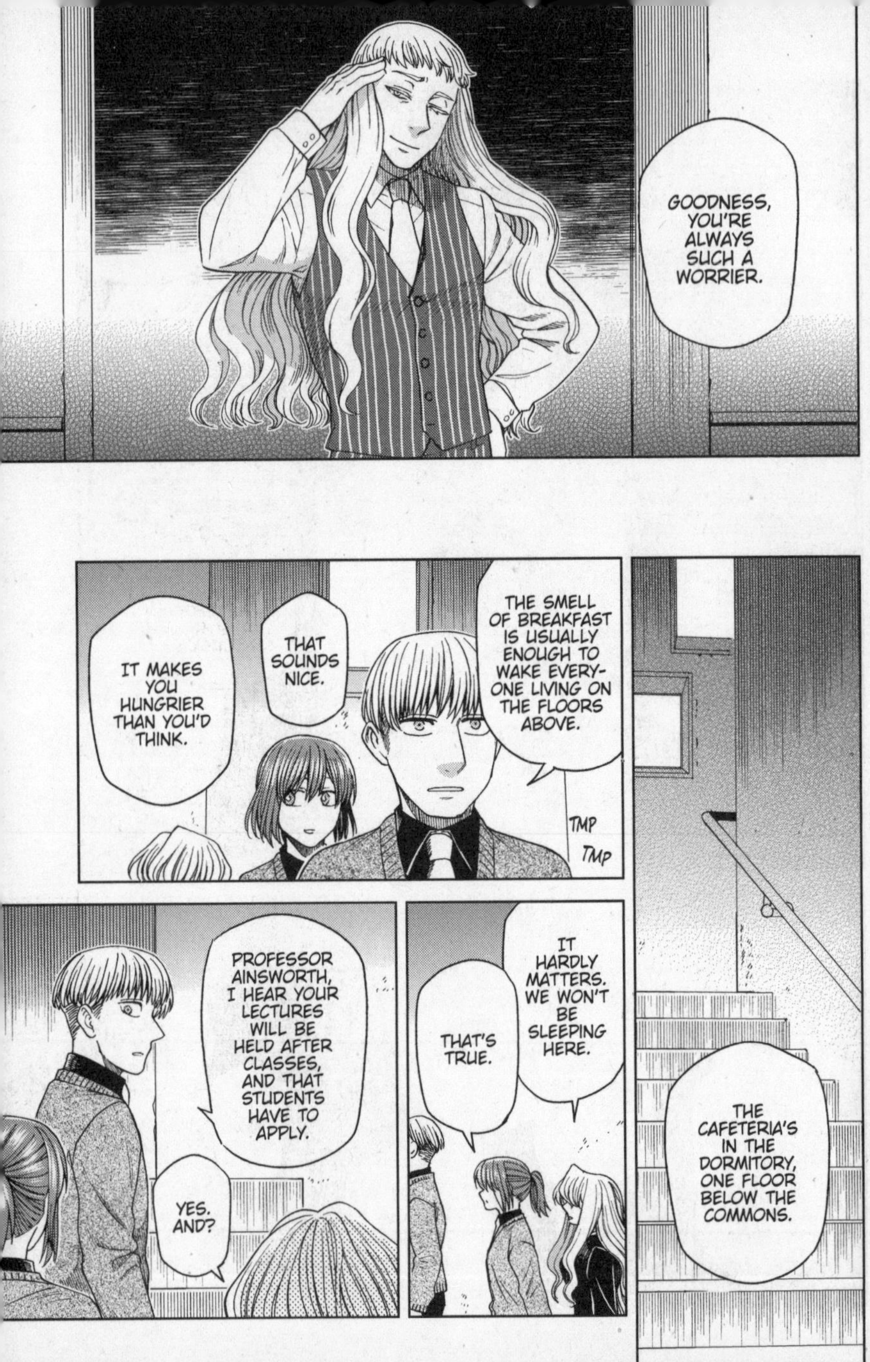
GOODNESS, YOU'RE ALWAYS SUCH A WORRIER.
THE CAFETERIA'S IN THE DORMITORY, ONE FLOOR BELOW THE COMMONS.
THE SMELL OF BREAKFAST IS USUALLY ENOUGH TO WAKE EVERY-ONE LIVING ON THE FLOORS ABOVE.
TMP
TMP
THAT SOUNDS NICE.
IT MAKES YOU HUNGRIER THAN YOU'D THINK.
IT HARDLY MATTERS. WE WON'T BE SLEEPING HERE.
THAT'S TRUE.
PROFESSOR AINSWORTH, I HEAR YOUR LECTURES WILL BE HELD AFTER CLASSES, AND THAT STUDENTS HAVE TO APPLY.
YES. AND?

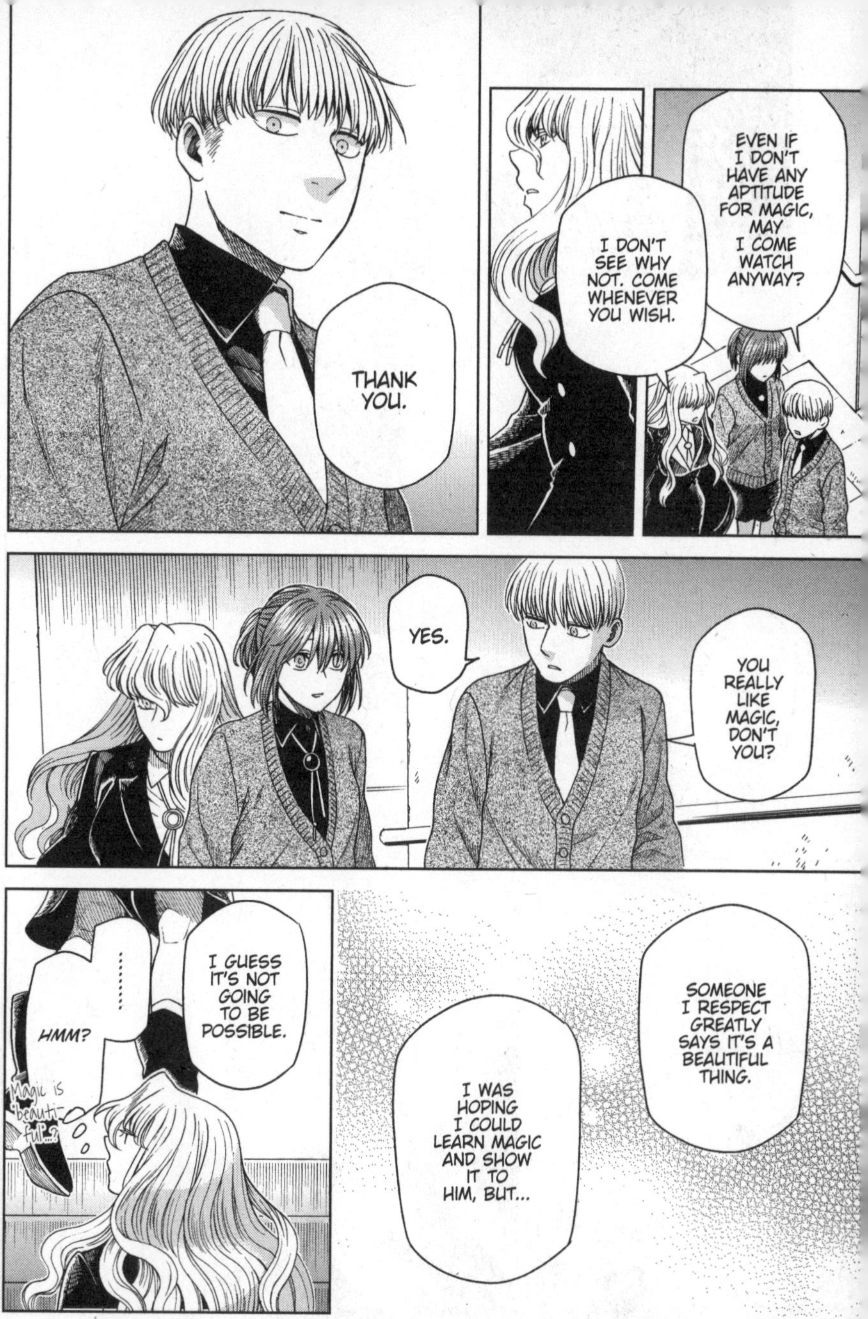
EVEN IF I DON'T HAVE ANY APTITUDE FOR MAGIC, MAY I COME WATCH ANYWAY?
I DON'T SEE WHY NOT. COME WHENEVER YOU WISH.
THANK YOU.
YOU REALLY LIKE MAGIC, DON'T YOU?
YES.
SOMEONE I RESPECT GREATLY SAYS IT'S A BEAUTIFUL THING.
I WAS HOPING I COULD LEARN MAGIC AND SHOW IT TO HIM, BUT...
I GUESS IT'S NOT GOING TO BE POSSIBLE.
......
HMM?
Magic is "beautiful"...?

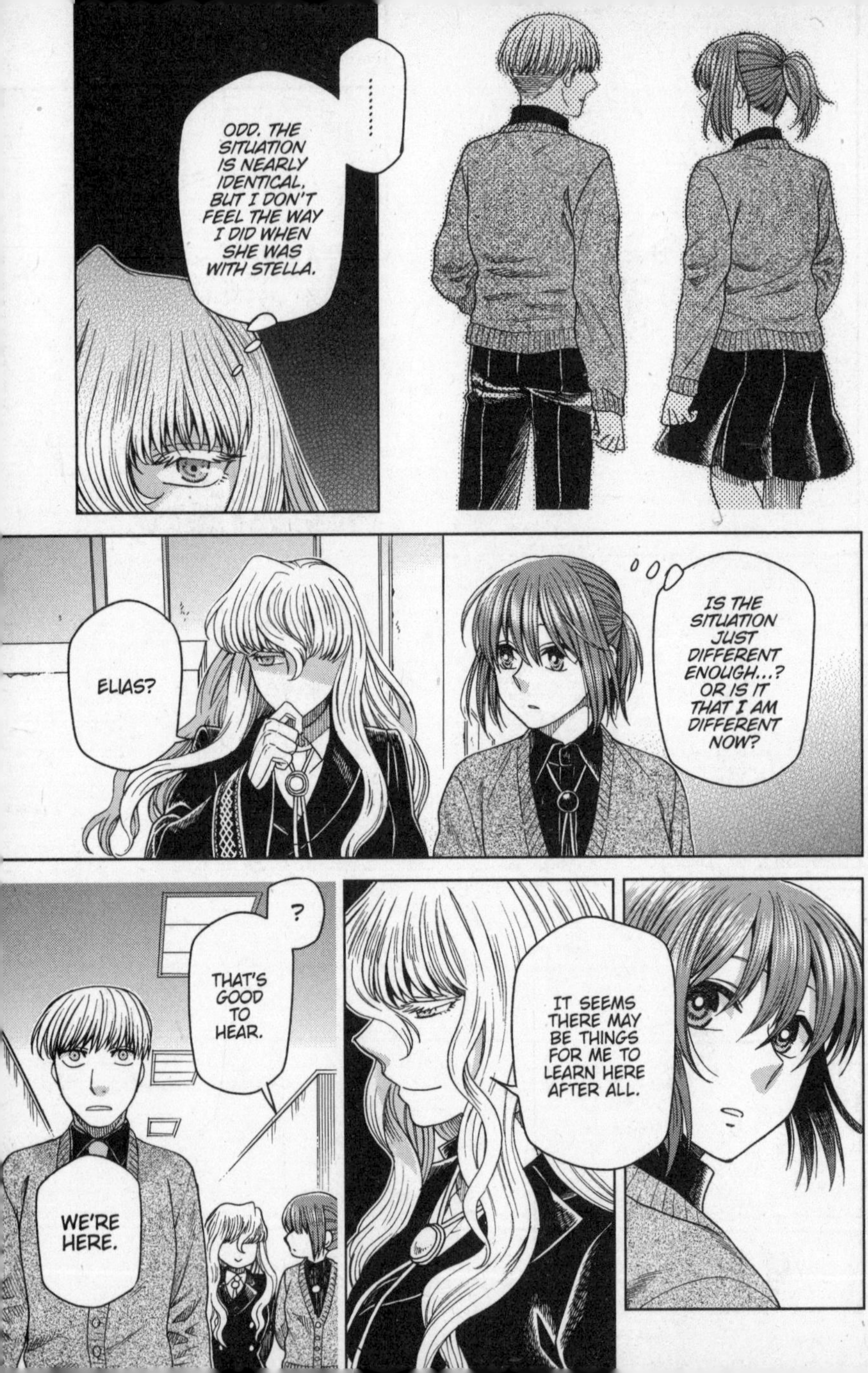
......
ODD. THE SITUATION IS NEARLY IDENTICAL, BUT I DON'T FEEL THE WAY I DID WHEN SHE WAS WITH STELLA.
IS THE SITUATION JUST DIFFERENT ENOUGH...? OR IS IT THAT I AM DIFFERENT NOW?
ELIAS?
IT SEEMS THERE MAY BE THINGS FOR ME TO LEARN HERE AFTER ALL.
?
THAT'S GOOD TO HEAR.
WE'RE HERE.

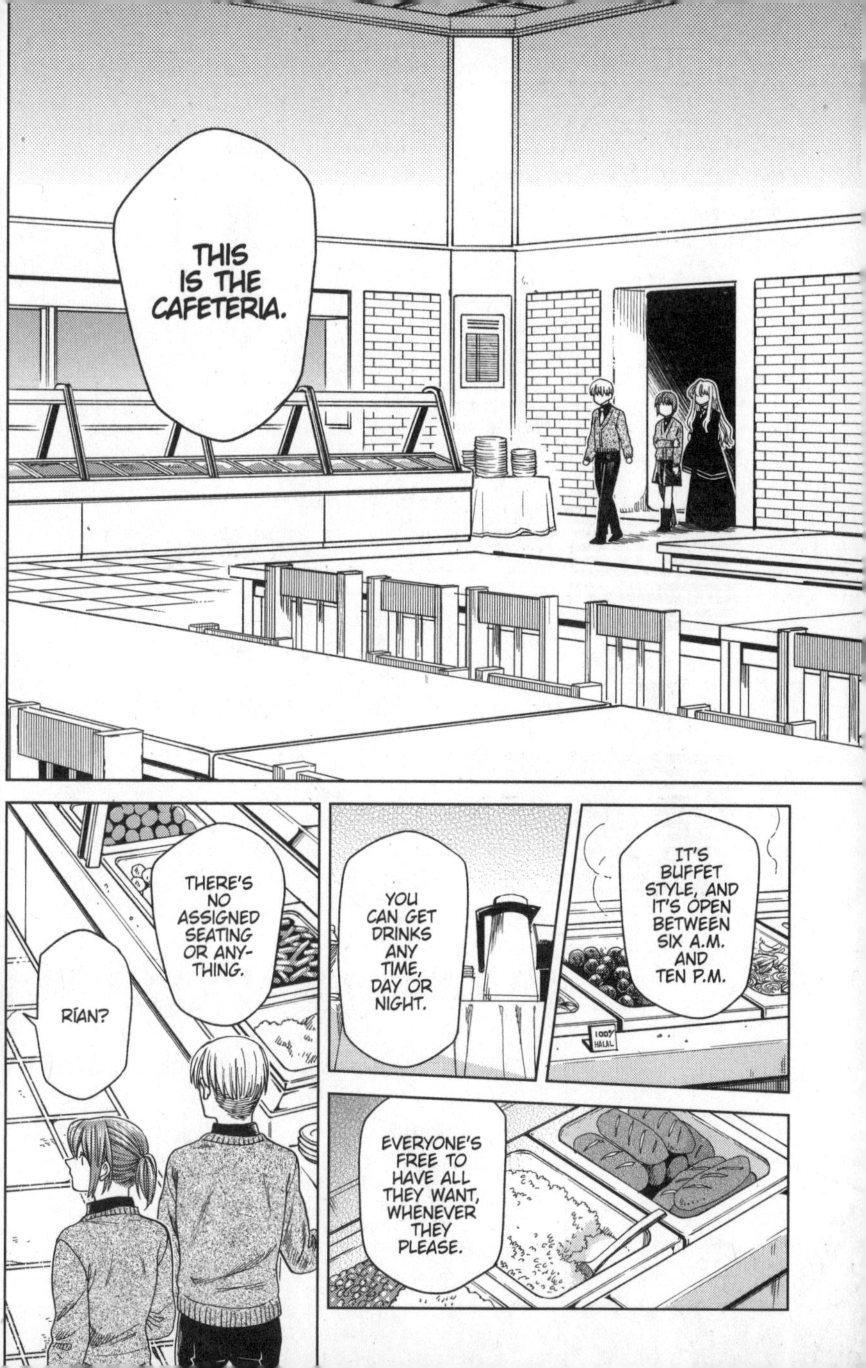
THIS IS THE CAFETERIA.
IT'S BUFFET STYLE, AND IT'S OPEN BETWEEN SIX A.M. AND TEN P.M.
100% HALAL
YOU CAN GET DRINKS ANY TIME, DAY OR NIGHT.
EVERYONE'S FREE TO HAVE ALL THEY WANT, WHENEVER THEY PLEASE.
THERE'S NO ASSIGNED SEATING OR ANY-THING.
RÍAN?

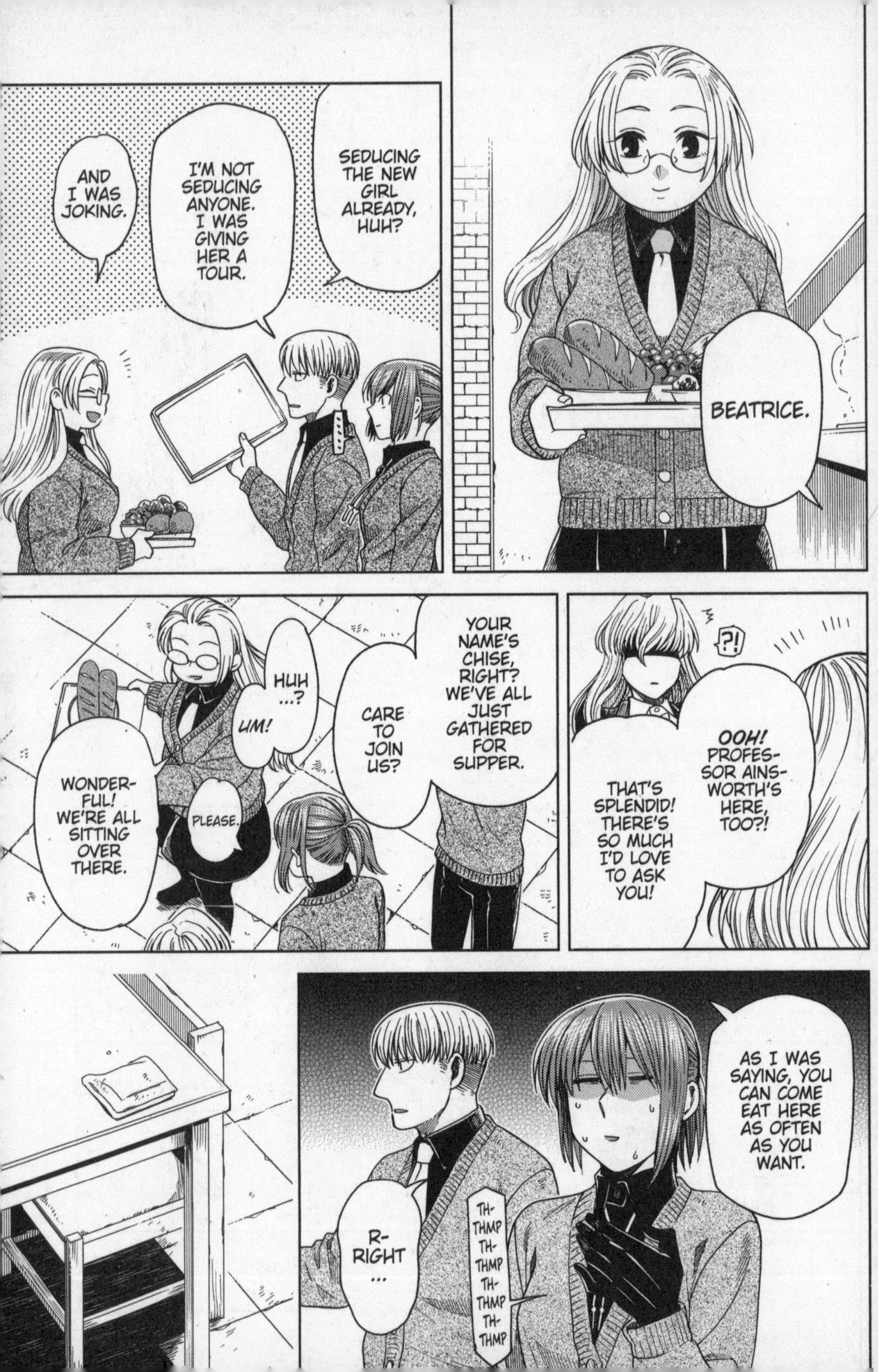
BEATRICE.
SEDUCING THE NEW GIRL ALREADY, HUH?
I'M NOT SEDUCING ANYONE. I WAS GIVING HER A TOUR.
AND I WAS JOKING.
?!
OOH! PROFESSOR AINSWORTH'S HERE, TOO?!
THAT'S SPLENDID! THERE'S SO MUCH I'D LOVE TO ASK YOU!
YOUR NAME'S CHISE, RIGHT? WE'VE ALL JUST GATHERED FOR SUPPER.
CARE TO JOIN US?
HUH ...?
UM!
PLEASE.
WONDERFUL! WE'RE ALL SITTING OVER THERE.
AS I WAS SAYING, YOU CAN COME EAT HERE AS OFTEN AS YOU WANT.
TH-THMP TH-THMP TH-THMP TH-THMP
R-RIGHT ...

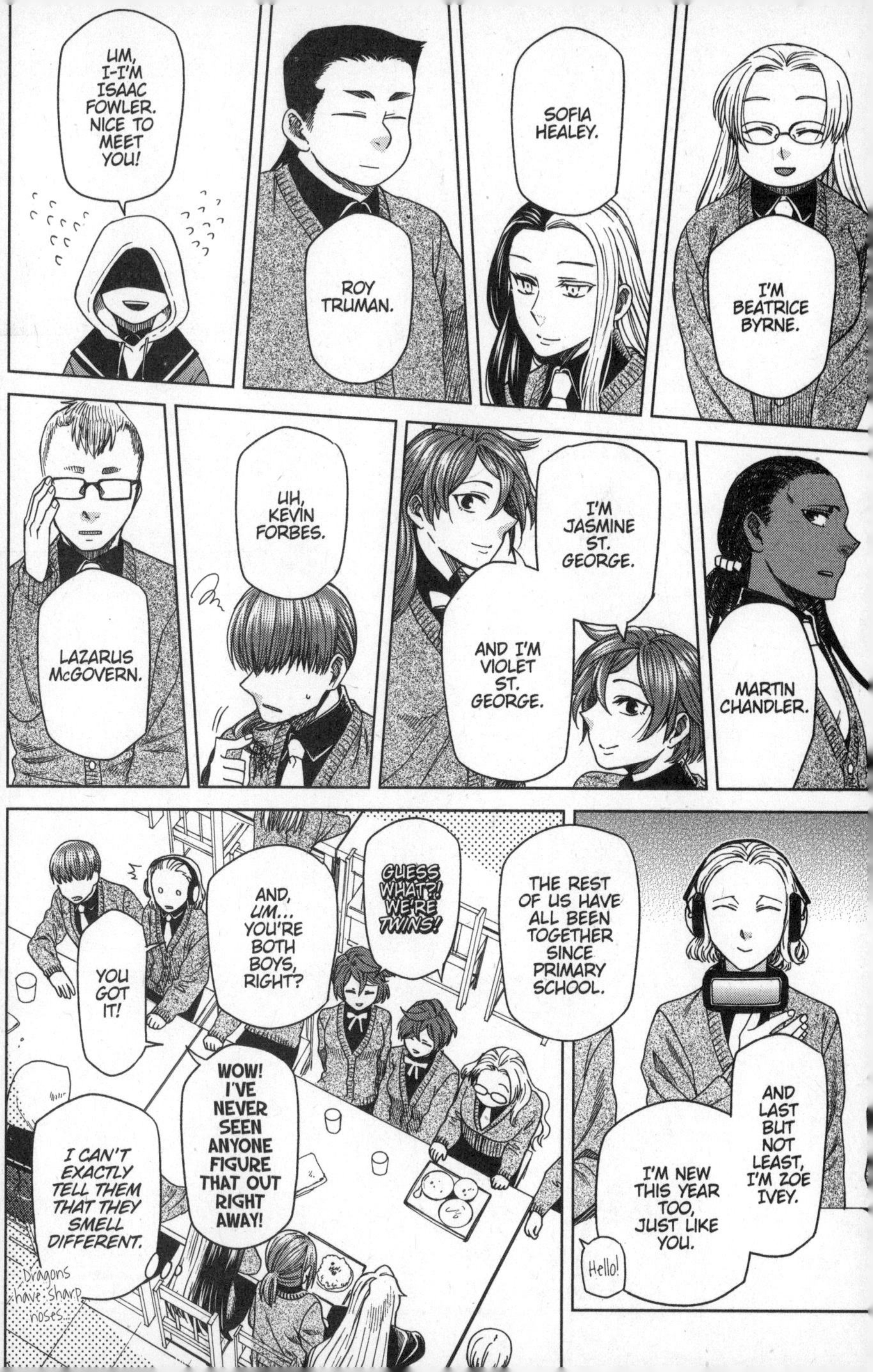
I'M BEATRICE BYRNE.
SOFIA HEALEY.
ROY TRUMAN.
UM, I-I'M ISAAC FOWLER. NICE TO MEET YOU!
MARTIN CHANDLER.
I'M JASMINE ST. GEORGE.
AND I'M VIOLET ST. GEORGE.
UH, KEVIN FORBES.
LAZARUS McGOVERN.
AND LAST BUT NOT LEAST, I'M ZOE IVEY.
I'M NEW THIS YEAR TOO, JUST LIKE YOU.
Hello!
THE REST OF US HAVE ALL BEEN TOGETHER SINCE PRIMARY SCHOOL.
GUESS WHAT?! WE'RE TWINS!
AND, UM... YOU'RE BOTH BOYS, RIGHT?
YOU GOT IT!
WOW! I'VE NEVER SEEN ANYONE FIGURE THAT OUT RIGHT AWAY!
I CAN'T EXACTLY TELL THEM THAT THEY SMELL DIFFERENT.
Dragons have sharp noses...

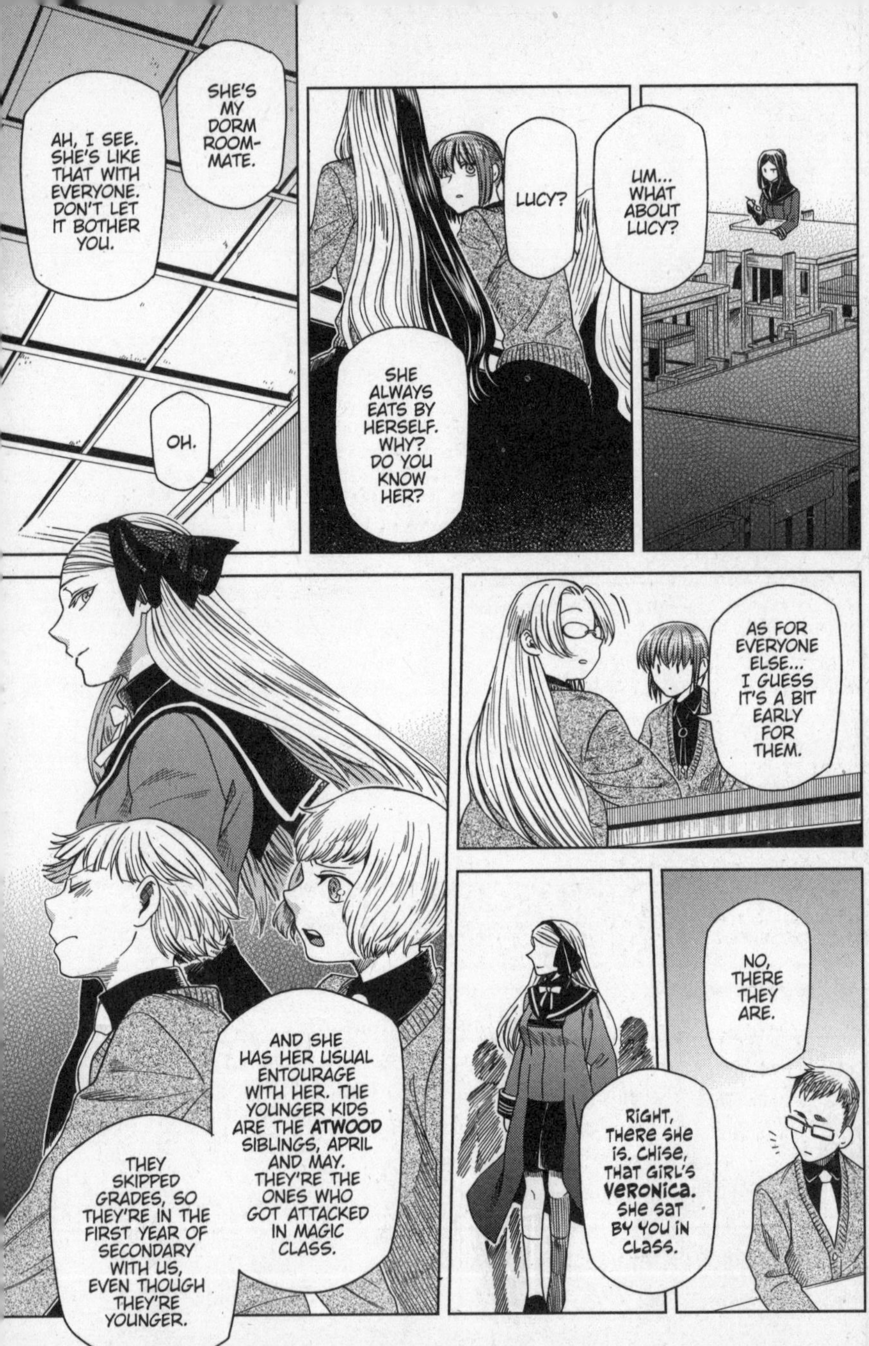
UM... WHAT ABOUT LUCY?
LUCY?
SHE ALWAYS EATS BY HERSELF. WHY? DO YOU KNOW HER?
SHE'S MY DORM ROOM-MATE.
AH, I SEE. SHE'S LIKE THAT WITH EVERYONE. DON'T LET IT BOTHER YOU.
OH.
AS FOR EVERYONE ELSE... I GUESS IT'S A BIT EARLY FOR THEM.
NO, THERE THEY ARE.
RIGHT, THERE SHE IS. CHISE, THAT GIRL'S **VERONICA.** SHE SAT BY YOU IN CLASS.
AND SHE HAS HER USUAL ENTOURAGE WITH HER. THE YOUNGER KIDS ARE THE **ATWOOD** SIBLINGS, APRIL AND MAY. THEY'RE THE ONES WHO GOT ATTACKED IN MAGIC CLASS.
THEY SKIPPED GRADES, SO THEY'RE IN THE FIRST YEAR OF SECONDARY WITH US, EVEN THOUGH THEY'RE YOUNGER.

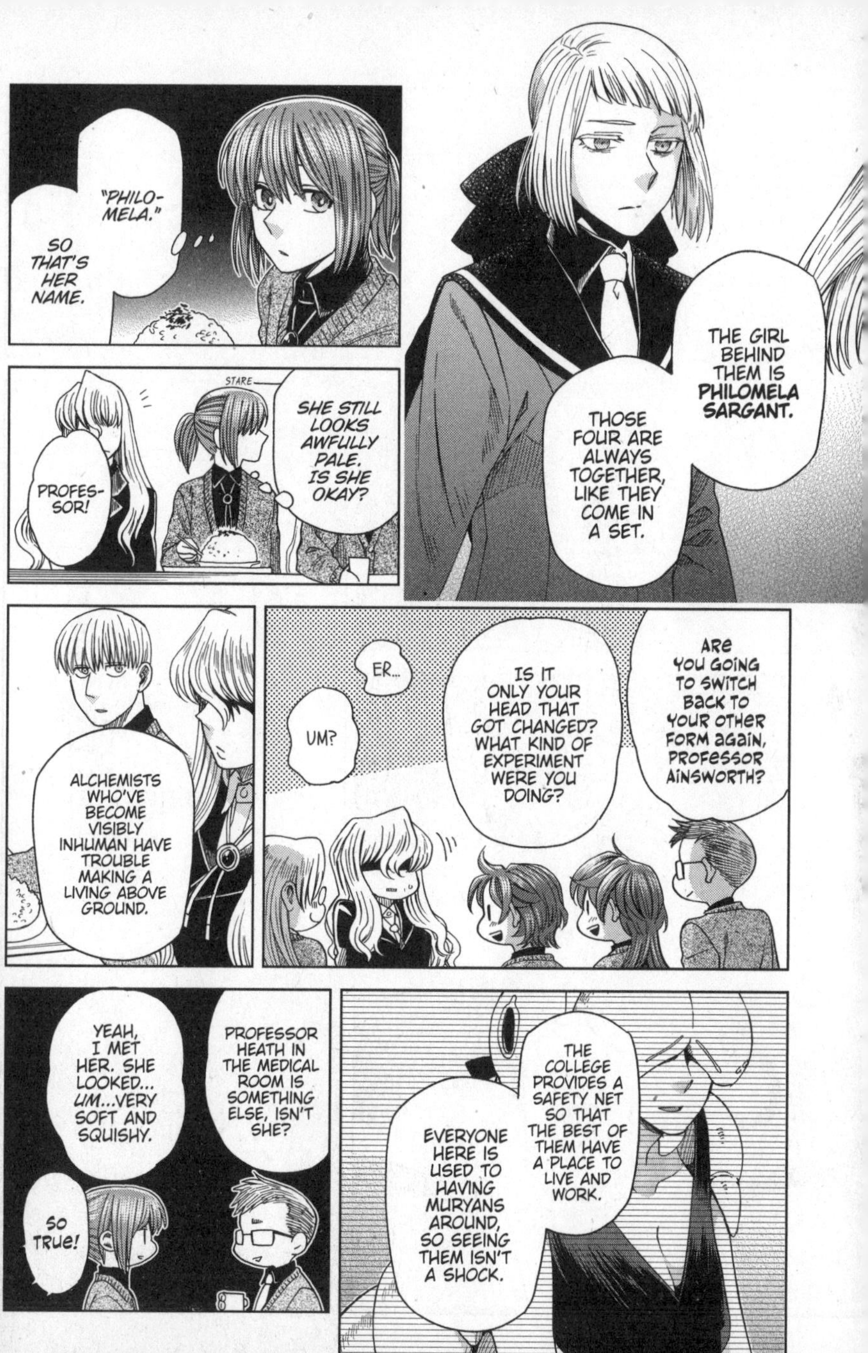
THE GIRL BEHIND THEM IS **PHILOMELA SARGANT.**
THOSE FOUR ARE ALWAYS TOGETHER, LIKE THEY COME IN A SET.
"PHILO-MELA."
...
SO THAT'S HER NAME.
STARE
SHE STILL LOOKS AWFULLY PALE. IS SHE OKAY?
PROFES-SOR!
ARE YOU GOING TO SWITCH BACK TO YOUR OTHER FORM AGAIN, PROFESSOR AINSWORTH?
IS IT ONLY YOUR HEAD THAT GOT CHANGED? WHAT KIND OF EXPERIMENT WERE YOU DOING?
ER...
UM?
ALCHEMISTS WHO'VE BECOME VISIBLY INHUMAN HAVE TROUBLE MAKING A LIVING ABOVE GROUND.
THE COLLEGE PROVIDES A SAFETY NET SO THAT THE BEST OF THEM HAVE A PLACE TO LIVE AND WORK.
EVERYONE HERE IS USED TO HAVING MURYANS AROUND, SO SEEING THEM ISN'T A SHOCK.
PROFESSOR HEATH IN THE MEDICAL ROOM IS SOMETHING ELSE, ISN'T SHE?
YEAH, I MET HER. SHE LOOKED... *UM*...VERY SOFT AND SQUISHY.
SO TRUE!

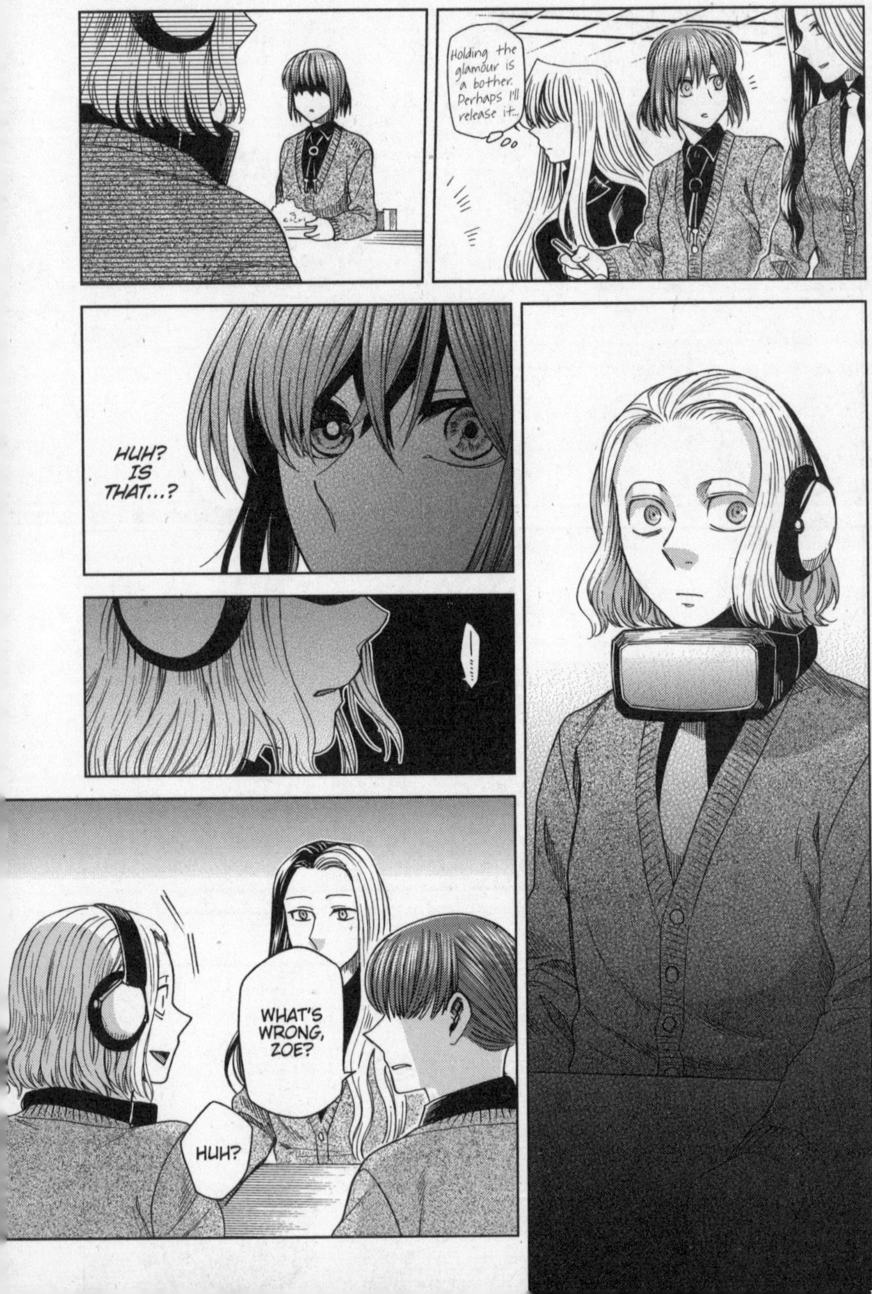
Holding the glamour is a bother. Perhaps I'll release it...
HUH? IS THAT...?
WHAT'S WRONG, ZOE?
HUH?

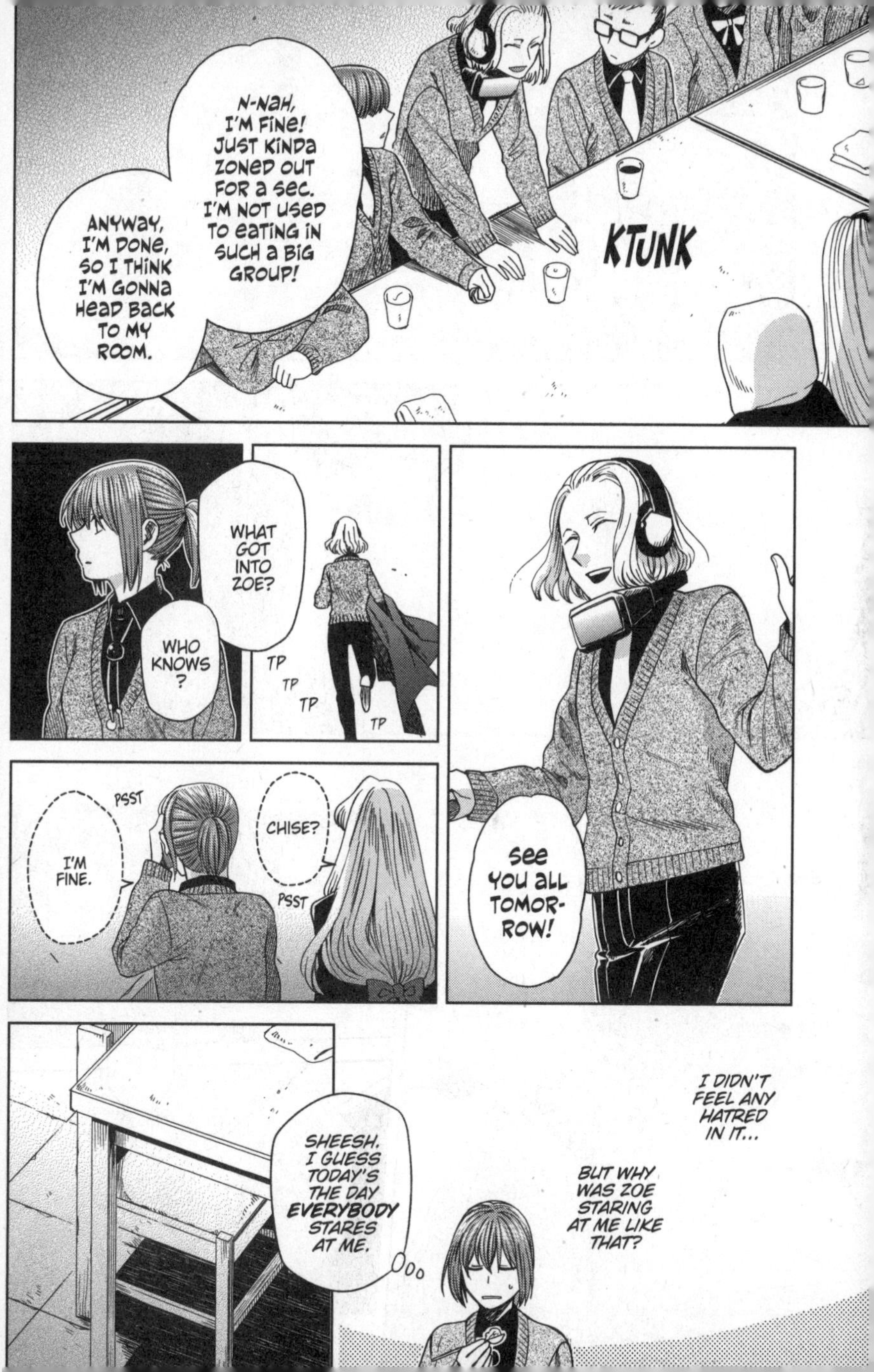
N-NAH, I'M FINE! JUST KINDA ZONED OUT FOR A SEC. I'M NOT USED TO EATING IN SUCH A BIG GROUP!
ANYWAY, I'M DONE, SO I THINK I'M GONNA HEAD BACK TO MY ROOM.
KTUNK
SEE YOU ALL TOMOR-ROW!
TP
TP
TP
TP
WHAT GOT INTO ZOE?
WHO KNOWS?
CHISE?
PSST
PSST
I'M FINE.
I DIDN'T FEEL ANY HATRED IN IT...
BUT WHY WAS ZOE STARING AT ME LIKE THAT?
SHEESH. I GUESS TODAY'S THE DAY EVERYBODY STARES AT ME.

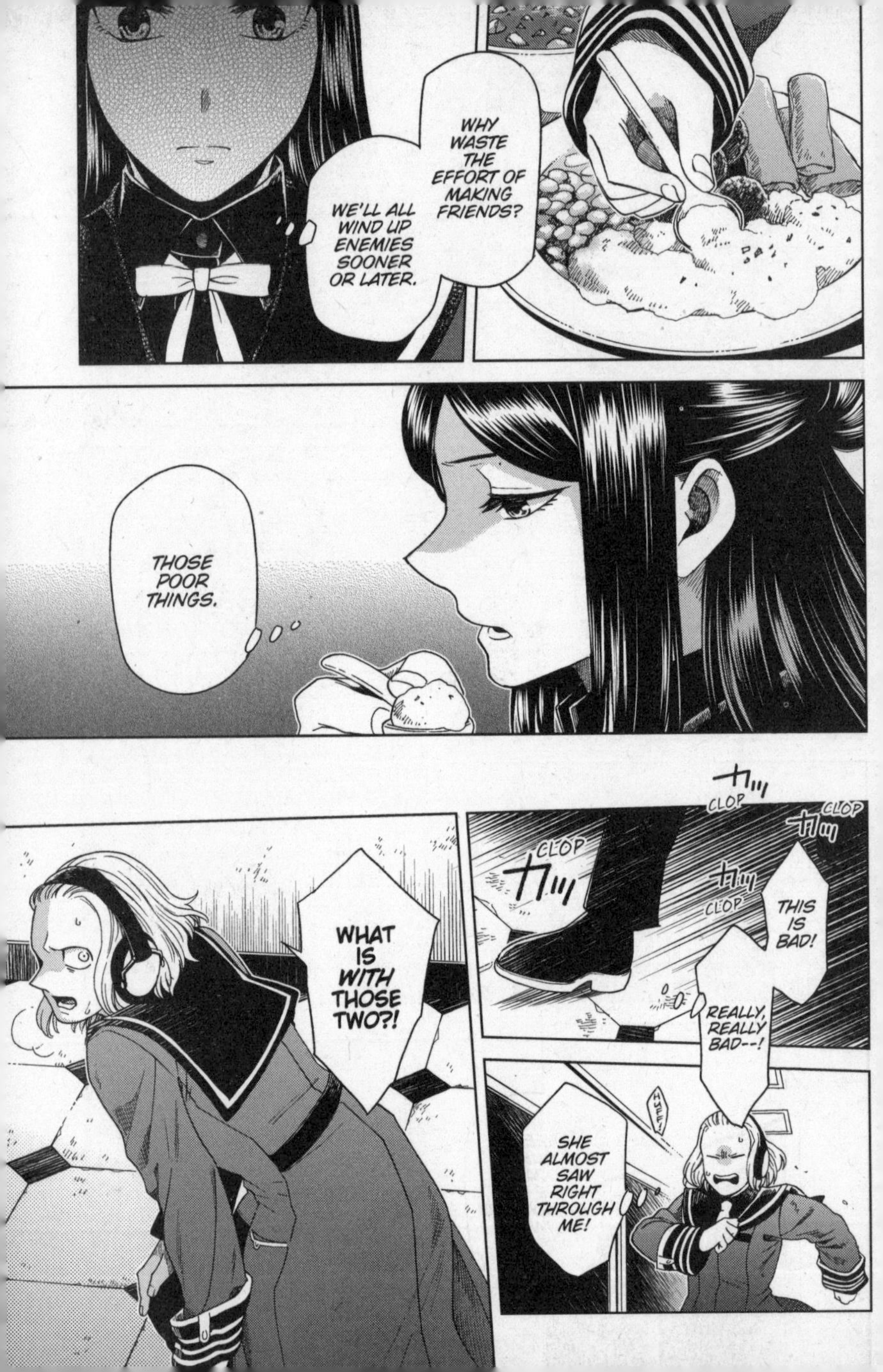
WHY WASTE THE EFFORT OF MAKING FRIENDS?
WE'LL ALL WIND UP ENEMIES SOONER OR LATER.
THOSE POOR THINGS.
カッ
CLOP
CLOP
カッ
CLOP
カッ
カッ
CLOP
THIS IS BAD!
REALLY, REALLY BAD--!
SHE ALMOST SAW RIGHT THROUGH ME!
WHAT IS WITH THOSE TWO?!

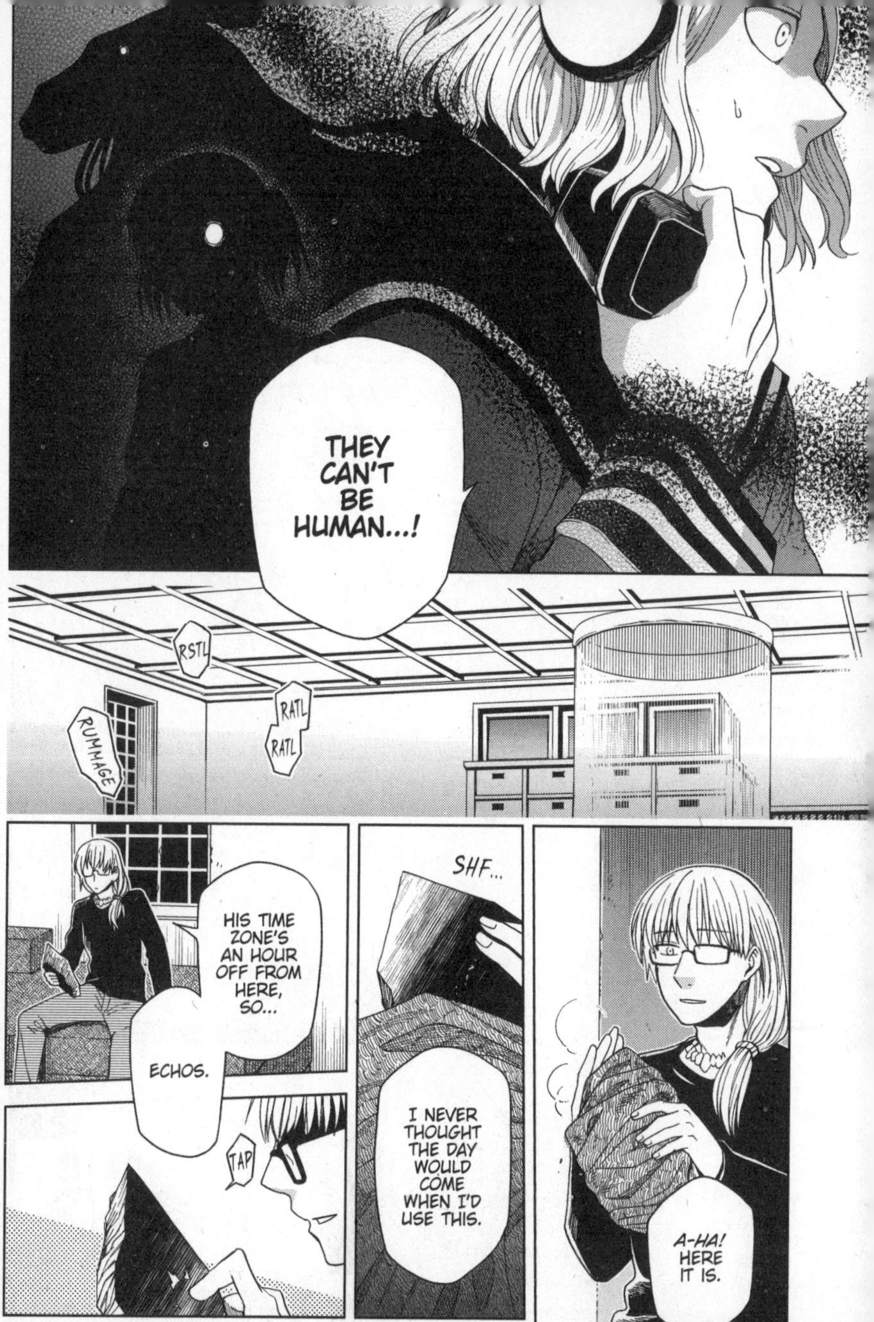
THEY CAN'T BE HUMAN...!
RATL
RATL
RSTL
RUMMAGE
A-HA! HERE IT IS.
SHF...
I NEVER THOUGHT THE DAY WOULD COME WHEN I'D USE THIS.
HIS TIME ZONE'S AN HOUR OFF FROM HERE, SO...
ECHOS.
TAP

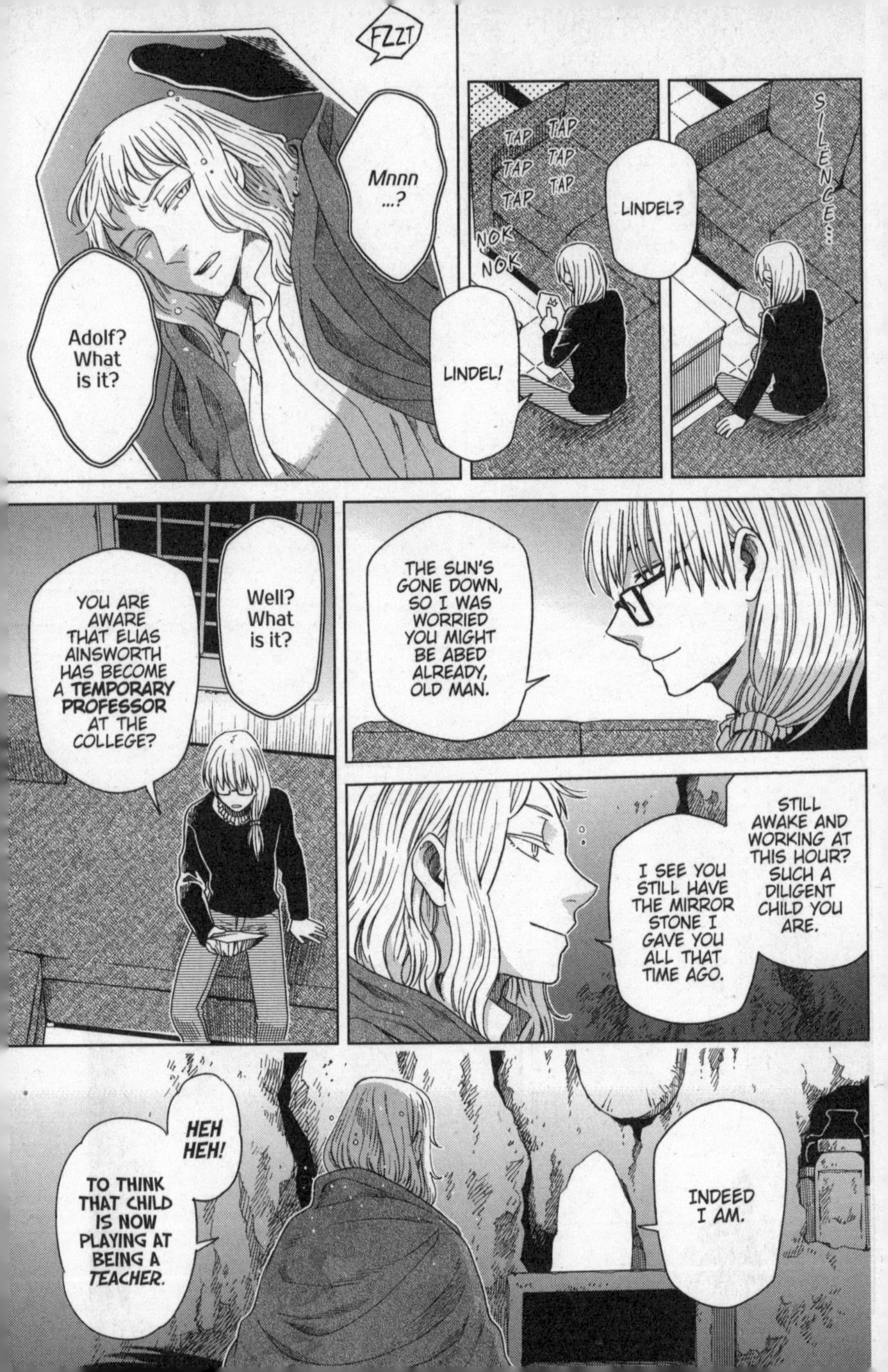
LINDEL?
SILENCE...
TAP TAP TAP TAP TAP TAP
NOK NOK
LINDEL!
FZZT
Mnnn ...?
Adolf? What is it?
THE SUN'S GONE DOWN, SO I WAS WORRIED YOU MIGHT BE ABED ALREADY, OLD MAN.
STILL AWAKE AND WORKING AT THIS HOUR? SUCH A DILIGENT CHILD YOU ARE.
I SEE YOU STILL HAVE THE MIRROR STONE I GAVE YOU ALL THAT TIME AGO.
Well? What is it?
YOU ARE AWARE THAT ELIAS AINSWORTH HAS BECOME A **TEMPORARY PROFESSOR** AT THE COLLEGE?
INDEED I AM.
HEH HEH!
TO THINK THAT CHILD IS NOW PLAYING AT BEING A *TEACHER*.

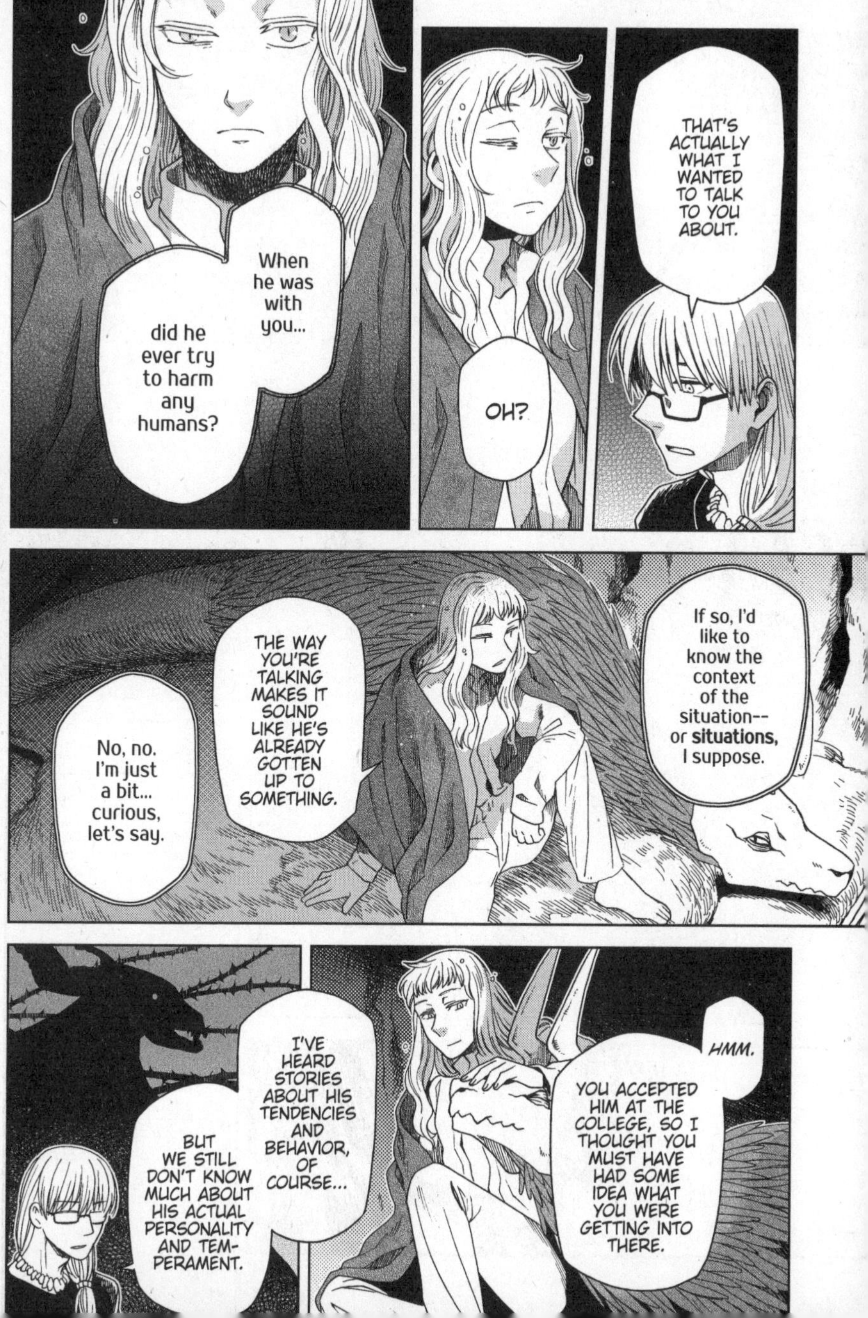
THAT'S ACTUALLY WHAT I WANTED TO TALK TO YOU ABOUT.
OH?
When he was with you...
did he ever try to harm any humans?
If so, I'd like to know the context of the situation-- or **situations,** I suppose.
THE WAY YOU'RE TALKING MAKES IT SOUND LIKE HE'S ALREADY GOTTEN UP TO SOMETHING.
No, no. I'm just a bit... curious, let's say.
HMM.
YOU ACCEPTED HIM AT THE COLLEGE, SO I THOUGHT YOU MUST HAVE HAD SOME IDEA WHAT YOU WERE GETTING INTO THERE.
I'VE HEARD STORIES ABOUT HIS TENDENCIES AND BEHAVIOR, OF COURSE...
BUT WE STILL DON'T KNOW MUCH ABOUT HIS ACTUAL PERSONALITY AND TEMPERAMENT.

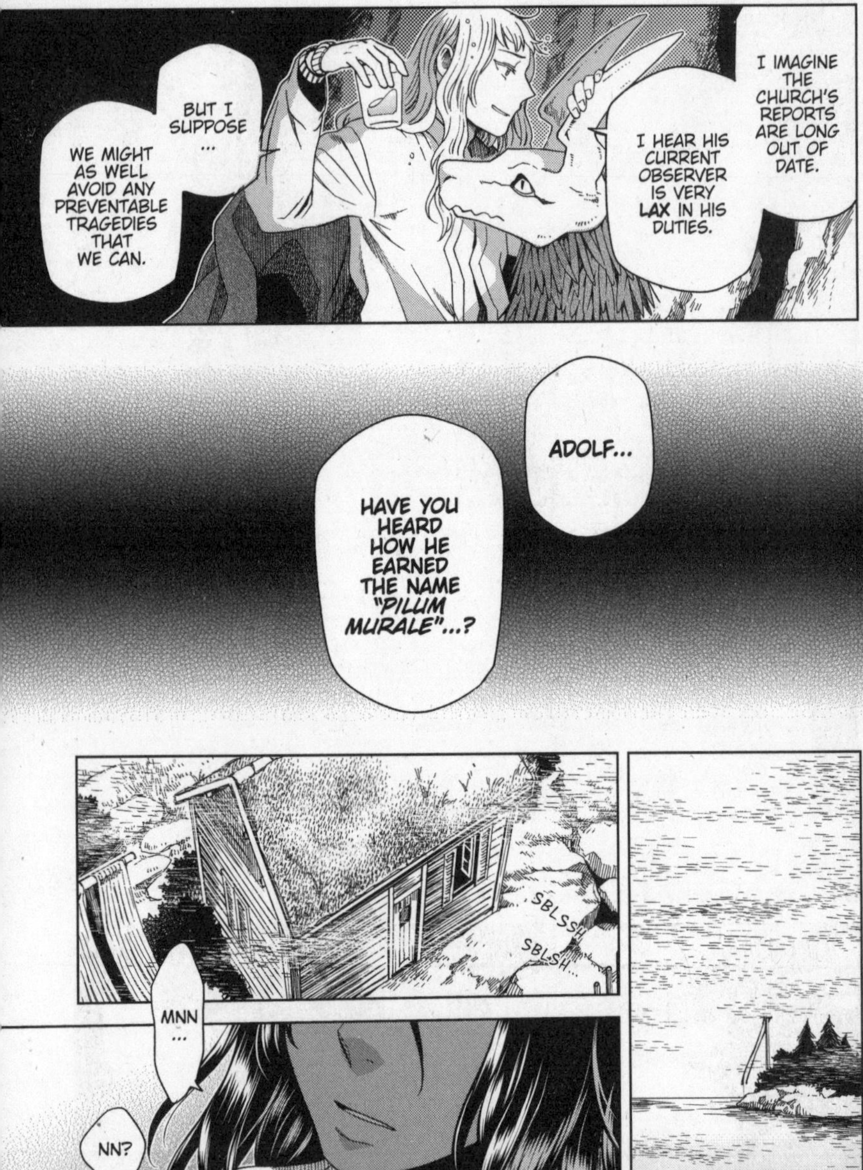
I IMAGINE THE CHURCH'S REPORTS ARE LONG OUT OF DATE.
I HEAR HIS CURRENT OBSERVER IS VERY **LAX** IN HIS DUTIES.
BUT I SUPPOSE ...
WE MIGHT AS WELL AVOID ANY PREVENTABLE TRAGEDIES THAT WE CAN.
ADOLF...
HAVE YOU HEARD HOW HE EARNED THE NAME *"PILUM MURALE"*...?
SBLSSH
SBLSH...
MNN ...
NN?

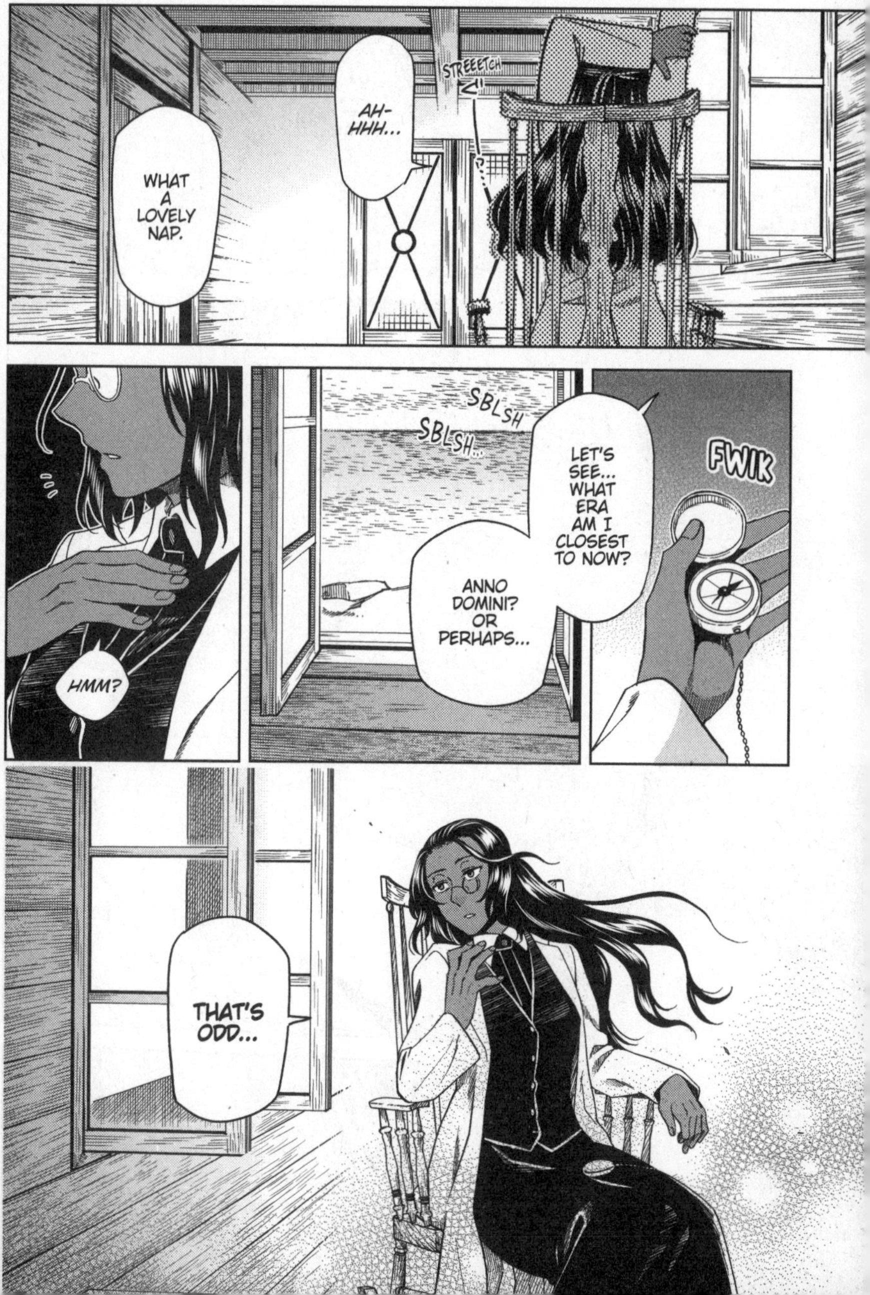
STREEETCH
AH-HHH...
WHAT A LOVELY NAP.
FWIK
LET'S SEE... WHAT ERA AM I CLOSEST TO NOW?
SBLSH
SBLSH...
ANNO DOMINI? OR PERHAPS...
HMM?
THAT'S ODD...

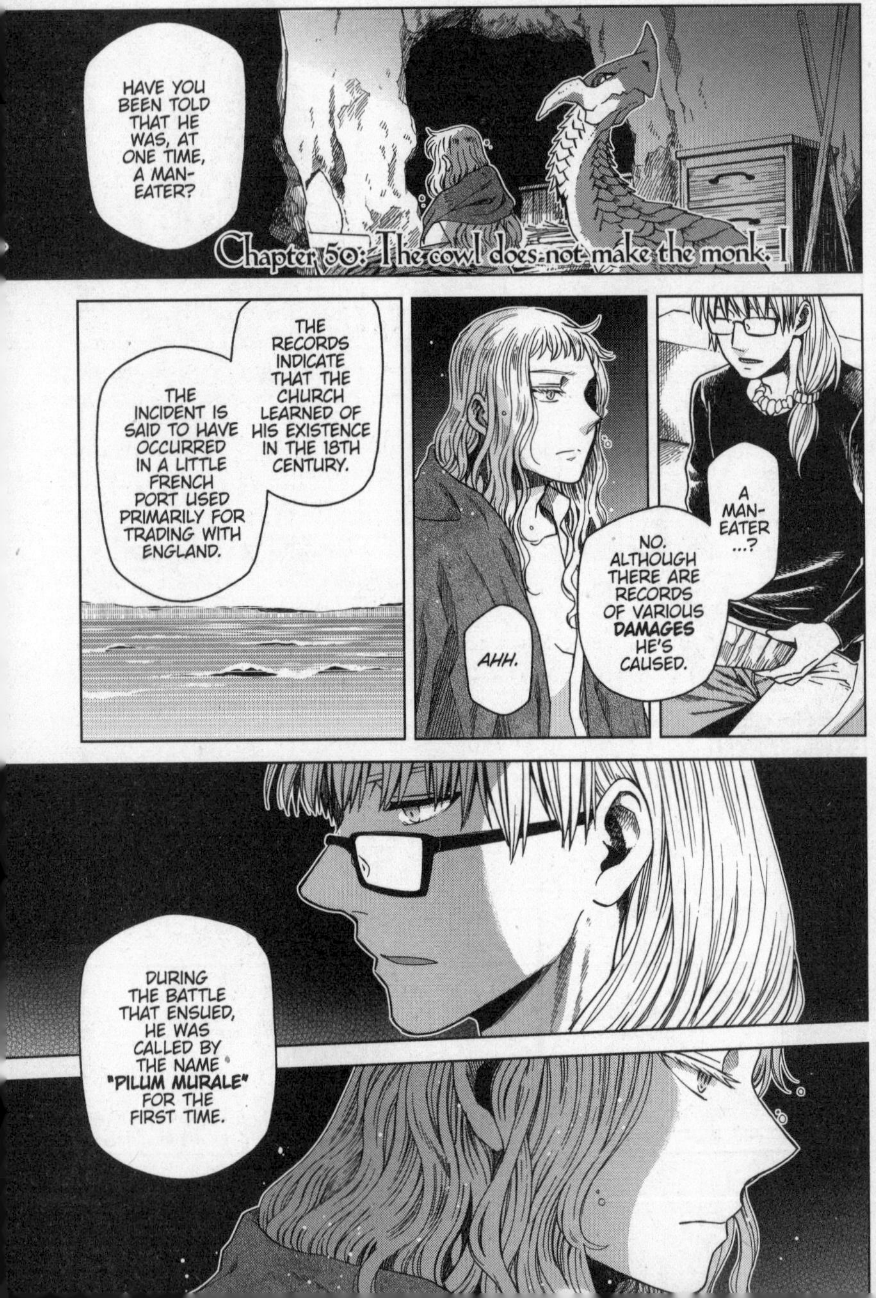
HAVE YOU BEEN TOLD THAT HE WAS, AT ONE TIME, A MAN-EATER?
Chapter 50: The cowl does not make the monk. I
A MAN-EATER ...?
NO. ALTHOUGH THERE ARE RECORDS OF VARIOUS **DAMAGES** HE'S CAUSED.
AHH.
THE RECORDS INDICATE THAT THE CHURCH LEARNED OF HIS EXISTENCE IN THE 18TH CENTURY.
THE INCIDENT IS SAID TO HAVE OCCURRED IN A LITTLE FRENCH PORT USED PRIMARILY FOR TRADING WITH ENGLAND.
DURING THE BATTLE THAT ENSUED, HE WAS CALLED BY THE NAME **"PILUM MURALE"** FOR THE FIRST TIME.

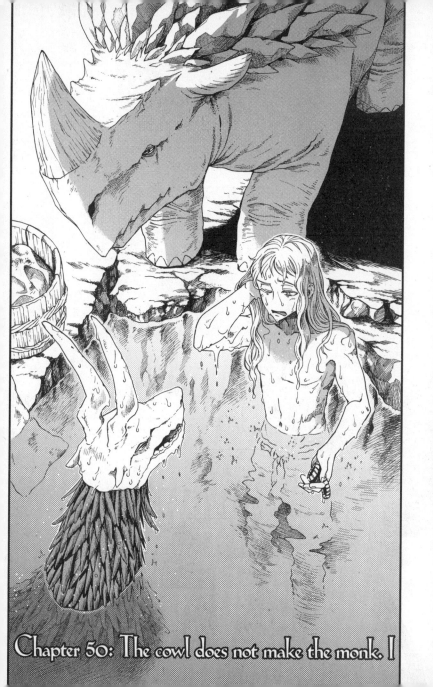

Chapter 50: The cowl does not make the monk. I

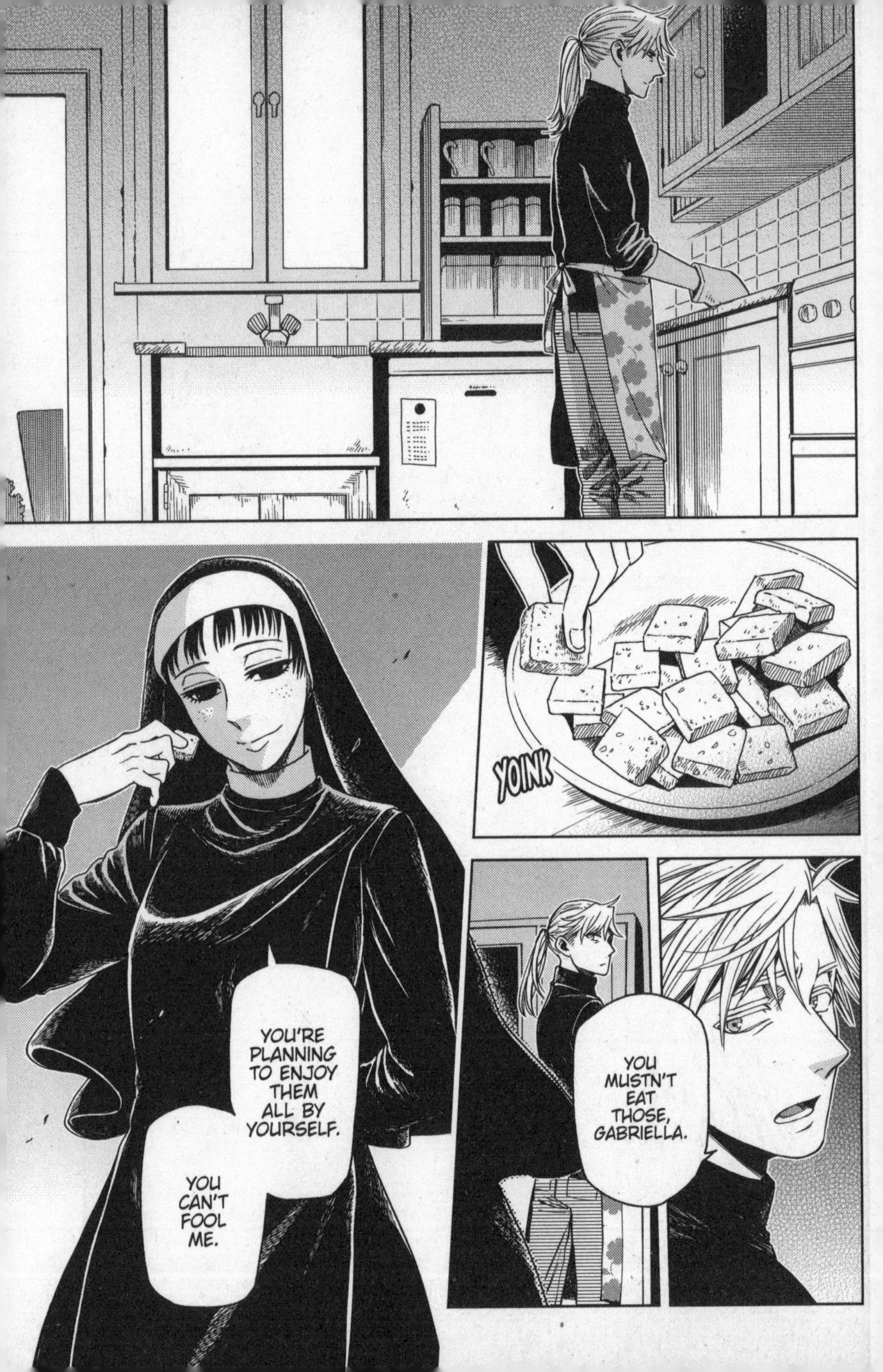
YOINK
YOU MUSTN'T EAT THOSE, GABRIELLA.
YOU'RE PLANNING TO ENJOY THEM ALL BY YOURSELF.
YOU CAN'T FOOL ME.

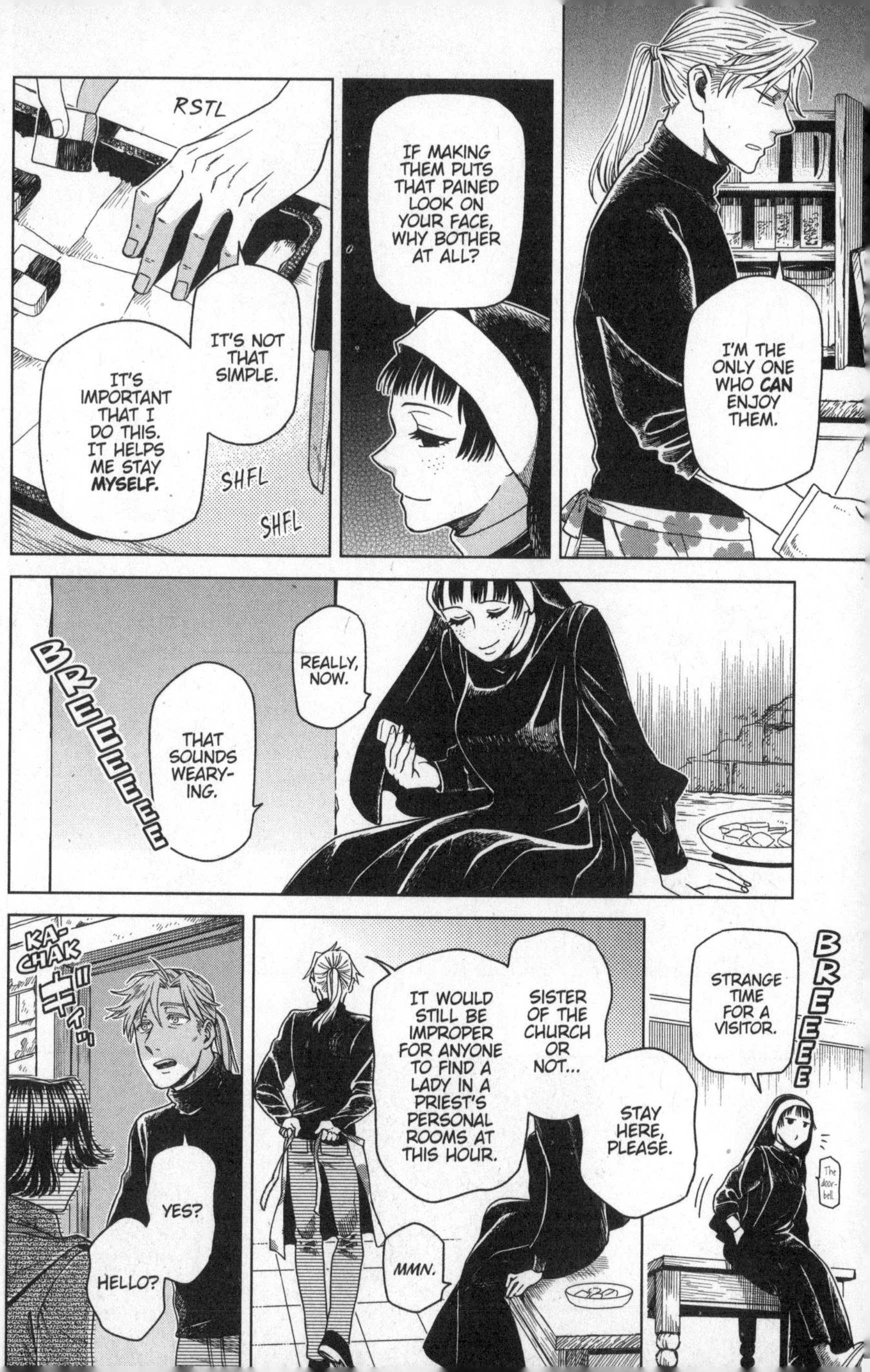
I'M THE ONLY ONE WHO **CAN** ENJOY THEM.
IF MAKING THEM PUTS THAT PAINED LOOK ON YOUR FACE, WHY BOTHER AT ALL?
RSTL
IT'S NOT THAT SIMPLE.
IT'S IMPORTANT THAT I DO THIS. IT HELPS ME STAY **MYSELF.**
SHFL
SHFL
REALLY, NOW.
THAT SOUNDS WEARY-ING.
BREEEEEEEE
BREEEE
STRANGE TIME FOR A VISITOR.
The door-bell.
SISTER OF THE CHURCH OR NOT...
IT WOULD STILL BE IMPROPER FOR ANYONE TO FIND A LADY IN A PRIEST'S PERSONAL ROOMS AT THIS HOUR.
STAY HERE, PLEASE.
MMN.
KA-CHAK
ギィ
YES?
HELLO?

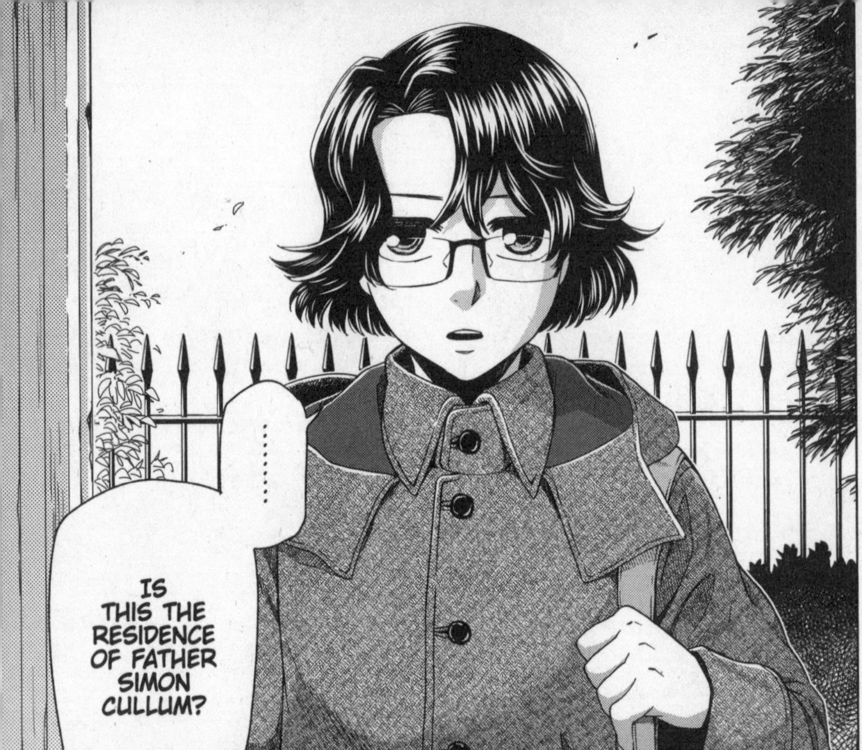
......
IS THIS THE RESIDENCE OF FATHER SIMON CULLUM?
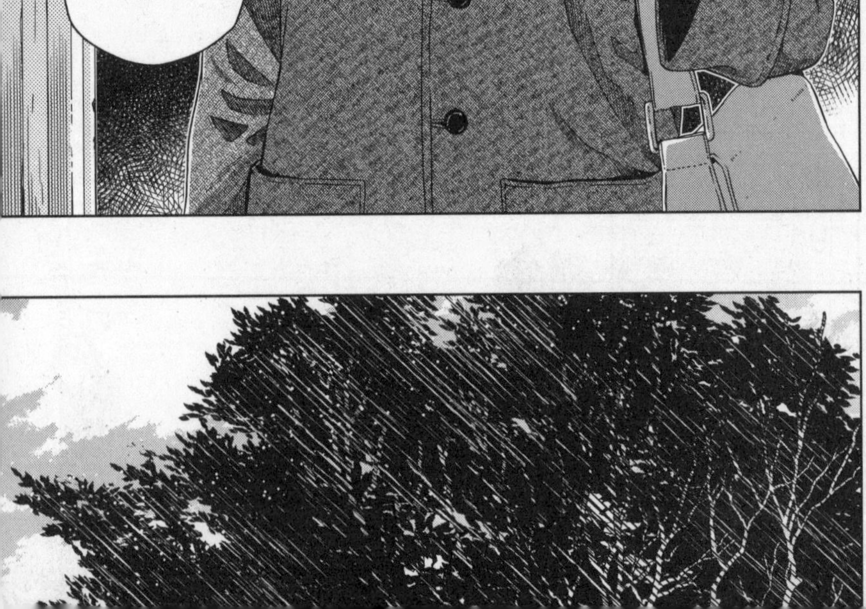

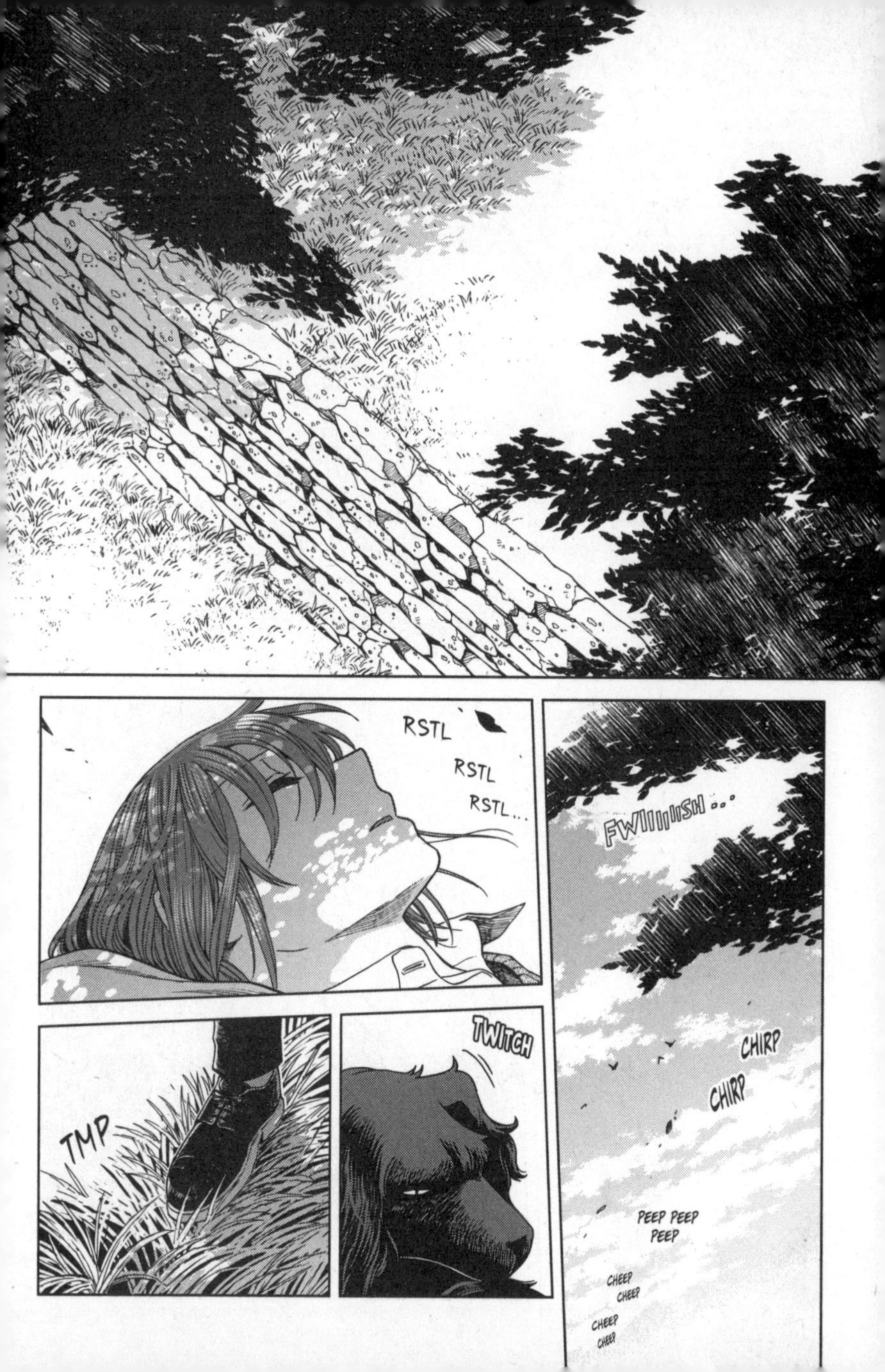
FWIIIIISH...
CHIRP
CHIRP
PEEP PEEP PEEP
CHEEP CHEEP
CHEEP CHEEP
RSTL
RSTL
RSTL...
TWITCH
TMP

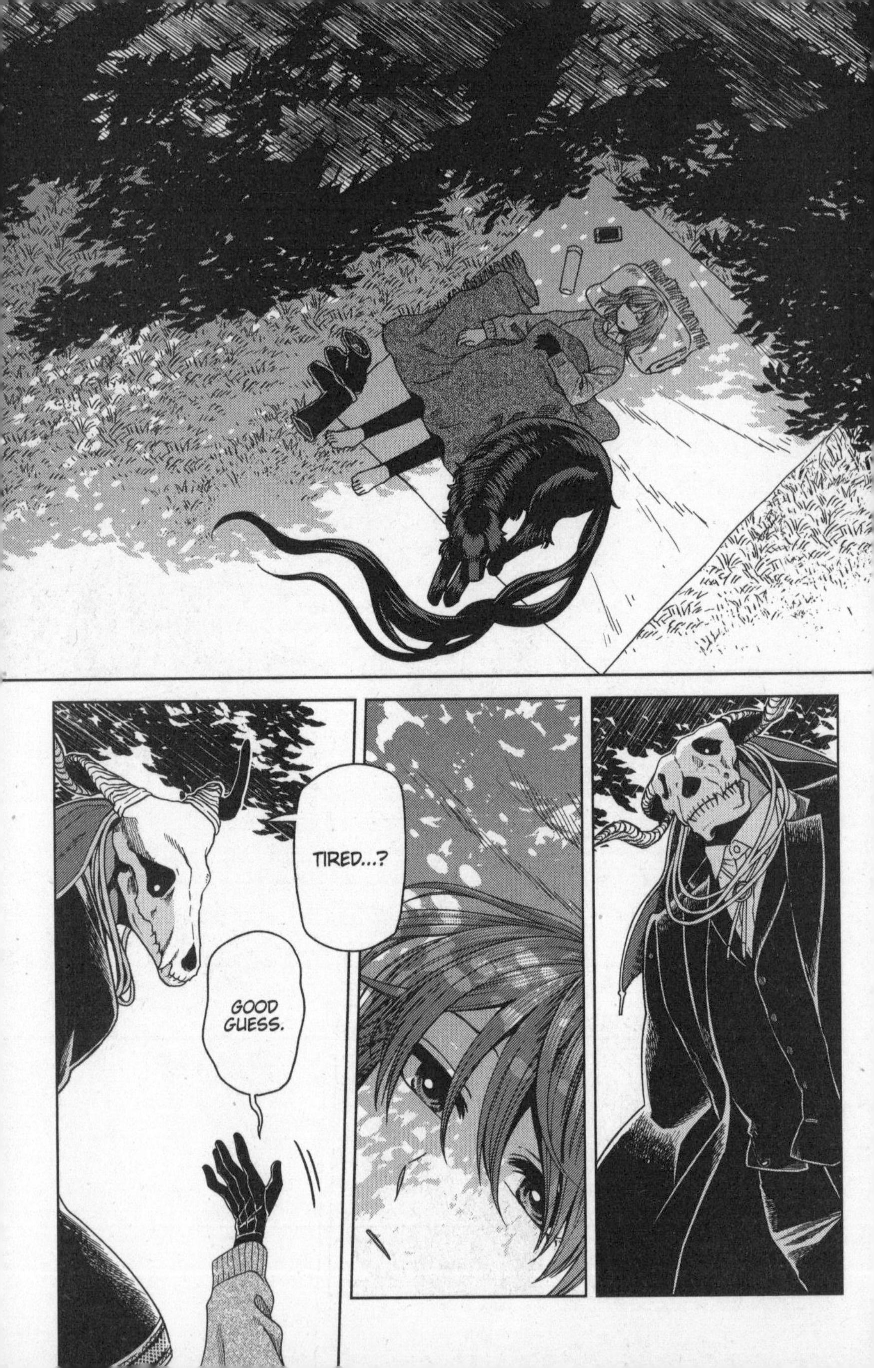
TIRED...?
GOOD GUESS.

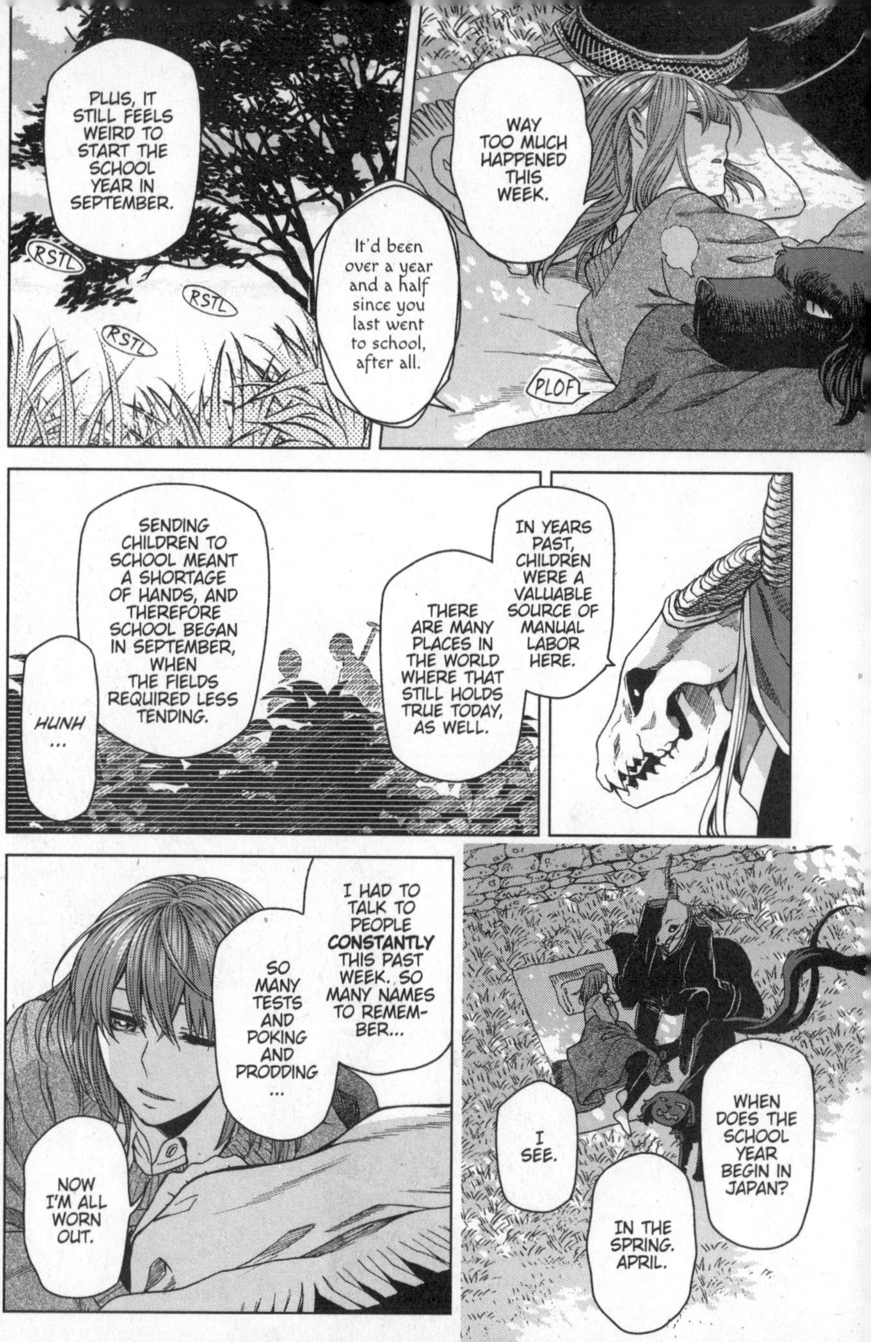
WAY TOO MUCH HAPPENED THIS WEEK.
PLOF
It'd been over a year and a half since you last went to school, after all.
PLUS, IT STILL FEELS WEIRD TO START THE SCHOOL YEAR IN SEPTEMBER.
RSTL
RSTL
RSTL
IN YEARS PAST, CHILDREN WERE A VALUABLE SOURCE OF MANUAL LABOR HERE.
THERE ARE MANY PLACES IN THE WORLD WHERE THAT STILL HOLDS TRUE TODAY, AS WELL.
SENDING CHILDREN TO SCHOOL MEANT A SHORTAGE OF HANDS, AND THEREFORE SCHOOL BEGAN IN SEPTEMBER, WHEN THE FIELDS REQUIRED LESS TENDING.
HUNH ...
WHEN DOES THE SCHOOL YEAR BEGIN IN JAPAN?
IN THE SPRING. APRIL.
I SEE.
I HAD TO TALK TO PEOPLE **CONSTANTLY** THIS PAST WEEK. SO MANY NAMES TO REMEMBER...
SO MANY TESTS AND POKING AND PRODDING ...
NOW I'M ALL WORN OUT.

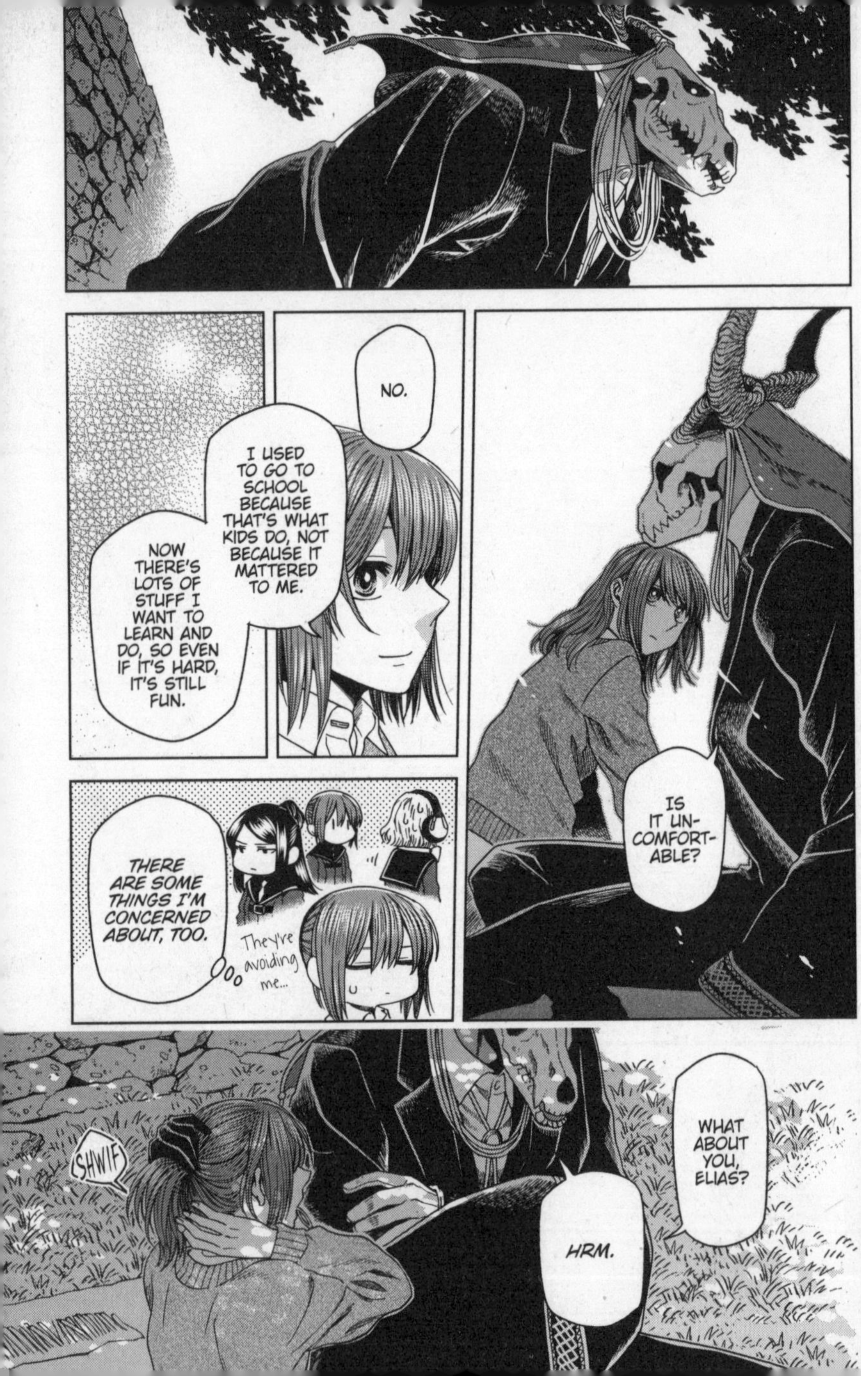

IS IT UN-COMFORTABLE?
NO.
I USED TO GO TO SCHOOL BECAUSE THAT'S WHAT KIDS DO, NOT BECAUSE IT MATTERED TO ME.
NOW THERE'S LOTS OF STUFF I WANT TO LEARN AND DO, SO EVEN IF IT'S HARD, IT'S STILL FUN.
THERE ARE SOME THINGS I'M CONCERNED ABOUT, TOO.
They're avoiding me...
WHAT ABOUT YOU, ELIAS?
HRM.
SHWIF

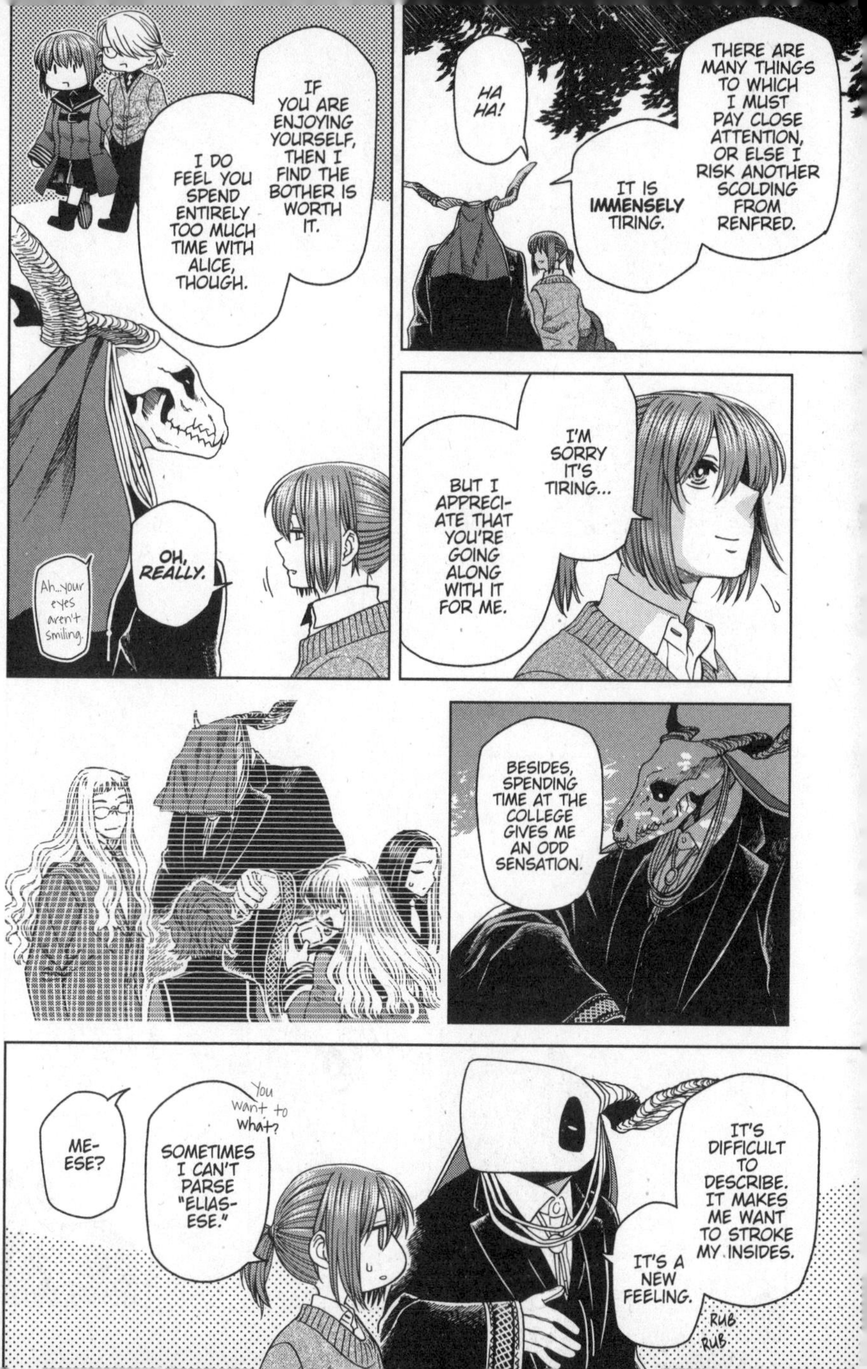

THERE ARE MANY THINGS TO WHICH I MUST PAY CLOSE ATTENTION, OR ELSE I RISK ANOTHER SCOLDING FROM RENFRED.
IT IS **IMMENSELY** TIRING.
HA HA!
I'M SORRY IT'S TIRING...
BUT I APPRECIATE THAT YOU'RE GOING ALONG WITH IT FOR ME.
IF YOU ARE ENJOYING YOURSELF, THEN I FIND THE BOTHER IS WORTH IT.
I DO FEEL YOU SPEND ENTIRELY TOO MUCH TIME WITH ALICE, THOUGH.
OH, REALLY.
Ah...your eyes aren't smiling.
BESIDES, SPENDING TIME AT THE COLLEGE GIVES ME AN ODD SENSATION.
IT'S DIFFICULT TO DESCRIBE. IT MAKES ME WANT TO STROKE MY INSIDES.
IT'S A NEW FEELING.
RUB RUB
You want to what?
SOMETIMES I CAN'T PARSE "ELIAS-ESE."
ME-ESE?

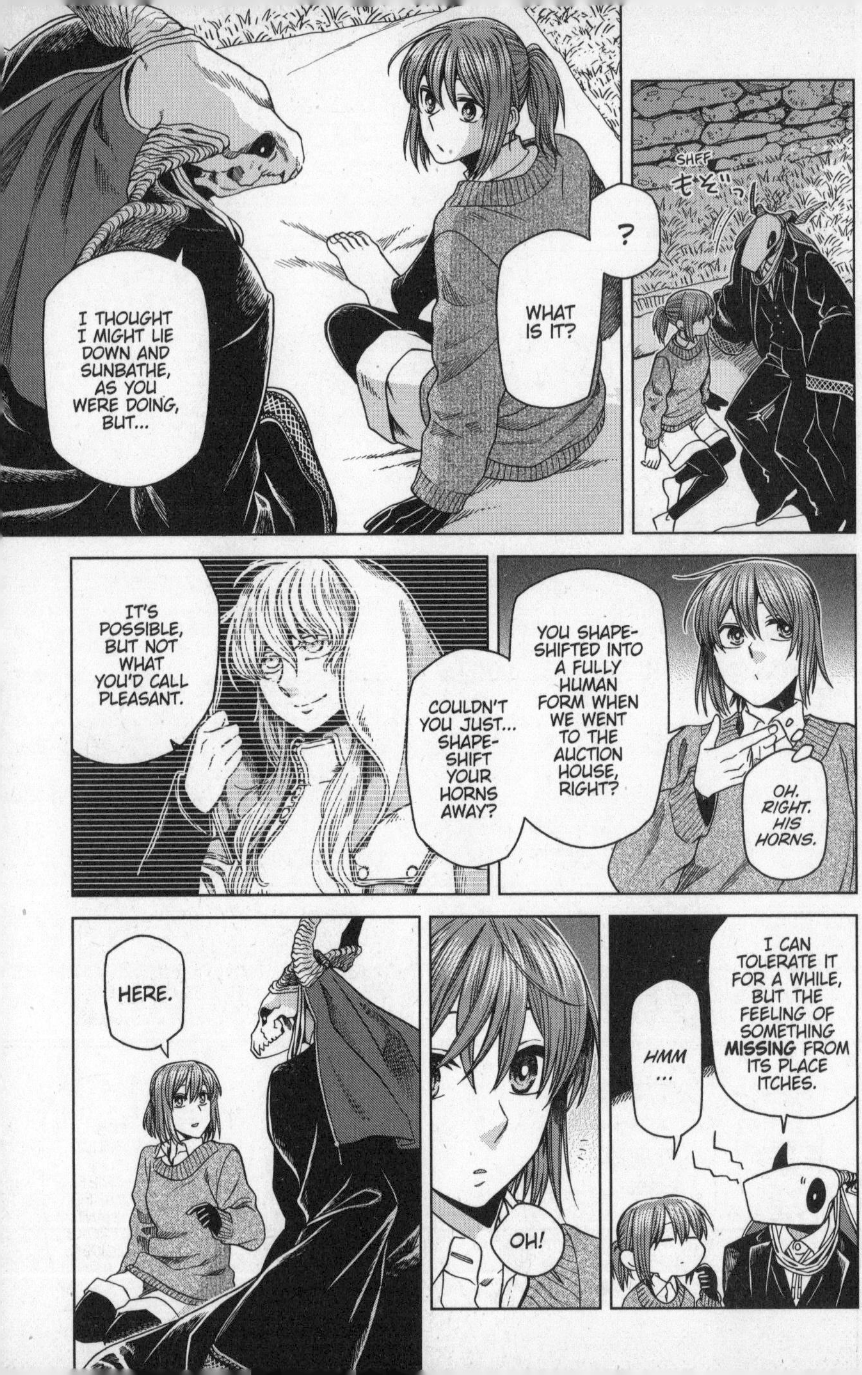
SHFF
もぞっ
?
WHAT IS IT?
I THOUGHT I MIGHT LIE DOWN AND SUNBATHE, AS YOU WERE DOING, BUT...
YOU SHAPE-SHIFTED INTO A FULLY HUMAN FORM WHEN WE WENT TO THE AUCTION HOUSE, RIGHT?
OH. RIGHT. HIS HORNS.
COULDN'T YOU JUST... SHAPE-SHIFT YOUR HORNS AWAY?
IT'S POSSIBLE, BUT NOT WHAT YOU'D CALL PLEASANT.
I CAN TOLERATE IT FOR A WHILE, BUT THE FEELING OF SOMETHING MISSING FROM ITS PLACE ITCHES.
HMM...
OH!
HERE.

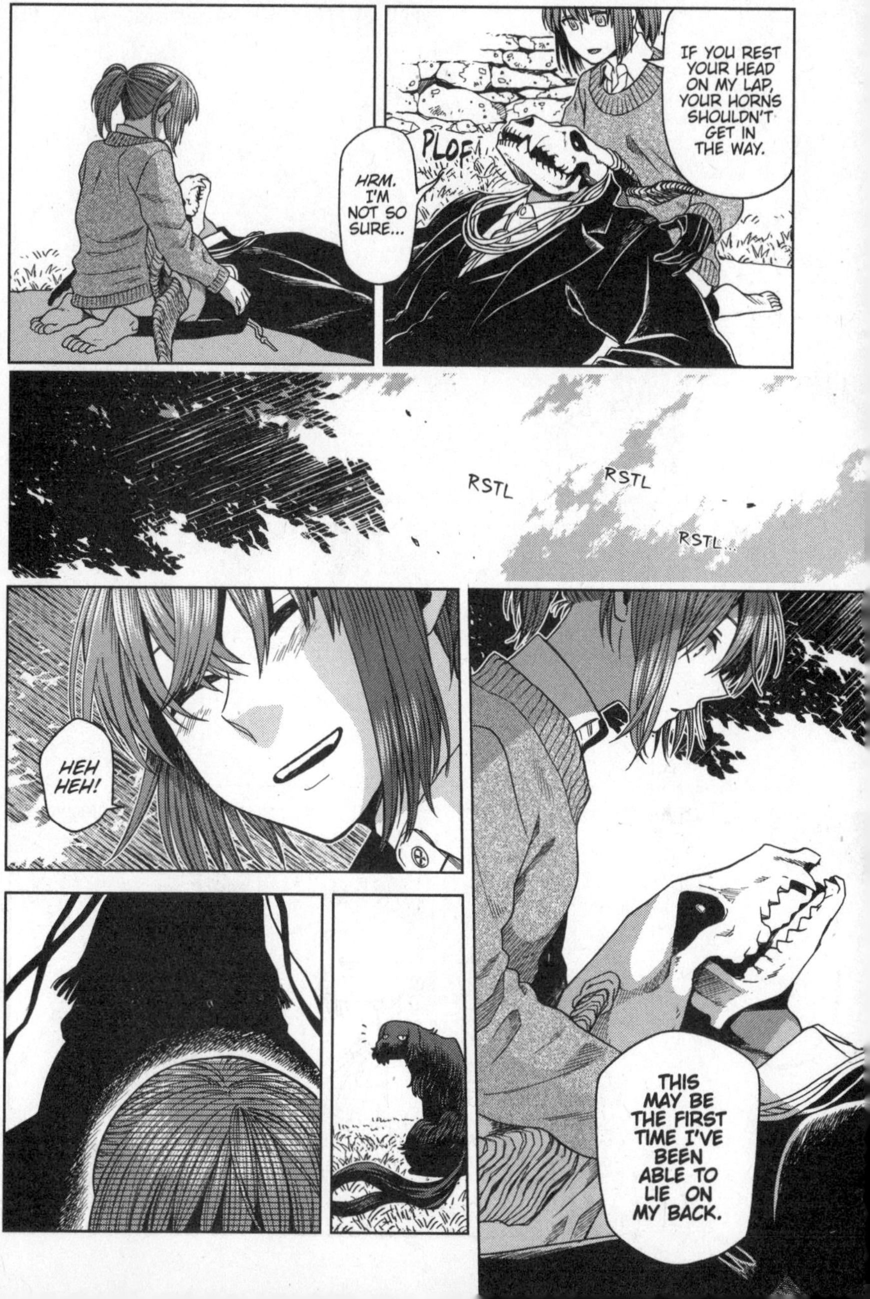
IF YOU REST YOUR HEAD ON MY LAP, YOUR HORNS SHOULDN'T GET IN THE WAY.
PLOF
HRM. I'M NOT SO SURE...
RSTL
RSTL
RSTL...
THIS MAY BE THE FIRST TIME I'VE BEEN ABLE TO LIE ON MY BACK.
HEH HEH!

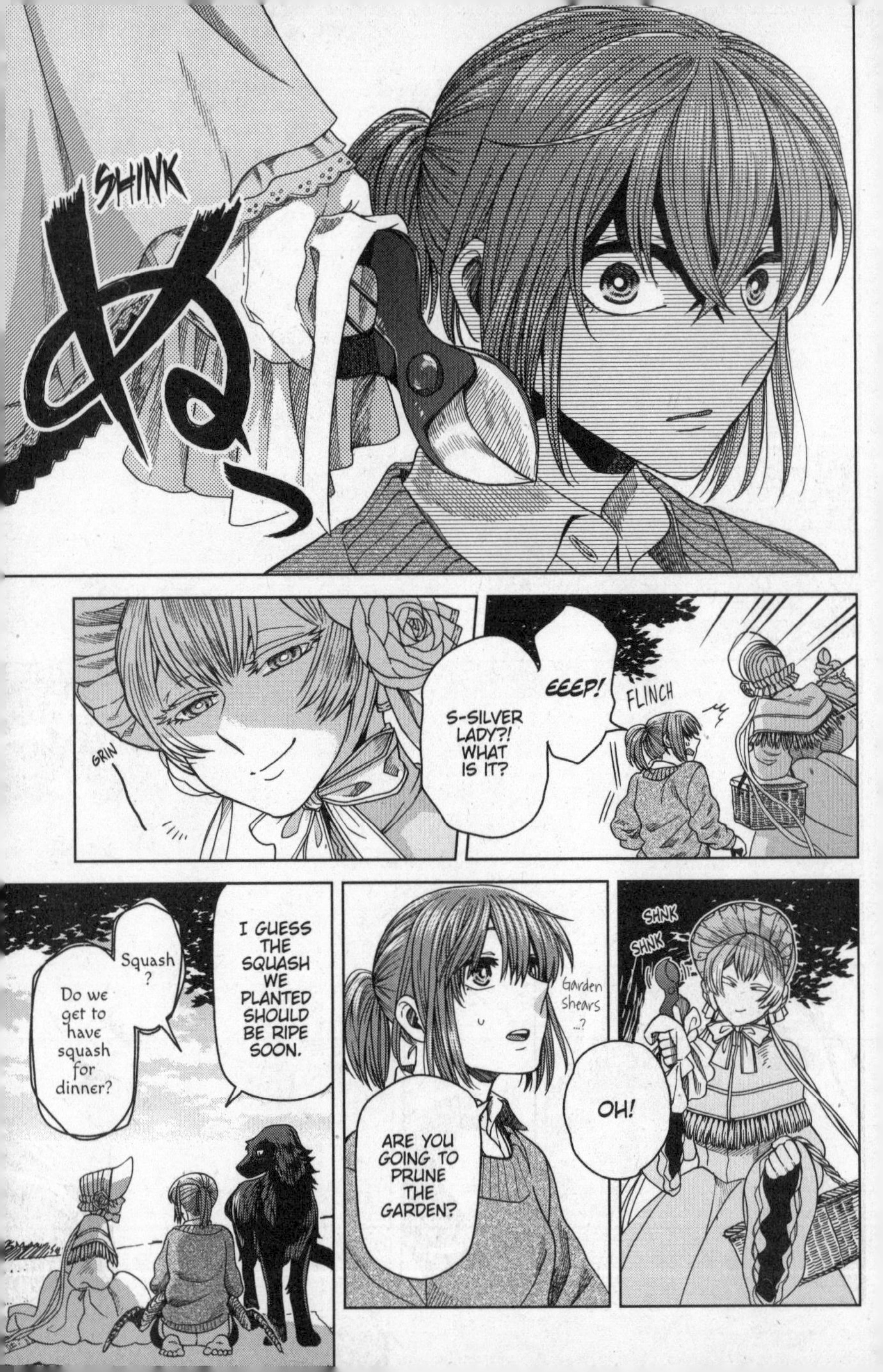
SHINK
EEEP!
FLINCH
S-SILVER LADY?! WHAT IS IT?
GRIN
SHNK
SHNK
Garden Shears ...?
OH!
ARE YOU GOING TO PRUNE THE GARDEN?
I GUESS THE SQUASH WE PLANTED SHOULD BE RIPE SOON.
Squash?
Do we get to have squash for dinner?

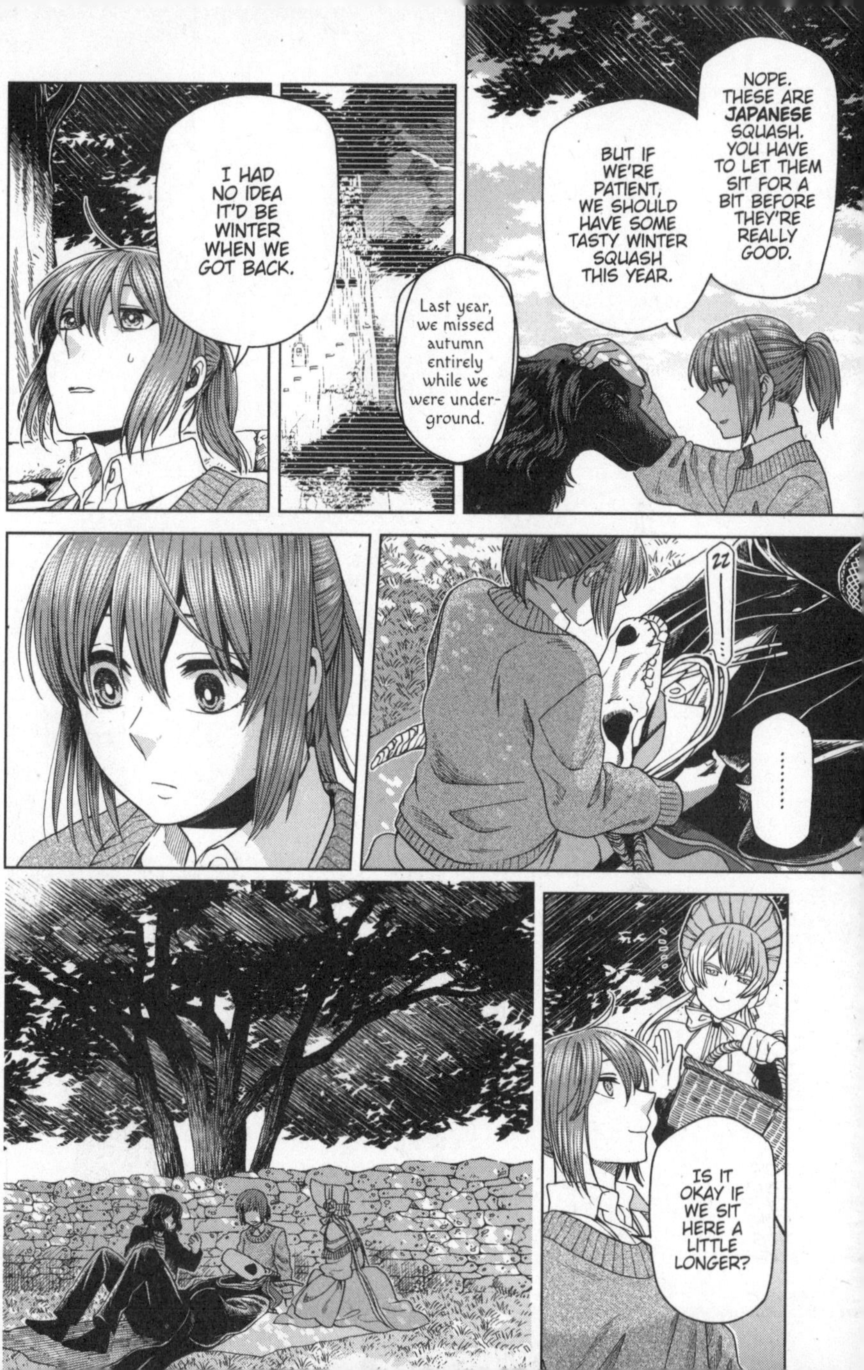
NOPE. THESE ARE JAPANESE SQUASH. YOU HAVE TO LET THEM SIT FOR A BIT BEFORE THEY'RE REALLY GOOD.
BUT IF WE'RE PATIENT, WE SHOULD HAVE SOME TASTY WINTER SQUASH THIS YEAR.
Last year, we missed autumn entirely while we were under-ground.
I HAD NO IDEA IT'D BE WINTER WHEN WE GOT BACK.
ZZ
!
......
IS IT OKAY IF WE SIT HERE A LITTLE LONGER?

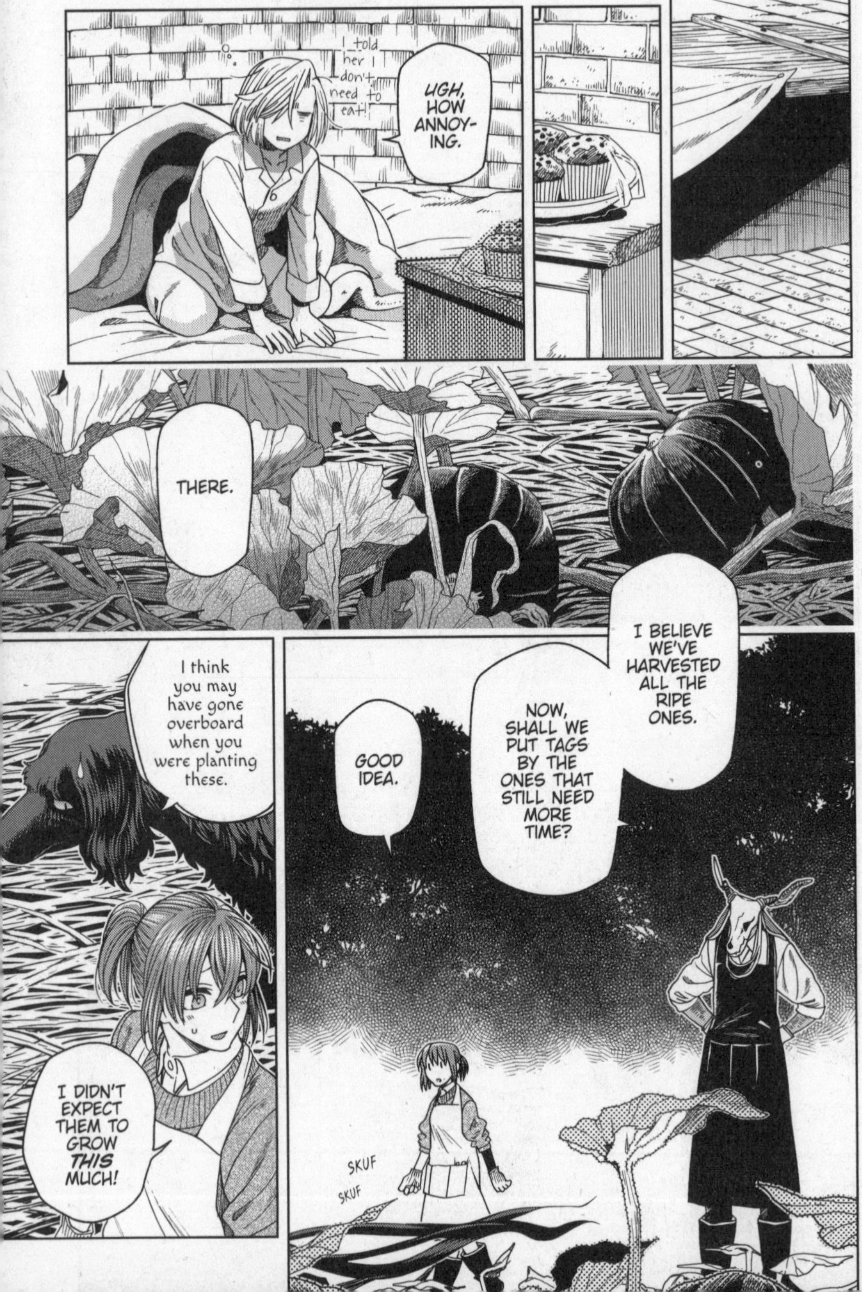
UGH, HOW ANNOYING.
I told her I don't need to eat!
THERE.
I BELIEVE WE'VE HARVESTED ALL THE RIPE ONES.
NOW, SHALL WE PUT TAGS BY THE ONES THAT STILL NEED MORE TIME?
GOOD IDEA.
SKUF
SKUF
I think you may have gone overboard when you were planting these.
I DIDN'T EXPECT THEM TO GROW *THIS* MUCH!

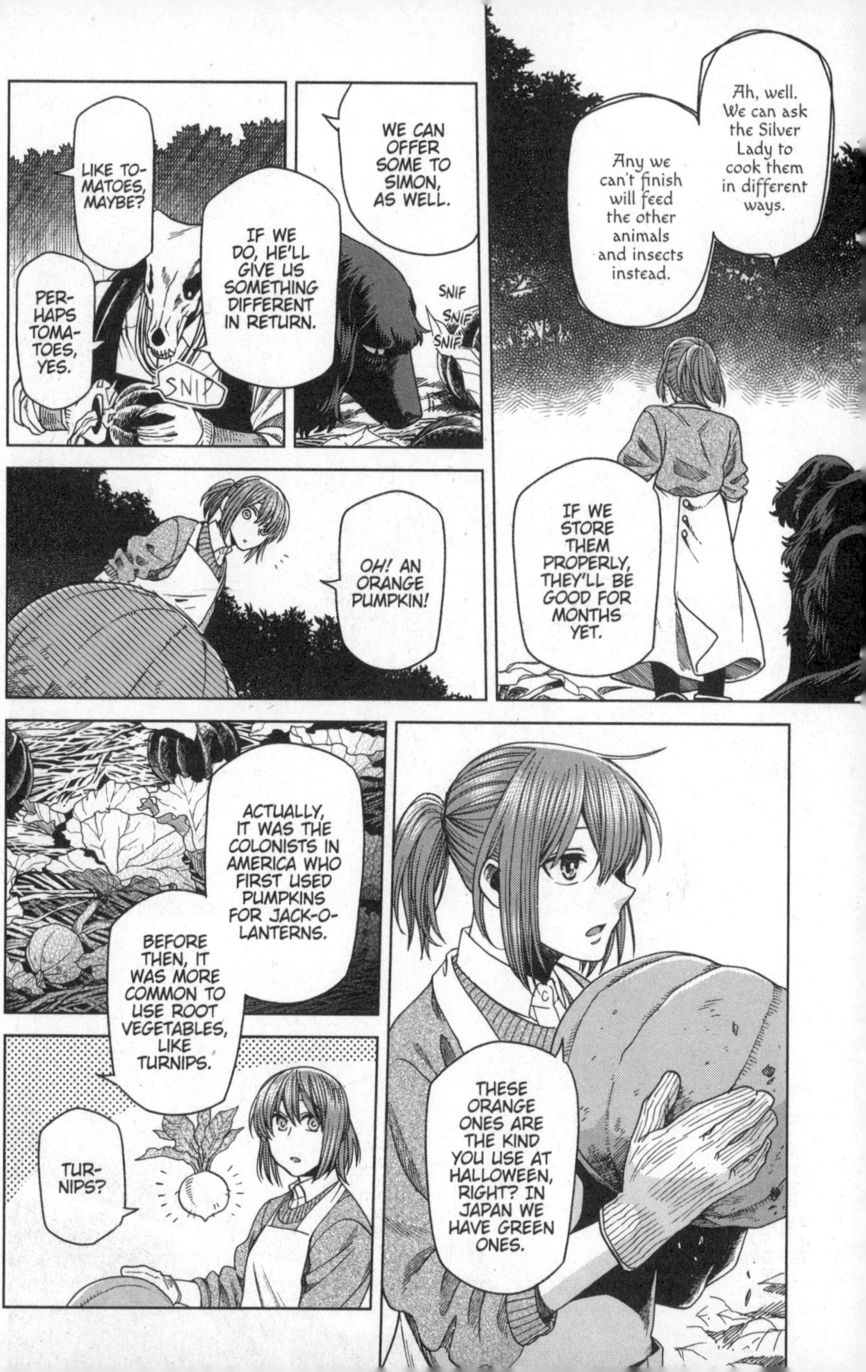
Ah, well. We can ask the Silver Lady to cook them in different ways.
Any we can't finish will feed the other animals and insects instead.
IF WE STORE THEM PROPERLY, THEY'LL BE GOOD FOR MONTHS YET.
WE CAN OFFER SOME TO SIMON, AS WELL.
SNIF SNIF SNIF
IF WE DO, HE'LL GIVE US SOMETHING DIFFERENT IN RETURN.
LIKE TO-MATOES, MAYBE?
PER-HAPS TOMA-TOES, YES.
SNIP
OH! AN ORANGE PUMPKIN!
THESE ORANGE ONES ARE THE KIND YOU USE AT HALLOWEEN, RIGHT? IN JAPAN WE HAVE GREEN ONES.
ACTUALLY, IT WAS THE COLONISTS IN AMERICA WHO FIRST USED PUMPKINS FOR JACK-O-LANTERNS.
BEFORE THEN, IT WAS MORE COMMON TO USE ROOT VEGETABLES, LIKE TURNIPS.
TUR-NIPS?

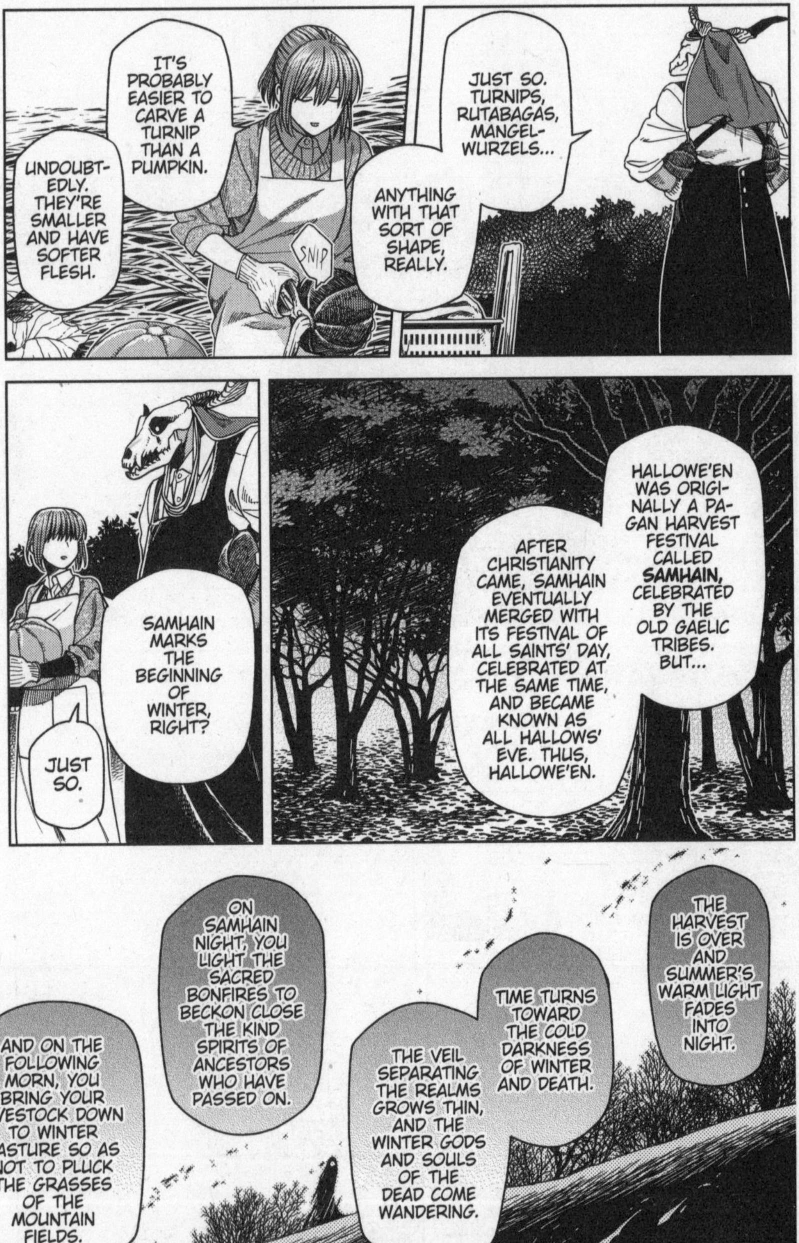
JUST SO. TURNIPS, RUTABAGAS, MANGEL-WURZELS...
ANYTHING WITH THAT SORT OF SHAPE, REALLY.
IT'S PROBABLY EASIER TO CARVE A TURNIP THAN A PUMPKIN.
SNIP
UNDOUBTEDLY. THEY'RE SMALLER AND HAVE SOFTER FLESH.
HALLOWE'EN WAS ORIGINALLY A PAGAN HARVEST FESTIVAL CALLED **SAMHAIN,** CELEBRATED BY THE OLD GAELIC TRIBES. BUT...
AFTER CHRISTIANITY CAME, SAMHAIN EVENTUALLY MERGED WITH ITS FESTIVAL OF ALL SAINTS' DAY, CELEBRATED AT THE SAME TIME, AND BECAME KNOWN AS ALL HALLOWS' EVE. THUS, HALLOWE'EN.
SAMHAIN MARKS THE BEGINNING OF WINTER, RIGHT?
JUST SO.
THE HARVEST IS OVER AND SUMMER'S WARM LIGHT FADES INTO NIGHT.
TIME TURNS TOWARD THE COLD DARKNESS OF WINTER AND DEATH.
THE VEIL SEPARATING THE REALMS GROWS THIN, AND THE WINTER GODS AND SOULS OF THE DEAD COME WANDERING.
ON SAMHAIN NIGHT, YOU LIGHT THE SACRED BONFIRES TO BECKON CLOSE THE KIND SPIRITS OF ANCESTORS WHO HAVE PASSED ON.
AND ON THE FOLLOWING MORN, YOU BRING YOUR LIVESTOCK DOWN TO WINTER PASTURE SO AS NOT TO PLUCK THE GRASSES OF THE MOUNTAIN FIELDS.

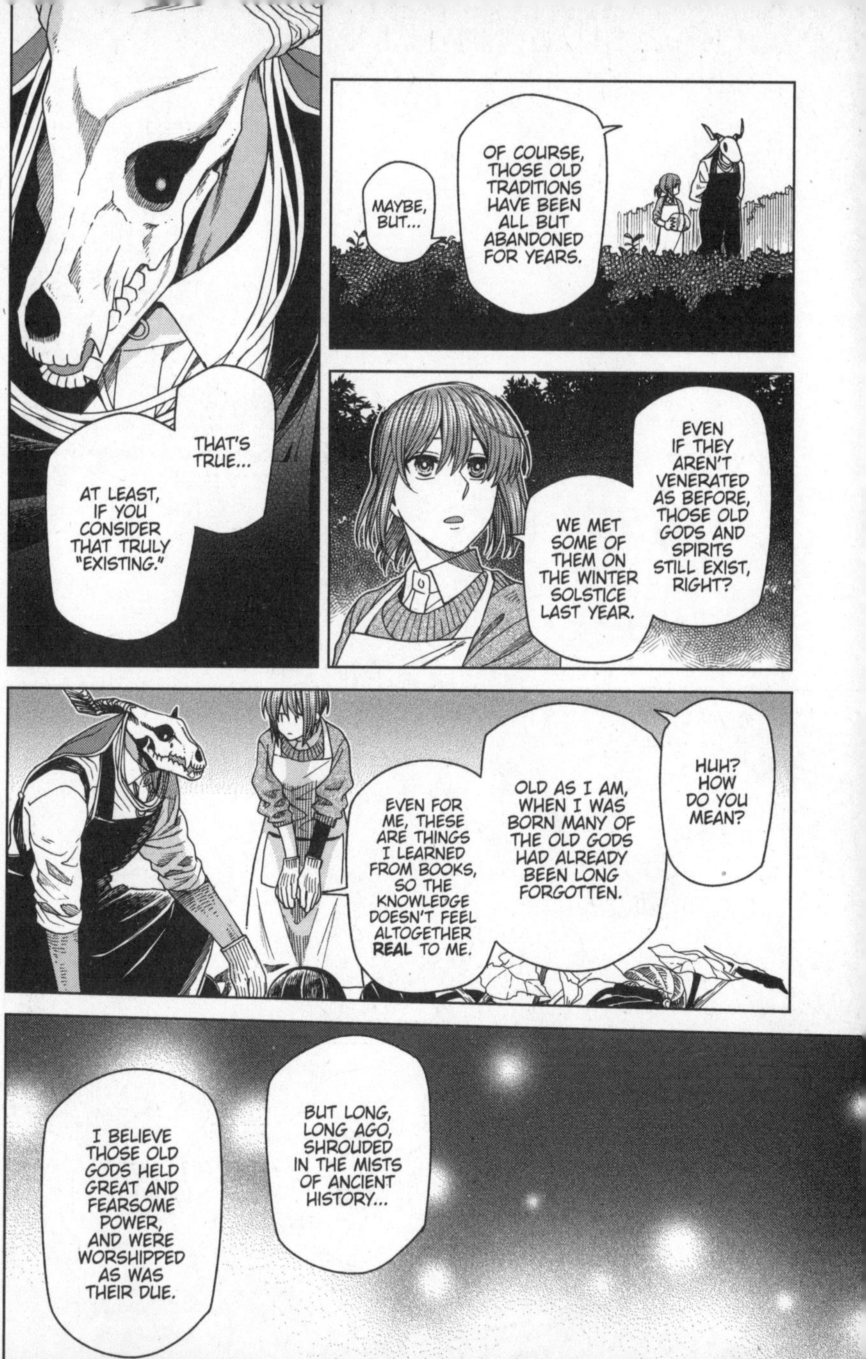

OF COURSE, THOSE OLD TRADITIONS HAVE BEEN ALL BUT ABANDONED FOR YEARS.
MAYBE, BUT...
EVEN IF THEY AREN'T VENERATED AS BEFORE, THOSE OLD GODS AND SPIRITS STILL EXIST, RIGHT?
WE MET SOME OF THEM ON THE WINTER SOLSTICE LAST YEAR.
THAT'S TRUE...
AT LEAST, IF YOU CONSIDER THAT TRULY "EXISTING."
HUH? HOW DO YOU MEAN?
OLD AS I AM, WHEN I WAS BORN MANY OF THE OLD GODS HAD ALREADY BEEN LONG FORGOTTEN.
EVEN FOR ME, THESE ARE THINGS I LEARNED FROM BOOKS, SO THE KNOWLEDGE DOESN'T FEEL ALTOGETHER **REAL** TO ME.
BUT LONG, LONG AGO, SHROUDED IN THE MISTS OF ANCIENT HISTORY...
I BELIEVE THOSE OLD GODS HELD GREAT AND FEARSOME POWER, AND WERE WORSHIPPED AS WAS THEIR DUE.

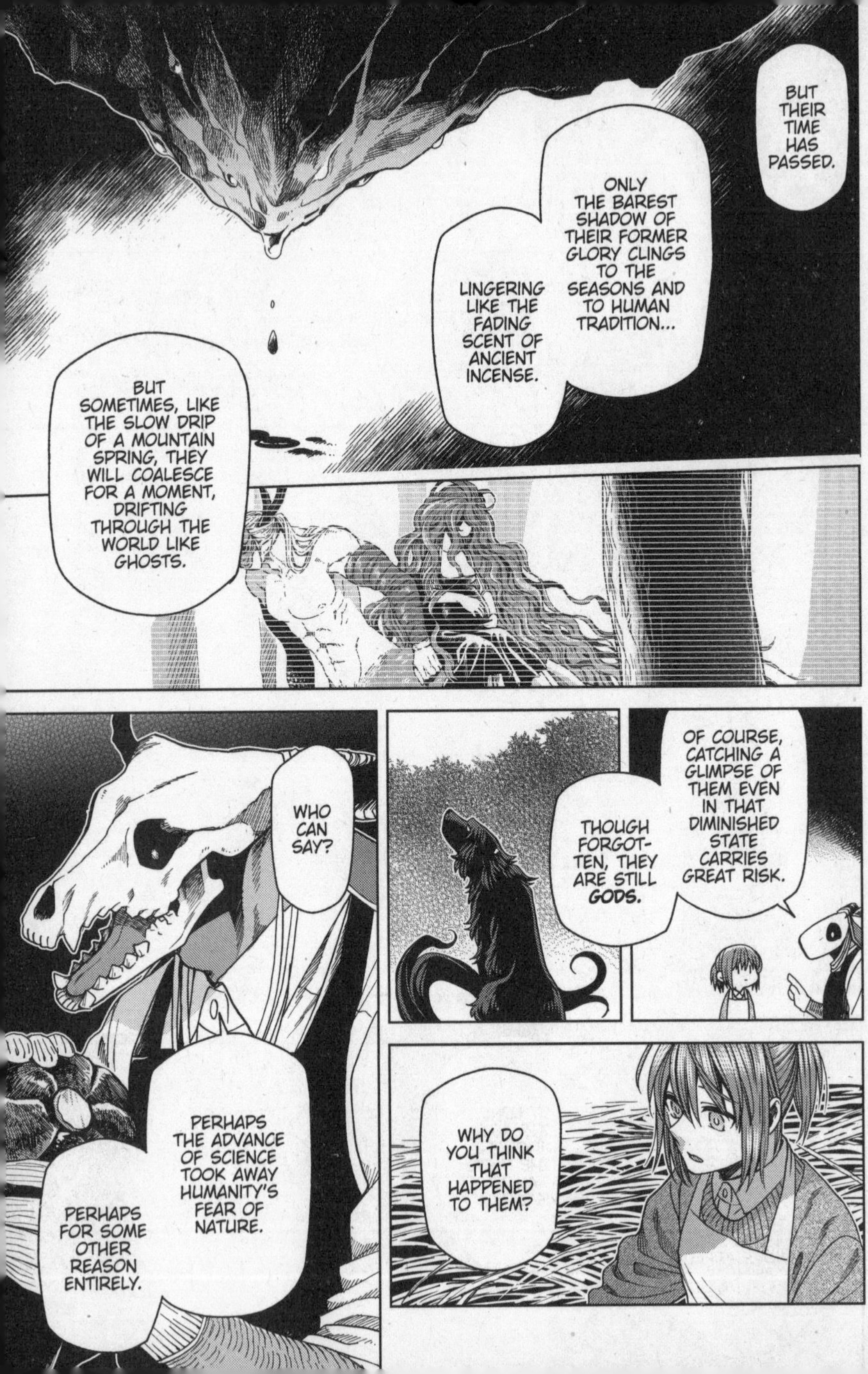
BUT THEIR TIME HAS PASSED.
ONLY THE BAREST SHADOW OF THEIR FORMER GLORY CLINGS TO THE SEASONS AND TO HUMAN TRADITION...
LINGERING LIKE THE FADING SCENT OF ANCIENT INCENSE.
BUT SOMETIMES, LIKE THE SLOW DRIP OF A MOUNTAIN SPRING, THEY WILL COALESCE FOR A MOMENT, DRIFTING THROUGH THE WORLD LIKE GHOSTS.
OF COURSE, CATCHING A GLIMPSE OF THEM EVEN IN THAT DIMINISHED STATE CARRIES GREAT RISK.
THOUGH FORGOT-TEN, THEY ARE STILL **GODS.**
WHY DO YOU THINK THAT HAPPENED TO THEM?
WHO CAN SAY?
PERHAPS THE ADVANCE OF SCIENCE TOOK AWAY HUMANITY'S FEAR OF NATURE.
PERHAPS FOR SOME OTHER REASON ENTIRELY.

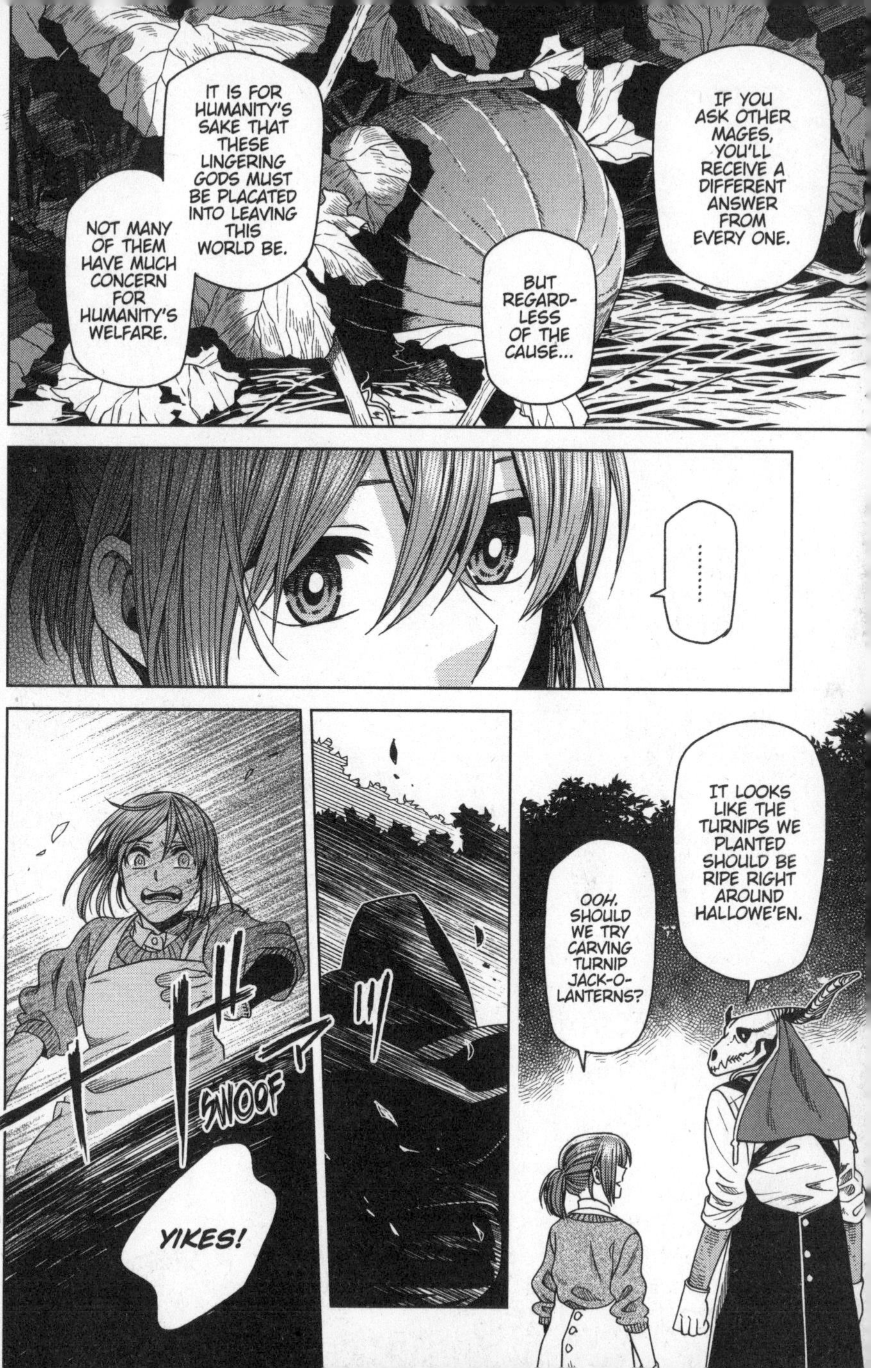
IF YOU ASK OTHER MAGES, YOU'LL RECEIVE A DIFFERENT ANSWER FROM EVERY ONE.
BUT REGARDLESS OF THE CAUSE...
IT IS FOR HUMANITY'S SAKE THAT THESE LINGERING GODS MUST BE PLACATED INTO LEAVING THIS WORLD BE.
NOT MANY OF THEM HAVE MUCH CONCERN FOR HUMANITY'S WELFARE.
......
IT LOOKS LIKE THE TURNIPS WE PLANTED SHOULD BE RIPE RIGHT AROUND HALLOWE'EN.
OOH. SHOULD WE TRY CARVING TURNIP JACK-O-LANTERNS?
SWOOF
YIKES!

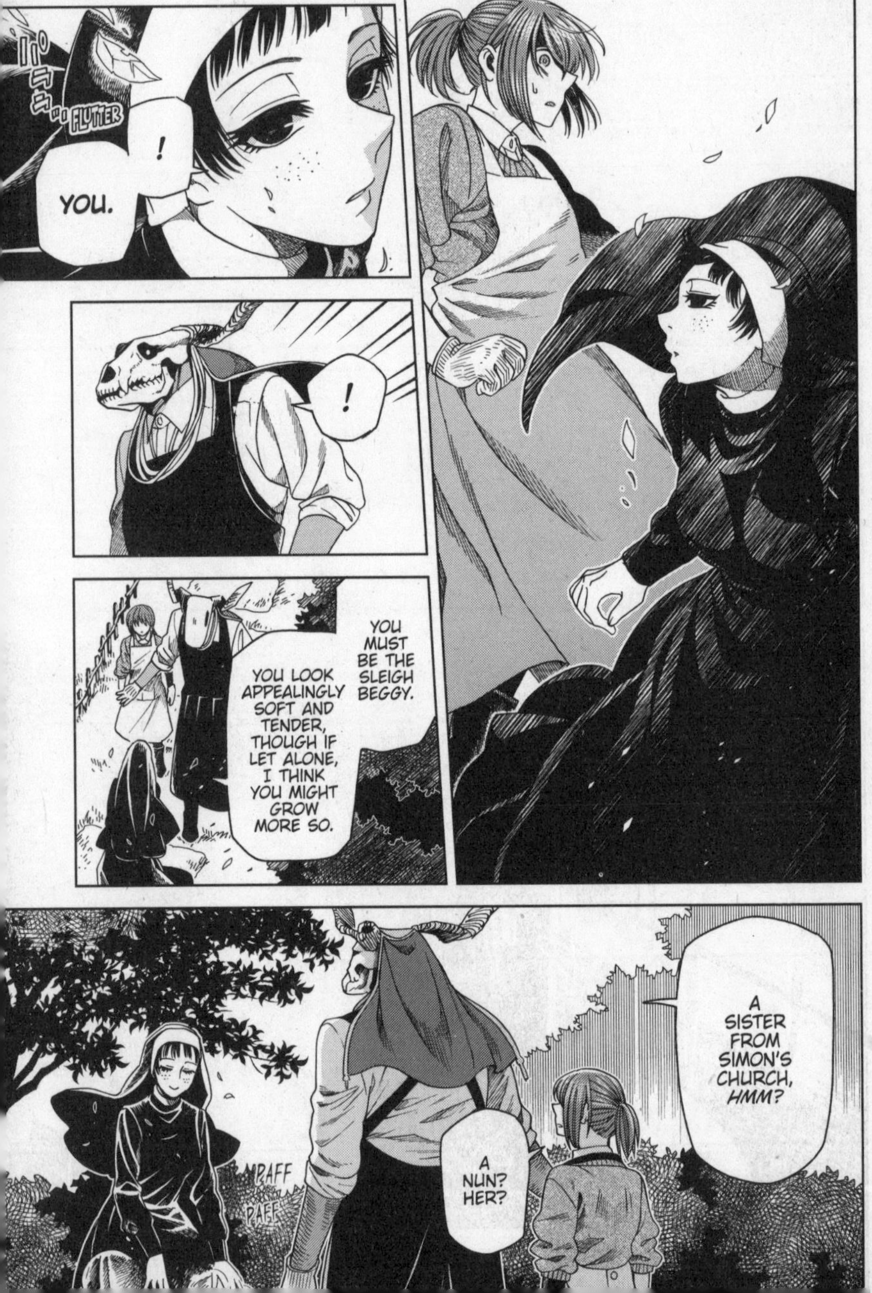
FLUTTER
!
YOU.
!
YOU MUST BE THE SLEIGH BEGGY.
YOU LOOK APPEALINGLY SOFT AND TENDER, THOUGH IF LET ALONE, I THINK YOU MIGHT GROW MORE SO.
A SISTER FROM SIMON'S CHURCH, *HMM?*
A NUN? HER?
PAFF
PAFF

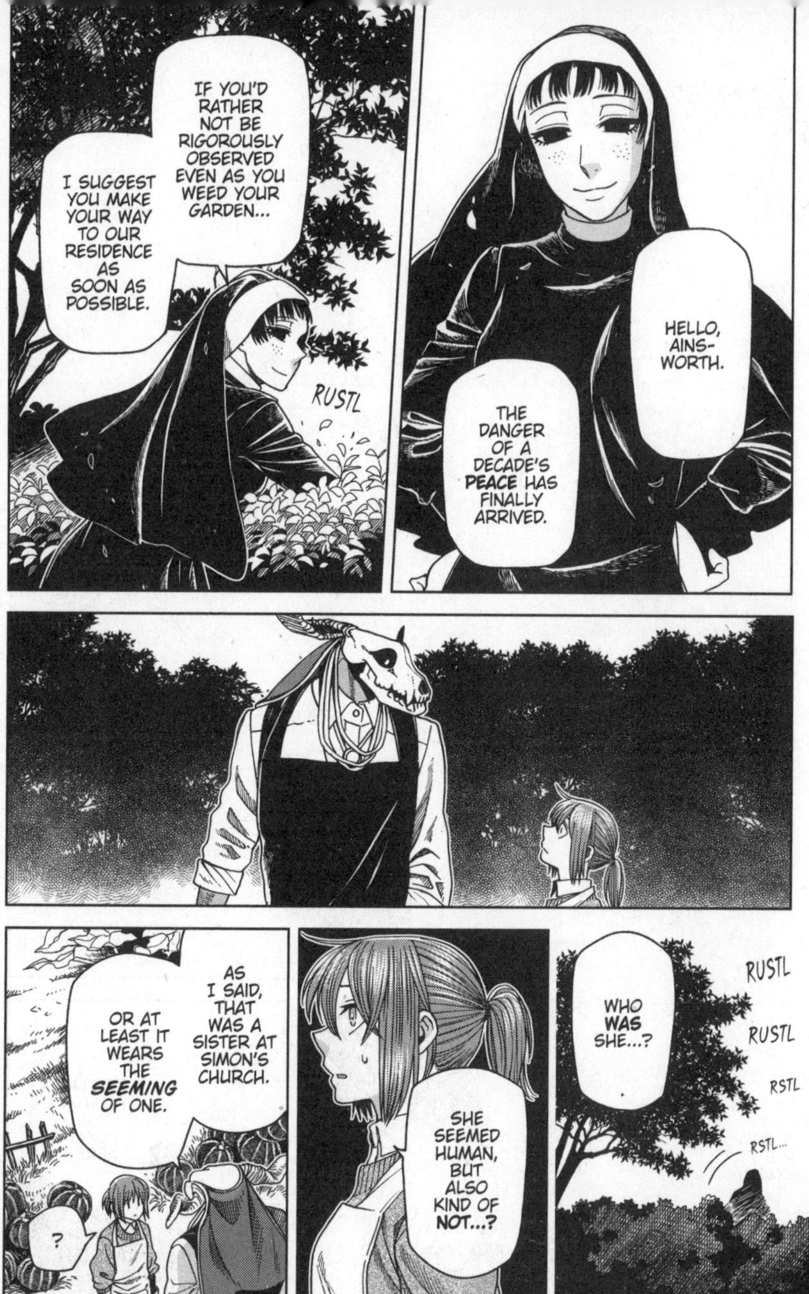
HELLO, AINS-WORTH.
THE DANGER OF A DECADE'S PEACE HAS FINALLY ARRIVED.
IF YOU'D RATHER NOT BE RIGOROUSLY OBSERVED EVEN AS YOU WEED YOUR GARDEN...
I SUGGEST YOU MAKE YOUR WAY TO OUR RESIDENCE AS SOON AS POSSIBLE.
RUSTL
RUSTL
WHO WAS SHE...?
RUSTL
RSTL
RSTL...
SHE SEEMED HUMAN, BUT ALSO KIND OF NOT...?
AS I SAID, THAT WAS A SISTER AT SIMON'S CHURCH.
OR AT LEAST IT WEARS THE SEEMING OF ONE.
?

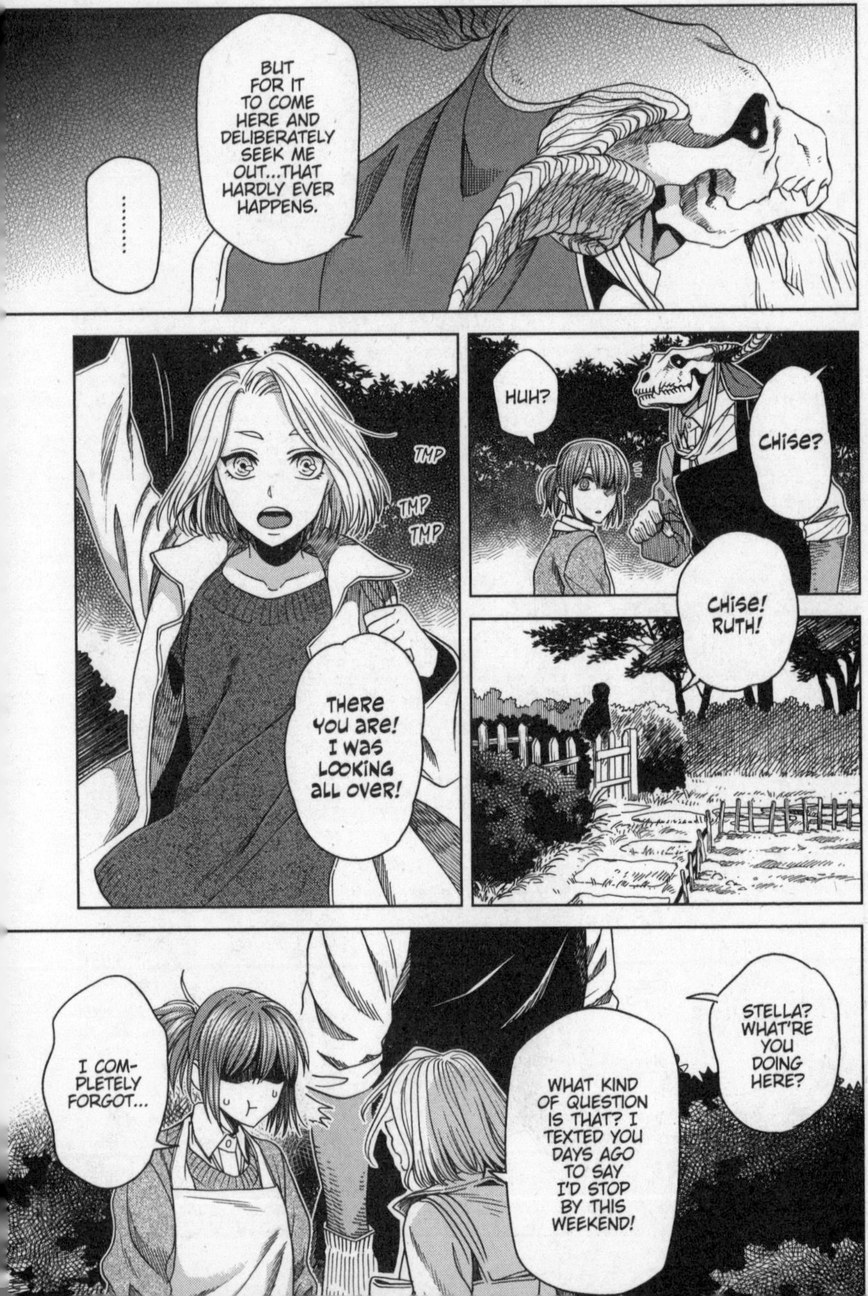
BUT FOR IT TO COME HERE AND DELIBERATELY SEEK ME OUT...THAT HARDLY EVER HAPPENS.
......
HUH?
CHISE?
CHISE! RUTH!
TMP
TMP
TMP
THERE YOU ARE! I WAS LOOKING ALL OVER!
STELLA? WHAT'RE YOU DOING HERE?
WHAT KIND OF QUESTION IS THAT? I TEXTED YOU DAYS AGO TO SAY I'D STOP BY THIS WEEKEND!
I COM-PLETELY FORGOT...

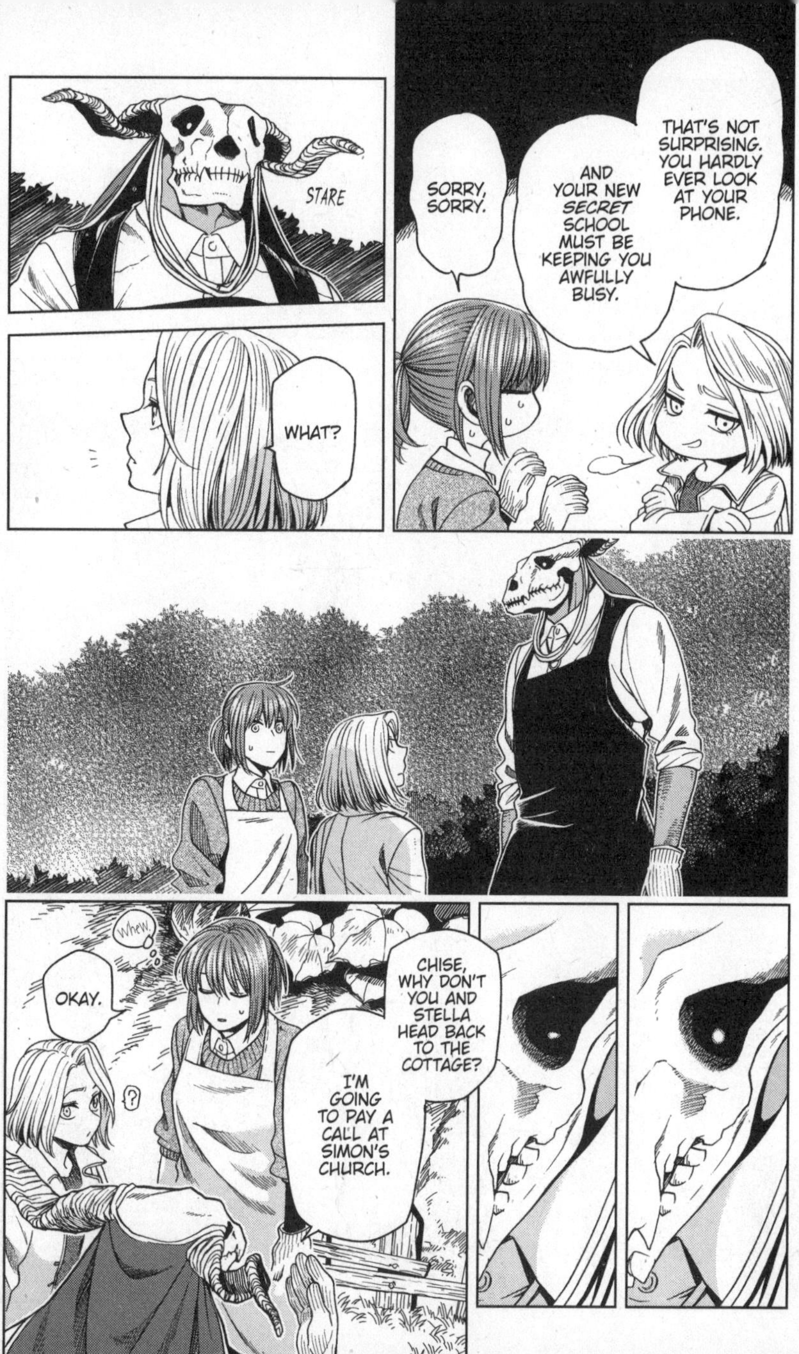
THAT'S NOT SURPRISING. YOU HARDLY EVER LOOK AT YOUR PHONE.
AND YOUR NEW *SECRET* SCHOOL MUST BE KEEPING YOU AWFULLY BUSY.
SORRY, SORRY.
STARE
WHAT?
CHISE, WHY DON'T YOU AND STELLA HEAD BACK TO THE COTTAGE?
I'M GOING TO PAY A CALL AT SIMON'S CHURCH.
Whew.
OKAY.
?

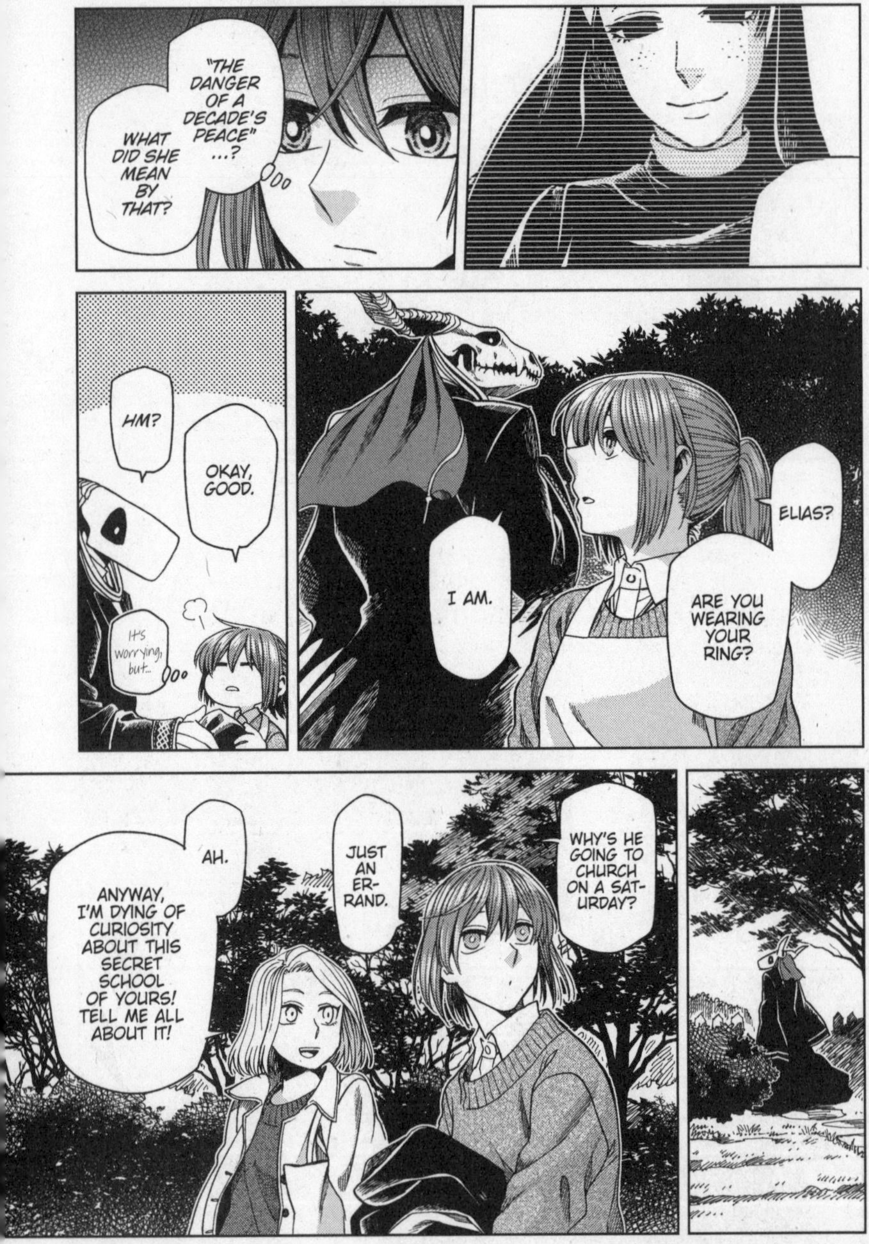
"THE DANGER OF A DECADE'S PEACE" ...?
WHAT DID SHE MEAN BY THAT?
ELIAS?
ARE YOU WEARING YOUR RING?
I AM.
HM?
OKAY, GOOD.
It's worrying, but...
WHY'S HE GOING TO CHURCH ON A SAT-URDAY?
JUST AN ER-RAND.
AH.
ANYWAY, I'M DYING OF CURIOSITY ABOUT THIS SECRET SCHOOL OF YOURS! TELL ME ALL ABOUT IT!

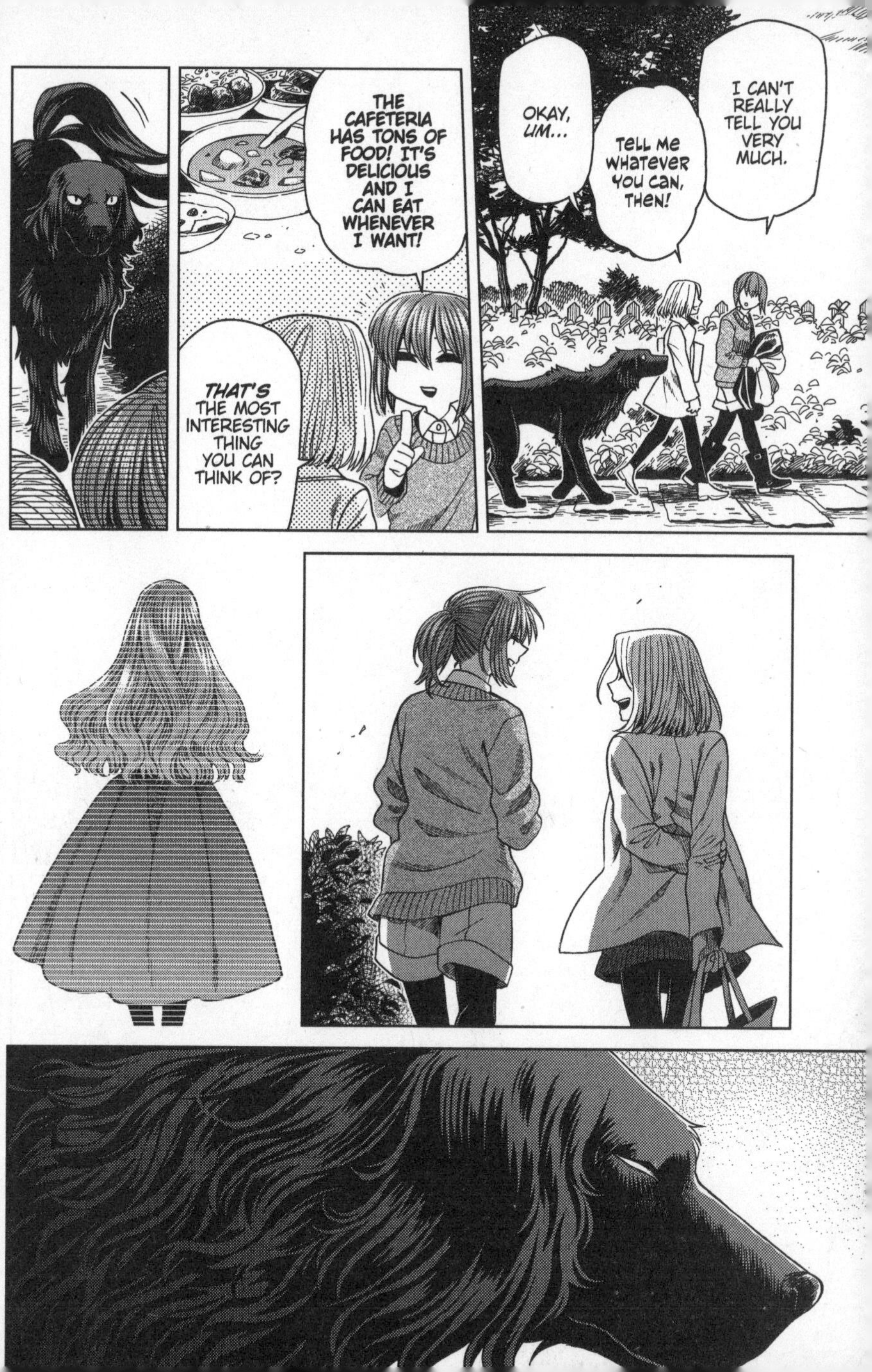
I CAN'T REALLY TELL YOU VERY MUCH.
TELL ME WHATEVER YOU CAN, THEN!
OKAY, UM...
THE CAFETERIA HAS TONS OF FOOD! IT'S DELICIOUS AND I CAN EAT WHENEVER I WANT!
THAT'S THE MOST INTERESTING THING YOU CAN THINK OF?

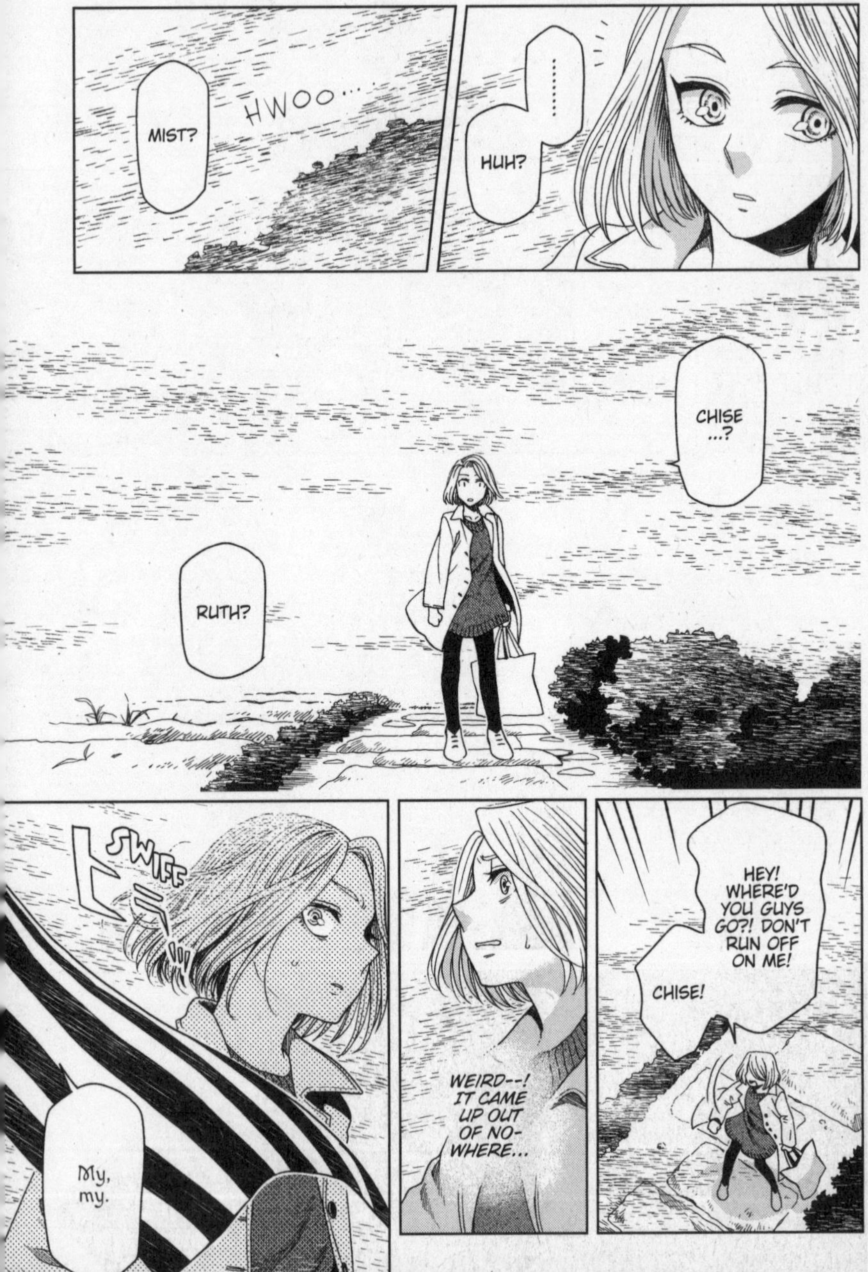
......
HUH?
HWOO....
MIST?
CHISE ...?
RUTH?
HEY! WHERE'D YOU GUYS GO?! DON'T RUN OFF ON ME!
CHISE!
WEIRD--! IT CAME UP OUT OF NO-WHERE...
SWIFF
My, my.

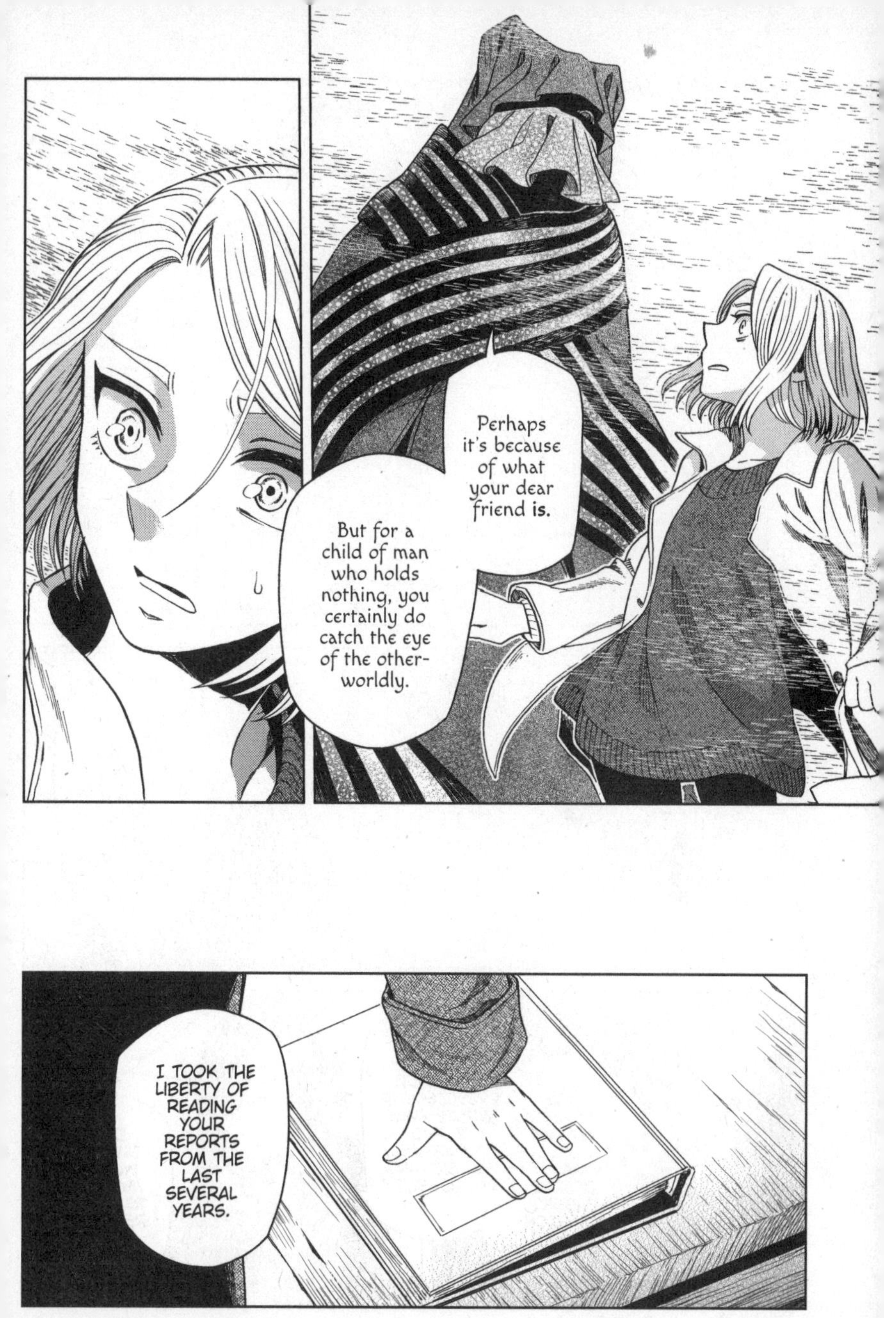
Perhaps it's because of what your dear friend is.
But for a child of man who holds nothing, you certainly do catch the eye of the other-worldly.
I TOOK THE LIBERTY OF READING YOUR REPORTS FROM THE LAST SEVERAL YEARS.

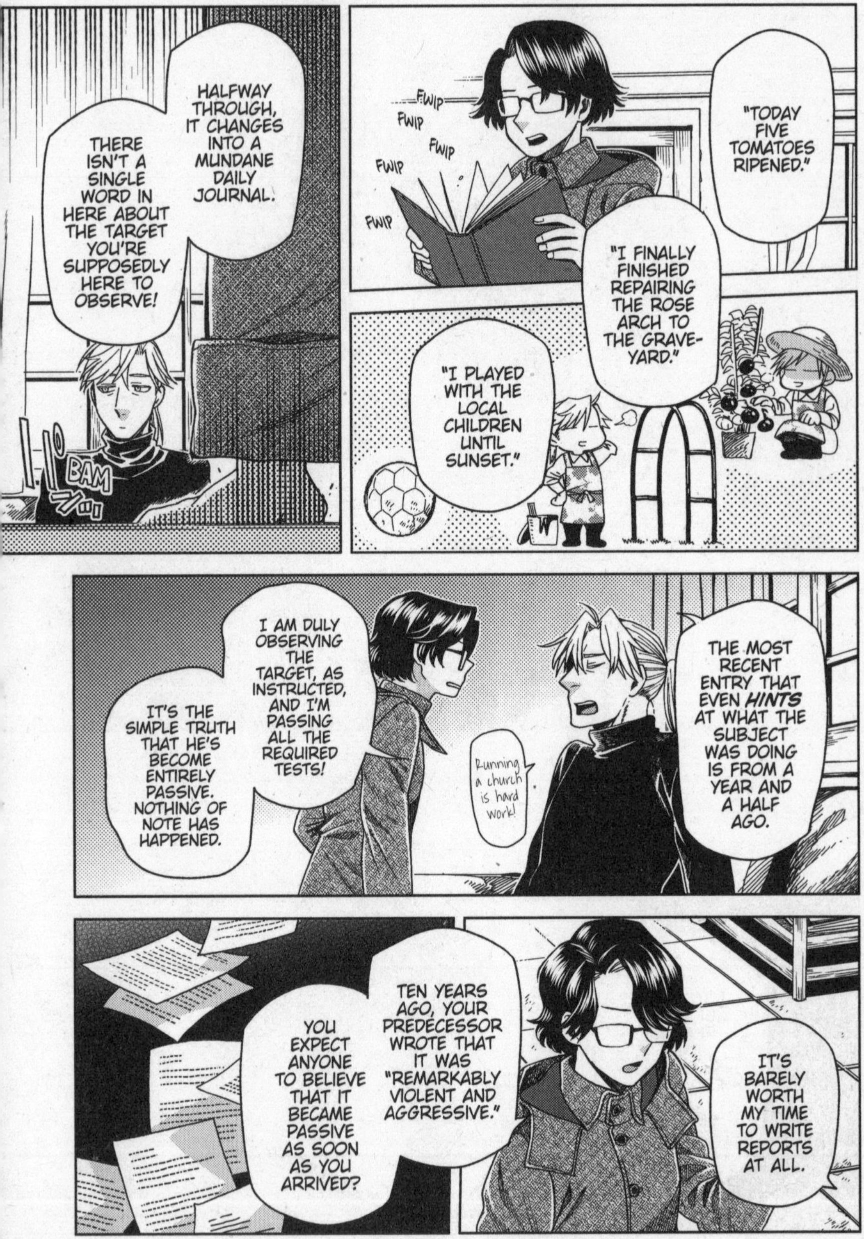
"TODAY FIVE TOMATOES RIPENED."
FWIP
FWIP
FWIP
FWIP
FWIP
"I FINALLY FINISHED REPAIRING THE ROSE ARCH TO THE GRAVEYARD."
"I PLAYED WITH THE LOCAL CHILDREN UNTIL SUNSET."
HALFWAY THROUGH, IT CHANGES INTO A MUNDANE DAILY JOURNAL.
THERE ISN'T A SINGLE WORD IN HERE ABOUT THE TARGET YOU'RE SUPPOSEDLY HERE TO OBSERVE!
BAM
THE MOST RECENT ENTRY THAT EVEN *HINTS* AT WHAT THE SUBJECT WAS DOING IS FROM A YEAR AND A HALF AGO.
Running a church is hard work!
I AM DULY OBSERVING THE TARGET, AS INSTRUCTED, AND I'M PASSING ALL THE REQUIRED TESTS!
IT'S THE SIMPLE TRUTH THAT HE'S BECOME ENTIRELY PASSIVE. NOTHING OF NOTE HAS HAPPENED.
IT'S BARELY WORTH MY TIME TO WRITE REPORTS AT ALL.
TEN YEARS AGO, YOUR PREDECESSOR WROTE THAT IT WAS "REMARKABLY VIOLENT AND AGGRESSIVE."
YOU EXPECT ANYONE TO BELIEVE THAT IT BECAME PASSIVE AS SOON AS YOU ARRIVED?

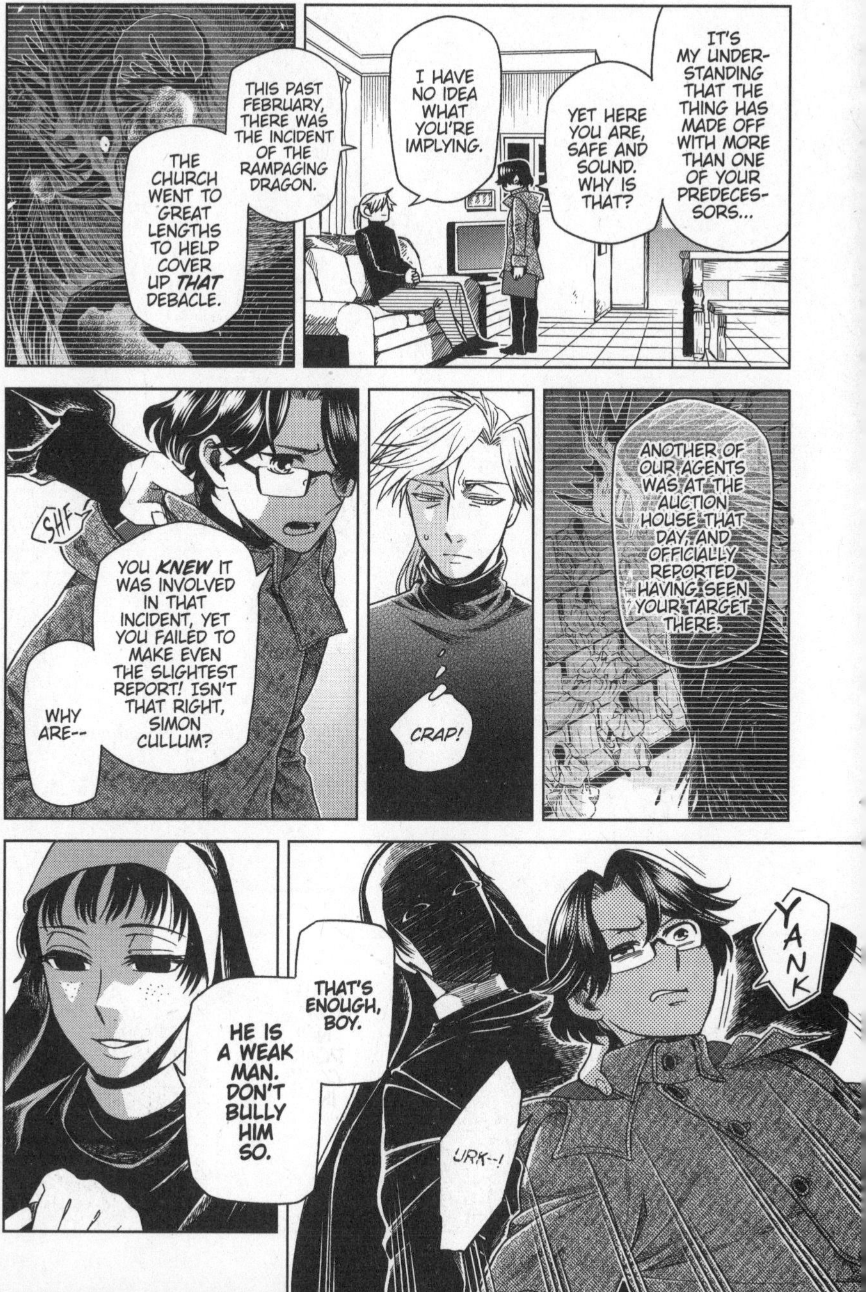
IT'S MY UNDERSTANDING THAT THE THING HAS MADE OFF WITH MORE THAN ONE OF YOUR PREDECESSORS...
YET HERE YOU ARE, SAFE AND SOUND. WHY IS THAT?
I HAVE NO IDEA WHAT YOU'RE IMPLYING.
THIS PAST FEBRUARY, THERE WAS THE INCIDENT OF THE RAMPAGING DRAGON.
THE CHURCH WENT TO GREAT LENGTHS TO HELP COVER UP *THAT* DEBACLE.
ANOTHER OF OUR AGENTS WAS AT THE AUCTION HOUSE THAT DAY, AND OFFICIALLY REPORTED HAVING SEEN YOUR TARGET THERE.
CRAP!
SHF
YOU **KNEW** IT WAS INVOLVED IN THAT INCIDENT, YET YOU FAILED TO MAKE EVEN THE SLIGHTEST REPORT! ISN'T THAT RIGHT, SIMON CULLUM?
WHY ARE--
YANK
THAT'S ENOUGH, BOY.
URK--!
HE IS A WEAK MAN. DON'T BULLY HIM SO.

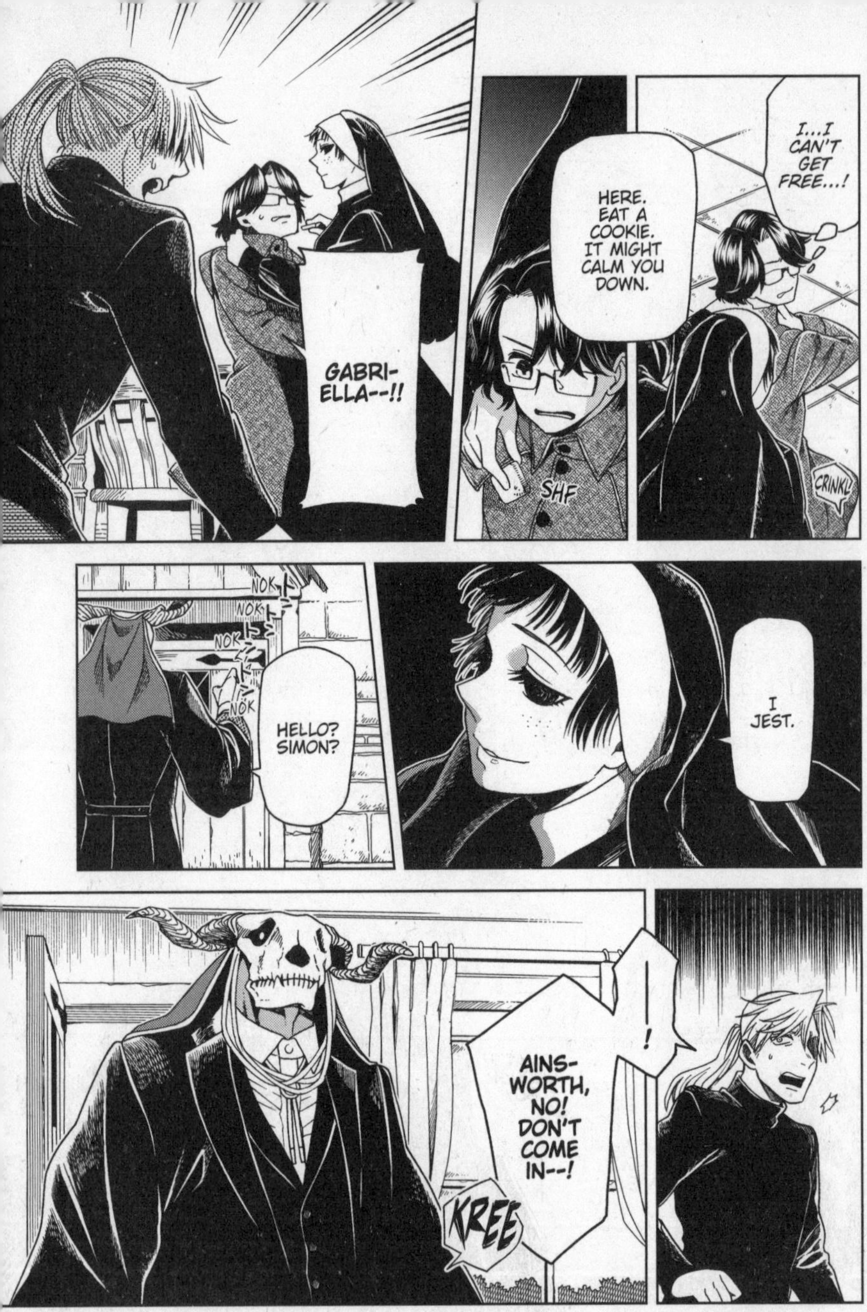
I...I CAN'T GET FREE...!
CRINKL!
HERE. EAT A COOKIE. IT MIGHT CALM YOU DOWN.
SHF
GABRI-ELLA--!!
I JEST.
NOK
NOK
NOK
NOK
HELLO? SIMON?
!
AINS-WORTH, NO! DON'T COME IN--!
KREE

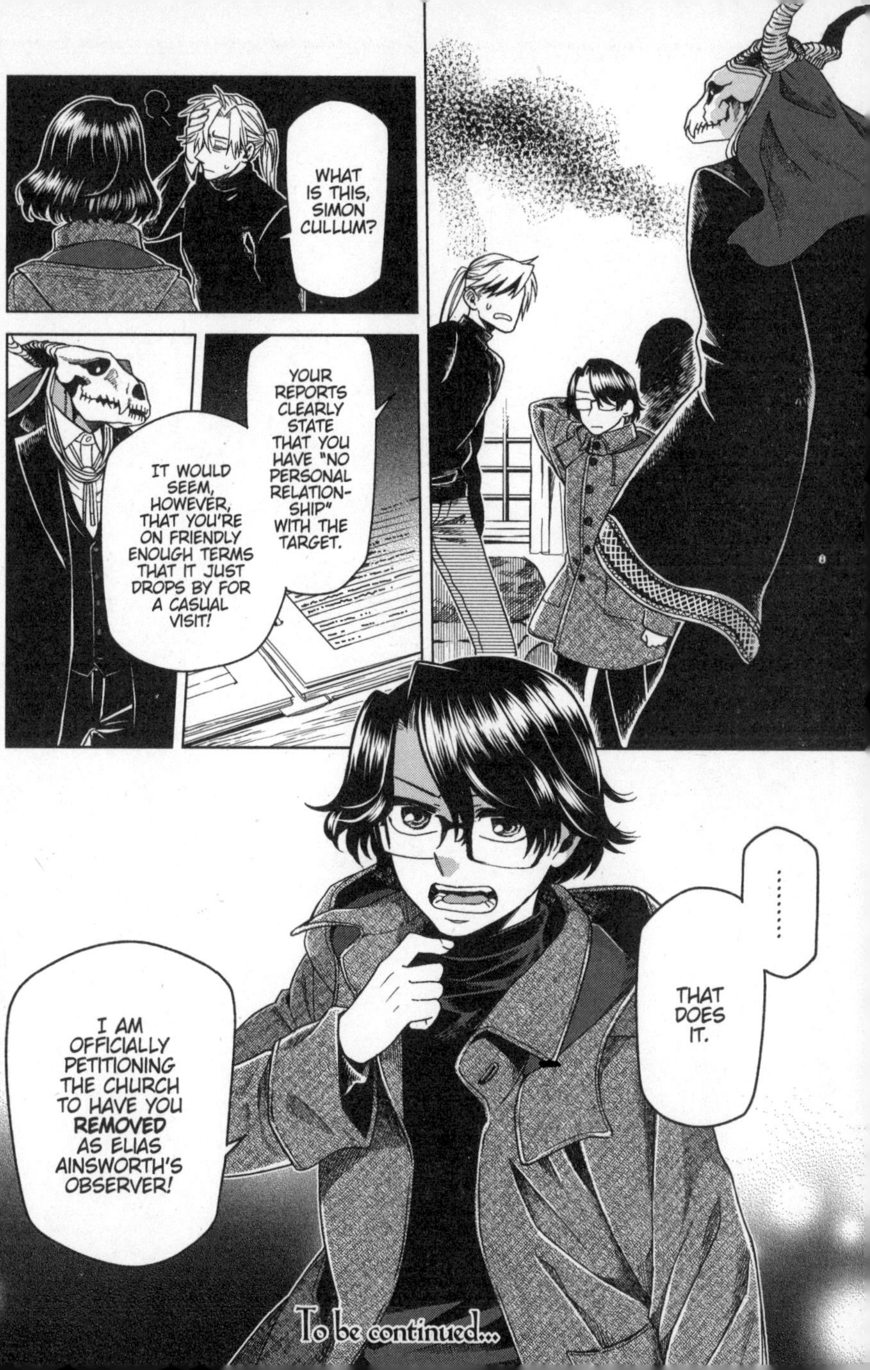
WHAT IS THIS, SIMON CULLUM?
YOUR REPORTS CLEARLY STATE THAT YOU HAVE "NO PERSONAL RELATIONSHIP" WITH THE TARGET.
IT WOULD SEEM, HOWEVER, THAT YOU'RE ON FRIENDLY ENOUGH TERMS THAT IT JUST DROPS BY FOR A CASUAL VISIT!
......
THAT DOES IT.
I AM OFFICIALLY PETITIONING THE CHURCH TO HAVE YOU **REMOVED** AS ELIAS AINSWORTH'S OBSERVER!
To be continued...

The Ancient Magus' Bride

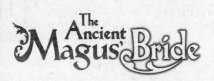

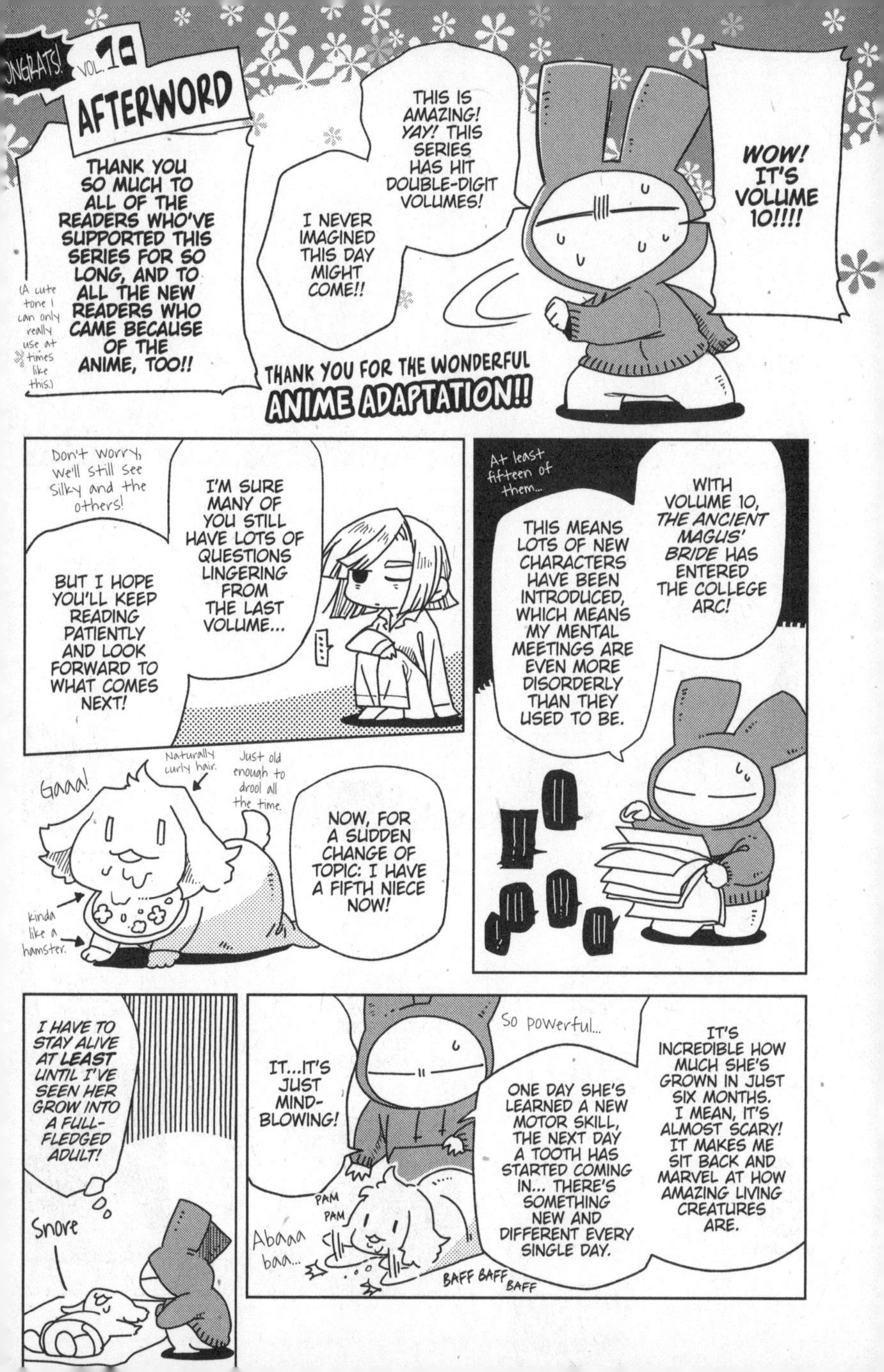

ONGRATS! VOL. 10
AFTERWORD
WOW! IT'S VOLUME 10!!!!
THIS IS AMAZING! YAY! THIS SERIES HAS HIT DOUBLE-DIGIT VOLUMES!
I NEVER IMAGINED THIS DAY MIGHT COME!!
THANK YOU SO MUCH TO ALL OF THE READERS WHO'VE SUPPORTED THIS SERIES FOR SO LONG, AND TO ALL THE NEW READERS WHO CAME BECAUSE OF THE ANIME, TOO!!
(A cute tone I can only really use at times like this.)
THANK YOU FOR THE WONDERFUL ANIME ADAPTATION!!
At least fifteen of them...
WITH VOLUME 10, THE ANCIENT MAGUS' BRIDE HAS ENTERED THE COLLEGE ARC!
THIS MEANS LOTS OF NEW CHARACTERS HAVE BEEN INTRODUCED, WHICH MEANS MY MENTAL MEETINGS ARE EVEN MORE DISORDERLY THAN THEY USED TO BE.
Don't worry, we'll still see Silky and the others!
I'M SURE MANY OF YOU STILL HAVE LOTS OF QUESTIONS LINGERING FROM THE LAST VOLUME...
BUT I HOPE YOU'LL KEEP READING PATIENTLY AND LOOK FORWARD TO WHAT COMES NEXT!
NOW, FOR A SUDDEN CHANGE OF TOPIC: I HAVE A FIFTH NIECE NOW!
Just old enough to drool all the time.
Naturally curly hair.
Gaaa!
Kinda like a hamster.
IT'S INCREDIBLE HOW MUCH SHE'S GROWN IN JUST SIX MONTHS. I MEAN, IT'S ALMOST SCARY! IT MAKES ME SIT BACK AND MARVEL AT HOW AMAZING LIVING CREATURES ARE.
So powerful...
ONE DAY SHE'S LEARNED A NEW MOTOR SKILL, THE NEXT DAY A TOOTH HAS STARTED COMING IN... THERE'S SOMETHING NEW AND DIFFERENT EVERY SINGLE DAY.
IT...IT'S JUST MIND-BLOWING!
PAM PAM
Abaaa baa...
BAFF BAFF BAFF
I HAVE TO STAY ALIVE AT LEAST UNTIL I'VE SEEN HER GROW INTO A FULL-FLEDGED ADULT!
Snore

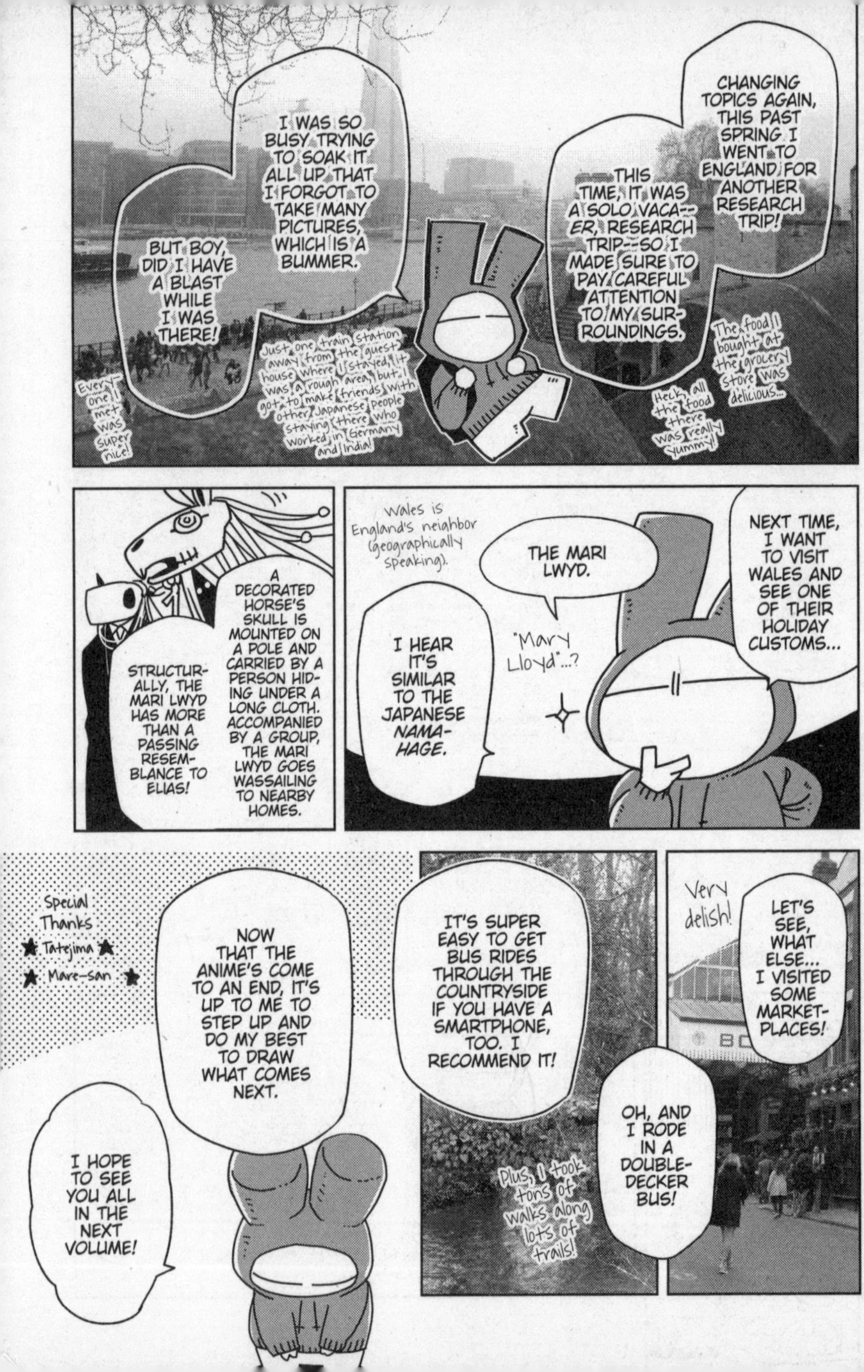
CHANGING TOPICS AGAIN, THIS PAST SPRING I WENT TO ENGLAND FOR ANOTHER RESEARCH TRIP!
THIS TIME, IT WAS A SOLO VACA-- ER, RESEARCH TRIP--SO I MADE SURE TO PAY CAREFUL ATTENTION TO MY SURROUNDINGS.
The food I bought at the grocery store was delicious...
Heck, all the food there was really yummy!
I WAS SO BUSY TRYING TO SOAK IT ALL UP THAT I FORGOT TO TAKE MANY PICTURES, WHICH IS A BUMMER.
BUT BOY, DID I HAVE A BLAST WHILE I WAS THERE!
Just one train station away from the guest house where I stayed, it was a rough area, but I got to make friends with other Japanese people staying there who worked in Germany and India!
Everyone I met was super nice!
NEXT TIME, I WANT TO VISIT WALES AND SEE ONE OF THEIR HOLIDAY CUSTOMS...
THE MARI LWYD.
Wales is England's neighbor (geographically speaking).
"Mary Lloyd"...?
I HEAR IT'S SIMILAR TO THE JAPANESE NAMAHAGE.
A DECORATED HORSE'S SKULL IS MOUNTED ON A POLE AND CARRIED BY A PERSON HIDING UNDER A LONG CLOTH. ACCOMPANIED BY A GROUP, THE MARI LWYD GOES WASSAILING TO NEARBY HOMES.
STRUCTURALLY, THE MARI LWYD HAS MORE THAN A PASSING RESEMBLANCE TO ELIAS!
Very delish!
LET'S SEE, WHAT ELSE... I VISITED SOME MARKETPLACES!
OH, AND I RODE IN A DOUBLE-DECKER BUS!
IT'S SUPER EASY TO GET BUS RIDES THROUGH THE COUNTRYSIDE IF YOU HAVE A SMARTPHONE, TOO. I RECOMMEND IT!
Plus, I took tons of walks along lots of trails!
NOW THAT THE ANIME'S COME TO AN END, IT'S UP TO ME TO STEP UP AND DO MY BEST TO DRAW WHAT COMES NEXT.
Special Thanks
★ Tatejima ★
★ Mare-san ★
I HOPE TO SEE YOU ALL IN THE NEXT VOLUME!

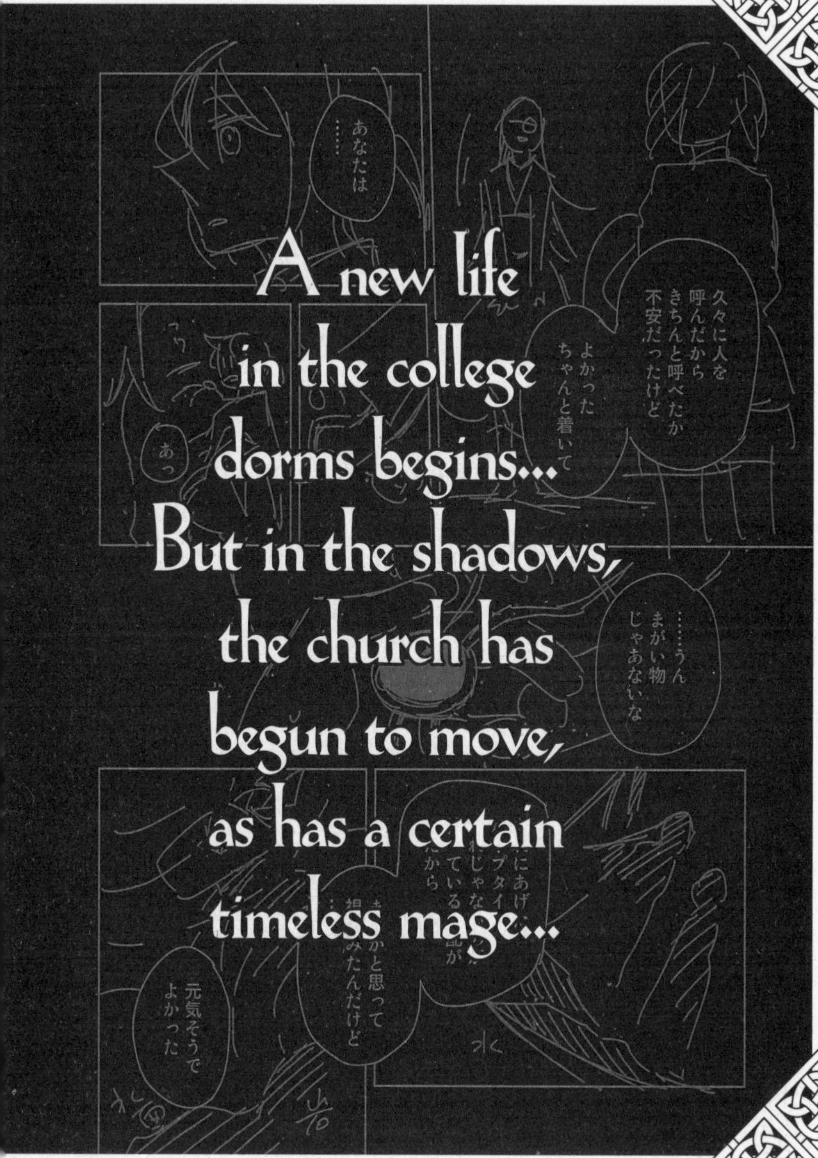
久々に人を呼んだからきちんと呼べたか不安だったけど
よかったちゃんと着いて
あなたは……
あっ
……うんまがい物じゃあないな
元気そうでよかった

A new life
in the college
dorms begins...
But in the shadows,
the church has
begun to move,
as has a certain
timeless mage...

Chise, now a student auditing
classes at the college, is changing.
As he watches over her and accepts
who she's becoming, Elias begins to
realize that he may be changing, too.

New school friends. The Seven Shields.
The Church. And Rahab, a mage
who wanders through time.

The stage is set and the actors
have taken their places.
Now it is time for the curtain to rise...

Volume 11 Coming Soon!

SEVEN SEAS ENTERTAINMENT PRESENTS

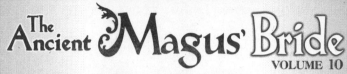

The Ancient Magus' Bride

VOLUME 10

story and art by KORE YAMAZAKI

TRANSLATION
Adrienne Beck

ADAPTATION
Ysabet Reinhardt MacFarlane

LETTERING AND RETOUCH
Lys Blakeslee

COVER DESIGN
Nicky Lim

PROOFREADER
Shanti Whitesides

ASSISTANT EDITOR
J.P. Sullivan

PRODUCTION ASSISTANT
CK Russell

PRODUCTION MANAGER
Lissa Pattillo

EDITOR-IN-CHIEF
Adam Arnold

PUBLISHER
Jason DeAngelis

Originally published in Japan in 2018 by MAG Garden Corporation, Tokyo.
English translation rights arranged through TOHAN CORPORATION, Tokyo.

Seven Seas books may be purchased in bulk for promotional, educational, or business use. Please contact your local bookseller or the Macmillan Corporate and Premium Sales Department at 1-800-221-7945, extension 5442, or by e-mail at MacmillanSpecialMarkets@macmillan.com.

ISBN: 978

Printed i

First Prin

10 9 8 7

FOLLOW US ONLINE: *www.sevenseasentertainment.com*

READING DIRECTIONS

This book reads from ***right to left***, Japanese style. If this is your first time reading manga, you start reading from the top right panel on each page and take it from there. If you get lost, just follow the numbered diagram here. It may seem backwards at first, but you'll get the hang of it! Have fun!!

1
2
3
4
5
6
7
8
9

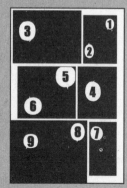

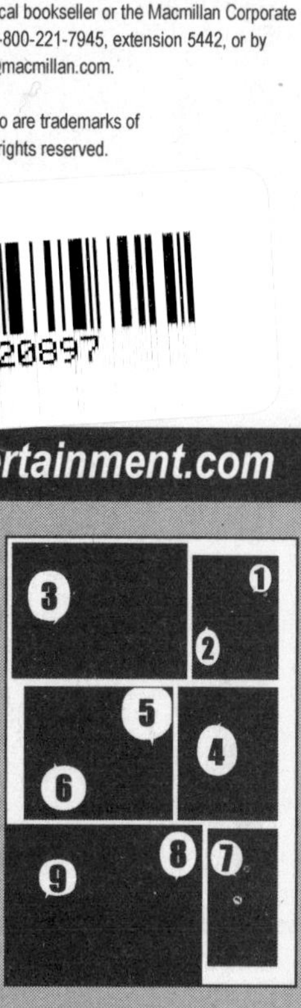